BERKELEY
ESSAY, PRINCIPLES, DIALOGUES
WITH SELECTIONS FROM OTHER WRITINGS

BERKELEY
ESSAY, PRINCIPLES, DIALOGUES
WITH SELECTIONS FROM OTHER WRITINGS

EDITED BY

MARY WHITON CALKINS

PROFESSOR OF PHILOSOPHY AND PSYCHOLOGY
WELLESLEY COLLEGE

CHARLES SCRIBNER'S SONS

NEW YORK

CONTENTS

VERSES

ON THE PROSPECT OF PLANTING ARTS AND LEARNING IN AMERICA

The Muse, disgusted at an age and clime
    Barren of every glorious theme,
In distant lands now waits a better time
    Producing subjects worthy fame:

In happy climes, where from the genial sun
    And virgin earth such scenes ensue,
The force of art by nature seems outdone,
    And fancied beauties by the true:

In happy climes, the seat of innocence,
    Where nature guides and virtue rules,
Where men shall not impose for truth and sense
    The pedantry of courts and schools:

There shall be sung another golden age,
    The rise of empire and of arts,
The good and great inspiring epic rage,
    The wisest heads and noblest hearts.

Not such as Europe breeds in her decay;
    Such as she bred when fresh and young,
When heavenly flame did animate her clay,
    By future poets shall be sung.

Westward the course of empire takes its way;
    The four first Acts already past,
A fifth shall close the Drama with the day;
    Time's noblest offspring is the last.

George Berkeley.

INTRODUCTION

THE LIFE OF BERKELEY

I

Two centuries ago, on a winter's day, the twenty-third
of January, 1729, a church service in Trinity Church of
Newport, Rhode Island, was cut short by the sighting
in the harbor of "a pretty large ship," which had sailed,
four months before, from Gravesend on the Thames.
"Dismissed with the blessing by their rector, Mr. Honey-
man, and led by him," the worshippers streamed to the
shore to welcome Dean George Berkeley on his romantic
mission to the Colonial and Indian youth of America.
Berkeley was nearly forty-five years old, newly married,
and, according to the *New England Weekly Courier*,
"a gentleman of middle stature, of an agreeable, pleasant, and erect aspect." He had come to Newport, a
town which in the early eighteenth century rivalled
Boston and New York, to buy land for the support of
the college which he purposed to establish in the Bermudas, and to make acquaintance with New Englanders
who might further his philanthropic purpose. Never
perhaps, since the days when Plato sought to set up in
the Sicilian court a philosopher-king, has a metaphysician entertained a more adventurous plan for the
upbuilding of the Great Society.

For nearly five years before he sailed into Newport
harbor Berkeley had lavished all his energy, his time,
and his fortune on this project of founding in the Sum-

ix

mer Islands a college which should serve for the instruction, both of the "English youth" of the colonies and of "a number of young American savages, in Christian religion, practical mathematics, and other liberal arts and sciences." The repeated attempts of Berkeley's contemporaries, to depict his personal charm and persuasiveness, pale beside the statement of the bare fact that his fiery pleading in behalf of this Utopian scheme had won for him private subscriptions of more than five thousand pounds from prelates and noblemen and distinguished ladies "who desire to be unknown," a vote of approval from the House of Commons (after Berkeley had privately talked with each member of it), a charter for the college of St. Paul in the Bermudas, and a promise from Sir Robert Walpole, Prime Minister, of a grant of twenty thousand pounds. Most amazing of all, a gently bred Irish lady, chosen by Berkeley for her "qualities of mind and her unaffected inclination to books," agreed "with great cheerfulness" to sail westward with him on this adventurous voyage.

II

Nothing in the record of Berkeley's early years prepares us for this astounding effort of his middle life. Of the external happenings of his childhood and youth, we know, in truth, little save that he was born in Kilcrin, Ireland, on March 12, 1685, attended the Kilkenny School, was matriculated in 1700 at Trinity College, Dublin, received the bachelor's degree in 1704 and, in 1707, that of master of arts, became a Fellow in 1707 and lived in residence, as Tutor, through the year 1712. In curious contrast to this uneventful chronicle is the fascinating record of Berkeley's animated thinking during his college years—a story which we construct for ourselves from the pages, first published only half a century ago, of a little manuscript volume, in Berkeley's own hand, called by its first editor, the *Commonplace Book*. The abbreviated memoranda, questions, notes, and comments succeed each other with no attempt at logical order and no thought of consistency. There are brief references to the doctrines of Locke and Hobbes, of Descartes, Malebranche and Spinoza; vigorous reactions to the mathematicians and scientists of the day, and, in particular, to Newton; anticipations of all the significant teachings of Berkeley's own system; indications of doctrines which more or less completely he later abandons. His first book, the *Essay toward a New Theory of Vision,* published in 1709, is a primarily psychological study of our consciousness of distance and magnitude but subtly suggests the metaphysical conclusion of the books which follow close upon it, the *Principles of Human Knowledge* and the *Dialogues between Hylas and Philonous*. In these volumes Berkeley, before he is thirty, makes his great contribution to modern philosophy drawing, in ineradicable outline, the conception of the universe as, through and through, mental.

III

When Berkeley went, in the wet spring of 1713, from Dublin to London, he carried in his hands the manuscript of the *Dialogues*. It may be conjectured that he carried in his heart the determination to win for his doctrine of ideas something better than the humorous and superficial misunderstanding with which his *Principles* had been received. But the story of his months in London contains few records of philosophical discussion. Berkeley was introduced by his countryman, Dean Swift, not only at the Court of Queen Anne but to London men of letters—to Addison, Steele and Swift; and we are told that Addison arranged a discussion between Berkeley and Samuel Clarke concerning the real existence of sensible things. But to Berkeley, at least, the meeting gave little satisfaction; and presently we find, somewhat to our surprise, that he is contributing to Steele's short-lived *Guardian* popular essays (at a guinea each) in criticism of the dogmatism of alleged "free-thinkers."

The London sojourn came to an end when in the fall of 1713 the eccentric Earl of Peterborough, hero of the war of the Succession in Spain, was appointed Ambassador Extraordinary to Victor Amodeus, newly crowned King of Sicily. For, commended by his good genius, Swift, Berkeley was made chaplain and secretary to the earl. His letters to his life-long friend, Thomas Prior, suggest the impressions and reflections of the months of travel. From Turin he writes, after a formidable crossing of Mont Cenis, "I am now hardened against wind and weather, earth and sea, frost and snow; can gallop all day long, and sleep but three or four hours at night." A second letter clearly indicates Berkeley's consuming concern for human welfare. Looking back upon his weeks in France, he writes, "I cannot help observing that the Jacobites have little to hope and others little to fear from that reduced nation. The king indeed looks as he neither wanted meat nor drink and his palaces are in good repair; but throughout the land there . . . are instances enough of poverty and distress to spoil the mirth of any one who feels for the sufferings of his fellow-creatures."

In August 1714, Queen Anne died and Peterborough was recalled. Berkeley spent the two following years in London, and his letters give evidence of his interest in the political issues of the day. From a mocking reference in a friend's letter, we learn of an illness during this period: "Poor philosopher Berkeley," says Arbuthnot, writing to Swift, "has now the *idea* of health which was very hard to produce in him; for he had an *idea* of a strange fever upon him, so strong that it was very hard to destroy it by introducing a contrary one." In 1715, Berkeley is again on his travels. He has become the companion of the son of Bishop Ashe, and his next five years are spent on the continent, largely in Italy. "Would you know how we pass the time at Naples?" he writes to Pope. "Our chief entertainment is the devotion of our neighbors. Besides the gaiety of the churches (where folks go to see what they call *una bella Devotione,* i.e., a sort of religious opera), they make fireworks almost every week out of devotion; [and] . . . the ladies invite gentlemen to their houses and treat them with music and sweetmeats out of devotion." But Berkeley was no mere sightseer. The manuscript volumes of his Italian journal contain not merely vivid narration of amusing experiences but references to the treasures of the Vatican Library, to the pictures and statues of the great palaces and galleries, to "the antiquities upon the Mount Esquiline" and "the remains of the Thermæ Constantini" as well as careful "observations and remarks on the eruption of Fire & Smoke from Mount Vesuvio." We are told, also, that Berkeley had collected materials for a natural history of Sicily which, along with the incomplete manuscript of the projected Second Part of his *Principles,* he lost on the journey from Sicily to Naples.

But for one fact we should, by this time, believe that Berkeley the philosopher had been completely metamorphosed into Berkeley the traveller. This is the publication, in 1720, on his homeward journey of a Latin book *De Motu*, an essay in defense of the thesis that the will, divine and human, is the cause of motion in the physical world. No reader of this closely reasoned argument can fail to realize that Berkeley has not given over metaphysical thinking. But his immediate concern on his return to England was with the lowered tone of public social morality. The wild speculation culminating in the disastrous failure of the "South Sea Scheme" seemed to him a symptom only, not the cause, of the sickness of the body politic. His published reaction to this desolating condition is his *Essay towards Preventing the Ruin of Great Britain* in which he emphasizes the need of individual right living. "Let us be industrious, frugal and religious," he says, "if we are to be saved at all." There is much to commend Fraser's conjecture that "the deep impression which this English catastrophe of 1720 made upon Berkeley" inspired or strengthened his colonial dream.

In 1723, Berkeley was startled to find himself co-heir with Robert Marshal of Esther Van Homrigh, Swift's Vanessa. More emphatic testimony to his personal charm and dignity could scarcely be found for Miss Van Homrigh had met him only once and casually at her mother's dinner table. There is satisfaction to be found in the fact that the tidings of the bequest of Vanessa, following on that of her tragic death, seems to have cast no shadow on the friendship between Swift and Berkeley. For, sixteen months later, when Berkeley, just appointed Dean of Derry, was begging to surrender his office in order to further his colonial project,

Swift writes in characteristic and approving fashion to the Lord Lieutenant of Ireland:—

"There is a gentleman of this kingdom just gone for England. It is Dr. George Berkeley, Dean of Derry, the best preferment among us, being worth £1100 a year. . . . He is an absolute philosopher with regard to money, titles and power; and for three years past has been struck with a notion of founding a University at the Bermudas. . . . He has seduced several of the hopefullest young clergymen here . . . all in the fairest way for preferment. . . . Your Excellency will see his whole scheme of a life academico-philosophical, of a college founded for Indian scholars and missionaries; where he most exorbitantly proposes a whole hundred pounds a year for himself, fifty pounds for a Fellow, and ten for a Student. His heart will break if his Deanery be not taken from him and left to your Excellency's disposal. . . . And therefore I humbly entreat your Excellency either to use such persuasions as will keep one of the first men in the Kingdom for learning and virtue quiet at home, or assist him by your credit to compass his romantic design."

IV

By a long circuit we have thus returned to Berkeley newly landed in Rhode Island, and to the story of his nearly three years' residence in America. Reluctantly we pass with merely casual glance the records of the friends he made, of the sermons he preached, and of the dignified but simple house he built, under the fruit trees, for himself and his wife and the children who were born to them. (The house with its low timbered ceiling and tiled fireplaces and gently sloping roof is still opened to Berkeley-lovers.) The early months of his stay were heartened by the preparations for the Bermuda College, but presently even before his hopeful eyes the vision faded and, when he was definitely assured that the endowment promised for the new university had been diverted by Walpole to a princess's marriage portion, he began to make preparation for return to England. But though the College of St. Paul was never built in the Summer Islands, Berkeley still influences the academic life of America. The rent of Rhode Island farmers still supports the Berkleian Scholars of Yale University; for to the "College at Newhaven" Berkeley made over the ninety-six acres of his Whitehall estate; and the Yale University library still prizes the books, nearly a thousand of them, sent by Berkeley shortly after his return to London. (A similar gift to the Harvard College Library was destroyed by fire.) In two other ways Berkeley's life in New England bore sound intellectual fruit. It deepened and widened Berkeley's influence, already exerted through the teaching of the *Principles,* on Samuel Johnson, Episcopal missionary at Stratford, Connecticut, former tutor of Yale College, years later the first president of King's College (now Columbia University), one of the great figures in the history of American philosophy. New England has furthermore the honor of being the birthplace of the important book, called *Alciphron,* in which Berkeley expounds his philosophy with special reference to its theistic basis and its moral applications. The *Alciphron* was published in Dublin but its scene is laid in Whitehall, Berkeley's Newport home, with its "prospect of a narrow bay or creek of the sea, enclosed on either side by coast beautified with rocks and woods, and green banks and farm-houses."

In the fall of 1731, Berkeley sailed back to England. The next two years he spent in London, and in 1734 he published the *Analyst,* an essay setting forth the unreasonableness of the free-thinking mathematician who presumes to say that "mysteries may not be objects of faith at the same time that he himself admits such obscure mysteries" as "infinitesimals each infinitely less than the foregoing and infinitely greater than the following . . . to be the object of science." Early in 1734 Berkeley was made Bishop of Cloyne and there is reason to believe that he owed his appointment to the interest of the "philosophic queen," Caroline, in his American book, the *Alciphron.*

The quiet diocese of Cloyne, in what Berkeley called the "remote corner of Inokelly," lies between hills and sea with the river Lee flowing to the West of it. Here Berkeley lived for nearly twenty years dividing his time between his philosophical studies, the education of his children, and his eager efforts in behalf of the dwellers in Cloyne. The enthusiasm with which he had undertaken to enrich the lives of colonial youth and "savage Americans" burned now for his Irish countrymen, especially for the native Irish. "Ireland," he wrote in a letter to an American friend, "contains ten times more objects of charity, whether we consider the souls or bodies of men, than are to be met with in New England." And, in frank opposition to the prevailing theory and practice which far outlasted his generation, he insisted that any "scheme for the welfare of the Irish nation" should "take in the whole inhabitants" instead of concerning itself with "the flourishing of our Protestant gentry, exclusive of the bulk of the natives." He proposed accordingly the admission of Romanists to the College of Dublin; and in 1749 appealed by his *Word to the Wise* to the Roman Catholic clergy of Ireland "to preach the gospel of work and self-reliance to their flocks." It is a satisfaction to read of the "sincere and hearty" response to this appeal.

In the three Parts of *The Querist,* successively published in 1735, 1736 and 1737, each Part consisting simply of a series of brief and pointed questions, Berkeley suggested his social philosophy It centred about the doctrine that "individual industry is the soul of social and economical prosperity." Berkeley's theories found expression not only in his books but in his conduct. He was perhaps as ardent an advocate as Ghandi of home industry and "chose to wear ill clothes and worse wigs rather than leave the poor of the town to be unemployed." But in the years of scarcity, famine, and disease which followed on the freezing of the river Lee, in 1739, Berkeley went further. He came down to breakfast one Sunday with not a grain of powder on his Cloyne-made wig. "We shall have a famine forthwith," he replied to his wife's remonstrance, "and I have desired that none of the servants put any powder in their wigs; neither will I."

The habit of prescribing for the ailments of his poor neighbors, starting with these years of distress, became an important factor of the last great concern of Berkeley's life. He had learned from American Indians the medicinal value of tar-water; he had long used tar-water as a family remedy; and he now began in good earnest to prescribe it for every sort of disease. A room in the Episcopal mansion was set apart for the manufacture of it, pamphlets were written to advocate its use, and Berkeley's "correspondence with patients that drink tar-water" obliged him to be "less punctual" in letters to his friends. Berkeley's latest book, *Siris,* a unique mixture of medical counsel and Platonizing idealism is compounded, on the one hand, of recipes and accounts of cure and, on the other hand, of grave disquisitions starting with the conception of tar as containing the "vital element" of the universe.

We have left to the end a reference to the home-life of this modest bishop's palace with its surrounding myrtle trees and its lovely outlook on Cork Harbor. Berkeley's letters give us enchanting glimpses of his home. To one correspondent he writes that he has asked "Dean Browne to look out for a six stringed bass viol of an old make and mellow tone." "The more," he adds, "we have of good instruments, the better. I have got an excellent master . . . and all my children not excepting my little daughter learn to play and are preparing to fill my house with harmony against all events; that if we have worse times we may have better spirits. . . . My wife, I am told, is this day inferior to no singer in the kingdom. . . . Music is at present the reigning passion at Cloyne. To be plain, we are musically mad. If you would know what that is, come and see." In another letter to the same friend, he declines the offer of certain books "which I should readily purchase and accept your kind offer of procuring them, if I did not apprehend that there might be some among them of too delicate a nature to be read by boys and girls, to whom my library, and particularly my French books, are open." A letter to Prior, several years later, describes Berkeley's "son William and his sister" as "both employed in copying pictures. Their stint," he adds, "on account of health is an hour and a half for painting." This is the same daughter who was learning to play with the excellent music master, "so bright a little gem," her father exclaimed, "that to prevent her doing mischief among the illiterate squires, I am resolved to treat her like a boy and make her study eight hours a day." And it is William of whom Berkeley writes in the most moving of his published letters:—

"I was a man retired from the amusement of politics, visits, and what the world calls pleasure. I had a little friend, educated always under mine own eye, whose painting delighted me, whose music ravished me, and whose lively gay spirit was a continuous feast. It has pleased God to take him hence. God I say, in mercy hath deprived me of this pretty, gay plaything. His parts and person, his innocence and piety, his particularly uncommon affection for me had gained too much upon me. Not content to be fond of him, I was vain of him. I had set my heart too much upon him."

In 1752, little more than a year after William's death, Berkeley left Cloyne for Oxford. Lover of university life, he had long pictured Oxford as ideal home of the scholar—"the most delightful place I have ever seen," he had described it; and he had now the added impetus of his desire to be near his son George who was entering on his university career in Oxford. Berkeley was eager, however, to resign his bishopric for, characteristically, he disapproved of non-resident prelates. But in this purpose he was foiled by none other than His Majesty. King George the Second. Berkeley, said the king, might live where he chose but, in spite of himself, he should die a bishop. But the visionary bishop lived only a few months longer, in the house near New College on Holywell Street, Oxford. He died, suddenly and peacefully, on a winter Sunday afternoon as he sat, drinking tea with his family, near the fire. His "dear wife Anne," we are told, had been reading from St. Paul's first letter to the Corinthians at the fifteenth chapter; and Berkeley's last words were in comment on that great hymn of immortality.

THE PHILOSOPHY OF BERKELEY [1]

I. THE CENTRAL DOCTRINES OF BERKELEY'S METAPHYSICS

i. Berkeley's Conception of the Physical World as Immaterial

Berkeley, like many others of us, was brought up to believe that the universe is made up in part of innumerable finite minds, in part of unnumbered material objects radically different from the minds but influencing and influenced by them, and all—minds and bodies alike—created by the Infinite Spirit, God. For this conception Berkeley substituted the doctrine of a world made up wholly of finite spirits created by God. In place of the belief that material things occasion our experiences of color, weight, motion and the like he proposed the doctrine that God causes in human minds such experiences, or ideas. Thus, the clear and involuntary ideas of finite minds, directly due to God, constitute the real but immaterial physical world.

The most striking feature of this doctrine is Berkeley's teaching that material things do not exist. To get at his meaning, it is necessary, first, to understand his use of terms. By *a spirit*, he means a primarily conscious and, in that sense, an active and permanent being; *ideas* he describes as mental but as "passive," that is, as dependent on spirit, and as "fleeting," or impermanent;

---

[1] The student is advised to postpone the reading of what follows, in particular of sections II-IV, until he has read both or either of the following works of Berkeley himself: *The Principles of Human Knowledge, Three Dialogues between Hylas and Philonous.*

matter he defines as that which is radically unlike and independent of mental reality, that which (in the words which Hume later used) "would exist though we and every sensible creature were absent or annihilated."

By four main considerations Berkeley seeks to undermine the belief that material objects, thus defined, exist. (1) Against the unsophisticated dualists of his day (and of ours), who insist naïvely that they directly see and touch and hear, and therefore know, the existence of material things, Berkeley argues that this assertion leads to the contradiction of supposing that a material object has no stable or constant nature of its own. Cool one hand and warm another, he directs, and then plunge them both into a basin of lukewarm water and, behold, you shall directly perceive what you call the material water as both hot and cold. And similarly, you may at different times or from different positions perceive the same fruit as sweet or as sour, the same building as large or as small. All this, Berkeley insists, is sheer absurdity from the standpoint of the naïve dualist, who conceives the material world as fixed and permanent, but is readily explained by the idealist, who claims that things are ideas and who points to the notorious changeableness of the same ideas.[1]

(2) Berkeley's second argument is urged against the academic dualist of his day who had accepted Locke's distinction, and Descartes's, of the secondary from the primary qualities. But the primary and secondary qualities, Berkeley points out, are "inseparably united" in the physical object. What we see is not the colored and the extended but the colored, extended object. What we touch is not the hard and the extended but the hard, extended object. Those, therefore, who agree with Locke

[1] *Three Dialogues*, I., THIS TEXT, pp. 233 ff; *Principles*, 11, 14.

and Descartes that the secondary qualities are mental, and this includes virtually all the scientists of Berkeley's day as of our own, must by parity of reasoning conclude that the primary qualities, extension and motion, are mental also.[1]

(3) Up to this point, Berkeley has contended merely that we have no right to claim direct perception of material things—in other words, that the objects of our direct sense-consciousness are themselves percepts. His third argument he directs against a strongly entrenched position of Descartes and of Locke. This is the doctrine, held by many of our own day also, that though we directly perceive only what is mental, namely our own percepts, we must none the less infer as causes of these percepts existent material objects. In opposition to this doctrine, Berkeley points out that causes must be held to resemble their effects; and accordingly that a material, that is a non-mental, thing can not in the nature of the case be conceived as cause of a percept which is mental. More than this, every cause, he insists, is active whereas matter is, by common consent, "passive and inert." For both reasons, because no material thing can be conceived to cause that which is mental (since the material is by definition radically unlike and independent of the mental) and because no inactive thing can be a cause at all, Berkeley rejects the conclusion that matter can be inferred to exist as cause of our percepts.[2]

(4) These three arguments, so briefly summarized in the preceding paragraphs, are greatly elaborated by Berkeley and drawn out over many pages. And yet he explicitly proposes to supplant them by a consideration of quite a different sort. Toward the end of the first of the *Three Dialogues*, Philonous, representing Berke-

---

[1] *Principles*, 10; *Three Dialogues*, I., This Text, p. 253.
[2] *Three Dialogues*, II., This Text, p. 282.

ley, says to Hylas, the dualist,[1] "I am content to put the whole upon this issue. If you can conceive it possible for any . . . sensible object whatever to exist without the mind, then I will grant it actually to be so." Hylas rises greedily to this bait. "What more easy," he exclaims, "than to conceive a tree or house existing by itself independent of, and unperceived by, any mind whatsoever?" But Philonous is quick to point out that the tree or house in question must be conceived by Hylas if he is to describe it in any way at all, even as existing independent of mind. And in the end Hylas reaches the following idealistic position: "As I was thinking of a tree in a solitary place . . . methought that was to conceive a tree as existing unperceived or unthought-of; not considering that I myself conceived it all the while. But now I plainly see that all I can do is to frame ideas in my own mind. . . . And this is far from proving that I can conceive them as *existing out of the minds of all Spirits*." In a word, Berkeley bases his idealism on the appeal to our consciousness which shows us that whatever we experience is part of our own experiencing, and accordingly mental.

ii. *Berkeley's Conception of the Universe as Spiritual*

The preceding pages have summarized only Berkeley's doctrine that the physical world is mental, not material. For aught that he has so far told us, physical objects are merely his own sense percepts. But his universe is at once enlarged through the discovery of an important difference between the percepts which constitute his physical world and other ideas which he calls the ideas of imagination. These last he can excite in his mind at his pleasure; but his percepts are actually imprinted

---

[1] THIS TEXT, p. 261 f. Cf. *Principles*, 22 f.

on his senses without dependence on his will.[1] To
explain the occurrence of these ideas of sense it is
necessary, Berkeley argues, to infer the existence of
some cause other-than-himself. The immediate problem concerns the nature of this cause. It is no longer
open to him to infer the existence of a material cause of
these sense-ideas. Nor is it possible, in the second place,
to argue that his sense-percepts are caused by still
other ideas. For ideas, Berkeley invariably teaches, are
passive, not active; and accordingly "the connexion of
ideas does not imply the relation of *cause* and *effect* but
only of a mark or *sign* with the *thing signified*. The fire
which I see," he continues, by way of illustration, "is
not the cause of the pain I suffer upon my approaching
it, but the mark that forewarns me of it." [2] Only one
path remains open. The cause of Berkeley's sense-ideas
must be another self, or spirit, and to explain the order,
regularity and nature of these sense-ideas it is necessary
to infer that this creative spirit is infinite. To sum-
marize his argument in his own words:—

"The ideas actually perceived by Sense have not . . .
dependence on *my* will. When in broad daylight I open
my eyes, it is not in my power to choose whether I shall
see or no . . . and so likewise as to the hearing and
other senses; the ideas imprinted on them are not
creatures of *my* will. There is therefore some other
Will or Spirit that produces them." And "if we attentively consider the constant regularity, order, and
concatenation of natural things," that is of the sense
ideas which constitute the nature-world, "the surprising
magnificence, beauty, and perfection of the larger, and
the exquisite contrivance of the smaller parts of the
creation, together with the exact harmony and correspondence of the whole . . ." we shall necessarily con-

[1] *Principles*, 28, 29.
[2] *Principles*, 65.

clude that the creator of this ordered world of percepts is God, "a really existing Spirit," infinitely powerful, wise, and good, "a thinking, intelligent being in the same sense with other spirits, though not in the same imperfect manner or degree." [1]

By a somewhat similar inference, Berkeley teaches, we infer the existence of other finite spirits. "A human spirit or person," he says, "is not perceived by sense. . . . When . . . we see the color, size, figure, and motions of a man we perceive only certain sensations or ideas excited in our own minds; and these . . . serve to mark out unto us the existence of finite and created spirits like ourselves." [2]

A subsidiary argument for the existence of God is so often stressed by Berkeley that it should be included in even so brief an outline of his doctrine. He uses it at all stages of his thinking but it is nowhere more persuasively set forth than in the Fourth Dialogue of the *Alciphron*. Protesting against Euphranor's assertion that "we have at least as clear, full, and immediate certainty of the being" of God "as of any one human soul whatsoever besides our own," Alciphron says: "Nothing so much convinces me of the existence of another person as *his speaking to me*" and adds, "You will not I suppose pretend that God speaks to man in the same clear and sensible manner as one man doth to another." But this, it turns out, is precisely what Euphranor, representing Berkeley, does pretend. The fact that we regularly infer from visual signs, in particular from the clearness or mistiness and the apparent size of objects, their nearness or distance and their tactual characters is conceived by Berkeley as a divine visual language. "The

[1] *Principles*, 29, 146; *Siris*, 323; *Alciphron*, IV., 22, THIS TEXT, p. 387. Cf. *Three Dialogues*, II., THIS TEXT, p. 276.

[2] *Principles*, 148.

great Mover and Author of Nature," Euphranor says to Alciphron, "constantly explaineth Himself to the eyes of men by the sensible intervention of arbitrary signs, which have no similitude or connexion with the things signified. . . . In consequence, I say, . . . you have as much reason to think the Universal Agent or God speaks to your eyes, as you can have for thinking any particular person speaks to your ears." [1]

Throughout, Berkeley teaches the uniformity of God's dealings with finite spirits. No scientific writer of his day or ours lays more stress on the pervasiveness of natural law, and no Humian more decisively refuses to attribute absolute necessity to the orderly sequence of phenomena on each other. "There are," he says, "certain general laws that run through the whole chain of natural effects: these are learned by the observation and study of nature. . . . Experience teaches us that such and such ideas are attended with such and such other ideas in the ordinary course of things. This gives us a sort of foresight, which enables us to regulate our actions for the benefit of life. . . . That food nourishes, sleep refreshes, and fire warms us; that to sow in the seed-time is the way to reap in the harvest . . . all this we know not by discovering any *necessary connexion* between our ideas, but only by the observation of the *settled laws* of nature." This wholly scientific conception of the laws of nature becomes an integral part of Berkeley's theistic system by the conclusion, demanded by his conception of the relation of God to the world, that these uniformities in the succession of nature-events (that is, of percepts on each other) are the "regular, constant methods of working observed by the Supreme Agent . . . the set rules or established methods

[1] *Alciphron*, IV., 5, 6, 12, THIS TEXT, pp. 357, 360, 370. Cf. *Principles*, 148 ff.

wherein the Mind we depend on excites in us the ideas of Sense." [1]

Such in brief outline is Berkeley's idealism, suggested in his earliest book, the *Essay toward a New Theory of Vision*, argued in detail in the two closely following works, the *Principles* and *The Three Dialogues between Hylas and Philonous*, amplified but never essentially modified in his later writings.

II. THE OUTLYING DOCTRINES OF BERKELEY'S METAPHYSICS

i. The preceding pages have concerned themselves exclusively with the core of Berkeley's doctrine: his theistic immaterialism. They have virtually ignored two striking features of his teaching, his sensationalism and his opposition to what he calls abstract ideas. By the term "sensationalism" is meant, on the one hand, Berkeley's emphasis upon perception, imagination, and upon the ideas imprinted by sense, and on the other hand his neglect of thought and of other-than-sense ideas. This sensationalistic tendency is early indicated, in the Commonplace Book, by statements such as this: [2] "I approve of this axiom of the Schoolmen, 'Nihil est in intellectu quod non prius fuit in sensu.' I wish they had stuck to it. It had never taught them the doctrine of abstract ideas." The same sensationalistic emphasis distinguishes not only Berkeley's earliest metaphysical books, *Essay, Principles*, and *Three Dialogues*, but all his mathematical writings as well, culminating in the *Analyst* of 1734.

Yet, as every close reader of Berkeley realizes, he was from the first more than a sensationalist. Inference

---

[1] *Principles*, 62 and 30-31.
[2] Cf. Fraser, *The Works of George Berkeley*, 1901, Vol. I., p. 48.

and reasoning are recognized both in *Principles* and in *Three Dialogues;* indeed, the very first paragraph of the *Principles* admits, in addition to the ideas imprinted on the senses, "such as are perceived by attending to the passions and operations of the mind." A more significant statement is made by Philonous in the early part of the *Third Dialogue* (1713): "I have," he declares, "though not an inactive idea yet in *myself* some sort of an active, thinking image of the Deity. And, though I perceive him not by sense, yet I have a notion of Him or know Him by reflexion and reasoning." [1] Nearly twenty years later, in 1734, Berkeley introduces, in the second edition of the *Principles,* this conception of notions, distinguished from ideas of sense (whether percepts or ideas) by having as their objects either spirits or (Berkeley now adds) relations. "We may be said," he asserts, "to have some knowledge or *notion* of our own minds, of spirits and active beings; whereof in a strict sense we have not *ideas*. In like manner we know and have a *notion* of relations between things or ideas" for "all relations" include "an act of the mind." And "relations are distinct from the ideas or things related, inasmuch as the latter may be perceived by us without our perceiving the former." [2]

Berkeley never goes beyond this bare assertion of an intellectual factor in knowledge, the notion, which on the one hand resembles the idea in being treated as dependent on mind and described as copy of a known object, but which, on the other hand, is contrasted with the idea as active whereas the notion is always described as passive. He never distinguishes the notional experience of awareness of self from the radically different notional experience of awareness of relation; nor does he ever

[1] THIS TEXT, p. 302.
[2] *Principles*, 89, 142.

distinguish one relational experience from another or anticipate Kant and Hegel by showing that our consciousness of physical objects is relational as well as sensational. With the years, however, he comes to estimate far more highly the intellectual as compared with the sense-factor in knowledge. In the *Siris*, accordingly, his latest work, we find many statements such as the following: "Sense at first besets and overbears the mind. The sensible appearances are all in all: our reasonings are employed about them: our desires terminate in them: we look no farther for realities or causes; till Intellect begins to dawn, and cast a ray on this shadowy scene. We then perceive the true principle of unity, identity, and existence. Those things that before seemed to constitute the whole of Being, upon taking an intellectual view of things, prove to be but fleeting phantoms." [1]

ii. Berkeley attacks what he knows as abstract ideas in everything he writes from the *Commonplace Book*, which briefly dismisses "abstract ideas" as "none at all," [2] to the *Siris* which disparages them as "compounded of inconsistencies." [3] His first detailed treatment of the subject occurs in the Introduction to the *Principles* and owes much of its difficulty to the fact that Berkeley really deals with three sorts of "abstraction" which he insufficiently distinguishes. His own statements of these three types of abstraction follow: (1) "It is agreed on all hands," he says, "that the *qualities* or *modes* of things . . . are . . . blended together, several in the same object. But, we are told, that the mind, being able to consider each quality singly, or abstracted from . . . other qualities, . . . does by that means frame to itself

---

[1] *Siris*, 294, THIS TEXT, p. 420. Cf. *Siris*, 264.
[2] Fraser, *op. cit.*, Vol. I., p. 57.
[3] *Siris*, 323.

abstract ideas. For example . . . the abstract ideas of extension, colour, and motion." This is obviously abstraction in the accurate psychological sense of attention-to-part-only-of-a-complex-experience, to its visual or its auditory or its affective aspect, for example. Berkeley expressly admits the occurrence of abstraction in this sense but he incorrectly limits it. "I may indeed," he says, "divide in my thoughts . . . those things which perhaps I never perceived by sense so divided. Thus I . . . conceive the smell of a rose without thinking on the rose itself." The qualifying statement that "abstraction . . . extends only to the conceiving separately such objects as it is possible may really exist asunder" [1] is plainly unjustified since we certainly abstract color from extension or pitch from loudness, for example, though the two can not "really exist asunder."

(2) Abstraction, in the second sense which Berkeley gives to the word, is really generalization, in one conception of the term. Berkeley describes it in the paragraph following at once on that last quoted. "We are told," he says, that "the mind having observed that in the particular extensions . . . there is something common and alike in all, and some other things peculiar, as this or that figure or magnitude . . . singles out by itself that which is common; making therof a most abstract idea of extension; which is neither line, surface, nor solid, nor has any figure or magnitude." [2] This conception Berkeley opposes in so far as it involves the doctrine of the general image. By this is meant the image which, as general, has no quality that does not belong to all members of the given class—the extension, for example, which is neither line, surface, nor solid or

---

[1] *Principles,* Introduction, 7; *Principles, 5.*

[2] *Principles,* Introduction, 7-8.

the triangle which (to quote from Locke's statement of this discredited theory) is "neither oblique nor rectangle, neither equilateral, equicrural, nor scalenon; but all and none of these at once." [1] Against this theory Berkeley urges the conception of the general notion as the idea which (itself a particular) has the function of suggesting similar ideas. "I do not deny," he says, that "there are *general ideas*. . . . An idea which considered in itself is particular, becomes general, by being made to represent or stand for all other particular ideas of the same sort. . . . For instance a black line of an inch in length . . . which in itself is a particular line" may represent "all particular lines whatsoever." [2]

(3) By abstraction, in the third place, Berkeley means no more nor less than the realistic denial that only the mental exists. This procedure he describes, curiously enough, as abstracting existence from perception. "Can there be a nicer strain of abstraction," he exclaims, "than to distinguish the existence of sensible objects from their being perceived, so as to conceive them existing unperceived?" [3] Abstraction in this misleading metaphysical meaning of the word, Berkeley of course most energetically opposes. Unfortunately in repudiating it he often tends, or seems to tend, to deny what he elsewhere rightly admits: (1) abstraction as distinguishing attention; (2) the abstract (or better, the general) as the representative notion.

It may well be noted in conclusion that Berkeley's criticisms of the mathematics of his day are throughout rooted either in his sensationalism or in his hostility to

---

[1] *Principles*, Introduction, 13. Quoted from Locke's *Essay Concerning Human Understanding*, Book IV., Chapter 7, §9.

[2] *Principles*, Introduction, 12.

[3] *Principles*, 5.

abstraction. He opposes, in the first place, the conception of infinitesimals and of infinite extension on the ground that both are unimaginable (in his phrase, inconceivable). "We cannot," he says, in the *Commonplace Book*, "imagine a line or space infinitely great—therefore absurd to talk or make propositions about it." [1] And, a little later: "No reasoning about things whereof we have no ideas; therefore no reasoning about infinitesimals." [2] Nearly thirty years later, he writes to the same effect in *The Analyst*: "To conceive a quantity infinitely small . . . is, I confess, above my capacity." [2]

In the second place, Berkeley of course sets himself squarely against the mathematicians' doctrine that space and time are absolute, or abstract, in the sense of being independent of any mind. "No general ideas," he exclaims in the *Commonplace Book*. "The contrary a cause of mistake or confusion in mathematiques, etc." [3] And, more definitely, in Query 7 of *The Analyst*: "Whether it be possible to free geometry from insuperable difficulties and absurdities, so long as either the abstract, general notion of extension, or absolute external extension be supposed its true object?" [4]

III. BERKELEY'S ETHICS

Berkeley's unique contribution to philosophy is his metaphysical theory. But Berkeley's concern through

[1] Fraser, *op. cit.*, Vol. I., p. 9.

[2] *The Analyst*, 5, Fraser, *op. cit.*, Vol. III., p. 20.

[3] Fraser, *op. cit.*, Vol. I., p. 7.

[4] Fraser, *op. cit.*, Vol. III., p. 53. For discussion of Berkeley's conception and treatment of mathematics, cf. G. A. Johnston, "The Development of Berkeley's Philosophy," Chapter II., pp. 75 ff and Chapter V. Especially to be noted is Johnston's emphasis (pp. 264 ff) on the fact that Berkeley has "no objection in the world to the calculus as such" but only to the calculus when held to involve the vague "conception of infinitely small quantities." Cf. *The Analyst*, 20.

long periods of his life was with practical, social, and economic issues; and Berkeley has an ethical doctrine which underlies his solutions of the concrete problems which he faces. As even the briefest of summaries will make evident, the chief contact between his ethics and his metaphysics is through his theology. In the *Commonplace Book* as in the *Alciphron,* latest of the systematically ethical writings, he teaches that "The 2 great principles of Morality" are "the being of a God and the freedom of man." [1]

The Discourse on Passive Obedience, published in 1712, summarizes at the outset most of the basal teachings of Berkeley's moral philosophy. Like that of Locke, it seems in the first place, to be rooted theoretically in a naïve form of egoistic hedonism. "Self-love," he says, "being a principle of all others the most universal, . . . it is natural for us to regard things as they are fitted to augment or impair our own happiness; and accordingly we denominate them *good* or *evil.*" But since, in the second place, it is "a truth, evident by the light of nature, that there is a sovereign omniscient Spirit who alone can make us for ever happy, or for ever miserable, it plainly follows that a conformity to His will . . . is the sole rule whereby every man who acts up to the principles of reason must govern and square his actions." Finally "when we inquire what that end is which [God] designs should be carried on by human actions" we find that it is the good "of His creatures." And "as nothing in a natural state can entitle one man more than another to the favour of God . . . it follows that . . . it is not . . . the private good of this or that man, nation, or age but the general well-being of all men, of all nations, of all ages of the world which God designs

[1] *Commonplace Book,* Fraser, Vol. I., p. 19.

should be procured by the concurring actions of each individual." [1]

In this ingenious fashion Berkelely combines radically diverse ethical theories. From an uncritically assumed hedonistic premise, supplemented by an elsewhere argued assertion of the existence of "God . . . a being of infinite goodness," he deduces a fully socialized ethical theory. He is next concerned to show that the pursuit of this moral ideal, "the well-being of mankind," demands "the observation of some determinate, established laws which, if universally practised have, from the nature of things, an essential fitness to procure the well-being of mankind." (To deny this would, he holds, commit us to the obviously absurd position of "obliging every one, upon each particular occasion," to determine what is for "the public good.") These laws, or "eternal rules of reason," he carefully distinguishes from scientific laws, general rules "which we observe to obtain in the works of nature, independent of the wills of men." [2]

On this foundation Berkeley rests all his specific ethical and social teachings. For example, he urges that submission to authority is a "law of nature." Such submission does not however involve the yielding of the right of private judgment. For Berkeley expressly recognizes two sorts of passive obedience, either "a punctual performance of what is enjoined" by civil laws "or, if that be inconsistent with reason or conscience, a patient submission to whatever penalties the supreme power hath annexed to the neglect or transgression of them." [3] Without obedience of one sort or the other, there is, he urges "no politeness, no order, no

---

[1] *Passive Obedience*, 5-7, This Text, pp. 432 ff.
[2] *Op. cit.*, 8-14, 33.
[3] *Op. cit.*, 3.

peace among men, but the world is one great heap of misery and confusion." [1]

The *Alciphron,* written twenty years later, implies throughout this same conception of the moral ideal, but in two ways, supplements the *Discourse.* In the first place, it argues in detail the doctrine, emphasized by Berkeley throughout his life, of freedom of choice. The argument takes the characteristic form of a reply to Berkeley's opponents. In the Seventh Dialogue, Alciphron throughout asserts that *"human liberty* [is] *a thing impossible"* and bases the statement on three considerations: first that volition is motion in the brain and that accordingly "those things which vulgarly pass for human actions are to be esteemed mechanical;" second that, "supposing the mind incorporeal," none the less, the "decree of the judgment doth necessarily determine the will;" and finally that granting, as of course Berkeley grants, that God foreknows our actions, "that which is certainly foreknown will certainly be. And what is certain is necessary. And necessary actions can not be the effect of free-will." In opposition Berkeley stoutly protests first, and briefly, against the materialistic assumption of Alciphron's first argument; second by a counter appeal to his own introspection "since," he says "it is evident to me, in the gross and concrete, that I am a free agent;" and finally by denying flatly that what is certain is therefore necessary: "If," he asks, "it is foreseen that such an action shall be done, may it not also be foreseen that it shall be an effect of human choice?" [2]

---

[1] *Op. cit.,* 16.

[2] *Alciphron,* Dialogue VII., Sects. 16-18. THIS TEXT, pp. 376 ff. Cf. *Three Dialogues between Hylas and Philonous,* III., THIS TEXT, p. 308; *Principles,* 153; also St. Augustine, City of God, Book 308.

In another fashion the *Alciphron* amplifies Berkeley's ethical teaching: by its prolonged criticism of two contemporary doctrines. The first of these is the ethical naturalism upheld by Mandeville, as Berkeley understood him. Against its conception of "private vice as public benefit," and its consequent account of vice as "a fine thing with an ugly name" and of virtue as "a trick of statesmen," Berkeley vigorously protests. With equal ardor (and with complete abandonment of the sensationalism of the *Commonplace Book*) he upholds against the naturalistic emphasis on sense-pleasures the doctrine that "reason being the principal part of our nature . . . rational pleasures" must be "more agreeable to human-kind than those of sense." [1]

Against Shaftesbury's conception of the moral experience as the disinterested intuition of beauty, Berkeley, by common consent of the critics, argues less discriminatingly. Yet there is undeniable force in the main consideration which he urges against this intuition theory: that "duty and virtue are in a fairer way of being practised if men are led by reason and judgment" and that "beauty . . . consists in . . . proportions" which, he adds, are "perceived only by reason," not by sense. The only moral "beauty," he contends, is that of "a system of spirits subordinate to the will, and under the direction of the Father of spirits, governing them by laws and conducting them by methods suitable to wise and good ends." [2]

[1] *Op. cit.*, Dialogue II, 3, 11, 14, Fraser, Vol. II., pp. 74, 86, 93. Cf., by way of contrast, the statement of Berkeley's *Commonplace Book* (Fraser, *op. cit.*, Vol. I., p. 47) "Sensual pleasure is the *summum bonum*."

[2] *Op. cit.*, Dialogue III., 5, 8, 11, Fraser, Vol. II., pp. 129, 133. 139.

IV. A CRITICAL DISCUSSION OF BERKELEY'S IDEALISTIC METAPHYSICS

In the concluding section of this Introduction, difficulties in the doctrine of Berkeley, urged by critics of his own day and of ours will be closely considered. It will appear that by far the greater number of these criticisms have been anticipated by Berkeley himself; and that some of them closely resemble those of the "ingenious friends" to whom Percival "did but name" the subject matter of the *Principles,* whereupon "they immediately treated it with ridicule, at the same time refusing to read it." [1] The difficulties may be roughly grouped under two heads: those which directly oppose Berkeley's doctrine that all objects are mental; and those which allege inconsistencies in Berkeley's conception of the universe as spiritual.

i. *Objections to Berkeley's Immaterialism*

(1) The more naïve of the critics of Berkeley's idealism have always urged that on his principles "all that is real and substantial in nature is banished out of the world." [2] Against this objection, Berkeley maintains that "whatever we see, feel, hear, or any wise conceive or understand, remains as secure as ever, and is as real as ever. That the things I see with my eyes and touch with my hands do exist, really exist," he continues, "I make not the least question." The reality of perceived things consists, he repeats, not in their independence of mind but in their independence of any

[1] *Berkeley and Percival. Correspondence,* edited by B. Rand, p. 80.

[2] *Principles,* 34, 35.

finite mind, in the fact that they are created by God and by him imprinted on my senses. In a similar fashion, Berkeley replies to critics who insist that the physical world of the idealist must be an impermanent universe of objects, annihilated when he turns his back upon them. "Sensible things," he says, "have an existence exterior to my mind; since I find them by experience to be independent of it. There is therefore some other Mind wherein they exist . . . as they did before my birth, and would do after my supposed annihilation." [1] And for Berkeley this other mind is, of course, the mind of God. In a word, Berkeley affirms the existence of a world of finite spirits, having precisely those involuntary and closely interrelated experiences which they all claim to have, yet owing these experiences not to "material," that is non-mental, objects but to the Infinite Spirit whose will creates the percepts within His own mind and the resembling and interconnected percepts in finite minds.

(2) Sophisticated critics nowadays direct their attention to the arguments by which Berkeley enforces his conclusion, and are first, and mainly, concerned to refute his two arguments against the existence of matter as immediately perceived. (a) The first of these is the relativity argument which, it will be remembered, sets forth that objects are not immediately perceived to be material for the reason that they may be characterized by opposite qualities—may be hot to the cooled hand and cold to the warmed hand, or blue at a distance and green when viewed from a nearer point. This argument is obviously based on the conception of the material object as stable and constant in its qualities; and this conception the twentieth century realist flatly repudi-

---

[1] *Three Dialogues between Hylas and Philonous*, III. THIS TEXT, p. 300.

ates. (b) The primary-secondary-quality argument, on the other hand, the modern realist neatly turns to his own use. He agrees with Berkeley that if the secondary qualities are mental so are the primary; but he adds that if the primary qualities are material so are the secondary. And he stoutly grasps the second horn of the dilemma. In other words he insists that the argument proves only that primary and secondary qualities must "row in the same boat," that is, must be conceived as alike material or alike mental.

Modern idealists take careful note of both criticisms. As regards the first of them they point out that the realistic conception of impermanent, unstable physical objects is fraught with great difficulties of its own.[1] The conclusion that the primary-secondary-quality distinction may tell as well for realism as idealism the Berkleian accepts—as Berkeley himself would have accepted it had he been writing for twentieth century readers and not for convinced followers of Locke. But the discriminating idealist is not greatly concerned for the fate of either argument. He bases idealism on no one of these subsidiary considerations but squarely, as Berkeley based it, on the one unchallengeable assertion: what I *directly* know, and all that I directly know, is a self (myself) experiencing. To state this central Berkleian position in slightly different fashion: what I am at any time unchallengeably, incontrovertibly certain of, when I assert the existence of a physical object —flower, desk or book—what I can maintain against anyone's denial is merely this, that I have such and such an idea, that I am experiencing in such and such

---

[1] Cf. the writer's *Persistent Problems of Philosophy*, 5th edition, pp. 414f. and 423ff., with references to Nunn, Broad, Russell, Alexander, and Pitkin, upholders of this theory, and to its critics, Drake and May Sinclair.

a fashion, sensationally, relationally, or affectively. Any other statement which I make may be disputed but no one on earth can challenge the assertions: "I see, hear, taste thus or thus," "I have such or such an idea," "I compare," "I relate causally." And each of these unchallengeable assertions has, as object, mental reality.

(3) Against each of the arguments by which Berkeley seeks to prove that matter can not validly be *inferred* to exist as cause of our percepts modern realists propose an objection. (a) In opposition to the argument, "the mental can not be caused by the non-mental," they rightly urge that it assumes what is a point at issue, the necessary likeness of cause and effect. (Modern idealists, accepting this criticism point out that Berkeley might, in Kantian fashion, have shown that cause is itself a form of experience.) (b) Against Berkeley's contention that matter is inactive, and accordingly noncausal, contemporary realists appeal to the modern dynamic conceptions of matter in terms of electrons moving with incomparable swiftness, with ceaseless energy. The idealist, on his side, hospitably welcomes the modern conceptions of matter. But he insists that the physical universe, thus described, is still reducible to the elemental factors which Berkeley discussed: that ions and electrons and atoms, as well as particles and planets, are spatial entities and are endowed with motion; that energy itself is motion, or capacity of motion; that force is ratio of motions or cause of motion—in a word, that there are no ultimately novel terms in which modern scientists describe their world. It follows that contemporary conceptions of matter are no less stateable than eighteenth century conceptions in Berkleian terms.

(4) Far more significant than any one of the preceding criticisms is the contention of contemporary

neo-realists that the idealistic position consists essentially in the fallacy of deducing from the truism "no unknown objects are known" the conclusion "no unknown objects exist." The first comment to be made on this criticism is that, like most of those already considered, it has been anticipated by Berkeley. Toward the end of the second of the *Three Dialogues between Hylas and Philonous*, Hylas proposes the conception of matter as "neither cause, instrument nor occasion but Something entirely unknown, distinct from all these." [1] Berkeley dismisses the conception on the following ground:— "Where," he says, "there is not so much as the most inadequate or faint idea pretended to—I will not indeed thence conclude against the reality of any notion, or existence of anything; but my inference shall be that you mean nothing at all." The discriminating idealist of our day will react in a similar fashion to the criticism in its modern form. He will admit that he himself and his fellow idealists have no right to deny forthwith the possible existence of unknown objects. But this, he will point out, is merely because no statement whatever should be made about anything conceived as literally unknown; and he will urge that the criticism cuts both ways and that consequently the realist has no more right than the idealist to make statements about unknown objects. This conclusion, however, obviously undermines the fundamental realistic teaching that objects exist both as unknown and as known. The idealist insists, accordingly, that his realistic critic must face the dilemma of Hylas: either he after all knows something of the objects which he calls unknown—that they exist, that they need not enter into the knowledge relation, and so on—or else he illicitly claims for himself the

[1] THIS TEXT, pp. 289, 291.

privilege, which he rightly denies to the idealist, of making assertions about that which is unknown.

ii. *Alleged Inconsistencies in Berkeley's Doctrine of the Universe as Spiritual*

(5) The criticisms so far considered have all been directed against Berkeley's doctrine of the objects of knowledge, in particular against his conception of the physical world as a system of ideas. Those which follow concern themselves not at all with his doctrine of physical objects but with his philosophy of spirits. The first of the criticisms to be discussed is that of Hume. With Berkeley's doctrine of the world of ideas Hume was completely in accord. "No man," Hume says, "who reflects, ever doubted that . . . *this house* and *that tree* are nothing but perceptions." [1] But Hume believes, in opposition to Berkeley, that only ideas exist, that the universe is merely a great and ordered collection of more or less vivid percepts and images. Accordingly he challenges Berkeley's doctrine of spirit or self, contending that mind, or spiritual substance, should have been outlawed along with matter. "All our perceptions," he says (and by "perceptions" he means precisely what Locke and Berkeley mean by "ideas") "may exist separately and have no need of anything else to support their existence." And he flatly denies the direct and intimate awareness of self which Descartes and Locke had strongly emphasized and Berkeley unequivocally asserted. "For my part," Hume says, in a very famous passage which follows on the words just quoted, "when I enter most intimately into what I call *myself* I always stumble on some particular perception or other of heat or cold, light or shade, love or hatred, pain or pleasure.

[1] *Inquiry Concerning Human Understanding,* Section XII.

I never can catch *myself* at any time without a perception. . . . When my perceptions are removed . . . I
. . . may be truly said not to exist." Accordingly,
Hume concludes, "what we call a *mind* is nothing but a
heap or collection of different perceptions." [1]

Against this move, however, Berkeley had already
countered. He was meditating on the concept of the
mind as "congeries of perceptions" [2] more than thirty
years before Hume published the *Treatise*. And in the
third of the *Dialogues between Hylas and Philonous*
he makes clear why he rejects this doctrine that the
mind is a "heap or collection" of ideas. "It seems,"
says Hylas, anticipating Hume's criticism, "that according to your own way of thinking, . . . it should follow
that *you* are only a system of floating ideas without any
substance to support them. Words are not to be used
without a meaning. And as there is no more meaning
in *spiritual Substance* than in *material Substance,* the
one is to be exploded as well as the other." To which
Philonous rejoins: "How often must I repeat that I
know or am conscious of my own being; and that *I myself* am not my ideas but somewhat . . . that perceives,
knows, wills, and operates about ideas. . . . I know
what I mean when I affirm that there is a spiritual substance or support of ideas, that is, that a spirit knows
and perceives ideas. But I do not know what is meant
when it is said that an unperceiving substance . . .
supports . . . ideas." [3] To this the twentieth century
idealist has nothing essential to add. He may indeed
point out that every Humian assumes a self in the very
denial of self, but he rests his case on the appeal to

[1] *Treatise of Human Understanding,* Book I., Part IV.,
Section vi.

[2] *Commonplace Book,* Fraser, *op. cit.,* Vol. I., p. 27.

[3] THIS TEXT, p. 304.

every man's direct and immediate experience of himself as being conscious, as having ideas.

(6) The difficulties next to be considered have to do with Berkeley's theistic position. All commentators, realists and idealists alike, are agreed that Berkeley is unsuccessful in his argument from Nature to God. He effectively argues, on the basis of his immaterialistic philosophy, that some spirit greater than himself exists as cause of his percepts. But he fails to prove, what is necessary to the final stage of his argument, that *only* an infinitely wise and good and powerful spirit could have caused the world as we find it, the community of finite spirits and the interlocking systems of their ordered ideas. On the contrary, the world as observed teems with mischances and miseries, with sins and stupidities, which it is crucially difficult, rather than inevitable, to attribute to an all-wise, all-good and all-powerful creator. Berkeley, to be sure, protests that experiences "which considered in themselves appear to be evil have the nature of good, when considered as linked with the whole system of beings." [1] But Berkeley has no right to this unqualified assertion. Had he already proved the existence of God, on quite other grounds, then indeed he might have pointed out that experiences, in themselves evil, may conceivably be parts of a whole that is good; and that consequently the existence of finite evils is compatible with that of an all-wise, all-good and all-powerful Creative Spirit. Instead, he unjustifiably makes the self-evident goodness of the world a postulate of his argument for the existence of God.

A second, less fundamental, difficulty in Berkeley's conception of God is a consequence not of his idealism but of the conventional type of his theism. It is his doctrine that God neither suffers pain nor perceives by

[1] *Principles*, 153.

sense, though he "knows or understands all things, and
. . . among other things what pain is." [1] But against
this conception must be urged the psychological impossibility of knowing what pain or taste or warmth or
any sensational experience really *is* without sensing it.
Berkeley's theism was not adventurous enough to achieve
the doctrine, essential to his own system, that God is both
a sensing and a suffering, though an infinite, being.

(7) By far the most serious of the criticisms on
Berkleian idealism concerns itself with the grounds of
his doctrine of our knowledge of spirits. The difficulty
in the form in which Berkeley tried to meet it is
pointedly put by Hylas towards the beginning of the
last of the *Three Dialogues*: "Answer me, Philonous.
Are all our ideas perfectly inert?" (And Philonous of
course replies that "they are altogether passive and
inert"). Hylas continues: "And is not God an agent, a
being purely active?"; to which Philonous once more
assents. On these admissions Hylas bases his argument.
Since no passive idea "can be like unto or represent" an
active spirit, we have therefore no idea of any spirit;
and accordingly Philonous can not even claim to know
his "own soul." [2]

A candid reader must admit that Hylas carried off the
honors in this philosophic tourney. Philonous, imper-
sonating Berkeley, has throughout implied that knowledge consists in the possession of an idea like its object;
and has stressed the contrast between passive ideas and
active spirits. And it certainly follows from this distinction that no idea can resemble a spirit and that

---

[1] *Three Dialogues between Hylas and Philonous,* III., THIS
TEXT, p. 313. Cf. *Alciphron,* IV., 24, THIS TEXT, p. 389.

[2] THIS TEXT, pp. 301 f., *Commonplace Book* (Fraser, *op.
cit.,* Vol. I., p. 38): "An idea being itself inactive cannot be
the resemblance or image of an active thing".

spirit, consequently, must remain unknown. Berkeley's effort, already considered, to evade the difficulty by proclaiming that he has an active "notion," not a passive "idea," of spirit is, as every one recognizes, a futile quibble; for he nowhere distinguishes notion from idea except by its function of resembling spirit (or relation). To the twentieth century idealist it is evident that there is only one way—but a clear way—out of the difficulty: to abandon, once and for all, the whole copy-theory of knowledge, by recognizing that ideas are ways in which minds are conscious, not copies distinct from mind of objects external to both. As a matter of fact, while at the same time inconsistently clinging to the mythical notion-doctrine of knowledge, Berkeley really takes this other way out. He reasserts his direct and immediate knowledge of his own existence and thus suggests the possibility of a knowledge of other selves which is from one point of view "mediate," because derived from his knowledge of himself, and yet from another point of view "direct," since it requires no intermediary idea. In other words, Berkeley virtually abandons the discredited view that a mind knows objects by possessing ideas which are like the objects known. Knowledge accordingly becomes for him an attitude of mind not an idea distinct from mind. And the illuminating, indisputable instance of direct knowledge is, as Berkeley reiterates, his knowledge of himself.

Present-day realists, unhampered by the copy-theory of knowledge, find a second difficulty in Berkeley's doctrine of knowledge of minds, or selves. Granting Berkeley's right to a certainty of his own existence, they contend that, on the basal principle of his idealism, he may know only his single, individual self—that other finite selves and God, as well as physical objects, reduce simply to ideas in his mind. In the writer's view, this criticism constitutes the one important contribution of contemporary realists to the great controversy between realists and idealists. The argument, as has just been stated, consists essentially in developing the implications of the fundamental idealistic position: I unchallengeably know only myself and my experience. From this it follows, the critic insists, not merely (as Berkeley had argued) that alleged material things are really my ideas but also that God and my fellow-men are my ideas. In a word, the metaphysical universe narrows to myself and my own experiences—I have no more right to infer the existence of other selves than to infer that of non-mental objects. Yet, on the other hand, the passivity of my perception, indeed all my involuntary experience, forces me to admit the existence of somewhat other-than-myself. The idealist is thus, his critic asserts, involved in a hopeless contradiction. On the one hand he insists that he is certain only of himself and his own experience. Yet, on the other hand, because of his directly experienced passivity, he is forced to admit the existence of something besides himself.

It can not be claimed that Berkeley met this criticism or even that he explicitly foresaw it. Twentieth century idealists adopt one of two attitudes toward it. The pluralists among them, those who conceive the universe as a great society of independent spirits, or persons, stressing the direct experience of passivity insist that the reality beyond me is more likely to resemble than to differ radically from the self directly known. In a word, they reason from analogy, or else they assume without reasoning, that the world is throughout mental. Monistic, or absolutistic, idealists on the other hand, believe that the paradox (involved in asserting both that I am certain only of myself and also that there exists reality outside myself) may be resolved by the conception of myself as identically part of an Including Self. So conceived, the other-than-self of which in my passivity I am directly conscious may be regarded as, in another sense, my own Greater Self. This doctrine can not properly be attributed to Berkeley but it may be argued that only by such a conception can Berkeley explain how the percepts which constitute his physical universe are at once his own and God's.

(8) The criticisms of Berkeley's idealism which the foregoing pages have discussed have been urged by realists, or jointly by realists and idealists. The difficulty to which these concluding pages call attention is one which almost all present-day idealists acutely feel. They point out that Berkeley, too closely following Locke's "new way by ideas," constantly tends to attribute to ideas a reality peculiarly their own and accordingly to obscure the subordinate relation of ideas to persons. In the *Commonplace Book* Berkeley had indeed written "Nothing properly but Persons, i.e. conscious things, do exist. All other things are not so much existences as manners of ye existence of persons." [1] But in *Principles* and *Dialogues* alike, the most systematic of Berkeley's metaphysical writings, he most often ignores this correct conception of the idea as a self's experiencing, treating it rather as a mental item or datum, essentially different from mind or self. When, for example, in the second paragraph of the *Principles,* he says explicitly that he denotes by *"mind, spirit, soul* or *myself* . . . a thing entirely distinct from them wherein they exist,"* the phrase "entirely distinct" is certainly with difficulty reconciled with the conception of ideas as ways in which the mind is conscious. The reiterated teaching that spirits are "active" and ideas "passive" has the same misleading tendency. For ideas

[1] Fraser, *op. cit.,* Vol. I., p. 59.

are "passive" only in the sense in which they are "dependent on" (that is, not independent of) mind; and they are dependent only as they are modes of the mind's awareness.

The mischievous tendency to attribute to ideas a reality of their own shows itself not only in the overstressed distinction of idea from mind but also in the artificial contrast of idea with object. The awkward copy-theory of knowledge, which so sharply separates knowing mind, representative idea, and object-known is one instance of this error. Another example is the seemingly dualistic implication of Berkeley's constant phrase "idea of." For these words seem clearly to imply, or at least to permit, the conception of the idea as distinct from, and opposed to, the object—fire, house, tree, or tulip—whereas, on Berkeley's principles the idea *is* the object. That Berkeley was not unaware of this confusion is clear from the following statement of the *Commonplace Book*: "The referring ideas to things which are not ideas, the using the term 'idea of' is one great cause of mistake." [1] But despite this warning to himself, it remains true that Berkeley's allusions to the "ideas of" objects are far more frequent than his unambiguous statements that "the things we see and feel . . . are . . . but so many sensations, notions, ideas." [2]

It may be suggested in conclusion that the preoccupation with ideas-as-such, which the preceding paragraphs have deprecated, may well account for Berkeley's unconcern for the personalistic conception of physical nature. This doctrine, put forward by Leibniz twenty

---

[1] Fraser, *op. cit.*, Vol. I., p. 35. Cf. pp. 30, 17.
[2] *Principles*, 5, which concludes with the words, omitted in the second edition, "In truth, the object and the sensation are the same thing."

years or so before Berkeley's day, regards the inorganic as well as the organic nature-object as sign of a distinct self. Berkeley conceives a human body not merely as his percept (and God's) but as a percept fitted to serve as "concomitant sign" of another human self. Leibniz goes further and conceives, not merely the human body, but every nature-object—every plant and stone, for example—as the body, or part of the body, of a distinct but extra-human spirit (or else as a collection of such bodies). Leibniz accordingly, unlike Berkeley, contrasts the physical with the human world, not as a system of ideas with the minds which possess the ideas, but rather as a world of relatively simple and incommunicative extra-human selves with the complex and intercommunicating selves which constitute human society. Toward such a personalistic doctrine of physical nature present-day idealism, whether theistic or non-theistic, pluralistic or monistic, seems to be tending.

The preceding pages have summarized and discussed the criticisms, old and new, of Berkeley's idealism. The outcome, in the view of the writer, is somewhat as follows: Berkeley has clearly formulated a conception, in its main outline self-consistent, of a world that is through and through mental. He has established, in opposition to his critics, his immaterialism and his personalism. With the difficulties inherent in his copy-theory of knowledge, his unwitting solipsism, his argument for the existence of God, and his over-rationalistic theism he has not satisfactorily dealt. Yet no one of these difficulties is necessarily involved in Berkeley's fundamental conception of the universe as personal, and each of them may be met by a modification of his teaching which is consistent with its basal principles.

MARY WHITON CALKINS.

BIBLIOGRAPHY

I. Chief Works of Berkeley

ARITHMETICA ABSQUE ALGEBRA AUT EUCLIDE DEMON-
  STRATA. Dublin, 1707.

MISCELLANEA MATHEMATICA. Dublin, 1707.

COMMONPLACE BOOK.
  Written, 1705-1708. First published, 1871.

AN ESSAY TOWARDS A NEW THEORY OF VISION. Dublin,
  1709.
  Second edition, 1709. Third edition, annexed to
Alciphron, 1732.

A TREATISE CONCERNING THE PRINCIPLES OF UNDER-
  STANDING. [Part I] Dublin, 1710.
  Second edition, 1734.

PASSIVE OBEDIENCE. London, 1712.
  Second unchanged edition, 1712. Third edition, 1713.

THREE DIALOGUES BETWEEN HYLAS AND PHILONOUS.
  London, 1713.
  Second unchanged edition, 1725. Third edition, 1734.

DE MOTU, sive de motus Principio et natura et de causa
  communicationis Motuum. London, 1721.
  Reprinted in the *Miscellany,* 1752.

AN ESSAY TOWARDS PREVENTING THE RUIN OF GREAT
  BRITAIN. London, 1721.
  Reprinted in the *Miscellany,* 1752.

A PROPOSAL for the better supplying of Churches in
  our Foreign Plantations and for converting the
  savage Americans to Christianity, by a College to
  be erected in the Summer Islands. London, 1725.
  Reprinted in the *Miscellany,* 1752.

ALCIPHRON; OR, THE MINUTE PHILOSOPHER.
> In Seven Dialogues. Containing an Apology for
> the Christian Religion, against those who are called
> Free-thinkers. Dublin, 1732.
> Second edition, 1732. Third edition, 1752.

THE THEORY OF VISION, OR VISUAL LANGUAGE, SHEWING
THE IMMEDIATE PRESENCE AND PROVIDENCE OF A
DEITY. London, 1733.

THE ANALYST; OR, A DISCOURSE ADDRESSED TO AN IN-
FIDEL MATHEMATICIAN. Dublin and London, 1734.

A DEFENCE OF FREE THINKING IN MATHEMATICS. 1735.

THE QUERIST. In Three Parts. Dublin, 1735, 1736,
1737.
> Second edition, with omissions and additions, Lon-
don, 1750.

[SIRIS] A CHAIN OF PHILOSOPHICAL REFLEXIONS AND
INQUIRIES CONCERNING THE VIRTUES OF TAR-WATER
AND DIVERS OTHER SUBJECTS Connected Together
and Arising from One Another. London and Dublin, 1744.
> Later editions, 1744, 1746, 1748.

A MISCELLANY CONTAINING SEVERAL TRACTS ON VARI-
OUS SUBJECTS. London and Dublin, 1752.
> (With the exception of the first, *Farther Thoughts on
> Tar Water,* these traits are all reprints of earlier
> publications. The *Miscellany* contains also the
> *Verses,* prefixed to this volume, which seem to have
> been written in 1726.)

II

The Works of George Berkeley, edited by A. C. Fraser.
Vols. I-IV. Oxford, 1901.

Life and Letters of George Berkeley. A. C. Fraser.
Oxford, 1871.

Beiträge zur Lebensgeschichte Berkeleys. Th. Lorenz, *Arch. für Geschichte der Philosophie,* vols. XIII., XIV., XVII., XVIII., and *Mind,* N. S. Vol. XIII.

Berkeley and Percival. Correspondence. Edited by B. Rand, 1914.

Three Men of Letters. M. C. Tyler, 1895.

III

The Development of Berkeley's Philosophy. G. A. Johnston. London, 1923.

George Berkeley. Leben Und Lehre (with bibliography). R. Metz. Stuttgart. 1925.

Berkeley's Life and Writings. J. S. Mill, In *Dissertations and Discussions,* Vol. IV.

The Persistent Problems of Philosophy. (chapters V., XI.) By M. W. Calkins. Fifth revised edition, 1925.

The text of this volume is, by permission of the Delegates of the Clarendon Press, that of Fraser's 1901 edition of The Works of George Berkeley. Heavy-faced square brackets enclose words or sentences added by Berkeley in second (or in still later) editions of the various works here reprinted; light-faced brackets contain material omitted in second or in later editions.

AN ESSAY

TOWARDS

A NEW THEORY OF VISION

TO THE

RT. HON. SIR JOHN PERCIVALE, BART.

ONE OF HER MAJESTY'S MOST HONOURABLE PRIVY COUNCIL
IN THE KINGDOM OF IRELAND.

SIR,

I COULD not, without doing violence to myself, forbear upon this occasion to give some public testimony of the great and well-grounded esteem I have conceived for you, ever since I had the honour and happiness of your acquaintance. The outward advantages of fortune, and the early honours with which you are adorned, together with the reputation you are known to have amongst the best and most considerable men, may well imprint veneration and esteem on the minds of those who behold you from a distance. But these are not the chief motives that inspire me with the respect I bear you. A nearer approach has given me the view of something in your person infinitely beyond the external ornaments of honour and estate. I mean, an intrinsic stock of virtue and good sense, a true concern for religion, and disinterested love of your country. Add to these an uncommon proficiency in the best and most useful parts of knowledge; together with (what in my mind is a perfection of the first rank) a surpassing goodness of nature. All which I have collected, not from the uncertain reports of fame, but from my own experience. Within these few months that I have the honour to be known unto you, the many delight-

3

ful hours I have passed in your agreeable and improving conversation have afforded me the opportunity of discovering in you many excellent qualities, which at once fill me with admiration and esteem. That one at those years, and in those circumstances of wealth and greatness, should continue proof against the charms of luxury and those criminal pleasures so fashionable and predominant in the age we live in; that he should preserve a sweet and modest behaviour, free from that insolent and assuming air so familiar to those who are placed above the ordinary rank of men; that he should manage a great fortune with that prudence and inspection, and at the same time expend it with that generosity and nobleness of mind, as to shew himself equally remote from a sordid parsimony and a lavish inconsiderate profusion of the good things he is intrusted with—this, surely, were admirable and praiseworthy. But, that he should, moreover, by an impartial exercise of his reason, and constant perusal of the sacred Scriptures, endeavour to attain a right notion of the principles of natural and revealed religion; that he should with the concern of a true patriot have the interest of the public at heart, and omit no means of informing himself what may be prejudicial or advantageous to his country, in order to prevent the one and promote the other; in fine, that, by a constant application to the most severe and useful studies, by a strict observation of the rules of honour and virtue, by frequent and serious reflections on the mistaken measures of the world, and the true end and happiness of mankind, he should in all respects qualify himself bravely to run the race that is set before him, to deserve the character of great and good in this life, and be ever happy hereafter—this were amazing and almost incredible. Yet all this, and more than this, Sir, might I justly say of you, did either your modesty

permit, or your character stand in need of it. I know it
might deservedly be thought a vanity in me to imagine
that anything coming from so obscure a hand as mine
could add a lustre to your reputation. But, I am withal
sensible how far I advance the interest of my own, by
laying hold on this opportunity to make it known that
I am admitted into some degree of intimacy with a person of your exquisite judgment. And, with that view,
I have ventured to make you an address of this nature,
which the goodness I have ever experienced in you
inclines me to hope will meet with a favourable reception at your hands. Though I must own I have your
pardon to ask, for touching on what may possibly be
offensive to a virtue you are possessed of in a very
distinguishing degree. Excuse me, SIR, if it was out of
my power to mention the name of SIR JOHN PERCIVALE
without paying some tribute to that extraordinary and
surprising merit whereof I have so clear and affecting
an idea, and which, I am sure, cannot be exposed in too
full a light for the imitation of others.

Of late I have been agreeably employed in considering the most noble, pleasant, and comprehensive of all
the senses. The fruit of that (labour shall I call it or)
diversion is what I now present you with, in hopes it
may give some entertainment to one who, in the midst
of business and vulgar enjoyments, preserves a relish
for the more refined pleasures of thought and reflexion.
My thoughts concerning Vision have led me into some
notions so far out of the common road that it had been
improper to address them to one of a narrow and contracted genius. But, you, SIR, being master of a large
and free understanding, raised above the power of those
prejudices that enslave the far greater part of mankind, may deservedly be thought a proper patron for an
attempt of this kind. Add to this, that you are no less

disposed to forgive than qualified to discern whatever
faults may occur in it. Nor do I think you defective
in any one point necessary to form an exact judgment
on the most abstract and difficult things, so much as
in a just confidence of your own abilities. And, in this
one instance, give me leave to say, you shew a manifest
weakness of judgment. With relation to the following
Essay, I shall only add that I beg your pardon for laying a trifle of that nature in your way, at a time when
you are engaged in the important affairs of the nation,
and desire you to think that I am, with all sincerity and
respect,

SIR,

Your most faithful and most humble servant,

GEORGE BERKELEY.

CONTENTS

7

138. The way wherein we apprehend motion by sight easily collected from what hath been said.

139. *Ques.* How visible and tangible ideas came to have the same name, if not of the same kind.

140. This accounted for without supposing them of the same kind.

141. *Obj.* That a tangible square is liker to a visible square than to a visible circle.

142. *Ans.* That a visible square is fitter than a visible circle to represent a tangible square.

143. But it doth not hence follow that a visible square is like a tangible square.

144. Why we are more apt to confound visible with tangible ideas, than other signs with the things signified.

145. Several other reasons hereof assigned.

146. Reluctancy in rejecting any opinion no argument of its truth.

147. Proper objects of Vision the Language of Nature.

148. In it there is much admirable and deserving our attention.

149. Question proposed concerning the object of geometry.

150. At first view we are apt to think visible extension the object of geometry.

151. Visible extension shewn not to be the object of geometry.

152. Words may as well be thought the object of geometry as visible extension.

153. It is proposed to inquire, what progress an intelligence that could see, but not feel, might make in geometry.

154. He cannot understand those parts which relate to solids, and their surfaces, and lines generated by their section.

155. Nor even the elements of plane geometry.

156. The proper objects of sight incapable of being managed as geometrical figures.

157. The opinion of those who hold plane figures to be the immediate objects of sight considered.

158. Planes no more the immediate objects of sight than solids.

159. Difficult to enter precisely into the thoughts of the above-mentioned intelligence.

160. The object of geometry, its not being sufficiently understood, cause of difficulty and useless labour in that science.

AN ESSAY

TOWARDS

A NEW THEORY OF VISION

1. My design is to shew the manner wherein we perceive by Sight the Distance, Magnitude, and Situation of objects: also to consider the difference there is betwixt the ideas of Sight and Touch, and whether there be any idea common to both senses.

2. It is, I think, agreed by all that Distance, of itself and immediately, cannot be seen. For, distance being a line directed endwise to the eye, it projects only one point in the fund of the eye, which point remains invariably the same, whether the distance be longer or shorter.

3. I find it also acknowledged that the estimate we make of the distance of objects considerably remote is rather an act of judgment grounded on experience than of sense. For example, when I perceive a great number of intermediate objects, such as houses, fields, rivers, and the like, which I have experienced to take up a considerable space, I thence form a judgment or conclusion, that the object I see beyond them is at a great distance. Again, when an object appears faint and small which at a near distance I have experienced to make a vigorous and large appearance, I instantly con-

clude it to be far off. And this, it is evident, is the result of experience; without which, from the faintness and littleness, I should not have inferred anything concerning the distance of objects.

4. But, when an object is placed at so near a distance as that the interval between the eyes bears any sensible proportion to it, the opinion of speculative men is, that the two optic axes (the fancy that we see only with one eye at once being exploded), concurring at the object, do there make an angle, by means of which, according as it is greater or lesser, the object is perceived to be nearer or farther off.

5. Betwixt which and the foregoing manner of estimating distance there is this remarkable difference:—that, whereas there was no apparent *necessary* connexion between small distance and a large and strong appearance, or between great distance and a little and faint appearance, there appears a very *necessary* connexion between an obtuse angle and near distance, and an acute angle and farther distance. It does not in the least depend upon experience, but may be evidently known by any one before he had experienced it, that the nearer the concurrence of the optic axes the greater the angle, and the remoter their concurrence is, the lesser will be the angle comprehended by them.

6. There is another way, mentioned by optic writers, whereby they will have us judge of those distances in respect of which the breadth of the pupil hath any sensible bigness. And that is the greater or lesser divergency of the rays which, issuing from the visible point, do fall on the pupil—that point being judged nearest which is seen by most diverging rays, and that remoter which is seen by less diverging rays, and so on; the apparent distance still increasing, as the divergency of the rays decreases, till at length it becomes infinite,

when the rays that fall on the pupil are to sense parallel. And after this manner it is said we perceive distance when we look only with one eye.

7. In this case also it is plain we are not beholden to experience: it being a certain necessary truth that, the nearer the direct rays falling on the eye approach to a parallelism, the farther off is the point of their intersection, or the visible point from whence they flow.

8. Now, though the accounts here given of perceiving *near* distance by sight are received for true, and accordingly made use of in determining the apparent places of objects, they do nevertheless seem to me very unsatisfactory, and that for these following reasons:—

9. [*First,*] It is evident that, when the mind perceives any idea not immediately and of itself, it must be by the means of some other idea. Thus, for instance, the passions which are in the mind of another are of themselves to me invisible. I may nevertheless perceive them by sight; though not immediately, yet by means of the colours they produce in the countenance. We often see shame or fear in the looks of a man, by perceiving the changes of his countenance to red or pale.

10. Moreover, it is evident that no idea which is not itself perceived can be to me the means of perceiving any other idea. If I do not perceive the redness or paleness of a man's face themselves, it is impossible I should perceive by them the passions which are in his mind.

11. Now, from sect. ii., it is plain that distance is in its own nature imperceptible, and yet it is perceived by sight. It remains, therefore, that it be brought into view by means of some other idea, that is itself immediately perceived in the act of vision.

12. But those lines and angles, by means whereof

some men pretend to explain the perception of distance, are themselves not at all perceived; nor are they in truth ever thought of by those unskilful in optics. I appeal to any one's experience, whether, upon sight of an object, he computes its distance by the bigness of the angle made by the meeting of the two optic axes? or whether he ever thinks of the greater or lesser divergency of the rays which arrive from any point to his pupil? nay, whether it be not perfectly impossible for him to perceive by sense the various angles wherewith the rays, according to their greater or lesser divergence, do fall on the eye? Every one is himself the best judge of what he perceives, and what not. In vain shall any man tell me, that I perceive certain lines and angles, which introduce into my mind the various ideas of distance, so long as I myself am conscious of no such thing.

13. Since therefore those angles and lines are not themselves perceived by sight, it follows, from sect. x., that the mind does not by them judge of the distance of objects.

14. [*Secondly,*] The truth of this assertion will be yet farther evident to any one that considers those lines and angles have no real existence in nature, being only an hypothesis framed by the mathematicians, and by them introduced into optics, that they might treat of that science in a geometrical way.

15. The [*third* and] last reason I shall give for rejecting that doctrine is, that though we should grant the real existence of those optic angles, &c., and that it was possible for the mind to perceive them, yet these principles would not be found sufficient to explain the phenomena of distance, as shall be shewn hereafter.

16. Now it being already shewn that distance is *suggested* to the mind, by the mediation of some other idea

which is itself perceived in the act of seeing, it remains that we inquire, what ideas or sensations there be that attend vision, unto which we may suppose the ideas of distance are connected, and by which they are introduced into the mind.

And, *first,* it is certain by experience, that when we look at a near object with both eyes, according as it approaches or recedes from us, we alter the disposition of our eyes, by lessening or widening the interval between the pupils. This disposition or turn of the eyes is attended with a sensation, which seems to me to be that which in this case brings the idea of greater or lesser distance into the mind.

17. Not that there is any natural or necessary connexion between the sensation we perceive by the turn of the eyes and greater or lesser distance. But—because the mind has, by constant experience, found the different sensations corresponding to the different dispositions of the eyes to be attended each with a different degree of distance in the object—there has grown an habitual or customary connexion between those two sorts of ideas: so that the mind no sooner perceives the sensation arising from the different turn it gives the eyes, in order to bring the pupils nearer or farther asunder, but it withal perceives the different idea of distance which was wont to be connected with that sensation. Just as, upon hearing a certain sound, the idea is immediately suggested to the understanding which custom had united with it.

18. Nor do I see how I can easily be mistaken in this matter. I know evidently that distance is not perceived of itself; that, by consequence, it must be perceived by means of some other idea, which is immediately perceived, and varies with the different degrees of distance I know also that the sensation arising from the turn of

the eyes is of itself immediately perceived; and various degrees thereof are connected with different distances, which never fail to accompany them into my mind, when I view an object distinctly with both eyes whose distance is so small that in respect of it the interval between the eyes has any considerable magnitude.

19. I know it is a received opinion that, by altering the disposition of the eyes, the mind perceives whether the angle of the optic axes, or the lateral angles comprehended between the interval of the eyes or the optic axes, are made greater or lesser; and that, accordingly, by a kind of natural geometry, it judges the point of their intersection to be nearer or farther off. But that this is not true I am convinced by my own experience; since I am not conscious that I make any such use of the perception I have by the turn of my eyes. And for me to make those judgments and draw those conclusions from it, without knowing that I do so, seems altogether incomprehensible.

20. From all which it follows, that the judgment we make of the distance of an object viewed with both eyes is entirely the result of experience. If we had not constantly found certain sensations, arising from the various disposition of the eyes, attended with certain degrees of distance, we should never make those sudden judgments from them concerning the distance of objects; no more than we would pretend to judge of a man's thoughts by his pronouncing words we had never heard before.

21. *Secondly,* an object placed at a certain distance from the eye, to which the breadth of the pupil bears a considerable proportion, being made to approach, is seen more confusedly. And the nearer it is brought the more confused appearance it makes. And this being found constantly to be so, there arises in the mind an habitual

connexion between the several degrees of confusion and distance; the greater confusion still implying the lesser distance, and the lesser confusion the greater distance of the object.

22. This confused appearance of the object doth therefore seem to be the medium whereby the mind judges of distance, in those cases wherein the most approved writers of optics will have it judge by the different divergency with which the rays flowing from the radiating point fall on the pupil. No man, I believe, will pretend to see or feel those imaginary angles that the rays are supposed to form, according to their various inclinations on his eye. But he cannot choose seeing whether the object appear more or less confused. It is therefore a manifest consequence from what has been demonstrated that, instead of the greater or lesser divergency of the rays, the mind makes use of the greater or lesser confusedness of the appearance, thereby to determine the apparent place of an object.

23. Nor doth it avail to say there is not any necessary connexion between confused vision and distance great or small. For I ask any man what necessary connexion he sees between the redness of a blush and shame? And yet no sooner shall he behold that colour to arise in the face of another but it brings into his mind the idea of that passion which hath been observed to accompany it.

24. What seems to have misled the writers of optics in this matter is, that they imagine men judge of distance as they do of a conclusion in mathematics; betwixt which and the premises it is indeed absolutely requisite there be an apparent necessary connexion. But it is far otherwise in the sudden judgments men make of distance. We are not to think that brutes and children, or even grown reasonable men, whenever they perceive

an object to approach or depart from them, do it by virtue of geometry and demonstration.

25. That one idea may suggest another to the mind, it will suffice that they have been observed to go together, without any demonstration of the *necessity* of their coexistence, or without so much as knowing what it is that makes them so to coexist. Of this there are innumerable instances, of which no one can be ignorant.

26. Thus, greater confusion having been constantly attended with nearer distance, no sooner is the former idea perceived but it suggests the latter to our thoughts. And, if it had been the ordinary course of nature that the farther off an object were placed the more confused it should appear, it is certain the very same perception that now makes us think an object approaches would then have made us to imagine it went farther off, that perception, abstracting from custom and experience, being equally fitted to produce the idea of great distance, or small distance, or no distance at all.

27. *Thirdly,* an object being placed at the distance above specified, and brought nearer to the eye, we may nevertheless prevent, at least for some time, the appearance's growing more confused, by straining the eye. In which case that sensation supplies the place of confused vision, in aiding the mind to judge of the distance of the object; it being esteemed so much the nearer by how much the effort or straining of the eye in order to distinct vision is greater.

28. I have here set down those sensations or ideas that seem to be the constant and general occasions of introducing into the mind the different ideas of near distance. It is true, in most cases, that divers other circumstances contribute to frame our idea of distance, viz. the particular number, size, kind, &c. of the things

seen. Concerning which, as well as all other the fore-mentioned occasions which suggest distance, I shall only observe, they have none of them, in their own nature, any relation or connexion with it: nor is it possible they should ever signify the various degrees thereof, other-wise than as by experience they have been found to be connected with them.

29. I shall proceed upon these principles to account for a phenomenon which has hitherto strangely puzzled the writers of optics, and is so far from being accounted for by any of their theories of vision, that it is, by their own confession, plainly repugnant to them; and of con-sequence, if nothing else could be objected, were alone sufficient to bring their credit in question. The whole difficulty I shall lay before you in the words of the learned Doctor Barrow, with which he concludes his *Optic Lectures:*—

'Hæc sunt, quæ circa partem opticæ præcipue mathe-maticam dicenda mihi suggessit meditatio. Circa reli-quas (quæ φυσικώτεραι sunt, adeoque sæpiuscule pro certis principiis plausibiles conjecturas venditare neces-sum habent) nihil fere quicquam admodum verisimile succurrit, a pervulgatis (ab iis, inquam, quæ Keplerus, Scheinerus, Cartesius, et post illos alii tradiderunt) alienum aut diversum. Atqui tacere malo, quam toties oblatam crambem reponere. Proinde receptui cano; nec ita tamen ut prorsus discedam, anteaquam improbam quandam difficultatem (pro sinceritate quam et vobis et veritati debeo minime dissimulandam) in medium protulero, quæ doctrinæ nostræ, hactenus inculcatæ, se objicit adversam, ab ea saltem nullam admittit solu-tionem. Illa, breviter, talis est. Lenti vel speculo cavo *EBF* exponatur punctum visibile *A,* ita distans, ut radii ex *A* manantes ex inflectione versus axem *AB* cogantur. Sitque radiationis limes (seu puncti *A* imago, qualem

supra passim statuimus) punctum *Z*. Inter hoc autem
et inflectentis verticem *B* uspiam positus concipiatur
oculus. Quæri jam potest, ubi loci debeat punctum *A*
apparere? Retrorsum ad punctum *Z* videri non fert
natura (cum omnis impressio sensum afficiens proveniat
a partibus *A*) ac experientia reclamat. Nostris autem
e placitis consequi videtur, ipsum ad partes anticas

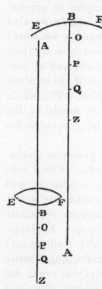

apparens, ab intervallo longissime
dissito (quod et maximum sensible
quodvis intervallum quodammodo ex-
superet), apparere. Cum enim quo
radiis minus divergentibus attingitur
objectum, eo (seclusis utique prænotionibus et præjudiciis) longius
abesse sentiatur; et quod parallelos
ad oculum radios projicit, remotis-
sime positum æstimetur: exigere ratio
videtur, ut quod convergentibus radiis apprehenditur, adhuc magis, si
fieri posset, quoad apparentiam elon-
getur. Quin et circa casum hunc
generatim inquiri possit, quidnam
omnino sit, quod apparentem puncti
A locum determinet, faciatque quod
constanti ratione nunc propius, nunc
remotius appareat? Cui itidem
dubio nihil quicquam ex hactenus
dictorum analogia responderi posse videtur, nisi debere
punctum *A* perpetuo longissime semotum videri. Verum
experientia secus attestatur, illud pro diversa oculi inter
puncta *B, Z,* positione varie distans, nunquam fere (si
unquam) longinquius ipso *A* libere spectato, subinde
vero multo propinquius adparere; quinimo, quo oculum
appellentes radii magis convergunt, eo speciem objecti
propius accedere. Nempe, si puncto *B* admoveatur

oculus, suo (ad lentem) fere nativo in loco conspicitur punctum *A* (vel æque distans, ad speculum); ad *O* reductus oculus ejusce speciem appropinquantem cernit; ad *P* adhuc vicinius ipsum existimat; ac ita sensim, donec alicubi tandem, velut ad *Q*, constituto oculo, objectum summe propinquum apparens in meram confusionem incipiat evanescere. Quæ sane cuncta rationibus atque decretis nostris repugnare videntur, aut cum iis saltem parum amice conspirant. Neque nostram tantum sententiam pulsat hoc experimentum, at ex æquo cæteras quas norim omnes: veterem imprimis ac vulgatam, nostræ præ reliquis affinem, ita convellere videtur, ut ejus vi coactus doctissimus *A*. Tacquetus isti principio (cui pene soli totam inædificaverat *Catoptricam* suam) ceu infido ac inconstanti renunciarit, adeoque suam ipse doctrinam labefactarit? id tamen, opinor, minime facturus, si rem totam inspexisset penitius, atque difficultatis fundum attigissit. Apud me vero non ita pollet hæc, nec eousque præpollebit ulla difficultas, ut ab iis quæ manifeste rationi consentanea video, discedam; præsertim quum, ut hic accidit, ejusmodi difficultas in singularis cujuspiam casus disparitate fundetur. Nimirum in præsente casu peculiare quiddam, naturæ subtilitati involutum, delitescit, ægre fortassis, nisi perfectius explorato videndi modo, detegendum. Circa quod nil, fateor, hactenus excogitare potui, quod adblandiretur animo meo, nedum plane satisfaceret. Vobis itaque nodum hunc, utinam feliciore conatu, resolvendum committo.'

In English as follows:

'I have here delivered what my thoughts have suggested to me concerning that part of optics which is more properly mathematical. As for the other parts of that science (which, being rather physical, do conse-

quently abound with plausible conjectures instead of
certain principles), there has in them scarce anything
occurred to my observation different from what has been
already said by Kepler, Scheinerus, Des Cartes, &c.
And methinks I had better say nothing at all than repeat that which has been so often said by others. I
think it therefore high time to take my leave of this
subject. But, before I quit it for good and all, the fair
and ingenuous dealing that I owe both to you and to
truth obliges me to acquaint you with a certain untoward difficulty, which seems directly opposite to the
doctrine I have been hitherto inculcating, at least admits of no solution from it. In short it is this. Before
the double convex glass or concave speculum *EBF,* let
the point *A* be placed at such a distance that the rays
proceeding from *A,* after refraction or reflection, be
brought to unite somewhere in the axis *AB.* And suppose the point of union (*i.e.* the image of the point *A,*
as hath been already set forth) to be *Z;* between which
and *B,* the vertex of the glass or speculum, conceive the
eye to be anywhere placed. The question now is, where
the point *A* ought to appear. Experience shews that it
doth not appear behind at the point *Z;* and it were contrary to nature that it should; since all the impression
which affects the sense comes from towards *A.* But,
from our tenets it should seem to follow that it would
appear before the eye at a vast distance off, so great
as should in some sort surpass all sensible distance. For
since, if we exclude all anticipations and prejudices,
every object appears by so much the farther off by
how much the rays it sends to the eye are less diverging; and that object is thought to be most remote from
which parallel rays proceed unto the eye; reason would
make one think that object should appear at yet a
greater distance which is seen by converging rays.

Moreover, it may in general be asked concerning this
case, what it is that determines the apparent place of
the point *A*, and maketh it to appear after a constant
manner, sometimes nearer, at other times farther off?
To which doubt I see nothing that can be answered
agreeable to the principles we have laid down, except
only that the point *A* ought always to appear extremely
remote. But, on the contrary, we are assured by experience, that the point *A* appears variously distant, according to the different situations of the eye between
the points *B* and *Z*. And that it doth almost never (if
at all) seem farther off than it would if it were beheld
by the naked eye; but, on the contrary, it doth sometimes appear much nearer. Nay, it is even certain that
by how much the rays falling on the eye do more converge, by so much the nearer does the object seem to
approach. For, the eye being placed close to the point
B, the object *A* appears nearly in its own natural place,
if the point *B* is taken in the glass, or at the same distance, if in the speculum. The eye being brought back
to *O*, the object seems to draw near; and, being come to
P, it beholds it still nearer: and so on by little and little,
till at length the eye being placed somewhere, suppose
at *Q*, the object appearing extremely near begins to
vanish into mere confusion. All which doth seem
repugnant to our principles; at least, not rightly to
agree with them. Nor is our tenet alone struck at by
this experiment, but likewise all others that ever came
to my knowledge are every whit as much endangered
by it. The ancient one especially (which is most commonly received, and comes nearest to mine) seems to
be so effectually overthrown thereby that the most
learned Tacquet has been forced to reject that principle,
as false and uncertain, on which alone he had built
almost his whole *Catoptrics*, and consequently, by tak-

ing away the foundation, hath himself pulled down the superstructure he had raised on it. Which, nevertheless, I do not believe he would have done, had he but considered the whole matter more thoroughly, and examined the difficulty to the bottom. But as for me, neither this nor any other difficulty shall have so great an influence on me, as to make me renounce that which I know to be manifestly agreeable to reason. Especially when, as it here falls out, the difficulty is founded in the peculiar nature of a certain odd and particular case. For, in the present case something peculiar lies hid, which, being involved in the subtilty of nature, will perhaps hardly be discovered till such time as the manner of vision is more perfectly made known. Concerning which, I must own I have hitherto been able to find out nothing that has the least show of probability, not to mention certainty. I shall therefore leave this knot to be untied by you, wishing you may have better success in it than I have had.'

30. The ancient and received principle, which Dr. Barrow here mentions as the main foundation of Tacquet's *Catoptrics,* is, that every 'visible point seen by reflection from a speculum shall appear placed at the intersection of the reflected ray and the perpendicular of incidence.' Which intersection in the present case happening to be behind the eye, it greatly shakes the authority of that principle whereon the aforementioned author proceeds throughout his whole *Catoptrics,* in determining the apparent place of objects seen by reflection from any kind of speculum.

31. Let us now see how this phenomenon agrees with our tenets. The eye, the nearer it is placed to the point B in the above figures, the more distinct is the appearance of the object: but, as it recedes to O, the appear-

ance grows more confused; and at *P* it sees the object yet more confused; and so on, till the eye, being brought back to *Z,* sees the object in the greatest confusion of all. Wherefore, by sect. 21, the object should seem to approach the eye gradually, as it recedes from the point *B;* that is, at *O* it should (in consequence of the principle I have laid down in the aforesaid section) seem nearer than it did at *B,* and at *P* nearer than at *O,* and at *Q* nearer than at *P,* and so on, till it quite vanishes at *Z.* Which is the very matter of fact, as any one that pleases may easily satisfy himself by experiment.

32. This case is much the same as if we should suppose an Englishman to meet a foreigner who used the same words with the English, but in a direct contrary signification. The Englishman would not fail to make a wrong judgment of the ideas annexed to those sounds, in the mind of him that used them. Just so in the present case, the object speaks (if I may so say) with words that the eye is well acquainted with, that is, confusions of appearance; but, whereas heretofore the greatest confusions were always wont to signify nearer distances, they have in this case a direct contrary signification, being connected with the greater distances. Whence it follows that the eye must unavoidably be mistaken, since it will take the confusions in the sense it has been used to, which is directly opposed to the true.

33. This phenomenon, as it entirely subverts the opinion of those who will have us judge of distance by lines and angles, on which supposition it is altogether inexplicable, so it seems to me no small confirmation of the truth of that principle whereby it is explained. But, in order to a more full explication of this point, and to shew how far the hypothesis of the mind's judging by the various divergency of rays may be of use in

determining the apparent place of an object, it will be
necessary to premise some few things, which are already
well known to those who have any skill in Dioptrics.

34. *First,* Any radiating point is then distinctly seen
when the rays proceeding from it are, by the refractive
power of the crystalline, accurately reunited in the
retina or fund of the eye. But if they are reunited
either before they arrive at the retina, or after they
have passed it, then there is confused vision.

35. *Secondly,* Suppose, in the adjacent figures, *NP*
represent an eye duly framed, and retaining its natural
figure. In fig. 1 the rays falling nearly parallel on the
eye, are, by the crystalline *AB*, refracted, so as their
focus, or point of union *F*, falls exactly on the retina.
But, if the rays fall sensibly diverging on the eye, as
in fig. 2, then their focus falls beyond the retina; or,
if the rays are made to converge by the lens *QS*, before
they come at the eye, as in fig. 3, their focus *F* will
fall before the retina. In which two last cases it is
evident, from the foregoing section, that the appearance
of the point *Z* is confused. And, by how much the
greater is the convergency or divergency of the rays
falling on the pupil, by so much the farther will the
point of their reunion be from the retina, either before
or behind it, and consequently the point *Z* will appear
by so much the more confused. And this, by the bye,
may shew us the difference between confused and faint
vision. Confused vision is, when the rays proceeding
from each distinct point of the object are not accurately
re-collected in one corresponding point on the retina,
but take up some space thereon—so that rays from
different points become mixed and confused together.
This is opposed to a distinct vision, and attends near
objects. Faint vision is when, by reason of the distance of the object, or grossness of the interjacent

medium, few rays arrive from the object to the eye. This is opposed to vigorous or clear vision, and attends remote objects. But to return.

36. The eye, or (to speak truly) the mind, perceiving only the confusion itself, without ever considering the cause from which it proceeds, doth constantly annex the same degree of distance to the same degree of con-

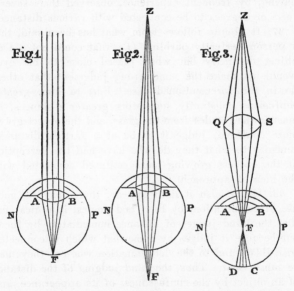

fusion. Whether that confusion be occasioned by converging or by diverging rays it matters not. Whence it follows that the eye, viewing the object Z through the glass QS (which by refraction causeth the rays ZQ, ZS, &c. to converge), should judge it to be at such a nearness, at which, if it were placed, it would radiate on the eye, with rays diverging to that degree as would produce the same confusion which is now produced by converging rays, *i.e.* would cover a portion of the retina equal to *DC*. (Vid. fig. 3, *sup.*) But then this must be understood (to use Dr. Barrow's phrase) 'seclusis prænotionibus et præjudiciis,' in case we abstract from all other circumstances of vision, such as the figure, size, faintness, &c. of the visible objects—all which do ordinarily concur to form our idea of distance, the mind having, by frequent experience, observed their several sorts or degrees to be connected with various distances.

37. It plainly follows from what has been said, that a person perfectly purblind (*i.e.* that could not see an object distinctly but when placed close to his eye) would not make the same wrong judgment that others do in the forementioned case. For, to him, greater confusions constantly suggesting greater distances, he must, as he recedes from the glass, and the object grows more confused, judge it to be at a farther distance; contrary to what they do who have had the perception of the objects growing more confused connected with the idea of approach.

38. Hence also it doth appear, there may be good use of computation, by lines and angles, in optics; not that the mind judges of distance immediately by them, but because it judges by somewhat which is connected with them, and to the determination whereof they may be subservient. Thus, the mind judging of the distance of an object by the confusedness of its appearance, and this confusedness being greater or lesser to the naked eye, according as the object is seen by rays more or less diverging, it follows that a man may make use of the divergency of the rays, in computing the apparent distance, though not for its own sake, yet on account of the confusion with which it is connected. But so it is, the confusion itself is entirely neglected by mathematicians, as having no necessary relation with distance,

such as the greater or lesser angles of divergency are
conceived to have. And these (especially for that they
fall under mathematical computation) are alone regarded, in determining the apparent places of objects,
as though they were the sole and immediate cause of the
judgments the mind makes of distance. Whereas, in
truth, they should not at all be regarded in themselves,
or any otherwise than as they are supposed to be the
cause of confused vision.

39. The not considering of this has been a fundamental and perplexing oversight. For proof whereof,
we need go no farther than the case before us. It
having been observed that the most diverging rays
brought into the mind the idea of nearest distance, and
that still as the divergency decreased the distance increased, and it being thought the connexion between
the various degrees of divergency and distance was immediate—this naturally leads one to conclude, from an
ill-grounded analogy, that converging rays shall make
an object appear at an immense distance, and that, as
the convergency increases, the distance (if it were possible) should do so likewise. That this was the cause
of Dr. Barrow's mistake is evident from his own words
which we have quoted. Whereas had the learned Doctor observed that diverging and converging rays, how
opposite soever they may seem, do nevertheless agree
in producing the same effect, to wit, confusedness of
vision, greater degrees whereof are produced indifferently, either as the divergency or convergency of the
rays increaseth; and that it is by this effect, which is
the same in both, that either the divergency or convergency is perceived by the eye—I say, had he but
considered this, it is certain he would have made a quite
contrary judgment, and rightly concluded that those
rays which fall on the eye with greater degrees of con-

vergency should make the object from whence they
proceed appear by so much the nearer. But it is plain
it was impossible for any man to attain to a right notion
of this matter so long as he had regard only to lines and
angles, and did not apprehend the true nature of vision,
and how far it was of mathematical consideration.

40. Before we dismiss this subject, it is fit we take
notice of a query relating thereto, proposed by the ingenious Mr. Molyneux, in his *Treatise of Dioptrics* (par.
i. prop. 31. sec. 9), where, speaking of the difficulty
we have been explaining, he has these words: 'And so
he (*i.e.* Dr. Barrow) leaves this difficulty to the solution of others, which I (after so great an example) shall
do likewise; but with the resolution of the same admirable author, of not quitting the evident doctrine which
we have before laid down, for determining the *locus
objecti*, on account of being pressed by one difficulty,
which seems inexplicable till a more intimate knowledge
of the visive faculty be obtained by mortals. In the
meantime I propose it to the consideration of the ingenious, whether the *locus apparens* of an object placed
as in this ninth section be not as much before the eye
as the distinct base is behind the eye?' To which query
we may venture to answer in the negative. For, in the
present case, the rule for determining the distance of
the distinct base, or respective focus from the glass is
this: *As the difference between the distance of the object
and focus is to the focus or focal length, so the distance
of the object from the glass is to the distance of the
respective focus or distinct base from the glass.* (Molyneux, *Dioptr.*, par. i. prop. 5.) Let us now suppose
the object to be placed at the distance of the focal
length, and one-half of the focal length from the glass,
and the eye close to the glass. Hence it will follow,
by the rule, that the distance of the distinct base behind

the eye is double the true distance of the object before the eye. If, therefore, Mr. Molyneux's conjecture held good, it would follow that the eye should see the object twice as far off as it really is; and in other cases at three or four times its due distance, or more. But this manifestly contradicts experience, the object never appearing, at farthest, beyond its due distance. Whatever, therefore, is built on this supposition (vid. corol. i. prop. 57. ibid.) comes to the ground along with it.

41. From what hath been premised, it is a manifest consequence, that a man born blind, being made to see, would at first have no idea of distance by sight: the sun and stars, the remotest objects as well as the nearer, would all seem to be in his eye, or rather in his mind. The objects intromitted by sight would seem to him (as in truth they are) no other than a new set of thoughts or sensations, each whereof is as near to him as the perceptions of pain or pleasure, or the most inward passions of his soul. For, our judging objects perceived by sight to be at any distance, or without the mind, is (vid. sect. xxviii.) entirely the effect of experience; which one in those circumstances could not yet have attained to.

42. It is indeed otherwise upon the common supposition—that men judge of distance by the angle of the optic axes, just as one in the dark, or a blind man by the angle comprehended by two sticks, one whereof he held in each hand. For, if this were true, it would follow that one blind from his birth, being made to see, should stand in need of no new experience, in order to perceive distance by sight. But that this is false has, I think, been sufficiently demonstrated.

43. And perhaps, upon a strict inquiry, we shall not find that even those who from their birth have grown

up in a continued habit of seeing are irrecoverably prejudiced on the other side, to wit, in thinking what they see to be at a distance from them. For, at this time it seems agreed on all hands, by those who have had any thoughts of that matter, that colours, which are the proper and immediate object of sight, are not without the mind.—But then, it will be said, by sight we have also the ideas of extension, and figure, and motion; all which may well be thought without and at some distance from the mind, though colour should not. In answer to this, I appeal to any man's experience, whether the visible extension of any object do not appear as near to him as the colour of that object; nay, whether they do not both seem to be in the very same place. Is not the extension we see coloured, and is it possible for us, so much as in thought, to separate and abstract colour from extension? Now, where the extension is, there surely is the figure, and there the motion too. I speak of those which are perceived by sight.

44. But for a fuller explication of this point, and to shew that the immediate objects of sight are not so much as the ideas or resemblances of things placed at a distance, it is requisite that we look nearer into the matter, and carefully observe what is meant in common discourse when one says, that which he sees is at a distance from him. Suppose, for example, that looking at the moon I should say it were fifty or sixty semidiameters of the earth distant from me. Let us see what moon this is spoken of. It is plain it cannot be the visible moon, or anything like the visible moon, or that which I see—which is only a round luminous plain, of about thirty visible points in diameter. For, in case I am carried from the place where I stand directly towards the moon, it is manifest the object varies still as

I go on; and, by the time that I am advanced fifty or sixty semidiameters of the earth, I shall be so far from being near a small, round, luminous flat that I shall perceive nothing like it—this object having long since disappeared, and, if I would recover it, it must be by going back to the earth from whence I set out. Again, suppose I perceive by sight the faint and obscure idea of something, which I doubt whether it be a man, or a tree, or a tower, but judge it to be at the distance of about a mile. It is plain I cannot mean that what I see is a mile off, or that it is the image or likeness of anything which is a mile off; since that every step I take towards it the appearance alters, and from being obscure, small, and faint, grows clear, large, and vigorous. And when I come to the mile's end, that which I saw first is quite lost, neither do I find anything in the likeness of it.

45. In these and the like instances, the truth of the matter, I find, stands thus:—Having of a long time experienced certain ideas perceivable by touch—as distance, tangible figure, and solidity—to have been connected with certain ideas of sight, I do, upon perceiving these ideas of sight, forthwith conclude what tangible ideas are, by the wonted ordinary course of nature, like to follow. Looking at an object, I perceive a certain visible figure and colour, with some degree of faintness and other circumstances, which, from what I have formerly observed, determine me to think that if I advance forward so many paces, miles, &c., I shall be affected with such and such ideas of touch. So that, in truth and strictness of speech, I neither see distance itself, nor anything that I take to be at a distance. I say, neither distance nor things placed at a distance are themselves, or their ideas, truly perceived by sight. This I am persuaded of, as to what concerns myself.

And I believe whoever will look narrowly into his own thoughts, and examine what he means by saying he sees this or that thing at a distance, will agree with me, that what he sees only suggests to his understanding that, after having passed a certain distance, to be measured by the motion of his body, which is perceivable by touch, he shall come to perceive such and such tangible ideas, which have been usually connected with such and such visible ideas. But, that one might be deceived by these suggestions of sense, and that there is no necessary connexion between visible and tangible ideas suggested by them, we need go no farther than the next looking-glass or picture to be convinced. Note that, when I speak of tangible ideas, I take the word idea for any immediate object of sense, or understanding—in which large signification it is commonly used by the moderns.

46. From what we have shewn, it is a manifest consequence that the ideas of space, outness, and things placed at a distance are not, strictly speaking, the object of sight; they are not otherwise perceived by the eye than by the ear. Sitting in my study I hear a coach drive along the street; I look through the casement and see it; I walk out and enter into it. Thus, common speech would incline one to think I heard, saw, and touched the same thing, to wit, the coach. It is nevertheless certain the ideas intromitted by each sense are widely different, and distinct from each other; but, having been observed constantly to go together, they are spoken of as one and the same thing. By the variation of the noise, I perceive the different distances of the coach, and know that it approaches before I look out. Thus, by the ear I perceive distance just after the same manner as I do by the eye.

47. I do not nevertheless say I hear distance, in like

manner as I say that I see it—tne ideas perceived by
hearing not being so apt to be confounded with the
ideas of touch as those of sight are. So likewise a man
is easily convinced that bodies and external things are
not properly the object of hearing, but only sounds, by
the mediation whereof the idea of this or that body, or
distance, is suggested to his thoughts. But then one is
with more difficulty brought to discern the difference
there is betwixt the ideas of sight and touch: though it
be certain, a man no more sees and feels the same thing,
than he hears and feels the same thing.

48. One reason of which seems to be this. It is
thought a great absurdity to imagine that one and the
same thing should have any more than one extension
and one figure. But, the extension and figure of a body
being let into the mind two ways, and that indifferently,
either by sight or touch, it seems to follow that we see
the same extension and the same figure which we feel.

49. But, if we take a close and accurate view of the
matter, it must be acknowledged that we never see and
feel one and the same object. That which is seen is one
thing, and that which is felt is another. If the visible
figure and extension be not the same with the tangible
figure and extension, we are not to infer that one and
the same thing has divers extensions. The true consequence is that the objects of sight and touch are two
distinct things. It may perhaps require some thought
rightly to conceive this distinction. And the difficulty
seems not a little increased, because the combination of
visible ideas hath constantly the same name as the
combination of tangible ideas wherewith it is connected
—which doth of necessity arise from the use and end
of language.

50. In order, therefore, to treat accurately and unconfusedly of vision, we must bear in mind that there

are two sorts of objects apprehended by the eye—the one primarily and immediately, the other secondarily and by intervention of the former. Those of the first sort neither are nor appear to be without the mind, or at any distance off. They may, indeed, grow greater or smaller, more confused, or more clear, or more faint. But they do not, cannot approach, [or even seem to approach] or recede from us. Whenever we say an object is at a distance, whenever we say it draws near, or goes farther off, we must always mean it of the latter sort, which properly belong to the touch, and are not so truly perceived as suggested by the eye, in like manner as thoughts by the ear.

51. No sooner do we hear the words of a familiar language pronounced in our ears but the ideas corresponding thereto present themselves to our minds: in the very same instant the sound and the meaning enter the understanding: so closely are they united that it is not in our power to keep out the one except we exclude the other also. We even act in all respects as if we heard the very thoughts themselves. So likewise the secondary objects, or those which are only suggested by sight, do often more strongly affect us, and are more regarded, than the proper objects of that sense; along with which they enter into the mind, and with which they have a far more strict connexion than ideas have with words. Hence it is we find it so difficult to discriminate between the immediate and mediate objects of sight, and are so prone to attribute to the former what belongs only to the latter. They are, as it were, most closely twisted, blended, and incorporated together. And the prejudice is confirmed and riveted in our thoughts by a long tract of time, by the use of language, and want of reflection. However, I doubt not but any one that shall attentively consider what we have already said, and shall say upon

this subject before we have done (especially if he pursue it in his own thoughts), may be able to deliver himself from that prejudice. Sure I am, it is worth some attention to whoever would understand the true nature of vision.

52. I have now done with Distance, and proceed to shew how it is that we perceive by sight the Magnitude of objects. It is the opinion of some that we do it by angles, or by angles in conjunction with distance. But, neither angles nor distance being perceivable by sight, and the things we see being in truth at no distance from us, it follows that, as we have shewn lines and angles not to be the medium the mind makes use of in apprehending the apparent place, so neither are they the medium whereby it apprehends the apparent magnitude of objects.

53. It is well known that the same extension at a near distance shall subtend a greater angle, and at a farther distance a lesser angle. And by this principle (we are told) the mind estimates the magnitude of an object, comparing the angle under which it is seen with its distance, and thence inferring the magnitude thereof. What inclines men to this mistake (beside the humour of making one see by geometry) is, that the same perceptions or ideas which suggest distance do also suggest magnitude. But, if we examine it, we shall find they suggest the latter as immediately as the former. I say, they do not first suggest distance and then leave it to the judgment to use that as a medium whereby to collect the magnitude; but they have as close and immediate a connexion with the magnitude as with the distance; and suggest magnitude as independently of distance, as they do distance independently of magnitude. All which will

be evident to whoever considers what has been already said and what follows.

54. It has been shewn there are two sorts of objects apprehended by sight, each whereof has its distinct magnitude, or extension—the one, properly tangible, *i.e.* to be perceived and measured by touch, and not immediately falling under the sense of seeing; the other, properly and immediately visible, by mediation of which the former is brought in view. Each of these magnitudes are greater or lesser, according as they contain in them more or fewer points, they being made up of points or minimums. For, whatever may be said of extension in abstract, it is certain sensible extension is not infinitely divisible. There is a *minimum tangibile,* and a *minimum visibile,* beyond which sense cannot perceive. This every one's experience will inform him.

55. The magnitude of the object which exists without the mind, and is at a distance, continues always invariably the same: but, the visible object still changing as you approach to or recede from the tangible object, it hath no fixed and determinate greatness. Whenever therefore we speak of the magnitude of any thing, for instance a tree or a house, we must mean the tangible magnitude; otherwise there can be nothing steady and free from ambiguity spoken of it. Now, though the tangible and visible magnitude do in truth belong to two distinct objects, I shall nevertheless (especially since those objects are called by the same name, and are observed to coexist), to avoid tediousness and singularity of speech, sometimes speak of them as belonging to one and the same thing.

56. Now, in order to discover by what means the magnitude of tangible objects is perceived by sight, I need only reflect on what passes in my own mind, and observe what those things be which introduce the ideas

of greater or lesser into my thoughts when I look on
any object. And these I find to be, *first*, the magnitude
or extension of the visible object, which, being immediately perceived by sight, is connected with that other
which is tangible and placed at a distance: *secondly*,
the confusion or distinctness: and *thirdly*, the vigorous-
ness or faintness of the aforesaid visible appearance.
Cæteris paribus, by how much the greater or lesser the
visible object is, by so much the greater or lesser do I
conclude the tangible object to be. But, be the idea
immediately perceived by sight never so large, yet, if it
be withal confused, I judge the magnitude of the thing
to be but small. If it be distinct and clear, I judge it
greater. And, if it be faint, I apprehend it to be yet
greater. What is here meant by confusion and faintness has been explained in sect. 35.

57. Moreover, the judgments we make of greatness
do, in like manner as those of distance, depend on the
disposition of the eye; also on the figure, number, and
[situation] of intermediate objects, and other circumstances that have been observed to attend great or small
tangible magnitudes. Thus, for instance, the very same
quantity of visible extension which in the figure of a
tower doth suggest the idea of great magnitude shall in
the figure of a man suggest the idea of much smaller
magnitude. That this is owing to the experience we
have had of the usual bigness of a tower and a man,
no one, I suppose, need be told.

58. It is also evident that confusion or faintness have
no more a necessary connexion with little or great
magnitude than they have with little or great distance.
As they suggest the latter, so they suggest the former
to our minds. And, by consequence, if it were not for
experience, we should no more judge a faint or confused
appearance to be connected with great or little magni-

tude than we should that it was connected with great or little distance.

59. Nor will it be found that great or small visible magnitude hath any necessary relation to great or small tangible magnitude—so that the one may certainly and infallibly be inferred from the other. But, before we come to the proof of this, it is fit we consider the difference there is betwixt the extension and figure which is the proper object of touch, and that other which is termed visible; and how the former is principally, though not immediately, taken notice of when we look at any object. This has been before mentioned, but we shall here inquire into the cause thereof. We regard the objects that environ us in proportion as they are adapted to benefit or injure our own bodies, and thereby produce in our minds the sensations of pleasure or pain. Now, bodies operating on our organs by an immediate application, and the hurt and advantage arising therefrom depending altogether on the tangible, and not at all on the visible, qualities of any object—this is a plain reason why those should be regarded by us much more than these. And for this end [chiefly] the visive sense seems to have been bestowed on animals, to wit, that, by the perception of visible ideas (which in themselves are not capable of affecting or anywise altering the frame of their bodies), they may be able to foresee (from the experience they have had what tangible ideas are connected with such and such visible ideas) the damage or benefit which is like to ensue upon the application of their own bodies to this or that body which is at a distance. Which foresight, how necessary it is to the preservation of an animal, every one's experience can inform him. Hence it is that, when we look at an object, the tangible figure and extension thereof are principally attended to; whilst there is small heed taken

of the visible figure and magnitude, which, though more immediately perceived, do less sensibly affect us, and are not fitted to produce any alteration in our bodies.

60. That the matter of fact is true will be evident to any one who considers that a man placed at ten foot distance is thought as great as if he were placed at the distance only of five foot; which is true, not with relation to the visible, but tangible greatness of the object: the visible magnitude being far greater at one station than it is at the other.

61. Inches, feet, &c. are settled, stated lengths, whereby we measure objects and estimate their magnitude. We say, for example, an object appears to be six inches, or six foot long. Now, that this cannot be meant of visible inches, &c. is evident; because a visible inch is itself no constant determinate magnitude, and cannot therefore serve to mark out and determine the magnitude of any other thing. Take an inch marked upon a ruler; view it successively, at the distance of half a foot, a foot, a foot and a half, &c. from the eye: at each of which, and at all the intermediate distances, the inch shall have a different visible extension, *i.e.* there shall be more or fewer points discerned in it. Now, I ask which of all these various extensions is that stated determinate one that is agreed on for a common measure of other magnitudes? No reason can be assigned why we should pitch on one more than another. And, except there be some invariable determinate extension fixed on to be marked by the word inch, it is plain it can be used to little purpose; and to say a thing contains this or that number of inches shall imply no more than that it is extended, without bringing any particular idea of that extension into the mind. Farther, an inch and a foot, from different distances, shall both exhibit the same visible magnitude, and yet at the same time

you shall say that one seems several times greater than the other. From all which it is manifest, that the judgments we make of the magnitude of objects by sight are altogether in reference to their tangible extension. Whenever we say an object is great or small, of this or that determinate measure, I say, it must be meant of the tangible and not the visible extension, which, though immediately perceived, is nevertheless little taken notice of.

62. Now, that there is no necessary connexion between these two distinct extensions is evident from hence—because our eyes might have been framed in such a manner as to be able to see nothing but what were less than the *minimum tangibile*. In which case it is not impossible we might have perceived all the immediate objects of sight the very same that we do now; but unto those visible appearances there would not be connected those different tangible magnitudes that are now. Which shews the judgments we make of the magnitude of things placed at a distance, from the various greatness of the immediate objects of sight, do arise not from any essential or necessary, but only a customary, tie which has been observed betwixt them.

63. Moreover, it is not only certain that any idea of sight might not have been connected with this or that idea of touch we now observe to accompany it, but also that the greater visible magnitudes might have been connected with and introduced into our minds lesser tangible magnitudes, and the lesser visible magnitudes greater tangible magnitudes. Nay, that it actually is so, we have daily experience—that object which makes a strong and large appearance not seeming near so great as another the visible magnitude whereof is much less, but more faint, [and the appearance upper, or which is the same thing, painted lower on the retina, which

faintness and situation suggest both greater magnitude and greater distance].

64. From which, and from sect. 57 and 58, it is manifest that, as we do not perceive the magnitude of objects immediately by sight, so neither do we perceive them by the mediation of anything which has a neces-- sary connexion with them. Those ideas that now sug- gest unto us the various magnitudes of external objects before we touch them might possibly have suggested no such thing; or they might have signified them in a direct contrary manner, so that the very same ideas on the perception whereof we judge an object to be small might as well have served to make us conclude it great; —those ideas being in their own nature equally fitted to bring into our minds the idea of small or great, or no size at all, of outward objects, just as the words of any language are in their own nature indifferent to signify this or that thing, or nothing at all.

65. As we see distance so we see magnitude. And we see both in the same way that we see shame or anger in the looks of a man. Those passions are themselves invisible; they are nevertheless let in by the eye along with colours and alterations of countenance which are the immediate object of vision, and which signify them for no other reason than barely because they have been observed to accompany them. Without which experi- ence we should no more have taken blushing for a sign of shame than of gladness.

66. We are nevertheless exceedingly prone to imagine those things which are perceived only by the mediation of others to be themselves the immediate objects of sight, or at least to have in their own nature a fitness to be suggested by them before ever they had been expe- rienced to co-exist with them. From which prejudice every one perhaps will not find it easy to emancipate

himself, by any the clearest convictions of reason. And there are some grounds to think that, if there was one only invariable and universal language in the world, and that men were born with the faculty of speaking it, it would be the opinion of some, that the ideas in other men's minds were properly perceived by the ear, or had at least a necessary and inseparable tie with the sounds that were affixed to them. All which seems to arise from want of a due application of our discerning faculty, thereby to discriminate between the ideas that are in our understandings, and consider them apart from each other; which would preserve us from confounding those that are different, and make us see what ideas do, and what do not, include or imply this or that other idea.

67. There is a celebrated phenomenon the solution whereof I shall attempt to give, by the principles that have been laid down, in reference to the manner wherein we apprehend by sight the magnitude of objects.—The apparent magnitude of the moon, when placed in the horizon, is much greater than when it is in the meridian, though the angle under which the diameter of the moon is seen be not observed greater in the former case than in the latter; and the horizontal moon doth not constantly appear of the same bigness, but at some times seemeth far greater than at others.

68. Now, in order to explain the reason of the moon's appearing greater than ordinary in the horizon, it must be observed that the particles which compose our atmosphere do intercept the rays of light proceeding from any object to the eye; and, by how much the greater is the portion of atmosphere interjacent between the object and the eye, by so much the more are the rays intercepted, and, by consequence, the appearance of

the object rendered more faint—every object appearing more vigorous or more faint in proportion as it sendeth more or fewer rays into the eye. Now, between the eye and the moon when situated in the horizon there lies a far greater quantity of atmosphere than there does when the moon is in the meridian. Whence it comes to pass, that the appearance of the horizontal moon is fainter, and therefore, by sect. 56, it should be thought bigger in that situation than in the meridian, or in any other elevation above the horizon.

69. Farther, the air being variously impregnated, sometimes more and sometimes less, with vapours and exhalations fitted to retund and intercept the rays of light, it follows that the appearance of the horizontal moon hath not always an equal faintness, and, by consequence, that luminary, though in the very same situation, is at one time judged greater than at another.

70. That we have here given the true account of the phenomena of the horizontal moon, will, I suppose, be farther evident to any one from the following considerations:—*First,* it is plain, that which in this case suggests the idea of greater magnitude, must be something which is itself perceived; for, that which is unperceived cannot suggest to our perception any other thing. *Secondly,* it must be something that does not constantly remain the same, but is subject to some change or variation; since the appearance of the horizontal moon varies, being at one time greater than at another. [*Thirdly,* it must not lie in the circumjacent or intermediate objects, such as mountains, houses, fields, &c.; because that when all those objects are excluded from sight the appearance is as great as ever.] And yet, *thirdly,*[1] it cannot be the visible figure or magnitude;

[1] "Fourthly" in the second edition which includes the bracketed sentence.

since that remains the same, or is rather lesser, by how much the moon is nearer to the horizon. It remains therefore, that the true cause is that affection or alteration of the visible appearance, which proceeds from the greater paucity of rays arriving at the eye, and which I term faintness: since this answers all the forementioned conditions, and I am not conscious of any other perception that does.

71. Add to this that in misty weather it is a common observation, that the appearance of the horizontal moon is far larger than usual, which greatly conspires with and strengthens our opinion. Neither would it prove in the least irreconcilable with what we have said, if the horizontal moon should chance sometimes to seem enlarged beyond its usual extent, even in more serene weather. For, we must not only have regard to the mist which happens to be in the place where we stand; we ought also to take into our thoughts the whole sum of vapours and exhalations which lie betwixt the eye and the moon: all which co-operating to render the appearance of the moon more faint, and thereby increase its magnitude, it may chance to appear greater than it usually does even in the horizontal position, at a time when, though there be no extraordinary fog or haziness just in the place where we stand, yet the air between the eye and the moon, taken altogether, may be loaded with a greater quantity of interspersed vapours and exhalations than at other times.

72. It may be objected that, in consequence of our principles, the interposition of a body in some degree opaque, which may intercept a great part of the rays of light, should render the appearance of the moon in the meridian as large as when it is viewed in the horizon. To which I answer, it is not faintness anyhow applied that suggests greater magnitude; there being no

necessary, but only an experimental, connexion between those two things. It follows that the faintness which enlarges the appearance must be applied in such sort, and with such circumstances, as have been observed to attend the vision of great magnitudes. When from a distance we behold great objects, the particles of the intermediate air and vapours, which are themselves unperceivable, do interrupt the rays of light, and thereby render the appearance less strong and vivid. Now, faintness of appearance, caused in this sort, hath been experienced to co-exist with great magnitude. But when it is caused by the interposition of an opaque sensible body, this circumstance alters the case; so that a faint appearance this way caused does not suggest greater magnitude, because it hath not been experienced to co-exist with it.

73. Faintness, as well as all other ideas or perceptions which suggest magnitude or distance, does it in the same way that words suggest the notions to which they are annexed. Now, it is known a word pronounced with certain circumstances, or in a certain context with other words, hath not always the same import and signification that it hath when pronounced in some other circumstances, or different context of words. The very same visible appearance, as to faintness and all other respects, if placed on high, shall not suggest the same magnitude that it would if it were seen at an equal distance on a level with the eye. The reason whereof is, that we are rarely accustomed to view objects at a great height; our concerns lie among things situated rather before than above us; and accordingly our eyes are not placed on the top of our heads, but in such a position as is most convenient for us to see distant objects standing in our way. And, this situation of them being a circumstance which usually attends the vision of distant

objects, we may from hence account for (what is commonly observed) an object's appearing of different magnitude, even with respect to its horizontal extension, on the top of a steeple, *e.g.* a hundred feet high, to one standing below, from what it would if placed at a hundred feet distance, on a level with his eye. For, it hath been shewn that the judgment we make on the magnitude of a thing depends not on the visible appearance only, but also on divers other circumstances, any one of which being omitted or varied may suffice to make some alteration in our judgment. Hence, the circumstance of viewing a distant object in such a situation as is usual and suits with the ordinary posture of the head and eyes, being omitted, and instead thereof a different situation of the object, which requires a different posture of the head, taking place—it is not to be wondered at if the magnitude be judged different. But it will be demanded, why a high object should constantly appear less than an equidistant low object of the same dimensions; for so it is observed to be. It may indeed be granted that the variation of some circumstances may vary the judgment made on the magnitude of high objects, which we are less used to look at; but it does not hence appear why they should be judged less rather than greater? I answer, that in case the magnitude of distant objects was suggested by the extent of their visible appearance alone, and thought proportional thereto, it is certain they would then be judged much less than now they seem to be. (Vid. sect. 79.) But, several circumstances concurring to form the judgment we make on the magnitude of distant objects, by means of which they appear far larger than others whose visible appearance hath an equal or even greater extension, it follows that upon the change or omission of any of those circumstances which are wont to attend the vision of distant objects, and so come to influence the judgments made on their magnitude, they shall proportionably appear less than otherwise they would. For, any of those things that caused an object to be thought greater than in proportion to its visible extension being either omitted, or applied without the usual circumstances, the judgment depends more entirely on the visible extension; and consequently the object must be judged less. Thus, in the present case the situation of the thing seen being different from what it usually is in those objects we have occasion to view, and whose magnitude we observe, it follows that the very same object being a hundred feet high, should seem less than if it was a hundred feet off, on (or nearly on) a level with the eye. What has been here set forth seems to me to have no small share in contributing to magnify the appearance of the horizontal moon, and deserves not to be passed over in the explication of it.

74. If we attentively consider the phenomenon before us, we shall find the not discerning between the mediate and immediate objects of sight to be the chief cause of the difficulty that occurs in the explication of it. The magnitude of the visible moon, or that which is the proper and immediate object of vision, is no greater when the moon is in the horizon than when it is in the meridian. How comes it, therefore, to seem greater in one situation than the other? What is it can put this cheat on the understanding? It has no other perception of the moon than what it gets by sight. And that which is seen is of the same extent—I say, the visible appearance hath the very same, or rather a less, magnitude, when the moon is viewed in the horizontal than when in the meridional position. And yet it is esteemed greater in the former than in the latter. Herein consists the difficulty; which doth vanish and admit of the most easy

solution, if we consider that as the visible moon is not greater in the horizon than in the meridian, so neither is it thought to be so. It hath been already shewn that, in any act of vision, the visible object absolutely, or in itself, is little taken notice of—the mind still carrying its view from that to some tangible ideas, which have been observed to be connected with it, and by that means come to be suggested by it. So that when a thing is said to appear great or small, or whatever estimate be made of the magnitude of any thing, this is meant not of the visible but of the tangible object. This duly considered, it will be no hard matter to reconcile the seeming contradiction there is, that the moon should appear of a different bigness, the visible magnitude thereof remaining still the same. For, by sect. 56, the very same visible extension, with a different faintness, shall suggest a different tangible extension. When therefore the horizontal moon is said to appear greater than the meridional moon, this must be understood, not of a greater visible extension, but of a greater tangible extension, which, by reason of the more than ordinary faintness of the visible appearance, is suggested to the mind along with it.

75. Many attempts have been made by learned men to account for this appearance. Gassendus, Des Cartes, Hobbes, and several others have employed their thoughts on that subject; but how fruitless and unsatisfactory their endeavours have been is sufficiently shewn in the *Philosophical Transactions* (Numb. 187, p. 314), where you may see their several opinions at large set forth and confuted, not without some surprise at the gross blunders that ingenious men have been forced into by endeavouring to reconcile this appearance with the ordinary principles of optics. Since the writing of which there hath been published in the *Transactions* (Numb. 187, p. 323)

another paper relating to the same affair, by the celebrated Dr. Wallis, wherein he attempts to account for that phenomenon; which, though it seems not to contain anything new, or different from what had been said before by others, I shall nevertheless consider in this place.

76. His opinion, in short, is this:—We judge not of the magnitude of an object by the optic angle alone, but by the optic angle in conjunction with the distance. Hence, though the angle remain the same, or even become less, yet, if withal the distance seem to have been increased, the object shall appear greater. Now, one way whereby we estimate the distance of anything is by the number and extent of the intermediate objects. When therefore the moon is seen in the horizon, the variety of fields, houses, &c. together with the large prospect of the wide extended land or sea that lies between the eye and the utmost limb of the horizon, suggest unto the mind the idea of greater distance, and consequently magnify the appearance. And this, according to Dr. Wallis, is the true account of the extraordinary largeness attributed by the mind to the horizontal moon, at a time when the angle subtended by its diameter is not one jot greater than it used to be.

77. With reference to this opinion, not to repeat what has been already said concerning distance, I shall only observe, *first,* that if the prospect of interjacent objects be that which suggests the idea of farther distance, and this idea of farther distance be the cause that brings into the mind the idea of greater magnitude, it should hence follow that if one looked at the horizontal moon from behind a wall, it would appear no bigger than ordinary. For, in that case, the wall interposing cuts off all that prospect of sea and land, &c. which might otherwise increase the apparent distance. and thereby the apparent

magnitude of the moon. Nor will it suffice to say, the memory doth even then suggest all that extent of land, &c. which lies within the horizon, which suggestion occasions a sudden judgment of sense, that the moon is farther off and larger than usual. For, ask any man who from such a station beholding the horizontal moon shall think her greater than usual, whether he hath at that time in his mind any idea of the intermediate objects, or long tract of land that lies between his eye and the extreme edge of the horizon? and whether it be that idea which is the cause of his making the aforementioned judgment? He will, without doubt, reply in the negative, and declare the horizontal moon shall appear greater than the meridional, though he never thinks of all or any of those things that lie between him and it. [And as for the absurdity of any idea's introducing into the mind another, whilst itself is not perceived, this has already fallen under our observation, and is too evident to need any farther enlargement on it.] *Secondly,* it seems impossible, by this hypothesis, to account for the moon's appearing, in the very same situation, at one time greater than at another; which, nevertheless, has been shewn to be very agreeable to the principles we have laid down, and receives a most easy and natural explication from them. [For the further clearing up of this point, it is to be observed, that what we immediately and properly see are only lights and colours in sundry situations and shades, and degrees of faintness and clearness, confusion and distinctness. All which visible objects are only in the mind; nor do they suggest aught external, whether distance or magnitude, otherwise than by habitual connexion, as words do things. We are also to remark, that beside the straining of the eyes, and beside the vivid and faint, the distinct and confused appearances (which, bearing some proportion to lines and angles, have been substituted instead of them in the fore-going part of this Treatise), there are other means which suggest both distance and magnitude—particularly the situation of visible points or objects, as upper or lower; the former suggesting a farther distance and greater magnitude, the latter a nearer distance and lesser magni-tude—all which is an effect only of custom and ex-perience, there being really nothing intermediate in the line of distance between the uppermost and the lower-most, which are both equidistant, or rather at no distance from the eye; as there is also nothing in upper or lower which by necessary connexion should suggest greater or lesser magnitude. Now, as these customary experi-mental means of suggesting distance do likewise suggest magnitude, so they suggest the one as immediately as the other. I say, they do not (vide sect. 53) first sug-gest distance, and then leave the mind from thence to infer or compute magnitude, but suggest magnitude as immediately and directly as they suggest distance.]

78. This phenomenon of the horizontal moon is a clear instance of the insufficiency of lines and angles for ex-plaining the way wherein the mind perceives and esti-mates the magnitude of outward objects. There is, nevertheless, a use of computation by them—in order to determine the apparent magnitude of things, so far as they have a connexion with and are proportional to those other ideas or perceptions which are the true and im-mediate occasions that suggest to the mind the apparent magnitude of things. But this in general may, I think, be observed concerning mathematical computation in optics—that it can never be very precise and exact, since the judgments we make of the magnitude of external things do often depend on several circumstances which are not proportional to or capabale of being defined by lines and angles.

79. From what has been said, we may safely deduce this consequence, to wit, that a man born blind, and made to see, would, at first opening of his eyes, make a very different judgment of the magnitude of objects intromitted by them from what others do. He would not consider the ideas of sight with reference to, or as having any connexion with, the ideas of touch. His view of them being entirely terminated within themselves, he can no otherwise judge them great or small than as they contain a greater or lesser number of visible points. Now, it being certain that any visible point can cover or exclude from view only one other visible point, it follows that whatever object intercepts the view of another hath an equal number of visible points with it; and consequently, they shall both be thought by him to have the same magnitude. Hence, it is evident one in those circumstances would judge his thumb, with which he might hide a tower, or hinder its being seen, equal to that tower; or his hand, the interposition whereof might conceal the firmament from his view, equal to the firmament: how great an inequality soever there may, in our apprehensions, seem to be betwixt those two things, because of the customary and close connexion that has grown up in our minds between the objects of sight and touch, whereby the very different and distinct ideas of those two senses are so blended and confounded together as to be mistaken for one and the same thing—out of which prejudice we cannot easily extricate ourselves.

80. For the better explaining the nature of vision, and setting the manner wherein we perceive magnitudes in a due light, I shall proceed to make some observations concerning matters relating therto, whereof the want of reflection, and duly separating between tangible and visible ideas, is apt to create in us mistaken and confused notions. And, *first*, I shall observe, that the *minimum*

visible is exactly equal in all beings whatsoever that are endowed with the visive faculty. No exquisite formation of the eye, no peculiar sharpness of sight, can make it less in one creature than in another; for, it not being distinguishable into parts, nor in anywise consisting of them, it must necessarily be the same to all. For, suppose it otherwise, and that the *minimum visibile* of a mite, for instance, be less than the *minimum visibile* of a man; the latter therefore may, by detraction of some part, be made equal to the former. It doth therefore consist of parts, which is inconsistent with the notion of a *minimum visibile* or point.

81. It will, perhaps, be objected, that the *minimum visibile* of a man doth really and in itself contain parts whereby it surpasses that of a mite, though they are not perceivable by the man. To which I answer, the *minimum visibile* having (in like manner as all other the proper and immediate objects of sight) been shewn not to have any existence without the mind of him who sees it, it follows there cannot be any part of it that is not actually perceived and therefore visible. Now, for any object to contain several distinct visible parts, and at the same time to be a *minimum visibile,* is a manifest contradiction.

82. Of these visible points we see at all times an equal number. It is every whit as great when our view is contracted and bounded by near objects as when it is extended to larger and remoter ones. For, it being impossible that one *minimum visibile* should obscure or keep out of sight more than one other, it is a plain consequence that, when my view is on all sides bounded by the walls of my study, I see just as many visible points as I could in case that, by the removal of the study-walls and all other obstructions, I had a full prospect of the circumjacent fields, mountains, sea, and open firmament.

For, so long as I am shut up within the walls, by their interposition every point of the external objects is covered from my view. But, each point that is seen being able to cover or exclude from sight one only other corresponding point, it follows that, whilst my sight is confined to those narrow walls, I see as many points, or *minima visibilia*, as I should were those walls away, by looking on all the external objects whose prospect is intercepted by them. Whenever, therefore, we are said to have a greater prospect at one time than another, this must be understood with relation, not to the proper and immediate, but the secondary and mediate objects of vision—which, as hath been shewn, do properly belong to the touch.

83. The visive faculty, considered with reference to its immediate objects, may be found to labour of two defects. *First,* in respect of the extent or number of visible points that are at once perceivable by it, which is narrow and limited to a certain degree. It can take in at one view but a certain determinate number of *minima visibilia,* beyond which it cannot extend its prospect. *Secondly,* our sight is defective in that its view is not only narrow, but also for the most part confused. Of those things that we take in at one prospect, we can see but a few at once clearly and unconfusedly; and the more we fix our sight on any one object, by so much the darker and more indistinct shall the rest appear.

84. Corresponding to these two defects of sight, we may imagine as many perfections, to wit, 1st. That of comprehending in one view a greater number of visible points; 2dly, of being able to view them all equally and at once, with the utmost clearness and distinction. That those perfections are not actually in some intelligences of a different order and capacity from ours, it is impossible for us to know.

85. In neither of those two ways do microscopes contribute to the improvement of sight. For, when we look through a microscope, we neither see more visible points, nor are the collateral points more distinct, than when we look with the naked eye at objects placed at a due distance. A microscope brings us, as it were, into a new world. It presents us with a new scene of visible objects, quite different from what we behold with the naked eye. But herein consists the most remarkable difference, to wit, that whereas the objects perceived by the eye alone have a certain connexion with tangible objects, whereby we are taught to foresee what will ensue upon the approach or application of distant objects to the parts of our own body—which much conduceth to its preservation—there is not the like connexion between things tangible and those visible objects that are perceived by help of a fine microscope.

86. Hence, it is evident that, were our eyes turned into the nature of microscopes, we should not be much benefitted by the change. We should be deprived of the forementioned advantage we at present received by the visive faculty, and have left us only the empty amusement of seeing, without any other benefit arising from it. But, in that case, it will perhaps be said, our sight would be endued with a far greater sharpness and penetration than it now hath. But I would fain know wherein consists that sharpness which is esteemed so great an excellency of sight. It is certain, from what we have already shewn, that the *minimum visibile* is never greater or lesser, but in all cases constantly the same. And in the case of microscopical eyes, I see only this difference, to wit, that upon the ceasing of a certain observable connexion betwixt the divers perceptions of sight and touch, which before enabled us to regulate our actions by the

eye, it would now be rendered utterly unserviceable to that purpose.

87. Upon the whole, it seems that if we consider the use and end of sight, together with the present state and circumstances of our being, we shall not find any great cause to complain of any defect or imperfection in it, or easily conceive how it could be mended. With such admirable wisdom is that faculty contrived, both for the pleasure and convenience of life.

88. Having finished what I intended to say concerning the Distance and Magnitude of objects, I come now to treat of the manner wherein the mind perceives by sight their Situation. Among the discoveries of the last age, it is reputed none of the least, that the manner of vision has been more clearly explained than ever it had been before. There is, at this day, no one ignorant that the pictures of external objects are painted on the retina or fund of the eye; that we can see nothing which is not so painted; and that, according as the picture is more distinct or confused, so also is the perception we have of the object. But then, in this explication of vision, there occurs one mighty difficulty, viz. the objects are painted in an inverted order on the bottom of the eye: the upper part of any object being painted on the lower part of the eye, and the lower part of the object on the upper part of the eye; and so also as to right and left. Since therefore the pictures are thus inverted, it is demanded, how it comes to pass that we see the objects erect and in their natural posture?

89. In answer to this difficulty, we are told that the mind, perceiving an impulse of a ray of light on the upper part of the eye, considers this ray as coming in a direct line from the lower part of the object; and, in like manner, tracing the ray that strikes on the lower

part of the eye, it is directed to the upper part of the
object. Thus, in the adjacent figure, C, the lower point
of the object ABC, is projected on c the upper part of
the eye. So likewise, the highest point A is projected
on a the lowest part of the eye; which makes the representation cba inverted. But the mind—considering the
stroke that is made on c as coming in the straight line
Cc from the lower end of the object; and the stroke or
impulse on a, as coming in the line Aa from the upper
end of the object—is directed to make a right judgment

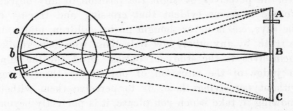

of the situation of the object ABC, notwithstanding the
picture of it be inverted. Moreover, this is illustrated
by conceiving a blind man, who, holding in his hands
two sticks that cross each other, doth with them touch
the extremities of an object, placed in a perpendicular
situation. It is certain this man will judge that to be
the upper part of the object which he touches with the
stick held in the undermost hand, and that to be the
lower part of the object which he touches with the stick
in his uppermost hand. This is the common explication
of the erect appearance of objects, which is generally
received and acquiesced in, being (as Mr. Molyneux
tells us, *Diopt.* part ii. ch. vii. p. 289) 'allowed by all
men as satisfactory.'

90. But this account to me does not seem in any degree true. Did I perceive those impulses, decussations,
and directions of the rays of light, in like manner as

hath been set forth, then, indeed, it would not at first view be altogether void of probability. And there might be some pretence for the comparison of the blind man and his cross sticks. But the case is far otherwise. I know very well that I perceive no such thing. And, of consequence, I cannot thereby make an estimate of the situation of objects. Moreover, I appeal to any one's experience, whether he be conscious to himself that he thinks on the intersection made by the radius pencils, or pursues the impulses they give in right lines, whenever he perceives by sight the position of any object? To me it seems evident that crossing and tracing of the rays, &c. is never thought on by children, idiots, or, in truth, by any other, save only those who have applied themselves to the study of optics. And for the mind to judge of the situation of objects by those things without perceiving them, or to perceive them without knowing it, take which you please, it is perfectly beyond my comprehension. Add to this, that the explaining the manner of vision by the example of cross sticks, and hunting for the object along the axes of the radius pencils, doth suppose the proper objects of sight to be perceived at a distance from us, contrary to what hath been demonstrated. [We may therefore venture to pronounce this opinion, concerning the way wherein the mind perceives the erect appearance of objects, to be of a piece with those other tenets of writers in optics, which in the foregoing parts of this treatise we have had occasion to examine and refute.]

91. It remains, therefore, that we look for some other explication of this difficulty. And I believe it not impossible to find one, provided we examine it to the bottom, and carefully distinguish between the ideas of sight and touch; which cannot be too oft inculcated in treating of vision. But, more especially throughout the

consideration of this affair, we ought to carry that distinction in our thoughts; for that from want of a right understanding thereof, the difficulty of explaining erect vision seems chiefly to arise.

92. In order to disentangle our minds from whatever prejudices we may entertain with relation to the subject in hand, nothing seems more apposite than the taking into our thoughts the case of one born blind, and afterwards, when grown up, made to see. And—though perhaps it may not be a task altogether easy and familiar to us, to divest ourselves entirely of the experiences received from sight, so as to be able to put our thoughts exactly in the posture of such a one's—we must, nevertheless, as far as possible, endeavour to frame true conceptions of what might reasonably be supposed to pass in his mind.

93. It is certain that a man actually blind, and who had continued so from his birth, would, by the sense of feeling, attain to have ideas of upper and lower. By the motion of his hand, he might discern the situation of any tangible object placed within his reach. That part on which he felt himself supported, or towards which he perceived his body to gravitate, he would term *lower,* and the contrary to this *upper*; and accordingly denominate whatsoever objects he touched.

94. But then, whatever judgments he makes concerning the situation of objects are confined to those only that are perceivable by touch. All those things that are intangible, and of a spiritual nature—his thoughts and desires, his passions, and in general all the modifications of his soul— to these he would never apply the terms upper and lower, except only in a metaphorical sense. He may perhaps, by way of allusion, speak of high or low thoughts: but those terms, in their proper signification, would never be applied to anything that

was not conceived to exist without the mind. For, a man born blind, and remaining in the same state, could mean nothing else by the words higher and lower than a greater or lesser distance from the earth; which distance he would measure by the motion or application of his hand, or some other part of his body. It is, therefore, evident that all those things which, in respect of each other, would by him be thought higher or lower, must be such as were conceived to exist without his mind, in the ambient space.[1]

95. Whence it plainly follows, that such a one, if we suppose him made to see, would not at first sight think that anything he saw was high or low, erect or inverted. For, it hath been already demonstrated, in sect. 41, that he would not think the things he perceived by sight to be at any distance from him, or without his mind. The objects to which he had hitherto been used to apply the terms up and down, high and low, were such only as affected, or were some way perceived by his touch. But the proper objects of vision make a new set of ideas, perfectly distinct and different from the former, and which can in no sort make themselves perceived by touch. There is, therefore, nothing at all that could induce him to think those terms applicable to them. Nor would he ever think it, till such time as he had observed their connexion with tangible objects, and the same prejudice began to insinuate itself into his understanding, which, from their infancy, had grown up in the understandings of other men.

96. To set this matter in a clearer light, I shall make use of an example. Suppose the above-mentioned blind person, by his touch, perceives a man to stand erect. Let us inquire into the manner of this. By the application of his hand to the several parts of a human body, he

[1] Cf. *Principles*, 44, for comment on this statement.

had perceived different tangible ideas; which being collected into sundry complex ones have distinct names annexed to them. Thus, one combination of a certain
tangible figure, bulk, and consistency of parts is called
the head; another the hand; a third the foot, and so of
the rest—all which complex ideas could, in his understanding, be made up only of ideas perceivable by touch.
He had also, by his touch, obtained an idea of earth or
ground, towards which he perceives the parts of his body
to have a natural tendency. Now—by *erect* nothing
more being meant than that perpendicular position of a
man wherein his feet are nearest to the earth—if the
blind person, by moving his hand over the parts of the
man who stands before him, do perceive the tangible
ideas that compose the head to be farthest from, and
those that compose the feet to be nearest to, that other
combination of tangible ideas which he calls earth, he
will denominate that man erect. But, if we suppose
him on a sudden to receive his sight, and that he behold
a man standing before him, it is evident, in that case, he
would neither judge the man he sees to be erect nor
inverted; for he, never having known those terms applied
to any other save tangible things, or which existed in the
space without him, and what he sees neither being tangible, nor perceived as existing without, he could not
know that, in propriety of language, they were applicable
to it.

97. Afterwards, when, upon turning his head or eyes
up and down to the right and left, he shall observe the
visible objects to change, and shall also attain to know
that they are called by the same names, and connected
with the objects perceived by touch; then, indeed, he will
come to speak of them and their situation in the same
terms that he has been used to apply to tangible things:
and those that he perceives by turning up his eyes he

will call upper, and those that by turning down his eyes he will call lower.

98. And this seems to me the true reason why he should think those objects uppermost that are painted on the lower part of his eye. For, by turning the eye up they shall be distinctly seen; as likewise they that are painted on the highest part of the eye shall be distinctly seen by turning the eye down, and are for that reason esteemed lowest. For we have shewn that to the immediate objects of sight, considered in themselves, he would not attribute the terms high and low. It must therefore be on account of some circumstances which are observed to attend them. And these, it is plain, are the actions of turning the eye up and down, which suggest a very obvious reason why the mind should denominate the objects of sight accordingly high or low. And, without this motion of the eye—this turning it up and down in order to discern different objects—doubtless *erect, inverse,* and other the like terms relating to the position of tangible objects, would never have been transferred, or in any degree apprehended to belong to the ideas of sight, the mere act of seeing including nothing in it to that purpose; whereas the different situations of the eye naturally direct the mind to make a suitable judgment of the situation of objects intromitted by it.

99. Farther, when he has by experience learned the connexion there is between the several ideas of sight and touch, he will be able, by the perception he has of the situation of visible things in respect of one another, to make a sudden and true estimate of the situation of outward, tangible things corresponding to them. And thus it is he shall perceive by sight the situation of external objects, which do not properly fall under that sense.

100. I know we are very prone to think that, if just

made to see, we should judge of the situation of visible things as we do now. But, we are also as prone to think that, at first sight, we should in the same way apprehend the distance and magnitude of objects, as we do now; which hath been shewn to be a false and groundless persuasion. And, for the like reasons, the same censure may be passed on the positive assurance that most men, before they have thought sufficiently of the matter, might have of their being able to determine by the eye, at first view, whether objects were erect or inverse.

101. It will perhaps be objected to our opinion, that a man, for instance, being thought erect when his feet are next the earth, and inverted when his head is next the earth, it doth hence follow that, by the mere act of vision, without any experience or altering the situation of the eye, we should have determined whether he were erect or inverted. For both the earth itself, and the limbs of the man who stands thereon, being equally perceived by sight, one cannot choose seeing what part of the man is nearest the earth, and what part farthest from it, *i.e.* whether he be erect or inverted.

102. To which I answer, the ideas which constitute the tangible earth and man are entirely different from those which constitute the visible earth and man. Nor was it possible, by virtue of the visive faculty alone, without superadding any experience of touch, or altering the position of the eye, ever to have known, or so much as suspected, there had been any relation or connexion between them. Hence, a man at first view would not denominate anything he saw, *earth,* or *head,* or *foot;* and consequently, he could not tell, by the mere act of vision, whether the head or feet were nearest the earth. Nor, indeed, would we have thereby any thought of earth or man, erect or inverse, at all—which will be made

yet more evident, if we nicely observe, and make a particular comparison between, the ideas of both senses.

103. That which I see is only variety of light and colours. That which I feel is hard or soft, hot or cold, rough or smooth. What similitude, what connexion, have those ideas with these? Or, how is it possible that any one should see reason to give one and the same name to combinations of ideas so very different, before he had experienced their co-existence? We do not find there is any necessary connexion betwixt this or that tangible quality, and any colour whatsoever. And we may sometimes perceive colours, where there is nothing to be felt. All which doth make it manifest that no man, at first receiving of his sight, would know there was any agreement between this or that particular object of his sight and any object of touch he had been already acquainted with. The colours therefore of the head would to him no more suggest the idea of head than they would the idea of feet.

104. Farther, we have at large shewn (vid. sect. 63 and 64) there is no discoverable necessary connexion between any given visible magnitude and any one particular tangible magnitude; but that it is entirely the result of custom and experience, and depends on foreign and accidental circumstances, that we can, by the perception of visible extension, inform ourselves what may be the extension of any tangible object connected with it. Hence, it is certain, that neither the visible magnitude of head or foot would bring along with them into the mind, at first opening of the eyes, the respective tangible magnitudes of those parts.

105. By the foregoing section, it is plain the visible figure of any part of the body hath no necessary connexion with the tangible figure thereof, so as at first sight to suggest it to the mind. For, figure is the ter-

mination of magnitude. Whence it follows that no visible magnitude having in its own nature an aptness to suggest any one particular tangible magnitude, so neither can any visible figure be inseparably connected with its corresponding tangible figure, so as of itself, and in a way prior to experience, it might suggest it to the understanding. This will be farther evident, if we consider that what seems smooth and round to the touch may to sight, if viewed through a microscope, seem quite otherwise.

106. From all which, laid together and duly considered, we may clearly deduce this inference:—In the first act of vision, no idea entering by the eye would have a perceivable connexion with the ideas to which the names earth, man, head, foot, &c. were annexed in the understanding of a person blind from his birth; so as in any sort to introduce them into his mind, or make themselves be called by the same names, and reputed the same things with them, as afterwards they come to be.

107. There doth, nevertheless, remain one difficulty, which to some may seem to press hard on our opinion, and deserve not to be passed over. For, though it be granted that neither the colour, size, nor figure of the visible feet have any necessary connexion with the ideas that compose the tangible feet, so as to bring them at first sight into my mind, or make me in danger of confounding them, before I had been used to and for some time experienced their connexion; yet thus much seems undeniable, namely, that the number of the visible feet being the same with that of the tangible feet, I may from hence, without any experience of sight, reasonably conclude that they represent or are connected with the feet rather than the head. I say, it seems the idea of two visible feet will sooner suggest to the mind the idea of two tangible feet than of one head—so that the blind

man, upon first reception of the visive faculty, might
know which were the feet or two, and which the head
or one.

108. In order to get clear of this seeming difficulty,
we need only observe that diversity of visible objects
does not necessarily infer diversity of tangible objects
corresponding to them. A picture painted with great
variety of colours affects the touch in one uniform manner; it is therefore evident that I do not, by any necessary consecution, independent of experience, judge of
the number of things tangible from the number of things
visible. I should not therefore at first opening my eyes
conclude that because I see two I shall feel two. How,
therefore, can I, before experience teaches me, know
that the visible legs, because two, are connected with
the tangible legs; or the visible head, because one, is
connected with the tangible head? The truth is, the
things I see are so very different and heterogeneous
from the things I feel that the perception of the one
would never have suggested the other to my thoughts,
or enabled me to pass the least judgment thereon, until
I had experienced their connexion.

109. But, for a fuller illustration of this matter, it
ought to be considered, that number (however some may
reckon it amongst the primary qualities) is nothing fixed
and settled, really existing in things themselves. It is
entirely the creature of the mind, considering either a
simple idea by itself, or any combination of simple ideas
to which it gives one name, and so makes it pass for a
unit. According as the mind variously combines its
ideas, the unit varies; and as the unit, so the number,
which is only a collection of units, doth also vary. We
call a window one, a chimney one; and yet a house,
in which there are many windows and many chimneys,
has an equal right to be called one; and many houses

go to the making of one city. In these and the like instances, it is evident the *unit* constantly relates to the particular draughts the mind makes of its ideas, to which it affixes names, and wherein it includes more or less, as best suits its own ends and purposes. Whatever therefore the mind considers as one, that is an unit. Every combination of ideas is considered as one thing by the mind, and in token thereof is marked by one name. Now, this naming and combining together of ideas is perfectly arbitrary, and done by the mind in such sort as experience shews it to be most convenient—without which our ideas had never been collected into such sundry distinct combinations as they now are.

110. Hence, it follows that a man born blind, and afterwards, when grown up, made to see, would not, in the first act of vision, parcel out the ideas of sight into the same distinct collections that others do who have experienced which do regularly co-exist and are proper to be bundled up together under one name. He would not, for example, make into one complex idea and thereby esteem and unite all those particular ideas which constitute the visible head or foot. For, there can be no reason assigned why he should do so, barely upon his seeing a man stand upright before him. There crowd into his mind the ideas which compose the visible man, in company with all the other ideas of sight perceived at the same time. But, all these ideas offered at once to his view he would not distribute into sundry distinct combinations, till such time as, by observing the motion of the parts of the man and other experiences, he comes to know which are to be separated and which are to be collected together.

111. From what hath been premised, it is plain the objects of sight and touch make, if I may so say, two

sets of ideas, which are widely different from each other. To objects of either kind we indifferently attribute the terms high and low, right and left, and such like, denoting the position or situation of things; but then we must well observe that the position of any object is determined with respect only to objects of the same sense. We say any object of touch is high or low, according as it is more or less distant from the tangible earth: and in like manner we denominate any object of sight high or low, in proportion as it is more or less distant from the visible earth. But, to define the situation of visible things with relation to the distance they bear from any tangible thing, or *vice versa,* this were absurd and perfectly unintelligible. For all visible things are equally in the mind, and take up no part of the external space; and consequently are equidistant from any tangible thing which exists without the mind.

112. Or rather, to speak truly, the proper objects of sight are at no distance, neither near nor far from any tangible thing. For, if we inquire narrowly into the matter, we shall find that those things only are compared together in respect of distance which exist after the same manner, or appertain unto the same sense. For, by the distance between any two points, nothing more is meant than the number of intermediate points. If the given points are visible, the distance between them is marked out by the number of the interjacent visible points; if they are tangible, the distance between them is a line consisting of tangible points; but, if they are one tangible and the other visible, the distance between them doth neither consist of points perceivable by sight nor by touch, *i.e.* it is utterly inconceivable. This, perhaps, will not find an easy admission into all men's understanding. However, I should gladly be informed whether it be not true, by any one who will

be at the pains to reflect a little, and apply it home to his thoughts.

113. The not observing what has been delivered in the two last sections, seems to have occasioned no small part of the difficulty that occurs in the business of direct appearances. The head, which is painted nearest the earth, seems to be farthest from it; and on the other hand, the feet, which are painted farthest from the earth, are thought nearest to it. Herein lies the difficulty, which vanishes if we express the thing more clearly and free from ambiguity, thus:—How comes it that, to the eye, the visible head, which is nearest the tangible earth, seems farthest from the earth; and the visible feet, which are farthest from the tangible earth, seem nearest the earth? The question being thus proposed, who sees not the difficulty is founded on a supposition that the eye or visive faculty, or rather the soul by means thereof, should judge of the situation of visible objects with reference to their distance from the tangible earth? Whereas, it is evident the tangible earth is not perceived by sight. And it hath been shewn, in the two last preceding sections, that the location of visible objects is determined only by the distance they bear from one another, and that it is nonsense to talk of distance, far or near, between a visible and tangible thing.

114. If we confine our thoughts to the proper objects of sight, the whole is plain and easy. The head is painted farthest from, and the feet nearest to, the visible earth; and so they appear to be. What is there strange or unaccountable in this? Let us suppose the pictures in the fund of the eye to be the immediate objects of sight. The consequence is that things should appear in the same posture they are painted in; and is it not so? The head which is seen seems farthest from

the earth which is seen; and the feet which are see., seem nearest to the earth which is seen. And just so they are painted.

115. But, say you, the picture of the man is inverted, and yet the appearance is erect. I ask, what mean you by the picture of the man, or, which is the same thing, the visible man's being inverted? You tell me it is inverted, because the heels are uppermost and the head undermost? Explain me this. You say that by the head's being undermost, you mean that it is nearest to the earth; and, by the heels being uppermost, that they are farthest from the earth. I ask again, what earth you mean? You cannot mean the earth that is painted on the eye or the visible earth—for the picture of the head is farthest from the picture of the earth, and the picture of the feet nearest to the picture of the earth; and accordingly the visible head is farthest from the visible earth, and the visible feet nearest to it. It remains, therefore, that you mean the tangible earth; and so determine the situation of visible things with respect to tangible things—contrary to what hath been demonstrated in sect. 111 and 112. The two distinct provinces of sight and touch should be considered apart, and as though their objects had no intercourse, no manner of relation to one another, in point of distance or position.

116. Farther, what greatly contributes to make us mistake in this matter is that, when we think of the pictures in the fund of the eye, we imagine ourselves looking on the fund of another's eye, or another looking on the fund of our own eye, and beholding the pictures painted thereon. Suppose two eyes, *A* and *B*. *A* from some distance looking on the pictures in *B* sees them inverted, and for that reason concludes they are inverted in *B*. But this is wrong. There are projected in little on the bottom of *A* the images of the pictures

of, suppose, man, earth, &c., which are painted on B.
And, besides these, the eye B itself, and the objects
which environ it, together with another earth, are projected in a larger size on A. Now, by the eye A these
larger images are deemed the true objects and the lesser
only pictures in miniature. And it is with respect to
those greater images that it determines the situation
of the smaller images; so that, comparing the little man
with the great earth, A judges him inverted, or that
the feet are farthest from and the head nearest to the
great earth. Whereas, if A compare the little man with
the little earth, then he will appear erect, *i.e.*, his head
shall seem farthest from and his feet nearest to the little
earth. But we must consider that B does not see two
earths as A does. It sees only what is represented by
the little pictures in A, and consequently shall judge
the man erect. For, in truth, the man in B is not inverted, for there the feet are next the earth; but it is
the representation of it in A which is inverted, for there
the head of the representation of the picture of the man
in B is next the earth, and the feet farthest from the
earth—meaning the earth which is without the representation of the pictures in B. For, if you take the
little images of the pictures in B, and consider them
by themselves, and with respect only to one another,
they are all erect and in their natural posture.

117. Farther, there lies a mistake in our imagining
that the pictures of external objects are painted on the
bottom of the eye. It has been shewn there is no
resemblance between the ideas of sight and things tangible. It hath likewise been demonstrated, that the
proper objects of sight do not exist without the mind.
Whence it clearly follows that the pictures painted on
the bottom of the eye are not the pictures of external
objects. Let any one consult his own thoughts, and

then tell me, what affinity, what likeness, there is between that certain variety and disposition of colours
which constitute the visible man, or picture of a man,
and that other combination of far different ideas, sensible by touch, which compose the tangible man. But,
if this be the case, how come they to be accounted pictures or images, since that supposes them to copy or
represent some originals or other?

118. To which I answer—In the forementioned instance, the eye *A* takes the little images, included within
the representation of the other eye *B*, to be pictures or
copies, whereof the archetypes are not things existing
without, but the larger pictures projected on its own
fund; and which by *A* are not thought pictures, but the
originals or true things themselves. Though if we suppose a third eye *C*, from a due distance, to behold the
fund of *A*, then indeed the things projected thereon
shall, to *C*, seem pictures or images, in the same sense
that those projected on *B* do to *A*.

119. Rightly to conceive the business in hand, we
must carefully distinguish between the ideas of sight
and touch, between the visible and tangible eye; for
certainly on the tangible eye nothing either is or seems
to be painted. Again, the visible eye, as well as all
other visible objects, hath been shewn to exist only in
the mind; which, perceiving its own ideas, and comparing them together, does call some pictures in respect to
others. What hath been said, being rightly comprehended and laid together, does, I think, afford a full
and genuine explication of the erect appearance of objects—which phenomenon, I must confess, I do not see
how it can be explained by any theories of vision hitherto made public.

120. In treating of these things, the use of language
is apt to occasion some obscurity and confusion, and

create in us wrong ideas. For, language being accommodated to the common notions and prejudices of men, it is scarce possible to deliver the naked and precise truth, without great circumlocution, impropriety, and (to an unwary reader) seeming contradictions. I do, therefore, once for all, desire whoever shall think it worth his while to understand what I have written concerning vision, that he would not stick in this or that phrase or manner of expression, but candidly collect my meaning from the whole sum and tenor of my discourse, and, laying aside the words as much as possible, consider the bare notions themselves, and then judge whether they are agreeable to truth and his own experience or no.

121. We have shewn the way wherein the mind, by mediation of visible ideas, doth perceive or apprehend the distance, magnitude, and situation of tangible objects. I come now to inquire more particularly concerning the difference between the ideas of sight and touch which are called by the same names, and see whether there be any idea common to both senses. From what we have at large set forth and demonstrated in the foregoing parts of this treatise, it is plain there is no one self-same numerical extension, perceived both by sight and touch; but that the particular figures and extensions perceived by sight, however they may be called by the same names, and reputed the same things with those perceived by touch, are nevertheless different, and have an existence very distinct and separate from them. So that the question is not now concerning the same numerical ideas, but whether there be any one and the same sort or species of ideas equally perceivable to both senses? or, in other words, whether extension, figure, and motion perceived by sight, are not specifi-

cally distinct from extension, figure, and motion perceived by touch?

122. But, before I come more particularly to discuss this matter, I find it proper to take into my thoughts extension in abstract. For of this there is much talk; and I am apt to think that when men speak of extension as being an idea common to two senses, it is with a secret supposition that we can single out extension from all other tangible and visible qualities, and form thereof an abstract idea, which idea they will have common both to sight and touch. We are therefore to understand by extension in abstract, an idea of extension—for instance, a line or surface entirely stripped of all other sensible qualities and circumstances that might determine it to any particular existence; it is neither black, nor white, nor red, nor hath it any colour at all, or any tangible quality whatsoever, and consequently it is of no finite determinate magnitude; for that which bounds or distinguishes one extension from another is some quality or circumstance wherein they disagree.

123. Now, I do not find that I can perceive, imagine, or anywise frame in my mind such an abstract idea as is here spoken of. A line or surface which is neither black, nor white, nor blue, nor yellow, &c.; nor long, nor short, nor rough, nor smooth, nor square, nor round, &c. is perfectly incomprehensible. This I am sure of as to myself; how far the faculties of other men may reach they best can tell.

124. It is commonly said that the object of geometry is abstract extension. But geometry centemplates figures: now, figure is the termination of magnitude; but we have shewn that extension in abstract hath no finite determinate magnitude; whence it clearly follows that it can have no figure, and consequently is not the

object of geometry. It is indeed a tenet, as well of the modern as the ancient philosophers, that all general truths are concerning universal abstract ideas; without which, we are told, there could be no science, no demonstration of any general proposition in geometry. But it were no hard matter, did I think it necessary to my present purpose, to shew that propositions and demonstrations in geometry might be universal, though they who make them never think of abstract general ideas of triangles or circles.

125. After reiterated efforts and pangs of thought to apprehend the general idea of a triangle, I have found it altogether incomprehensible. And surely, if any one were able to let that idea into my mind, it must be the author of the *Essay concerning Human Understanding:* he, who has so far distinguished himself from the generality of writers, by the clearness and significancy of what he says. Let us therefore see how this celebrated author describes the general or [which is the same thing, the] abstract idea of a triangle. 'It must be,' says he, 'neither oblique nor rectangle, neither equilateral, equicrural, nor scalenum; but all and none of these at once. In effect it is somewhat imperfect that cannot exist; an idea, wherein some parts of several different and inconsistent ideas are put together.' (*Essay on Human Understanding,* B. iv. ch. 7. s. 9.) This is the idea which he thinks needful for the enlargement of knowledge, which is the subject of mathematical demonstration, and without which we could never come to know any general proposition concerning triangles. [Sure I am, if this be the case, it is impossible for me to attain to know even the first elements of geometry: since I have not the faculty to frame in my mind such an idea as is here described.] That author acknowledges it doth 'require some pains and skill to form this

general idea of a triangle.' (*Ibid.*) But, had he called
to mind what he says in another place, to wit, 'that
ideas of mixed modes wherein any inconsistent ideas
are put together, cannot so much as exist in the mind,
i.e. be conceived,' (vid. B. iii. ch. 10. s. 33, *ibid.*)—I say,
had this occurred to his thoughts, it is not improbable
he would have owned it above all the pains and skill
he was master of, to form the above-mentioned idea of
a triangle, which is made up of manifest staring contradictions. That a man [of such a clear understanding],
who thought so much and so well, and laid so great a
stress on clear and determinate ideas, should nevertheless talk at this rate, seems very surprising. But the
wonder will lessen, if it be considered that the source
when this opinion [of abstract figures and extension]
flows is the prolific womb which has brought forth innumerable errors and difficulties, in all parts of philosophy, and in all the sciences. But this matter, taken in
its full extent, were a subject too vast and comprehensive to be insisted on in this place. [I shall only
observe that your metaphysicians and men of speculation seem to have faculties distinct from those of
ordinary men, when they talk of general or abstracted
triangles and circles, &c., and so peremptorily declare
them to be the subject of all the eternal, immutable,
universal truths in geometry.] And so much for extension in abstract.

126. Some, perhaps, may think pure space, vacuum,
or trine dimension, to be equally the object of sight and
touch. But, though we have a very great propension to
think the ideas of outness and space to be the immediate object of sight, yet, if I mistake not, in the foregoing parts of this *Essay,* that hath been clearly
demonstrated to be a mere delusion, arising from the

quick and sudden suggestion of fancy, which so closely
connects the idea of distance with those of sight, that
we are apt to think it is itself a proper and immediate
object of that sense, till reason corrects the mistake.

127. It having been shewn that there are no abstract
ideas of figure, and that it is impossible for us, by any
precision of thought, to frame an idea of extension separate from all other visible and tangible qualities, which
shall be common both to sight and touch—the question
now remaining is, whether the particular extensions,
figures, and motions perceived by sight, be of the same
kind with the particular extensions, figures, and motions
perceived by touch? In answer to which I shall venture
to lay down the following proposition:—*The extension,
figures, and motions perceived by sight are specifically
distinct from the ideas of touch, called by the same
names; nor is there any such thing as one idea, or kind
of idea, common to both senses.* This proposition may,
without much difficulty, be collected from what hath
been said in several places of this Essay. But, because
it seems so remote from, and contrary to the received
notions and settled opinion of mankind, I shall attempt
to demonstrate it more particularly and at large by the
following arguments:—

128. [*First,*] When, upon perception of an idea, I
range it under this or that sort, it is because it is perceived after the same manner, or because it has a likeness or conformity with, or affects me in the same way
as the ideas of the sort I rank it under. In short, it
must not be entirely new, but have something in it old
and already perceived by me. It must, I say, have
so much, at least, in common with the ideas I have
before known and named, as to make me give it the
same name with them. But, it has been, if I mistake
not, clearly made out that a man born blind would not,

at first reception of his sight, think the things he saw were of the same nature with the objects of touch, or had anything in common with them; but that they were a new set of ideas, perceived in a new manner, and entirely different from all he had ever perceived before. So that he would not call them by the same name, nor repute them to be of the same sort, with anything he had hitherto known. [And surely the judgment of such an unprejudiced person is more to be relied on in this case than the sentiments of the generality of men; who, in this as in almost everything else, suffer themselves to be guided by custom, and the erroneous suggestions of prejudice, rather than reason and sedate reflection.]

129. *Secondly,* Light and colours are allowed by all to constitute a sort or species entirely different from the ideas of touch; nor will any man, I presume, say they can make themselves perceived by that sense. But there is no other immediate object of sight besides light and colours. It is therefore a direct consequence, that there is no idea common to both senses.

130. It is a prevailing opinion, even amongst those who have thought and writ most accurately concerning our ideas, and the ways whereby they enter into the understanding, that something more is perceived by sight than barely light and colours with their variations. [The excellent] Mr. Locke termeth sight 'the most comprehensive of all our senses, conveying to our minds the ideas of light and colours, which are peculiar only to that sense; and also the far different ideas of space, figure, and motion.' (*Essay on Human Understanding,* B. iii. ch. 9. s. 9.) Space or distance, we have shewn, is no otherwise the object of sight than of hearing. (Vid. sect. 46.) And, as for figure and extension, I leave it to any one that shall calmly attend to his own clear and distinct ideas to decide whether he has any

idea intromitted immediately and properly by sight save only light and colours: or, whether it be possible for him to frame in his mind a distinct abstract idea of visible extension, or figure, exclusive of all colour; and, on the other hand, whether he can conceive colour without visible extension? For my own part, I must confess, I am not able to attain so great a nicety of abstraction. I know very well that, in a strict sense, I see nothing but light and colours, with their several shades and variations. He who beside these doth also perceive by sight ideas far different and distinct from them, hath that faculty in a degree more perfect and comprehensive than I can pretend to. It must be owned, indeed, that, by the mediation of light and colours, other far different ideas are suggested to my mind. [But so they are by hearing.] But then, upon this score, I see no reason why the sight should be thought more comprehensive than the hearing, which, beside sounds which are peculiar to that sense, doth, by their mediation, suggest not only space, figure, and motion, but also all other ideas whatsoever that can be signified by words.

131. *Thirdly,* It is, I think, an axiom universally received, that 'quantities of the same kind may be added together and make one entire sum.' Mathematicians add lines together; but they do not add a line to a solid, or conceive it as making one sum with a surface. These three kinds of quantity being thought incapable of any such mutual addition, and consequently of being compared together in the several ways of proportion, are by them for that reason esteemed entirely disparate and heterogeneous. Now let any one try in his thoughts to add a visible line or surface to a tangible line or surface, so as to conceive them making one continued sum or whole. He that can do this may think them homogeneous; but he that cannot must, by the foregoing

axiom, think them heterogeneous. [I acknowledge myself to be of the latter sort.] A blue and a red line I can conceive added together into one sum and making one continued line; but, to make, in my thoughts, one continued line of a visible and tangible line added together, is, I find, a task far more difficult, and even insurmountable—and I leave it to the reflection and experience of every particular person to determine for himself.

132. A farther confirmation of our tenet may be drawn from the solution of Mr. Molyneux's problem, published by Mr. Locke in his *Essay:* which I shall set down as it there lies, together with Mr. Locke's opinion of it:—'Suppose a man born blind, and now adult, and taught by his touch to distinguish between a cube and a sphere of the same metal, and nighly of the same bigness, so as to tell when he felt one and the other, which is the cube, and which the sphere. Suppose then the cube and sphere placed on a table, and the blind man made to see: Quære, Whether by his sight, before he touched them, he could now distinguish, and tell, which is the globe, which the cube. To which the acute and judicious proposer answers: Not. For, though he has obtained the experience of how a globe, how a cube affects his touch; yet he has not yet attained the experience, that what affects his touch so or so must affect his sight so or so: or that a protuberant angle in the cube, that pressed his hand unequally, shall appear to his eye as it doth in the cube. I agree with this thinking gentleman, whom I am proud to call my friend, in his answer to this his problem; and am of opinion that the blind man, at first sight, would not be able with certainty to say, which was the globe, which the cube, whilst he only saw them.' (*Essay on Human Understanding,* B. ii. ch. 9. s. 8.)

133. Now, if a square surface perceived by touch be of the same sort with a square surface perceived by sight, it is certain the blind man here mentioned might know a square surface as soon as he saw it. It is no more but introducing into his mind, by a new inlet, an idea he has been already well acquainted with. Since therefore he is supposed to have known by his touch that a cube is a body terminated by square surfaces; and that a sphere is not terminated by square surfaces—upon the supposition that a visible and tangible square differ only *in numero,* it follows that he might know, by the unerring mark of the square surfaces, which was the cube, and which not, while he only saw them. We must therefore allow, either that visible extension and figures are specifically distinct from tangible extension and figures, or else, that the solution of this problem, given by those two [very] thoughtful and ingenious men, is wrong.

134. Much more might be laid together in proof of the proposition I have advanced. But, what has been said is, if I mistake not, sufficient to convince any one that shall yield a reasonable attention. And, as for those that will not be at the pains of a little thought, no multiplication of words will ever suffice to make them understand the truth, or rightly conceive my meaning.

135. I cannot let go the above-mentioned problem without some reflection on it. It hath been made evident that a man blind from his birth would not, at first sight, denominate anything he saw, by the names he had been used to appropriate to ideas of touch. (Vid. sect. 106.) Cube, sphere, table are words he has known applied to things perceivable by touch, but to things perfectly intangible he never knew them applied. Those words, in their wonted application, always marked out to his mind bodies or solid things which were perceived

by the resistance they gave. But there is no solidity, no resistance or protrusion, perceived by sight. In short, the ideas of sight are all new perceptions, to which there be no names annexed in his mind; he cannot therefore understand what is said to him concerning them. And, to ask of the two bodies he saw placed on the table, which was the sphere, which the cube, were to him a question downright bantering and unintelligible; nothing he sees being able to suggest to his thoughts the idea of body, distance, or, in general, of anything he had already known.

136. It is a mistake to think the same thing affects both sight and touch. If the same angle or square which is the object of touch be also the object of vision, what should hinder the blind man, at first sight, from knowing it? For, though the manner wherein it affects the sight be different from that wherein it affected his touch, yet, there being, beside this manner or circumstance, which is new and unknown, the angle or figure, which is old and known, he cannot choose but discern it.

137. Visible figure and extension having been demonstrated to be of a nature entirely different and heterogeneous from tangible figure and extension, it remains that we inquire concerning motion. Now, that visible motion is not of the same sort with tangible motion seems to need no farther proof; it being an evident corollary from what we have shewn concerning the difference there is betwixt visible and tangible extension. But, for a more full and express proof hereof, we need only observe that one who had not yet experienced vision would not at first sight know motion. Whence it clearly follows that motion perceivable by sight is of a sort distinct from motion perceivable by touch. The antecedent I prove thus—By touch he could not perceive any motion but what was up or down, to the right of left, nearer or

farther from him; besides these, and their several
varieties or complications, it is impossible he should
have any idea of motion. He would not therefore think
anything to be motion, or give the name motion to any
idea, which he could not range under some or other of
those particular kinds thereof. But, from sect. 95, it is
plain that, by the mere act of vision, he could not know
motion upwards or downwards, to the right or left, or
in any other possible direction. From which I conclude,
he would not know motion at all at first sight. As for the
idea of motion in abstract, I shall not waste paper about
it, but leave it to my reader to make the best he can of
it. To me it is perfectly unintelligible.

138. The consideration of motion may furnish a new
field for inquiry. But, since the manner wherein the
mind apprehends by sight the motion of tangible objects,
with the various degrees thereof, may be easily collected
from what has been said concerning the manner wherein
that sense doth suggest their various distances, magnitudes, and situations, I shall not enlarge any farther on
this subject, but proceed to inquire what may be alleged,
with greatest appearance of reason, against the proposition we have demonstrated to be true; for, where there
is so much prejudice to be encountered, a bare and naked
demonstration of the truth will scarce suffice. We must
also satisfy the scruples that men may start in favour
of their preconceived notions, shew whence the mistake
arises, how it came to spread, and carefully disclose
and root out those false persuasions that an early prejudice might have implanted in the mind.

139. *First,* therefore, it will be demanded how visible
extension and figures come to be called by the same name
with tangible extension and figures, if they are not of the
same kind with them? It must be something more than
humour or accident that could occasion a custom so con-

stant and universal as this, which has obtained in all ages
and nations of the world, and amongst all ranks of men,
the learned as well as the illiterate.

140. To which I answer, we can no more argue a
visible and tangible square to be of the same species,
from their being called by the same name, than we can
that a tangible square, and the monosyllable consisting of
six letters whereby it is marked, are of the same species,
because they are both called by the same name. It is
customary to call written words, and the things they
signify, by the same name: for, words not being regarded
in their own nature, or otherwise than as they are marks
of things, it had been superfluous, and beside the design
of language, to have given them names distinct from
those of the things marked by them. The same reason
holds here also. Visible figures are the marks of tangible
figures; and, from sect. 59, it is plain that in themselves
they are little regarded, or upon any other score than
for their connexion with tangible figures, which by nature
they are ordained to signify. And, because this language
of nature does not vary in different ages or nations, hence
it is that in all times and places visible figures are called
by the same names as the respective tangible figures suggested by them; and not because they are alike, or of the
same sort with them.

141. But, say you, surely a tangible square is liker to
a visible square than to a visible circle; it has four
angles, and as many sides; so also has the visible square
—but the visible circle has no such thing, being bounded
by one uniform curve, without right lines or angles, which
makes it unfit to represent the tangible square, but very
fit to represent the tangible circle. Whence it clearly
follows, that visible figures are patterns of, or of the
same species with, the respective tangible figures represented by them; that they are like unto them, and of their

own nature fitted to represent them, as being of the same sort; and that they are in no respect arbitrary signs, as words.

142. I answer, it must be acknowledged the visible square is fitter than the visible circle to represent the tangible square, but then it is not because it is liker, or more of a species with it; but, because the visible square contains in it several distinct parts, whereby to mark the several distinct corresponding parts of a tangible square, whereas the visible circle doth not. The square perceived by touch hath four distinct equal sides, so also hath it four distinct equal angles. It is therefore necessary that the visible figure which shall be most proper to mark it contain four distinct equal parts, corresponding to the four sides of the tangible square; as likewise four other distinct and equal parts, whereby to denote the four equal angles of the tangible square. And accordingly we see the visible figures contain in them distinct visible parts, answering to the distinct tangible parts of the figures signified or suggested by them.

143. But, it will not hence follow that any visible figure is like unto or of the same species with its corresponding tangible figure—unless it be also shewn that not only the number, but also the kind of the parts be the same in both. To illustrate this, I observe that visible figures represent tangible figures much after the same manner that written words do sounds. Now, in this respect, words are not arbitrary; it not being indifferent what written word stands for any sound. But, it is requisite that each word contain in it as many distinct characters as there are variations in the sound it stands for. Thus, the single letter *a* is proper to mark one simple uniform sound; and the word *adultery* is accommodated to represent the sound annexed to it—in the formation whereof there being eight different col-

lisions or modifications of the air by the organs of speech, each of which produces a difference of sound, it was fit the word representing it should consist of as many distinct characters, thereby to mark each particular difference or part of the whole sound. And yet nobody, I presume, will say the single letter *a,* or the word *adultery,* are alike unto or of the same species with the respective sounds by them represented. It is indeed arbitrary that. in general, letters of any language represent sounds at all; but, when that is once agreed, it is not arbitrary what combination of letters shall represent this or that particular sound. I leave this with the reader to pursue, and apply it in his own thoughts.

144. It must be confessed that we are not so apt to confound other signs with the things signified, or to think them of the same species, as we are visible and tangible ideas. But, a little consideration will shew us how this may well be, without our supposing them of a like nature. These signs are constant and universal; their connexion with tangible ideas has been learnt at our first entrance into the world; and ever since, almost every moment of our lives, it has been occurring to our thoughts, and fastening and striking deeper on our minds. When we observe that signs are variable, and of human institution; when we remember there was a time they were not connected in our minds with those things they now so readily suggest, but that their signification was learned by the slow steps of experience: this preserves us from confounding them. But, when we find the same signs suggest the same things all over the world; when we know they are not of human institution, and cannot remember that we ever learned their signification, but think that at first sight they would have suggested to us the same things they do now: all this persuades us they are of the same species as the

things respectively represented by them, and that it is by a natural resemblance they suggest them to our minds.

145. Add to this that whenever we make a nice survey of any object, successively directing the optic axis to each point thereof, there are certain lines and figures, described by the motion of the head or eye, which, being in truth perceived by feeling, do nevertheless so mix themselves, as it were, with the ideas of sight that we can scarce think but they appertain to that sense. Again, the ideas of sight enter into the mind several at once, more distinct and unmingled than is usual in the other senses beside the touch. Sounds, for example, perceived at the same instant, are apt to coalesce, if I may so say, into one sound: but we can perceive, at the same time, great variety of visible objects, very separate and distinct from each other. Now, tangible extension being made up of several distinct co-existent parts, we may hence gather another reason that may dispose us to imagine a likeness or analogy between the immediate objects of sight and touch. But nothing, certainly, does more contribute to blend and confound them together, than the strict and close connexion they have with each other. We cannot open our eyes but the ideas of distance, bodies, and tangible figures are suggested by them. So swift, and sudden, and unperceived is the transit from visible to tangible ideas that we can scare forbear thinking them equally the immediate object of vision.

146. The prejudice which is grounded on these, and whatever other causes may be assigned thereof, sticks so fast on our understandings, that it is impossible, without obstinate striving and labour of the mind, to get entirely clear of it. But then the reluctancy we find in rejecting any opinion can be no argument of its truth, to whoever

considers what has been already shewn with regard to the prejudices we entertain concerning the distance, magnitude, and situation of objects; prejudices so familiar to our minds, so confirmed and inveterate, as they will hardly give way to the clearest demonstration.

147. Upon the whole, I think we may fairly conclude that the proper objects of Vision constitute the Universal Language of Nature; whereby we are instructed how to regulate our actions, in order to attain those things that are necessary to the preservation and well-being of our bodies, as also to avoid whatever may be hurtful and destructive of them. It is by their information that we are principally guided in all the transactions and concerns of life. And the manner wherein they signify and mark out unto us the objects which are at a distance is the same with that of languages and signs of human appointment; which do not suggest the things signified by any likeness or identity of nature, but only by an habitual connexion that experience has made us to observe between them.

148. Suppose one who had always continued blind be told by his guide that after he has advanced so many steps he shall come to the brink of a precipice, or be stopped by a wall; must not this to him seem very admirable and surprising? He cannot conceive how it is possible for mortals to frame such predictions as these, which to him would seem as strange and unaccountable as prophecy does to others. Even they who are blessed with the visive faculty may (though familiarity make it less observed) find therein sufficient cause of admiration. The wonderful art and contrivance wherewith it is adjusted to those ends and purposes for which it was apparently designed; the vast extent, number, and variety of objects that are at once, with so much ease,

and quickness, and pleasure, suggested by it—all these afford subject for much and pleasing speculation, and may, if anything, give us some glimmering analogous prænotion of things, that are placed beyond the certain discovery and comprehension of our present state.

149. I do not design to trouble myself much with drawing corollaries from the doctrine I have hitherto laid down. If it bears the test, others may, so far as they shall think convenient, employ their thoughts in extending it farther, and applying it to whatever purposes it may be subservient to. Only, I cannot forbear making some inquiry concerning the object of geometry, which the subject we have been upon does naturally lead one to. We have shewn there is no such idea as that of extension in abstract; and that there are two kinds of sensible extension and figures, which are entirely distinct and heterogeneous from each other. Now, it is natural to inquire which of these is the object of geometry.

150. Some things there are which, at first sight, incline one to think geometry conversant about visible extension. The constant use of the eyes, both in the practical and speculative parts of that science, doth very much induce us thereto. It would, without doubt, seem odd to a mathematician to go about to convince him the diagrams he saw upon paper were not the figures, or even the likeness of the figures, which make the subject of the demonstration—the contrary being held an unquestionable truth, not only by mathematicians, but also by those who apply themselves more particularly to the study of logic; I mean who consider the nature of science, certainty, and demonstration; it being by them assigned as one reason of the extraordinary clearness and evidence of geometry, that in that science the reasonings are free

from those inconveniences which attend the use of arbitrary signs, the very ideas themselves being copied out, and exposed to view upon paper. But, by the bye, how well this agrees with what they likewise assert of abstract ideas being the object of geometrical demonstration I leave to be considered.

151. To come to a resolution in this point, we need only observe what has been said in sect. 59, 60, 61, where it is shewn that visible extensions in themselves are little regarded, and have no settled determinate greatness, and that men measure altogether by the application of tangible extension to tangible extension. All which makes it evident that visible extension and figures are not the object of geometry.

152. It is therefore plain that visible figures are of the same use in geometry that words are. And the one may as well be accounted the object of that science as the other; neither of them being any otherwise concerned therein than as they represent or suggest to the mind the particular tangible figures connected with them. There is, indeed, this difference betwixt the signification of tangible figures by visible figures, and of ideas by words—that whereas the latter is variable and uncertain, depending altogether on the arbitrary appointment of men, the former is fixed, and, immutably the same in all times and places. A visible square, for instance, suggests to the mind the same tangible figure in Europe that it does in America. Hence it is, that the voice of nature, which speaks to our eyes, is not liable to that misinterpretation and ambiguity that languages of human contrivance are unavoidably subject to. From which may, in some measure, be derived that peculiar evidence and clearness of geometrical demonstrations.

153. Though what has been said may suffice to shew what ought to be determined with relation to the object

of geometry, I shall, nevertheless, for the fuller illustration thereof, take into my thoughts the case of an intelligence or unbodied spirit, which is supposed to see perfectly well, *i.e.* to have a clear perception of the proper and immediate objects of sight, but to have no sense of touch. Whether there be any such being in nature or no, is beside my purpose to inquire; it suffices, that the supposition contains no contradiction in it. Let us now examine what proficiency such a one may be able to make in geometry. Which speculation will lead us more clearly to see whether the ideas of sight can possibly be the object of that science.

154. *First,* then, it is certain the aforesaid intelligence could have no idea of a solid or quantity of three dimensions, which follows from its not having any idea of distance. We, indeed, are prone to think that we have by sight the ideas of space and solids; which arises from our imagining that we do, strictly speaking, see distance, and some parts of an object at a greater distance than others; which has been demonstrated to be the effect of the experience we have had what ideas of touch are connected with such and such ideas attending vision. But the intelligence here spoken of is supposed to have no experience of touch. He would not, therefore, judge as we do, nor have any idea of distance, outness, or profundity, nor consequently of space or body, either immediately or by suggestion. Whence it is plain he can have no notion of those parts of geometry which relate to the mensuration of solids, and their convex or concave surfaces, and contemplate the properties of lines generated by the section of a solid. The conceiving of any part whereof is beyond the reach of his faculties.

155. *Farther,* he cannot comprehend the manner wherein geometers describe a right line or circle; the rule and compass, with their use, being things of which

it is impossible he should have any notion. Nor is it an easier matter for him to conceive the placing of one plane or angle on another, in order to prove their equality; since that supposes some idea of distance, or external space. All which makes it evident our pure intelligence could never attain to know so much as the first elements of plain geometry. And perhaps, upon a nice inquiry, it will be found he cannot even have an idea of plain figures any more than he can of solids; since some idea of distance is necessary to form the idea of a geometrical plane, as will appear to whoever shall reflect a little on it.

156. All that is properly perceived by the visive faculty amounts to no more than colours with their variations, and different proportions of light and shade—but the perpetual mutability and fleetingness of those immediate objects of sight render them incapable of being managed after the manner of geometrical figures; nor is it in any degree useful that they should. It is true there be divers of them perceived at once; and more of some, and less of others: but accurately to compute their magnitude, and assign precise determinate proportions between things so variable and inconstant, if we suppose it possible to be done, must yet be a very trifling and insignificant labour.

157. I must confess, it seems to be the opinion of some very ingenious men that flat or plane figures are immediate objects of sight, though they acknowledge solids are not. And this opinion of theirs is grounded on what is observed in painting, wherein (say they) the ideas immediately imprinted in the mind are only of planes variously coloured, which, by a sudden act of the judgment, are changed into solids: but, with a little attention, we shall find the planes here mentioned as the immediate objects of sight are not visible but tangible planes. For,

when we say that pictures are planes, we mean thereby
that they appear to the touch smooth and uniform. But
then this smoothness and uniformity, or, in other words,
this planeness of the picture is not perceived immediately
by vision; for it appeareth to the eye various and multi-
form.

158. From all which we may conclude that planes are
no more the immediate object of sight than solids. What
we strictly see are not solids, nor yet planes variously
coloured—they are only diversity of colours. And some
of these suggest to the mind solids, and others plane
figures; just as they have been experienced to be connected with the one or the other: so that we see plains
in the same way that we see solids—both being equally
suggested by the immediate objects of sight, which accordingly are themselves denominated planes and solids.
But, though they are called by the same names with the
things marked by them, they are, nevertheless, of a
nature entirely different, as hath been demonstrated.

159. What has been said is, if I mistake not, sufficient
to decide the question we proposed to examine, concerning the ability of a pure spirit, such as we have described, to know geometry. It is, indeed, no easy matter for us to enter precisely into the thoughts of such an
intelligence; because we cannot, without great pains,
cleverly separate and disentangle in our thoughts the
proper objects of sight from those of touch which are
connected with them. This, indeed, in a complete degree seems scarce possible to be performed; which will
not seem strange to us, if we consider how hard it is for
any one to hear the words of his native language, which
is familiar to him, pronounced in his ears without understanding them. Though he endeavour to disunite the
meaning from the sound, it will nevertheless intrude into
his thoughts, and he shall find it extreme difficult, if not

impossible, to put himself exactly in the posture of a foreigner that never learnt the language, so as to be affected barely with the sounds themselves, and not perceive the signification annexed to them.

160. By this time, I suppose, it is clear that neither abstract nor visible extension makes the object of geometry; the not discerning of which may, perhaps, have created some difficulty and useless labour in mathematics. [Sure I am that somewhat relating thereto has occurred to my thoughts; which, though after the most anxious and repeated examination I am forced to think it true, doth, nevertheless, seem so far out of the common road of geometry, that I know not whether it may not be thought presumption if I should make it public, in an age wherein that science hath received such mighty improvements by new methods; great part whereof, as well as of the ancient discoveries, may perhaps lose their reputation, and much of that ardour with which men study the abstruse and fine geometry be abated, if what to me, and those few to whom I have imparted it, seems evidently true, should really prove to be so.]

A TREATISE

CONCERNING THE

PRINCIPLES OF HUMAN KNOWLEDGE

[PART I]

WHEREIN THE CHIEF CAUSES OF ERROR AND
DIFFICULTY IN THE SCIENCES, WITH THE
GROUNDS OF SCEPTICISM, ATHEISM, AND
IRRELIGION, ARE INQUIRED INTO

THOMAS, EARL OF PEMBROKE, &c.

KNIGHT OF THE MOST NOBLE ORDER OF THE GARTER, AND ONE OF
THE LORDS OF HER MAJESTY'S MOST HONOURABLE
PRIVY COUNCIL

MY LORD,

You will perhaps wonder that an obscure person, who
has not the honour to be known to your lordship, should
presume to address you in this manner. But that a man
who has written something with a design to promote
Useful Knowledge and Religion in the world should
make choice of your lordship for his patron, will not be
thought strange by any one that is not altogether unac-
quainted with the present state of the church and learning, and consequently ignorant how great an ornament
and support you are to both. Yet, nothing could have
induced me to make you this present of my poor endeavours, were I not encouraged by that candour and
native goodness which is so bright a part in your lordship's character. I might add, my lord, that the extraordinary favour and bounty you have been pleased to
shew towards our Society [1] gave me hopes you would
not be unwilling to countenance the studies of one of its
members. These considerations determined me to lay
this treatise at your lordship's feet, and the rather because I was ambitious to have it known that I am with
the truest and most profound respect, on account of that

[1] Trinity College, Dublin.

learning and virtue which the world so justly admires
in your lordship,
> My Lord,
>> Your lordship's most humble
>> and most devoted servant,
>>> GEORGE BERKELEY.

THE PREFACE

WHAT I here make public has, a long and scrupulous
inquiry, seemed to me evidently true and not unuseful
to be known; particularly to those who are tainted with
Scepticism, or want a demonstration of the existence
and immateriality of God, or the natural immortality of
the Soul. Whether it be so or no I am content the
reader should impartially examine; since I do not think
myself any farther concerned for the success of what I
have written than as it is agreeable to truth. But, to the
end this may not suffer, I make it my request that the
reader suspend his judgment till he has once at least
read the whole through, with that degree of attention
and thought which the subject-matter shall seem to deserve. For, as there are some passages that, taken by
themselves, are very liable (nor could it be remedied)
to gross misinterpretation, and to be charged with most
absurd consequences, which, nevertheless, upon an entire
perusal will appear not to follow from them; so likewise, though the whole should be read over, yet, if this
be done transiently, it is very probable my sense may be
mistaken: but to a thinking reader, I flatter myself it
will be throughout clear and obvious.

As for the characters of novelty and singularity which
some of the following notions may seem to bear, it is, I
hope, needless to make any apology on that account. He
must surely be either very weak, or very little acquainted

with the sciences, who shall reject a truth that is capable of demonstration, for no other reason but because it is newly known, and contrary to the prejudices of mankind.

Thus much I thought fit to premise, in order to prevent, if possible, the hasty censures of a sort of men who are too apt to condemn an opinion before they rightly comprehend it.

INTRODUCTION

1. PHILOSOPHY being nothing else but the study of Wisdom and Truth, it may with reason be expected that those who have spent most time and pains in it should enjoy a greater calm and serenity of mind, a greater clearness and evidence of knowledge, and be less disturbed with doubts and difficulties than other men. Yet, so it is, we see the illiterate bulk of mankind, that walk the highroad of plain common sense, and are governed by the dictates of nature, for the most part easy and undisturbed. To them nothing that is familiar appears unaccountable or difficult to comprehend. They complain not of any want of evidence in their senses, and are out of all danger of becoming Sceptics. But no sooner do we depart from sense and instinct to follow the light of a superior principle—to reason, meditate, and reflect on the nature of things, but a thousand scruples spring up in our minds, concerning those things which before we seemed fully to comprehend. Prejudices and errors of sense do from all parts discover themselves to our view; and, endeavouring to correct these by reason, we are insensibly drawn into uncouth paradoxes, difficulties, and inconsistencies, which multiply and grow upon us as we advance in speculation; till at length, having wandered through many intricate mazes, we find our-

selves just where we were, or, which is worse, sit down in a forlorn Scepticism.

2. The cause of this is thought to be the obscurity of things, or the natural weakness and imperfection of our understandings. It is said the faculties we have are few, and those designed by nature for the support and pleasure of life, and not to penetrate into the inward essence and constitution of things: besides, the mind of man being finite, when it treats of things which partake of Infinity, it is not to be wondered at if it run into absurdities and contradictions, out of which it is impossible it should ever extricate itself; it being of the nature of Infinite not to be comprehended by that which is finite.

3. But, perhaps, we may be too partial to ourselves in placing the fault originally in our faculties, and not rather in the wrong use we make of them. It is a hard thing to suppose that right deductions from true principles should ever end in consequences which cannot be maintained or made consistent. We should believe that God has dealt more bountifully with the sons of men than to give them a strong desire for that knowledge which he had placed quite out of their reach. This were not agreeable to the wonted indulgent methods of Providence, which, whatever appetites it may have implanted in the creatures, doth usually furnish them with such means as, if rightly made use of, will not fail to satisfy them. Upon the whole, I am inclined to think that the far greater part, if not all, of those difficulties which have hitherto amused philosophers, and blocked up the way to knowledge, are entirely owing to ourselves. We have first raised a dust, and then complain we cannot see.

4. My purpose therefore is, to try if I can discover what those Principles are which have introduced all that doubtfulness and uncertainty, those absurdities and

contradictions, into the several sects of philosophy; insomuch that the wisest men have thought our ignorance incurable, conceiving it to arise from the natural dulness and limitation of our faculties. And surely it is a work well deserving our pains to make a strict inquiry concerning the First Principles of Human Knowledge; to sift and examine them on all sides: especially since there may be some grounds to suspect that those lets and difficulties, which stay and embarrass the mind in its search after truth, do not spring from any darkness and intricacy in the objects, or natural defect in the understanding, so much as from false Principles which have been insisted on, and might have been avoided.

5. How difficult and discouraging soever this attempt may seem, when I consider what a number of very great and extraordinary men have gone before me in the like designs, yet I am not without some hopes; upon the consideration that the largest views are not always the clearest, and that he who is short-sighted will be obliged to draw the object nearer, and may, perhaps, by a close and narrow survey, discern that which had escaped far better eyes.

6. In order to prepare the mind of the reader for the easier conceiving what follows, it is proper to premise somewhat, by way of Introduction, concerning the nature and abuse of Language. But the unravelling this matter leads me in some measure to anticipate my design, by taking notice of what seems to have had a chief part in rendering speculation intricate and perplexed, and to have occasioned innumerable errors and difficulties in almost all parts of knowledge. And that is the opinion that the mind hath a power of framing *abstract* ideas or notions of things. He who is not a perfect stranger to the writings and disputes of philosophers must needs

acknowledge that no small part of them are spent about abstract ideas. These are in a more especial manner thought to be the object of those sciences which go by the name of logic and metaphysics, and of all that which passes under the notion of the most abstracted and sublime learning; in all which one shall scarce find any question handled in such a manner as does not suppose their existence in the mind, and that it is well acquainted with them.

7. It is agreed on all hands that the *qualities* or *modes* of things do never really exist each of them apart by itself, and separated from all others, but are mixed, as it were, and blended together, several in the same object. But, we are told, the mind, being able to consider each quality singly, or abstracted from those other qualities with which it is united, does by that means frame to itself *abstract ideas*. For example, there is conceived by sight an object extended, coloured, and moved: this mixed or compound idea the mind resolving into its simple, constituent parts, and viewing each by itself, exclusive of the rest, does frame the abstract ideas of extension, colour, and motion. Not that it is possible for colour or motion to exist without extension; but only that the mind can frame to itself by abstraction the idea of colour exclusive of extension, and of motion exclusive of both colour and extension.

8. Again, the mind having observed that in the particular extensions perceived by sense there is something common and alike in all, and some other things peculiar, as this or that figure or magnitude, which distinguish them one from another, it considers apart, or singles out by itself, that which is common; making thereof a most abstract idea of extension; which is neither line, surface, nor solid, nor has any figure or magnitude, but is an idea

entirely prescinded from all these. So likewise the mind, by leaving out of the particular colours perceived by sense that which distinguishes them one from another, and retaining that only which is common to all, makes an idea of colour in abstract; which is neither red, nor blue, nor white, nor any other determinate colour. And, in like manner, by considering motion abstractedly, not only from the body moved, but likewise from the figure it describes, and all particular directions and velocities, the abstract idea of motion is framed; which equally corresponds to all particular motions whatsoever that may be perceived by sense.

9. And as the mind frames to itself abstract ideas of *qualities* or *modes,* so does it, by the same precision, or mental separation, attain abstract ideas of the more compounded *beings* which include several co-existent qualities. For example, the mind having observed that Peter, James, and John resemble each other in certain common agreements of shape and other qualities, leaves out of the complex or compound idea it has of Peter, James, and any other particular man, that which is peculiar to each, retaining only what is common to all, and so makes an abstract idea, wherein all the particulars equally partake; abstracting entirely from and cutting off all those circumstances and differences which might determine it to any particular existence. And after this manner it is said we come by the abstract idea of *man,* or, if you please, humanity, or human nature; wherein it is true there is included colour, because there is no man but has some colour, but then it can be neither white, nor black, nor any particular colour, because there is no one particular colour wherein all men partake. So likewise there is included stature, but then it is neither tall stature, nor low stature, nor yet middle stature, but something abstracted from all these. And so of the rest. Moreover,

there being a great variety of other creatures that partake in some parts, but not all, of the complex idea of man, the mind, leaving out those parts which are peculiar to men, and retaining those only which **are common to** all the living creatures, frames the idea of *animal;* which abstracts not only from all particular men, but also all birds, beasts, fishes, and insects. The constituent parts of the abstract idea of animal are body, life, sense, and spontaneous motion. By *body* is meant body without any particular shape or figure, there being no one shape or figure common to all animals; without covering, either of hair, or feathers, or scales, &c., nor yet naked: hair, feathers, scales, and nakedness being the distinguishing properties of particular animals, and for that reason left out of the abstract idea. Upon the same account, the spontaneous motion must be neither walking, nor flying, nor creeping; it is nevertheless a motion, but what that motion is it is not easy to conceive.

10. Whether others have this wonderful faculty of abstracting their ideas, they best can tell. For myself, [I dare be confident I have it not]. I find indeed I have a faculty of imagining, or representing to myself, the ideas of those particular things I have perceived, and of variously compounding and dividing them. I can imagine a man with two heads; or the upper parts of a man joined to the body of a horse. I can consider the hand, the eye, the nose, each by itself abstracted or separated from the rest of the body. But then whatever hand or eye I imagine, it must have some particular shape and colour. Likewise the idea of man that I frame to myself must be either of a white, or a black, or a tawny, a straight, or a crooked, a tall, or a low, or a middle-sized man. I cannot by any effort of thought conceive the abstract idea above described. And it is equally impossible for me to form the abstract idea of

motion distinct from the body moving, and which is neither swift nor slow, curvilinear nor rectilinear; and the like may be said of all other abstract general ideas whatsoever. To be plain, I own myself able to abstract in one sense, as when I consider some particular parts or qualities separated from others, with which, though they are united in some object, yet it is possible they may really exist without them. But I deny that I can abstract from one another, or conceive separately, those qualities which it is impossible should exist so separated; or that I can frame a general notion, by abstracting from particulars in the manner aforesaid—which last are the two proper acceptations of *abstraction*. And there is ground to think most men will acknowledge themselves to be in my case. The generality of men which are simple and illiterate never pretend to abstract notions. It is said they are difficult and not to be attained without pains and study. We may therefore reasonably conclude that, if such there be, they are confined only to the learned.

11. I proceed to examine what can be alleged in defence of the doctrine of abstraction, and try if I can discover what it is that inclines the men of speculation to embrace an opinion so remote from common sense as that seems to be. There has been a late [excellent and] deservedly esteemed philosopher [1] who, no doubt, has given it very much countenance, by seeming to think the having abstract general ideas is what puts the widest difference in point of understanding betwixt man and beast. 'The having of general ideas,' saith he, 'is that which puts a perfect distinction betwixt man and brutes, and is an excellency which the faculties of brutes do by no means attain unto. For it is evident we observe no

[1] The reference is to Locke.

foot-steps in them of making use of general signs for universal ideas; from which we have reason to imagine that they have not the faculty of abstracting, or making general ideas, since they have no use of words, or any other general signs.' And a little after:—'Therefore, I think, we may suppose, that it is in this that the species of brutes are discriminated from man: and it is that proper difference wherein they are wholly separated, and which at last widens to so wide a distance. For if they have any ideas at all, and are not bare machines (as some would have them [1]), we cannot deny them to have some reason. It seems as evident to me that they do, some of them, in certain instances, reason, as that they have sense; but it is only in particular ideas, just as they receive them from their senses. They are the best of them tied up within those narrow bounds, and have not (as I think) the faculty to enlarge them by any kind of abstraction.'—*Essay on Human Understanding,* B. II. ch. 11. § 10 and 11. I readily agree with this learned author, that the faculties of brutes can by no means attain to abstraction. But then if this be made the distinguishing property of that sort of animals, I fear a great many of those that pass for men must be reckoned into their number. The reason that is here assigned, why we have no grounds to think brutes have abstract general ideas, is, that we observe in them no use of words, or any other general signs; which is built on this supposition, to wit, that the making use of words implies having general ideas. From which it follows that men who use language are able to abstract or generalize their ideas. That this is the sense and arguing of the author will further appear by his answering the question he in another place puts: 'Since all things that

---

[1] The reference is to Descartes. Cf. his *Discourse on Method,* V.

exist are only particulars, how come we by general terms?' His answer is: 'Words become general by being made the signs of general ideas.'—*Essay on Human Understanding,* B. III. ch. 3. § 6. But it seems that a word becomes general by being made the sign, not of an abstract general idea, but of several particular ideas, any one of which it indifferently suggests to the mind. For example, when it is said 'the change of motion is proportional to the impressed force,' or that 'whatever has extension is divisible,' these propositions are to be understood of motion and extension in general; and nevertheless it will not follow that they suggest to my thoughts an *idea* of motion without a body moved, or any determinate direction and velocity; or that I must conceive an *abstract general idea* of extension, which is neither line, surface, nor solid, neither great nor small, black, white, nor red, nor of any other determinate colour. It is only implied that whatever particular motion I consider, whether it be swift or slow, perpendicular, horizontal, or oblique, or in whatever object, the axiom concerning it holds equally true. As does the other of every particular extension; it matters not whether line, surface, or solid, whether of this or that magnitude or figure.

12. By observing how ideas become general, we may the better judge how words are made so. And here it is to be noted that I do not deny absolutely there are *general ideas,* but only that there are any *abstract general ideas.* For, in the passages we have quoted wherein there is mention of general ideas, it is always supposed that they are formed by abstraction, after the manner set forth in sections 8 and 9. Now, if we will annex a meaning to our words, and speak only of what we can conceive, I believe we shall acknowledge that an idea, which considered in itself is particular, becomes general,

by being made to represent or stand for all other particular ideas of the same sort. To make this plain by an example. Suppose a geometrician is demonstrating the method of cutting a line in two equal parts. He draws, for instance, a black line of an inch in length: this, which in itself is a particular line, is nevertheless *with regard to its signification* general; since, as it is there used, it represents all particular lines whatsoever; so that what is demonstrated of it is demonstrated of all lines, or, in other words, of a line in general. And, as *that particular line* becomes general by being made a sign, so the *name* line, which taken absolutely is particular, by being a sign, is made general. And as the former owes its generality, not to its being the sign of an abstract or general line, but of all particular right lines that may possibly exist, so the latter must be thought to derive its generality from the same cause, namely, the various particular lines which it indifferently denotes.

13. To give the reader a yet clearer view of the nature of abstract ideas, and the uses they are thought necessary to, I shall add one more passage out of the *Essay on Human Understanding,* which is as follows:—'Abstract ideas are not so obvious or easy to children, or the yet unexercised mind, as particular ones. If they seem so to grown men, it is only because by constant and familiar use they are made so. For, when we nicely reflect upon them, we shall find that general ideas are fictions and contrivances of the mind, that carry difficulty with them, and do not so easily offer themselves as we are apt to imagine. For example, does it not require some pains and skill to form the general idea of a triangle (which is yet none of the most abstract, comprehensive, and difficult); for it must be neither oblique nor rectangle, neither equilateral, equicrural, nor scalenon; but all and none of these at once? In effect, it is something imper-

fect, that cannot exist; an idea wherein some parts of several different and inconsistent ideas are put together. It is true the mind, in this imperfect state, has need of such ideas, and makes all the haste to them it can, for the conveniency of communication and enlargement of knowledge; to both which it is naturally very much inclined. But yet one has reason to suspect such ideas are marks of our imperfection. At least this is enough to shew that the most abstract and general ideas are not those that the mind is first and most easily acquainted with, nor such as its earliest knowledge is conversant about.'—B. iv. ch. 7. § 9. If any man has the faculty of framing in his mind such an idea of a triangle as is here described, it is in vain to pretend to dispute him out of it, nor would I go about it. All I desire is that the reader would fully and certainly inform himself whether he has such an idea or no. And this, methinks, can be no hard task for any one to perform. What more easy than for any one to look a little into his own thoughts, and there try whether he has, or can attain to have, an idea that shall correspond with the description that is here given of the general idea of a triangle— which is neither oblique nor rectangle, equilateral, equicrural nor scalenon, but all and none of these at once?

14. Much is here said of the difficulty that abstract ideas carry with them, and the pains and skill requisite to the forming them. And it is on all hands agreed that there is need of great toil and labour of the mind, to emancipate our thoughts from particular objects, and raise them to those sublime speculations that are conversant about abstract ideas. From all which the natural consequence should seem to be, that so difficult a thing as the forming abstract ideas was not necessary for *communication*, which is so easy and familiar to all sorts of men. But, we are told, if they seem obvious

and easy to grown men, it is only because by constant and familiar use they are made so. Now, I would fain know at what time it is men are employed in surmounting that difficulty, and furnishing themselves with those necessary helps for discourse. It cannot be when they are grown up; for then it seems they are not conscious of any such painstaking. It remains therefore to be the business of their childhood. And surely the great and multiplied labour of framing abstract notions will be found a hard task for that tender age. Is it not a hard thing to imagine that a couple of children cannot prate together of their sugar-plums and rattles and the rest of their little trinkets, till they have first tacked together numberless inconsistencies, and so framed in their minds abstract general ideas, and annexed them to every common name they make use of?

15. Nor do I think them a whit more needful for the *enlargement of knowledge* than for communication. It is, I know, a point much insisted on, that all knowledge and demonstration are about universal notions, to which I fully agree. But then it does not appear to me that those notions are formed by abstraction in the manner premised—*universality,* so far as I can comprehend, not consisting in the absolute, positive nature or conception of anything, but in the relation it bears to the particulars signified or represented by it; by virtue whereof it is that things, names, or notions, being in their own nature *particular,* are *rendered universal.* Thus, when I demonstrate any proposition concerning triangles, it is supposed that I have in view the universal idea of a triangle: which ought not to be understood as if I could frame an *idea* of a triangle which was neither equilateral, nor scalenon, nor equicrural; but only that the particular triangle I consider, whether of this or that sort it matters not, doth equally stand for and represent

all rectilinear triangles whatsoever, and is in that sense universal. All which seems very plain and not to include any difficulty in it.

16. But here it will be demanded, how we can know any proposition to be true of all particular triangles, except we have first seen it demonstrated of the abstract idea of a triangle which equally agrees to all? For, because a property may be demonstrated to agree to some one particular triangle, it will not thence follow that it equally belongs to any other triangle which in all respects is not the same with it. For example, having demonstrated that the three angles of an isosceles rectangular triangle are equal to two right ones, I cannot therefore conclude this affection agrees to all other triangles which have neither a right angle nor two equal sides. It seems therefore, that, to be certain this proposition is universally true, we must either make a particular demonstration for every particular triangle, which is impossible; or once for all demonstrate it of the abstract idea of a triangle, in which all the particulars do indifferently partake, and by which they are all equally represented. To which I answer, that, though the idea I have in view whilst I make the demonstration be, for instance, that of an isosceles rectangular triangle whose sides are of a determinate length, I may nevertheless be certain it extends to all other rectilinear triangles, of what sort or bigness soever. And that because neither the right angle, nor the equality, nor determinate length of the sides are at all concerned in the demonstration. It is true the diagram I have in view includes all these particulars; but then there is not the least mention made of *them* in the proof of the proposition. It is not said the three angles are equal to two right ones, because one of them is a right angle, or because the sides comprehending it are of the same length. Which

sufficiently shews that the right angle might have been
oblique, and the sides unequal, and for all that the demonstration have held good.   And for this reason it is
that I conclude that to be true of any obliquangular or
scalenon which I had demonstrated of a particular right-
angled equicrural triangle, and not because I demonstrated the proposition of the abstract idea of a triangle.
[And here it must be acknowledged that a man may
consider a figure merely as triangular; without attending
to the particular qualities of the angles, or relations of
the sides. *So far he may abstract.* But this will never
prove that he can frame an abstract, general, inconsistent *idea* of a triangle.   In like manner we may consider
Peter so far forth as man, or so far forth as animal,
without framing the forementioned abstract idea, either
of man or of animal; inasmuch as all that is perceived
is not considered.]

17. It were an endless as well as an useless thing to
trace the Schoolmen, those great masters of abstraction,
through all the manifold inextricable labyrinths of error
and dispute which their doctrine of abstract natures and
notions seems to have led them into. What bickerings
and controversies, and what a learned dust have been
raised about those matters, and what mighty advantage
has been from thence derived to mankind, are things at
this day too clearly known to need being insisted on.
And it had been well if the ill effects of that doctrine
were confined to those only who make the most avowed
profession of it.   When men consider the great pains,
industry, and parts that have for so many ages been laid
out on the cultivation and advancement of the sciences,
and that notwithstanding all this the far greater part of
them remain full of darkness and uncertainty, and disputes that are like never to have an end; and even those
that are thought to be supported by the most clear and

cogent demonstrations contain in them paradoxes which are perfectly irreconcilable to the understandings of men; and that, taking all together, a very small portion of them does supply any real benefit to mankind, otherwise than by being an innocent diversion and amusement —I say, the consideration of all this is apt to throw them into a despondency and perfect contempt of all study. But this may perhaps cease upon a view of the false Principles that have obtained in the world; amongst all which there is none, methinks, hath a more wide influence over the thoughts of speculative men than this of *abstract general ideas*.

18. I come now to consider the *source* of this prevailing notion, and that seems to me to be *language*. And surely nothing of less extent than reason itself could have been the source of an opinion so universally received. The truth of this appears as from other reasons so also from the plain confession of the ablest patrons of abstract ideas, who acknowledge that they are made in order to naming; from which it is clear consequence that if there had been no such thing as speech or universal signs, there never had been any thought of abstraction. See B. iii. ch. 6. § 39, and elsewhere of the *Essay on Human Understanding*.

Let us examine the manner wherein Words have contributed to the origin of that mistake.—First then, it is thought that every name has, or ought to have, one only precise and settled signification; which inclines men to think there are certain abstract determinate ideas that constitute the true and only immediate signification of each general name; and that it is by the mediation of these abstract ideas that a general name comes to signify any particular thing. Whereas, in truth, there is no such thing as one precise and definite signification annexed to any general name, they all signifying indifferently a great number of particular ideas. All which does evidently follow from what has been already said, and will clearly appear to any one by a little reflexion. To this it will be objected that every name that has a definition is thereby restrained to one certain signification. For example, a triangle is defined to be 'a plain surface comprehended by three right lines'; by which that name is limited to denote one certain idea and no other. To which I answer, that in the definition it is not said whether the surface be great or small, black or white, nor whether the sides are long or short, equal or unequal, nor with what angles they are inclined to each other; in all which there may be great variety, and consequently there is no one settled idea which limits the signification of the word triangle. It is one thing for to keep a name constantly to the same *definition,* and another to make it stand everywhere for the same *idea:* the one is necessary, the other useless and impracticable.

19. But, to give a farther account how words came to produce the doctrine of abstract ideas, it must be observed that it is a received opinion that language has no other end but the communicating ideas, and that every significant name stands for an idea. This being so, and it being withal certain that names which yet are not thought altogether insignificant do not always mark out particular conceivable ideas, it is straightway concluded that they stand for abstract notions. That there are many names in use amongst speculative men which do not always suggest to others determinate, particular ideas, or in truth anything at all, is what nobody will deny. And a little attention will discover that it is not necessary (even in the strictest reasonings) that significant names which stand for ideas should, every time they are used, excite in the understanding the ideas they

are made to stand for: in reading and discoursing, names being for the most part used as letters are in Algebra, in which, though a particular quantity be marked by each letter, yet to proceed right it is not requisite that in every step each letter suggest to your thoughts that particular quantity it was appointed to stand for.

20. Besides, the communicating of ideas marked by words is not the chief and only end of language, as is commonly supposed. There are other ends, as the raising of some passion, the exciting to or deterring from an action, the putting the mind in some particular disposition; to which the former is in many cases barely subservient, and sometimes entirely omitted, when these can be obtained without it, as I think doth not unfrequently happen in the familiar use of language. I entreat the reader to reflect with himself, and see if it doth not often happen, either in hearing or reading a discourse, that the passions of fear, love, hatred, admiration, and disdain, and the like, arise immediately in his mind upon the perception of certain words, without any ideas coming between. At first, indeed, the words might have occasioned ideas that were fitting to produce those emotions; but, if I mistake not, it will be found that, when language is once grown familiar, the hearing of the sounds or sight of the characters is oft immediately attended with those passions which at first were wont to be produced by the intervention of ideas that are now quite omitted. May we not, for example, be affected with the promise of a *good thing,* though we have not an idea of what it is? Or is not the being threatened with danger sufficient to excite a dread, though we think not of any particular evil likely to befall us, nor yet frame to ourselves an idea of danger in abstract? If any one shall join ever so little reflection of his own to what has been said, I believe that it will

evidently appear to him that general names are often used in the propriety of language without the speakers designing them for marks of ideas in his own, which he would have them raise in the mind of the hearer. Even proper names themselves do not seem always spoken with a design to bring into our view the ideas of those individuals that are supposed to be marked by them. For example, when a schoolman tells me 'Aristotle hath said it,' all I conceive he means by it is to dispose me to embrace his opinion with the deference and submission which custom has annexed to that name. And this effect may be so instantly produced in the minds of those who are accustomed to resign their judgment to authority of that philosopher, as it is impossible any idea either of his person, writings, or reputation should go before. [So close and immediate a connexion may custom establish betwixt the very word Aristotle and the motions of assent and reverence in the minds of some men.] Innumerable examples of this kind may be given, but why should I insist on those things which every one's experience will, I doubt not, plentifully suggest unto him?

21. We have, I think, shewn the impossibility of Abstract Ideas. We have considered what has been said for them by their ablest patrons; and endeavoured to shew they are of no use for those ends to which they are thought necessary. And lastly, we have traced them to the source from whence they flow, which appears evidently to be Language.

It cannot be denied that words are of excellent use, in that by their means all that stock of knowledge which has been purchased by the joint labours of inquisitive men in all ages and nations may be drawn into the view and made the possession of one single person. But [at the same time it must be owned that] most parts of knowledge have been [so] strangely perplexed and darkened by the abuse of words, and general ways of speech wherein they are delivered, [that it may almost be made a question whether language has contributed more to the hindrance or advancement of the sciences]. Since therefore words are so apt to impose on the understanding, [I am resolved in my inquiries to make as little use of them as possibly I can:] whatever ideas I consider, I shall endeavour to take them bare and naked into my view; keeping out of my thoughts, so far as I am able, those names which long and constant use hath so strictly united with them. From which I may expect to derive the following advantages:—

22. *First,* I shall be sure to get clear of all controversies purely verbal, the springing up of which weeds in almost all the sciences has been a main hindrance to the growth of true and sound knowledge. *Secondly,* this seems to be a sure way to extricate myself out of that fine and subtle net of abstract ideas, which has so miserably perplexed and entangled the minds of men; and that with this peculiar circumstance, that by how much the finer and more curious was the wit of any man, by so much the deeper was he likely to be ensnared and faster held therein. *Thirdly,* so long as I confine my thoughts to my own ideas, divested of words, I do not see how I can easily be mistaken. The objects I consider, I clearly and adequately know. I cannot be deceived in thinking I have an idea which I have not. It is not possible for me to imagine that any of my own ideas are alike or unlike that are not truly so. To discern the agreements or disagreements there are between my ideas, to see what ideas are included in my compound idea and what not, there is nothing more requisite than an attentive perception of what passes in my own understanding.

23. But the attainment of all these advantages does presuppose an entire deliverance from the deception of words; which I dare hardly promise myself, so difficult a thing it is to dissolve an union so early begun, and confirmed by so long a habit as that betwixt words and ideas. Which difficulty seems to have been very much increased by the doctrine of *abstraction*. For, so long as men thought *abstract* ideas were annexed to their words, it does not seem strange that they should use words for ideas; it being found an impracticable thing to lay aside the word, and retain the *abstract* idea in the mind; which in itself was perfectly inconceivable. This seems to me the principle cause why those who have so emphatically recommended to others the laying aside all use of words in their meditations, and contemplating their bare ideas, have yet failed to perform it themselves. Of late many have been very sensible of the absurd opinions and significant disputes which grow out of the abuse of words. And, in order to remedy these evils, they advise well, that we attend to the ideas signified, and draw off our attention from the words which signify them. But, how good soever this advice may be they have given others, it is plain they could not have a due regard to it themselves, so long as they thought the only immediate use of words was to signify ideas, and that the immediate signification of every general name was a determinate abstract idea.

24. But these being known to be mistakes, a man may with greater ease prevent his being imposed on by words. He that knows he has no other than *particular* ideas, will not puzzle himself in vain to find out and conceive the *abstract* idea annexed to any name. And he that knows names do not always stand for ideas will spare himself the labour of looking for ideas where there are none to be had. It were, therefore, to be

wished that every one would use his utmost endeavours to obtain a clear view of the ideas he would consider; separating from them all that dress and incumbrance of words which so much contribute to blind the judgment and divide the attention. In vain do we extend our view into the heavens and pry into the entrails of the earth, in vain do we consult the writings of learned men and trace the dark footsteps of antiquity. We need only draw the curtain of words, to behold the fairest tree of knowledge, whose fruit is excellent, and within the reach of our hand.

25. Unless we take care to clear the First Principles of Knowledge from the embarras and delusion of Words, we may make infinite reasonings upon them to no purpose; we may draw consequences from consequences, and be never the wiser. The farther we go, we shall only lose ourselves the more irrecoverably, and be the deeper entangled to difficulties and mistakes. Whoever therefore designs to read the following sheets, I entreat him that he would make my words the occasion of his own thinking, and endeavour to attain the same train of thoughts in reading that I had in writing them. By this means it will be easy for him to discover the truth or falsity of what I say. He will be out of all danger of being deceived by my words. And I do not see how he can be led into an error by considering his own naked, undisguised ideas.

OF THE

PRINCIPLES

OF

HUMAN KNOWLEDGE

PART FIRST

1. It is evident to any one who takes a survey of the *objects of human knowledge,* that they are either *ideas* actually imprinted on the senses; or else such as are perceived by attending to the passions and operations of the mind; or lastly, *ideas* formed by help of memory and imagination—either compounding, dividing, or barely representing those originally perceived in the aforesaid ways. By sight I have the ideas of light and colours, with their several degrees and variations. By touch I perceive hard and soft, heat and cold, motion and resistance; and of all these more and less either as to quantity or degree. Smelling furnishes me with odours; the palate with tastes; and hearing conveys sounds to the mind in all their variety of tone and composition.

And as several of these are observed to accompany each other, they come to be marked by one name, and so to be reputed as one *thing*. Thus, for example, a certain colour, taste, smell, figure and consistence having been observed to go together, are accounted one distinct thing, signified by the name apple; other collections of

ideas constitute a stone, a tree, a book, and the like
sensible things; which as they are pleasing or disagreeable excite the passions of love, hatred, joy, grief, and
so forth.

2. But, besides all that endless variety of ideas or objects of knowledge, there is likewise Something which
knows or perceives them; and exercises divers operations,
as willing, imagining, remembering, about them. This
perceiving, active being is what I call *mind, spirit, soul,*
or *myself.* By which words I do not denote any one of
my ideas, but a thing entirely distinct from them,
wherein they exist, or, which is the same thing, whereby
they are perceived; for the existence of an idea consists
in being perceived.

3. That neither our thoughts, nor passions, nor ideas
formed by the imagination, exist without the mind is
what everybody will allow. And to me it seems no less
evident that the various sensations or ideas imprinted
on the Sense, however blended or combined together
(that is, whatever objects they compose), cannot exist
otherwise than in a mind perceiving them. I think an
intuitive knowledge may be obtained of this, by any one
that shall attend to what is meant by the term *exist* when
applied to sensible things. The table I write on I say
exists; that is, I see and feel it: and if I were out of
my study I should say it existed; meaning thereby that
if I was in my study I might perceive it, or that some
other spirit actually does perceive it. There was an
odour, that is, it was smelt; there was a sound, that is,
it was heard; a colour or figure, and it was perceived by
sight or touch. This is all that I can understand by
these and the like expressions. For as to what is said
of the *absolute* existence of unthinking things, without
any relation to their being perceived, that is to me per-

fectly unintelligible. Their *esse* is *percipi;* nor is it possible they should have any existence out of the minds or thinking things which perceive them.

4. It is indeed an opinion strangely prevailing amongst men, that houses, mountains, rivers, and in a word all sensible objects, have an existence, natural or real, distinct from their being perceived by the understanding. But, with how great an assurance and acquiescence soever this Principle may be entertained in the world, yet whoever shall find in his heart to call it in question may, if I mistake not, perceive it to involve a manifest contradiction. For, what are the forementioned objects but the things we perceive by sense? and what do we perceive besides our own ideas or sensations? and is it not plainly repugnant that any one of these, or any combination of them, should exist unperceived?

5. If we thoroughly examine this tenet it will, perhaps, be found at bottom to depend on the doctrine of *abstract ideas.* For can there be a nicer strain of abstraction than to distinguish the existence of sensible objects from their being perceived, so as to conceive them existing unperceived? Light and colours, heat and cold, extension and figures—in a word the things we see and feel —what are they but so many sensations, notions, ideas, or impressions on the sense? and is it possible to separate, even in thought, any of these from perception? For my part, I might as easily divide a thing from itself. I may, indeed, divide in my thoughts, or conceive apart from each other, those things which perhaps I never perceived by sense so divided. Thus, I imagine the trunk of a human body without the limbs, or conceive the smell of a rose without thinking on the rose itself. So far, I will not deny, I can abstract; if that may properly be called *abstraction* which extends only

to the conceiving separately such objects as it is possible may really exist or be actually perceived asunder. But my conceiving or imagining power does not extend beyond the possibility of real existence or perception. Hence, as it is impossible for me to see or feel anything without an actual sensation of that thing, so is it impossible for me to conceive in my thoughts any sensible thing or object distinct from the sensation or perception of it. [In truth, the object and the sensation are the same thing, and cannot therefore be abstracted from each other.]

6. Some truths there are so near and obvious to the mind that a man need only open his eyes to see them. Such I take this important one to be, viz. that all the choir of heaven and furniture of the earth, in a word all those bodies which compose the mighty frame of the world, have not any subsistence without a mind; that their *being* is to be perceived or known; that consequently so long as they are not actually perceived by me, or do not exist in my mind, or that of any other created spirit, they must either have no existence at all, or else subsist in the mind of some Eternal Spirit: it being perfectly unintelligible, and involving all the absurdity of abstraction, to attribute to any single part of them an existence independent of a spirit. [To be convinced of which, the reader need only reflect, and try to separate in his own thoughts the *being* of a sensible thing from its *being perceived*.]

7. From what has been said it is evident there is not any other Substance than *Spirit*, or that which perceives. But, for the fuller proof of this point, let it be considered the sensible qualities are colour, figure, motion, smell, taste, and such like, that is, the ideas perceived by sense. Now, for an idea to exist in an unperceiving thing is a manifest contradiction; for to have an idea is

all one as to perceive: that therefore wherein colour, figure, and the like qualities exist must perceive them. Hence it is clear there can be no unthinking substance or *substratum* of those ideas.

8. But, say you, though the ideas themselves do not exist without the mind, yet there may be things like them, whereof they are copies or resemblances; which things exist without the mind, in an unthinking substance. I answer, an idea can be like nothing but an idea; a colour or figure can be like nothing but another colour or figure. If we look but never so little into our thoughts, we shall find it impossible for us to conceive a likeness except only between our ideas. Again, I ask whether those supposed *originals,* or external things, of which our ideas are the pictures or representations, be themselves perceivable or no? If they are, then *they* are ideas, and we have gained our point: but if you say they are not, I appeal to any one whether it be sense to assert a colour is like something which is invisible; hard or soft, like something which is intangible; and so of the rest.

9. Some there are who make a distinction betwixt *primary* and *secondary* qualities. By the former they mean extension, figure, motion, rest, solidity or impenetrability, and number; by the latter they denote all other sensible qualities, as colours, sounds, tastes, and so forth. The ideas we have of these last they acknowledge not to be the resemblances of anything existing without the mind, or unperceived; but they will have our ideas of the *primary qualities* to be patterns or images of things which exist without the mind, in an unthinking substance which they call Matter. By Matter, therefore, we are to understand an inert, senseless substance, in which

extension, figure, and motion do actually subsist. But it is evident, from what we have already shewn, that extension, figure and motion are only ideas existing in the mind, and that an idea can be like nothing but another idea; and that consequently neither they nor their archetypes can exist in an unperceiving substance. Hence, it is plain that the very notion of what is called *Matter* or *corporeal substance,* involves a contradiction in it. [Insomuch that I should not think it necessary to spend more time in exposing its absurdity. But, because the tenet of the existence of Matter seems to have taken so deep a root in the minds of philosophers, and draws after it so many ill consequences, I choose rather to be thought prolix and tedious than omit anything that might conduce to the full discovery and extirpation of that prejudice.]

10. They who assert that figure, motion, and the rest of the primary or original qualities do exist without the mind, in unthinking substances, do at the same time acknowledge that colours, sounds, heat, cold, and such-like secondary qualities, do not; which they tell us are sensations, existing in the mind alone, that depend on and are occasioned by the different size, texture, and motion of the minute particles of matter. This they take for an undoubted truth, which they can demonstrate beyond all exception. Now, if it be certain that those *original* qualities are inseparably united with the other sensible qualities, and not, even in thought, capable of being abstracted from them, it plainly follows that *they* exist only in the mind. But I desire any one to reflect, and try whether he can, by any abstraction of thought, conceive the extension and motion of a body without all other sensible qualities. For my own part, I see evidently that it is not in my power to frame an idea of a body extended and moving, but I must withal give it

some colour or other sensible quality, which is acknowledged to exist only in the mind. In short, extension, figure, and motion, abstracted from all other qualities, are inconceivable. Where therefore the other sensible qualities are, there must these be also, to wit, in the mind and nowhere else.

11. Again, *great* and *small, swift* and *slow,* are allowed to exist nowhere without the mind; being entirely relative, and changing as the frame or position of the organs of sense varies. The extension therefore which exists without the mind is neither great nor small, the motion neither swift nor slow; that is, they are nothing at all. But, say you, they are extension in general, and motion in general. Thus we see how much the tenet of extended moveable substances existing without the mind depends on that strange doctrine of *abstract ideas.* And here I cannot but remark how nearly the vague and indeterminate description of Matter, or corporeal substance, which the modern philosophers are run into by their own principles, resembles that antiquated and so much ridiculed notion of *materia prima,* to be met with in Aristotle and his followers. Without extension solidity cannot be conceived: since therefore it has been shewn that extension exists not in an unthinking substance, the same must also be true of solidity.

12. That *number* is entirely the creature of the mind, even though the other qualities be allowed to exist without, will be evident to whoever considers that the same thing bears a different denomination of number as the mind views it with different respects. Thus, the same extension is one, or three, or thirty-six, according as the mind considers it with reference to a yard, a foot, or an inch. Number is so visibly relative, and dependent on men's understanding, that it is strange to think how any one should give it an absolute existence without the

mind. We say one book, one page, one line, &c.; all these are equally units, though some contain several of the others. And in each instance, it is plain, the unit relates to some particular combination of ideas *arbitrarily* put together by the mind.

13. Unity I know some will have to be a simple or uncompounded idea, accompanying all other ideas into the mind. That I have any such idea answering the word *unity* I do not find; and if I had, methinks I could not miss finding it; on the contrary, it should be the most familiar to my understanding, since it is said to accompany all other ideas, and to be perceived by all the ways of sensation and reflexion. To say no more, it is an *abstract idea*.

14. I shall farther add, that, after the same manner as modern philosophers prove certain sensible qualities to have no existence in Matter, or without the mind, the same thing may be likewise proved of all other sensible qualities whatsoever. Thus, for instance, it is said that heat and cold are affections only of the mind, and not at all patterns of real beings, existing in the corporeal substances which excite them; for that the same body which appears cold to one hand seems warm to another. Now, why may we not as well argue that figure and extension are not patterns or resemblances of qualities existing in Matter; because to the same eye at different stations, or eyes of a different texture at the same station, they appear various, and cannot therefore be the images of anything settled and determinate without the mind? Again, it is proved that sweetness is not really in the sapid thing; because the thing remaining unaltered the sweetness is changed into bitter, as in case of a fever or otherwise vitiated palate. Is it not as reasonable to say that motion is not without the mind; since if the succession of ideas in the mind become swifter,

the motion, it is acknowledged, shall appear slower, without any alteration in any external object?

15. In short, let any one consider those arguments which are thought manifestly to prove that colours and tastes exist only in the mind, and he shall find they may with equal force be brought to prove the same thing of extension, figure, and motion. Though it must be confessed this method of arguing does not so much prove that there is no extension or colour in an outward object, as that we do not know by sense which is the true extension or colour of the object. But the arguments foregoing plainly shew it to be impossible that any colour or extension at all, or other sensible quality whatsoever, should exist in an unthinking subject without the mind, or in truth that there should be any such thing as an outward object.

16. But let us examine a little the received opinion. It is said extension is a *mode* or *accident* of Matter, and that Matter is the *substratum* that supports it. Now I desire that you would explain to me what is meant by Matter's *supporting* extension. Say you, I have no idea of Matter; and therefore cannot explain it. I answer, though you have no positive, yet, if you have any meaning at all, you must at least have a relative idea of Matter; though you know not what it is, yet you must be supposed to know what relation it bears to accidents, and what is meant by its supporting them. It is evident *support* cannot here be taken in its usual or literal sense, as when we say that pillars support a building. In what sense therefore must it be taken? [For my part, I am not able to discover any sense at all that can be applicable to it.]

17. If we inquire into what the most accurate philosophers declare themselves to mean by *material substance,* we shall find them acknowledge they have no other mean-

ing annexed to those sounds but the idea of Being in general, together with the relative notion of its supporting accidents. The general idea of Being appeareth to me the most abstract and incomprehensible of all other; and as for its supporting accidents, this, as we have just now observed, cannot be understood in the common sense of those words: it must therefore be taken in some other sense, but what that is they do not explain. So that when I consider the two parts or branches which make the signification of the words *material substance,* I am convinced there is no distinct meaning annexed to them. But why should we trouble ourselves any farther, in discussing this material *substratum* or support of figure and motion and other sensible qualities? Does it not suppose they have an existence without the mind? And is not this a direct repugnancy, and altogether inconceivable?

18. But, though it were possible that solid, figured, moveable substances may exist without the mind, corresponding to the ideas we have of bodies, yet how is it possible for us to know this? Either we must know it by Sense or by Reason. As for our senses, by them we have the knowledge only of our sensations, ideas, or those things that are immediately perceived by sense, call them what you will: but they do not inform us that things exist without the mind, or unperceived, like to those which are perceived. This the materialists themselves acknowledge.—It remains therefore that if we have any knowledge at all of external things, it must be by reason inferring their existence from what is immediately perceived by sense. But [I do not see] what reason can induce us to believe the existence of bodies without the mind, from what we perceive, since the very patrons of Matter themselves do not pretend there is any necessary connexion betwixt them and our

ideas? I say it is granted on all hands (and what happens in dreams, frensies, and the like, puts it beyond dispute) that it is possible we might be affected with all the ideas we have now, though no bodies existed without resembling them. Hence it is evident the supposition of external bodies is not necessary for the producing our ideas; since it is granted they are produced sometimes, and might possibly be produced always, in the same order we see them in at present, without their concurrence.

19. But, though we might possibly have all our sensations without them, yet perhaps it may be thought easier to conceive and explain the manner of their production, by supposing external bodies in their likeness rather than otherwise; and so it might be at least probable there are such things as bodies that excite their ideas in our minds. But neither can this be said. For, though we give the materialists their external bodies, they by their own confession are never the nearer knowing how our ideas are produced; since they own themselves unable to comprehend in what manner body can act upon spirit, or how it is possible it should imprint any idea in the mind. Hence it is evident the production of ideas or sensations in our minds, can be no reason why we should suppose Matter or corporeal substances; since that is acknowledged to remain equally inexplicable with or without this supposition. If therefore it were possible for bodies to exist without the mind, yet to hold they do so must needs be a very precarious opinion; since it is to suppose, without any reason at all, that God has created innumerable beings that are entirely useless, and serve to no manner of purpose.

20. In short, if there were external bodies, it is impossible we should ever come to know it; and if there were not, we might have the very same reasons to think

there were that we have now. Suppose—what no one can deny possible—an intelligence, without the help of external bodies, to be affected with the same train of sensations or ideas that you are, imprinted in the same order and with like vividness in his mind. I ask whether that intelligence hath not all the reason to believe the existence of Corporeal Substances, represented by his ideas, and exciting them in his mind, that you can possibly have for believing the same thing? Of this there can be no question. Which one consideration were enough to make any reasonable person suspect the strength of whatever arguments he may think himself to have, for the existence of bodies without the mind.

21. Were it necessary to add any farther proof against the existence of Matter, after what has been said, I could instance several of those errors and difficulties (not to mention impieties) which have sprung from that tenet. It has occasioned numberless controversies and disputes in philosophy, and not a few of far greater moment in religion. But I shall not enter into the detail of them in this place, as well because I think arguments *a posteriori* are unnecessary for confirming what has been, if I mistake not, sufficiently demonstrated *a priori*, as because I shall hereafter find occasion to speak somewhat of them.

22. I am afraid I have given cause to think I am needlessly prolix in handling this subject. For, to what purpose is it to dilate on that which may be demonstrated with the utmost evidence in a line or two, to any one that is capable of the least reflexion? It is but looking into your own thoughts, and so trying whether you can conceive it possible for a sound, or figure, or motion, or colour to exist without the mind or unperceived. This easy trial may perhaps make you see that

what you contend for is a downright contradiction. Insomuch that I am content to put the whole upon this issue:—If you can but conceive it possible for one extended moveable substance, or in general for any one idea, or anything like an idea, to exist otherwise than in a mind perceiving it, I shall readily give up the cause. And, as for all that compages of external bodies you contend for, I shall grant you its existence, though you cannot either give me any reason why you believe it exists, or assign any use to it when it is supposed to exist. I say, the bare possibility of your opinions being true shall pass for an argument that it is so.

23. But, say you, surely there is nothing easier than for me to imagine trees, for instance, in a park, or books existing in a closet, and nobody by to perceive them. I answer, you may so, there is no difficulty in it. But what is all this, I beseech you, more than framing in your mind certain ideas which you call *books* and *trees,* and at the same time omitting to frame the idea of any one that may perceive them? But do not you yourself perceive or think of them all the while? This therefore is nothing to the purpose: it only shews you have the power of imagining, or forming ideas in your mind; but it does not shew that you can conceive it possible the objects of your thought may exist without the mind. To make out this, it is necessary that you conceive them existing unconceived or unthought of; which is a manifest repugnancy. When we do our utmost to conceive the existence of external bodies, we are all the while only contemplating our own ideas. But the mind, taking no notice of itself, is deluded to think it can and does conceive bodies existing unthought of, or without the mind, though at the same time they are apprehended by, or exist in, itself. A little attention will discover to any one the truth and evidence of what is here

said, and make it unnecessary to insist on any other proofs against the existence of *material substance*.

24. [Could men but forbear to amuse themselves with words, we should, I believe, soon come to an agreement in this point.] It is very obvious, upon the least inquiry into our own thoughts, to know whether it be possible for us to understand what is meant by the *absolute existence of sensible objects in themselves, or without the mind*. To me it is evident those words mark out either a direct contradiction, or else nothing at all. And to convince others of this, I know no readier or fairer way than to entreat they would calmly attend to their own thoughts; and if by this attention the emptiness or repugnancy of those expressions does appear, surely nothing more is requisite for their conviction. It is on this therefore that I insist, to wit, that the *absolute existence of unthinking things* are words without a meaning, or which include a contradiction. This is what I repeat and inculcate, and earnestly recommend to the attentive thoughts of the reader.

25. All our ideas, sensations, notions, or the things which we perceive, by whatsoever names they may be distinguished, are visibly inactive: there is nothing of power or agency included in them. So that one idea or object of thought cannot produce or make any alteration in another. To be satisfied of the truth of this, there is nothing else requisite but a bare observation of our ideas. For, since they and every part of them exist only in the mind, it follows that there is nothing in them but what is perceived: but whoever shall attend to his ideas, whether of sense or reflexion, will not perceive in them any power or activity; there is, therefore, no such thing contained in them. A little attention will discover to us that the very being of an idea implies

passiveness and inertness in it; insomuch that it is impossible for an idea to do anything, or, strictly speaking, to be the cause of anything: neither can it be the resemblance or pattern of any active being, as is evident from sect. 8. Whence it plainly follows that extension, figure, and motion cannot be the cause of our sensations. To say, therefore, that these are the effects of powers resulting from the configuration, number, motion, and size of corpuscles, must certainly be false.

26. We perceive a continual succession of ideas; some are anew excited, others are changed or totally disappear. There is therefore, *some* cause of these ideas, whereon they depend, and which produces and changes them. That this cause cannot be any quality or idea or combination of *ideas,* is clear from the preceding section. It must therefore be a *substance;* but it has been shewn that there is no corporeal or material substance: it remains therefore that the cause of ideas is an incorporeal active substance or Spirit.

27. A Spirit is one simple, undivided, active being—as it perceives ideas it is called the *understanding,* and as it produces or otherwise operates about them it is called the *will.* Hence there can be no *idea* formed of a soul or spirit; for all ideas whatever, being passive and inert (vid. sect. 25), they cannot represent unto us, by way of image or likeness, that which acts. A little attention will make it plain to any one, that to have an idea which shall be *like* that active Principle of motion and change of ideas is absolutely impossible. Such is the nature of Spirit, or that which acts, that it cannot be of itself perceived, but only by the effects which it produceth. If any man shall doubt of the truth of what is here delivered, let him but reflect and try if he can frame the idea of any power or active being; and whether he has ideas of two principal powers, marked by the

names *will* and *understanding,* distinct from each other, as well as from a third idea of Substance or Being in general, with a relative notion of its supporting or being the subject of the aforesaid powers—which is signified by the name *soul* or *spirit.* This is what some hold; but, so far as I can see, the words *will,* [*understanding, mind,*] *soul, spirit,* do not stand for different ideas, or, in truth, for any idea at all, but for something which is very different from ideas, and which, being an agent, cannot be like unto, or represented by, any idea whatsoever. [Though it must be owned at the same time that we have some *notion* of soul, spirit, and the operations of the mind, such as willing, loving, hating—inasmuch as we know or understand the meaning of these words.]

28. I find I can excite ideas in my mind at pleasure, and vary and shift the scene as oft as I think fit. It is no more than *willing,* and straightway this or that idea arises in my fancy; and by the same power it is obliterated and makes way for another. This making and unmaking of ideas doth very properly denominate the mind active. Thus much is certain and grounded on experience: but when we talk of unthinking agents, or of exciting ideas exclusive of volition, we only amuse ourselves with words.

29. But, whatever power I may have over my own thoughts, I find the ideas actually perceived by Sense have not a like dependence of *my* will. When in broad daylight I open my eyes, it is not in my power to choose whether I shall see or no, or to determine what particular objects shall present themselves to my view: and so likewise as to the hearing and other senses; the ideas imprinted on them are not creatures of *my* will. There is therefore some other Will or Spirit that produces them.

30. The ideas of Sense are more strong, lively, and distinct than those of the Imagination; they have likewise a steadiness, order, and coherence, and are not excited at random, as those which are the effects of human wills often are, but in a regular train or series —the admirable connexion whereof sufficiently testifies the wisdom and benevolence of its Author. Now the set rules, or established methods, wherein the Mind we depend on excites in us the ideas of Sense, are called *the laws of nature;* and these we learn by experience, which teaches us that such and such ideas are attended with such and such other ideas, in the ordinary course of things.

31. This gives us a sort of foresight, which enables us to regulate our actions for the benefit of life. And without this we should be eternally at a loss: we could not know how to act anything that might procure us the least pleasure, or remove the least pain of sense. That food nourishes, sleep refreshes, and fire warms us; that to sow in the seed-time is the way to reap in the harvest; and in general that to obtain such or such ends, such or such means are conducive—all this we know, not by discovering any *necessary connexion* between our ideas, but only by the observation of the *settled laws* of nature; without which we should be all in uncertainty and confusion, and a grown man no more know how to manage himself in the affairs of life than an infant just born.

32. And yet this consistent uniform working, which so evidently displays the Goodness and Wisdom of that Governing Spirit whose Will constitutes the laws of nature, is so far from leading our thoughts to Him, that it rather sends them wandering after second causes. For, when we perceive certain ideas of Sense constantly followed by other ideas, and we know this is not of our

own doing, we forthwith attribute power and agency to the ideas themselves, and make one the cause of another, than which nothing can be more absurd and unintelligible. Thus, for example, having observed that when we perceive by sight a certain round luminous figure, we at the same time perceive by touch the idea or sensation called heat, we do from thence conclude the sun to be the *cause* of heat. And in like manner perceiving the motion and collision of bodies to be attended with sound, we are inclined to think the latter the *effect* of the former.

33. The ideas imprinted on the Senses by the Author of nature are called *real things:* and those excited in the imagination, being less regular, vivid, and constant, are more properly termed *ideas* or *images of* things, which they copy and represent. But then our *sensations,* be they never so vivid and distinct, are nevertheless ideas: that is, they exist in the mind, or are perceived by it, as truly as the ideas of its own framing. The ideas of Sense are allowed to have more reality in them, that is, to be more strong, orderly, and coherent than the creatures of the mind; but this is no argument that they exist without the mind. They are also less dependent on the spirit or thinking substance which perceives them, in that they are excited by the will of another and more powerful Spirit: yet still they are *ideas:* and certainly no idea, whether faint or strong, can exist otherwise than in a mind perceiving it.

34. Before we proceed any farther it is necessary we spend some time in answering Objections which may probably be made against the Principles we have hitherto laid down. In doing of which, if I seem too prolix to those of quick apprehensions, I desire I may be excused, since all men do not equally apprehend things of this

nature; and I am willing to be understood by every one.

First, then, it will be objected that by the foregoing principles all that is real and substantial in nature is banished out of the world, and instead thereof a chimerical scheme of *ideas* takes place. All things that exist exist only in the mind; that is, they are purely notional. What therefore becomes of the sun, moon, and stars? What must we think of houses, rivers, mountains, trees, stones; nay, even of our own bodies? Are all these but so many chimeras and illusions on the fancy?—To all which, and whatever else of the same sort may be objected, I answer, that by the Principles premised we are not deprived of any one thing in nature. Whatever we see, feel, hear, or any wise conceive or understand, remains as secure as ever, and is as real as ever. There is a *rerum natura,* and the distinction between realities and chimeras retains its full force. This is evident from sect. 29, 30, and 33, where we have shewn what is meant by *real things,* in opposition to *chimeras* or *ideas of our own framing;* but then they both equally exist in the mind, and in that sense are alike *ideas.*

35. I do not argue against the existence of any one thing that we can apprehend, either by sense or reflection. That the things I see with my eyes and touch with my hands do exist, really exist, I make not the least question. The only thing whose existence we deny is that which *philosophers* call Matter or corporeal substance. And in doing of this there is no damage done to the rest of mankind, who, I dare say, will never miss it. The Atheist indeed will want the colour of an empty name to support his impiety; and the Philosophers may possibly find they have lost a great handle for trifling and disputation. [But that is all the harm that I can see done.]

36. If any man thinks this detracts from the existence or reality of things, he is very far from understanding what hath been premised in the plainest terms I could think of. Take here an abstract of what has been said: —There are spiritual substances, minds, or human souls, which will or excite ideas in themselves at pleasure; but these are faint, weak, and unsteady in respect of others they perceive by sense: which, being impressed upon them according to certain rules or laws of nature, speak themselves the effects of a Mind more powerful and wise than human spirits. These latter are said to have *more reality* in them than the former;—by which is meant that they are more affecting, orderly, and distinct, and that they are not fictions of the mind perceiving them. And in this sense the sun that I see by day is the real sun, and that which I imagine by night is the idea of the former. In the sense here given of *reality,* it is evident that every vegetable, star, mineral, and in general each part of the mundane system, is as much a *real being* by our principles as by any other. Whether others mean anything by the term *reality* different from what I do, I entreat them to look into their own thoughts and see.

37. It will be urged that thus much at least is true, to wit, that we take away all *corporeal substances.* To this my answer is, that if the word *substance* be taken in the vulgar sense, for a *combination* of sensible qualities, such as extension, solidity, weight, and the like—this we cannot be accused of taking away: but if it be taken in a philosophic sense, for the support of accidents or qualities without the mind—then indeed I acknowledge that we take it away, if one may be said to take away that which never had any existence, not even in the imagination.

38. But after all, say you, it sounds very harsh to say

we eat and drink ideas, and are clothed with ideas. I acknowledge it does so—the word *idea* not being used in common discourse to signify the several combinations of sensible qualities which are called *things;* and it is certain that any expression which varies from the familiar use of language will seem harsh and ridiculous. But this doth not concern the truth of the proposition, which in other words is no more than to say, we are fed and clothed with those things which we perceive immediately by our senses. The hardness or softness, the colour, taste, warmth, figure, and suchlike qualities, which combined together constitute the several sorts of victuals and apparel, have been shewn to exist only in the mind that perceives them: and this is all that is meant by calling them *ideas;* which word, if it was as ordinarily used as *thing,* would sound no harsher nor more ridiculous than it. I am not for disputing about the propriety, but the truth of the expression. If therefore you agree with me that we eat and drink and are clad with the immediate objects of sense, which cannot exist unperceived or without the mind, I shall readily grant it is more proper or conformable to custom that they should be called *things* rather than *ideas.*

39. If it be demanded why I make use of the word *idea,* and do not rather in compliance with custom call them *things;* I answer, I do it for two reasons:—First, because the term *thing,* in contradistinction to *idea,* is generally supposed to denote somewhat existing without the mind: Secondly, because *thing* hath a more comprehensive signification than *idea,* including spirits, or thinking things, as well as ideas. Since therefore the objects of sense exist only in the mind, and are withal thoughtless and inactive, I chose to mark them by the word *idea;* which implies those properties.

40. But, say what we can, some one perhaps may be

apt to reply, he will still believe his senses, and never suffer any arguments, how plausible soever, to prevail over the certainty of them. Be it so; assert the evidence of sense as high as you please, we are willing to do the same. That what I see, hear, and feel doth exist, that is to say, is perceived by me, I no more doubt than I do of my own being. But I do not see how the testimony of sense can be alleged as a proof for the existence of anything which is *not* perceived by sense. We are not for having any man turn sceptic and disbelieve his senses; on the contrary, we give them all the stress and assurance imaginable; nor are there any principles more opposite to Scepticism than those we have laid down, as shall be hereafter clearly shewn.

41. *Secondly,* it will be objected that there is a great difference betwixt real fire for instance, and the idea of fire, betwixt dreaming or imagining oneself burnt, and actually being so. [If you suspect it to be only the idea of fire which you see, do but put your hand into it and you will be convinced with a witness.] This and the like may be urged in opposition to our tenets.—To all which the answer is evident from what hath been already said; and I shall only add in this place, that if real fire be very different from the idea of fire, so also is the real pain that it occasions very different from the idea of the same pain, and yet nobody will pretend that real pain either is, or can possibly be, in an unperceiving thing, or without the mind, any more than its idea.

42. *Thirdly,* it will be objected that we see things actually without or at a distance from us, and which consequently do not exist in the mind; it being absurd that those things which are seen at the distance of several miles should be as near to us as our own thoughts.—

In answer to this, I desire it may be considered that in a dream we do oft perceive things as existing at a great distance off, and yet for all that, those things are acknowledged to have their existence only in the mind.

43. But, for the fuller clearing of this point, it may be worth while to consider how it is that we perceive distance, and things placed at a distance, by sight. For, that we should in truth *see* external space, and bodies actually existing in it, some nearer, others farther off, seems to carry with it some opposition to what hath been said of their existing nowhere without the mind. The consideration of this difficulty it was that gave birth to my *Essay towards a New Theory of Vision,* which was published not long since. Wherein it is shewn that distance or outness is neither immediately of itself perceived by sight, nor yet apprehended or judged of by lines and angles, or anything that hath a necessary connexion with it; but that it is only suggested to our thoughts by certain visible ideas, and sensations attending vision, which in their own nature have no manner of similitude or relation either with distance or things placed at a distance; but, by a connexion taught us by experience, they come to signify and suggest them to us, after the same manner that words of any language suggest the ideas they are made to stand for. Insomuch that a man born blind, and afterwards made to see, would not, at first sight, think the things he saw to be without his mind, or at any distance from him. See sect. 41 of the forementioned treatise.

44. The ideas of sight and touch make two species entirely distinct and heterogeneous. The former are marks and prognostics of the latter. That the proper objects of sight neither exist without the mind, nor are the images of external things, was shewn even in that treatise. Though throughout the same the contrary

be supposed true of *tangible objects;*—not that to suppose that vulgar error was necessary for establishing the notion therein laid down, but because it was beside my purpose to examine and refute it, in a discourse concerning *Vision.* So that in strict truth the ideas of sight, when we apprehend by them distance, and things placed at a distance, do not suggest or mark out to us things actually existing at a distance, but only admonish us what ideas of touch will be imprinted in our minds at such and such distances of time, and in consequence of such or such actions. It is, I say, evident, from what has been said in the foregoing parts of this Treatise, and in sect. 147 and elsewhere of the Essay concerning Vision, that visible ideas are the Language whereby the Governing Spirit on whom we depend informs us what tangible ideas he is about to imprint upon us, in case we excite this or that motion in our own bodies. But for a fuller information in this point I refer to the Essay itself.

45. *Fourthly,* it will be objected that from the foregoing principles it follows things are every moment annihilated and created anew. The objects of sense exist only when they are perceived: the trees therefore are in the garden, or the chairs in the parlour, no longer than while there is somebody by to perceive them. Upon shutting my eyes all the furniture in the room is reduced to nothing, and barely upon opening them it is again created.—In answer to all which, I refer the reader to what has been said in sect. 3, 4, &c.; and desire he will consider whether he means anything by the actual existence of an idea distinct from its being perceived. For my part, after the nicest inquiry I could make, I am not able to discover that anything else is meant by those words; and I once more entreat the reader to sound his

own thoughts, and not suffer himself to be imposed on by words. If he can conceive it possible either for his ideas or their archetypes to exist without being perceived, then I give up the cause. But if he cannot, he will acknowledge it is unreasonable for him to stand up in defence of he knows not what, and pretend to charge on me as an absurdity, the not assenting to those propositions which at bottom have no meaning in them.

46. It will not be amiss to observe how far the received principles of philosophy are themselves chargeable with those pretended absurdities. It is thought strangely absurd that upon closing my eyelids all the visible objects around me should be reduced to nothing; and yet is not this what philosophers commonly acknowledge, when they agree on all hands that light and colours, which alone are the proper and immediate objects of sight, are mere sensations that exist no longer than they are perceived? Again, it may to some perhaps seem very incredible that things should be every moment creating; yet this very notion is commonly taught in the schools. For the Schoolmen, though they acknowledge the existence of Matter, and that the whole mundane fabric is framed out of it, are nevertheless of opinion that it cannot subsist without the divine conservation; which by them is expounded to be a continual creation.

47. Farther, a little thought will discover to us that, though we allow the existence of Matter or corporeal substance, yet it will unavoidably follow, from the principles which are now generally admitted, that the particular bodies, of what kind soever, do none of them exist whilst they are not perceived. For, it is evident, from sect. 11 and the following sections, that the Matter philosophers contend for is an incomprehensible Somewhat, which hath none of those particular qualities

whereby the bodies falling under our senses are distinguished one from another. But, to make this more plain, it must be remarked that the infinite divisibility of Matter is now universally allowed, at least by the most approved and considerable philosophers, who on the received principles demonstrate it beyond all exception. Hence, it follows there is an infinite number of parts in each particle of Matter which are not perceived by sense. The reason therefore that any particular body seems to be of a finite magnitude, or exhibits only a finite number of parts to sense, is, not because it contains no more, since in itself it contains an infinite number of parts, but because the sense is not acute enough to discern them. In proportion therefore as the sense is rendered more acute, it perceives a greater number of parts in the object, that is, the object appears greater; and its figure varies, those parts in its extremities which were before unperceivable appearing now to bound it in very different lines and angles from those perceived by an obtuser sense. And at length, after various changes of size and shape, when the sense becomes infinitely acute, the body shall seem infinite. During all which there is no alteration in the body, but only in the sense. Each body therefore, considered in itself, is infinitely extended, and consequently void of all shape and figure. From which it follows that, though we should grant the existence of Matter to be never so certain, yet it is withal as certain, the materialists themselves are by their own principles forced to acknowledge, that neither the particular bodies perceived by sense, nor anything like them, exists without the mind. Matter, I say, and each particle thereof, is according to them infinite and shapeless; and it is the mind that frames all that variety of bodies which compose the visible world, any one whereof does not exist longer than it is perceived.

48. But, after all, if we consider it, the objection proposed in sect. 45 will not be found reasonably charged on the Principles we have premised, so as in truth to make any objection at all against our notions. For. though we hold indeed the objects of sense to be nothing else but ideas which cannot exist unperceived, yet we may not hence conclude they have no existence except only while they are perceived by *us;* since there may be some other spirit that perceives them though we do not. Wherever bodies are said to have no existence without the mind, I would not be understood to mean this or that particular mind, but all minds whatsoever. It does not therefore follow from the foregoing Principles that bodies are annihilated and created every moment, or exist not at all during the intervals between *our* perception of them.

49. *Fifthly,* it may perhaps be objected that if extension and figure exist only in the mind, it follows that the mind is extended and figured; since extension is a mode or attribute which (to speak with the Schools) is predicated of the subject in which it exists.—I answer, those qualities are in the mind only as they are perceived by it;—that is, not by way of *mode* or *attribute,* but only by way of *idea.* And it no more follows the soul or mind is extended, because extension exists in it alone, than it does that it is red or blue, because those colours are on all hands acknowledged to exist in it, and nowhere else. As to what philosophers say of subject and mode, that seems very groundless and unintelligible. For instance, in this proposition 'a die is hard, extended, and square,' they will have it that the

word *die* denotes a subject or substance, distinct from the hardness, extension, and figure which are predicated of it, and in which they exist. This I cannot comprehend: to me a die seems to be nothing distinct from those things which are termed its modes or accidents. And, to say a die is hard, extended, and square is not to attribute those qualities to a subject distinct from and supporting them, but only an explication of the meaning of the word *die*.

50. *Sixthly,* you will say there have been a great many things explained by matter and motion; take away these and you destroy the whole corpuscular philosophy, and undermine those mechanical principles which have been applied with so much success to account for the phenomena. In short, whatever advances have been made, either by accident or modern philosophers, in the study of nature do all proceed on the supposition that corporeal substance or Matter doth really exist.—To this I answer that there is not any one phenomenon explained on that supposition which may not as well be explained without it, as might easily be made appear by an induction of particulars. To explain the phenomena, is all one as to shew why, upon such and such occasions, we are affected with such and such ideas. But how Matter should operate on a Spirit, or produce any idea in it, is what no philosopher will pretend to explain; it is therefore evident there can be no use of Matter in natural philosophy. Besides, they who attempt to account for things do it, not by corporeal substance, but by figure, motion, and other qualities; which are in truth no more than mere ideas, and therefore cannot be the cause of anything, as hath been already shewn. See sect. 25.

51. *Seventhly,* it will upon this be demanded whether it does not seem absurd to take away natural causes, and ascribe everything to the immediate operation of spirits? We must no longer say upon these principles that fire heats, or water cools, but that a spirit heats, and so forth. Would not a man be deservedly laughed at, who should talk after this manner?—I answer, he would so: in such things we ought to think with the learned, and speak with the vulgar. They who to demonstration are convinced of the truth of the Copernican system do nevertheless say 'the sun rises,' 'the sun sets,' or 'comes to the meridian'; and if they affected a contrary style in common talk it would without doubt appear very ridiculous. A little reflection on what is here said will make it manifest that the common use of language would receive no manner of alteration or disturbance from the admission of our tenets.

52. In the ordinary affairs of life, any phrases may be retained, so long as they excite in us proper sentiments, or dispositions to act in such a manner as is necessary for our well-being, how false soever they may be if taken in a strict and speculative sense. Nay, this is unavoidable, since, propriety being regulated by custom, language is suited to the received opinions, which are not always the truest. Hence it is impossible—even in the most rigid, philosophic reasonings—so far to alter the bent and genius of the tongue we speak as never to give a handle for cavillers to pretend difficulties and inconsistencies. But, a fair and ingenuous reader will collect the sense from the scope and tenor and connexion of a discourse, making allowances for those inaccurate modes of speech which use has made inevitable.

53. As to the opinion that there are no corporeal causes, this has been heretofore maintained by some of the Schoolmen, as it is of late by others among the

modern philosophers; who though they allow Matter to exist, yet will have God alone to be the immediate efficient cause of all things. These men saw that amongst all the objects of sense there was none which had any power or activity included in it; and that by consequence this was likewise true of whatever bodies they supposed to exist without the mind, like unto the immediate objects of sense. But then, that they should suppose an innumerable multitude of created beings, which they acknowledge are not capable of producing any one effect in nature, and which therefore are made to no manner of purpose, since God might have done everything as well without them—this I say, though we should allow it possible, must yet be a very unaccountable and ex·travagant supposition.

54. In the *eighth* place, the universal concurrent assent of mankind may be thought by some an invincible argument in behalf of Matter, or the existence of external things. Must we suppose the whole world to be mistaken? And if so, what cause can be assigned of so widespread and predominant an error?—I answer, first, that, upon a narrow inquiry, it will not perhaps be found so many as is imagined do really believe the existence of Matter or things without the mind. Strictly speaking, to believe that which involves a contradiction, or has no meaning in it, is impossible; and whether the foregoing expressions are not of that sort, I refer it to the impartial examination of the reader. In one sense, indeed, men may be said to believe that Matter exists; that is, they act as if the immediate cause of their sensations, which affects them every moment, and is so nearly present to them, were some senseless unthinking being. But, that they should clearly apprehend any meaning marked by those words, and form thereof a settled speculative

opinion, is what I am not able to conceive. This is not the only instance wherein men impose upon themselves, by imagining they believe those propositions which they have often heard, though at bottom they have no meaning in them.

55. But secondly, though we should grant a notion to be never so universally and stedfastly adhered to, yet this is but a weak argument of its truth to whoever considers what a vast number of prejudices and false opinions are everywhere embraced with the utmost tenaciousness, by the unreflecting (which are the far greater) part of mankind. There was a time when the antipodes and motion of the earth were looked upon as monstrous absurdities even by men of learning: and if it be considered what a small proportion they bear to the rest of mankind, we shall find that at this day those notions have gained but a very inconsiderable footing in the world.

56. But it is demanded that we assign a cause of this prejudice, and account for its obtaining in the world. To this I answer, that men knowing they perceived several ideas, whereof they themselves were not the authors, as not being excited from within, nor depending on the operation of their wills, this made them maintain *those* ideas or objects of perception, had an existence independent of and without the mind, without ever dreaming that a contradiction was involved in those words. But, philosophers having plainly seen that the immediate objects of perception do not exist without the mind, they in some degree corrected the mistake of the vulgar; but at the same time run into another, which seems no less absurd, to wit, that there are certain objects really existing without the mind, or having a subsistence distinct from being perceived, of which our ideas are only images or resemblances, imprinted by

those objects on the mind. And this notion of the philosophers owes its origin to the same cause with the former, namely, their being conscious that *they* were not the authors of their own sensations; which they evidently knew were imprinted from without, and which therefore must have *some* cause, distinct from the minds on which they are imprinted.

57. But why they should suppose the ideas of sense to be excited in us by things in their likeness, and not rather have recourse to *Spirit,* which alone can act, may be accounted for. First, because they were not aware of the repugnancy there is, as well in supposing things like unto our ideas existing without, as in attributing to them power or activity. Secondly, because the Supreme Spirit which excites those ideas in our minds, is not marked out and limited to our view by any particular finite collection of sensible ideas, as human agents are by their size, complexion, limbs, and motions. And thirdly, because His operations are regular and uniform. Whenever the course of nature is interrupted by a miracle, men are ready to own the presence of a Superior Agent. But, when we see things go on in the ordinary course, they do not excite in us any reflexion; their order and concatenation, though it be an argument of the greatest wisdom, power, and goodness in their Creator, is yet so constant and familiar to us, that we do not think them the immediate effects of a *Free Spirit;* especially since inconsistency and mutability in acting, though it be an imperfection, is looked on as a mark of *freedom.*

58. *Tenthly,* it will be objected that the notions we advance are inconsistent with several sound truths in philosophy and mathematics. For example, the motion of the earth is now universally admitted by astronomers as a truth grounded on the clearest and most convincing

reasons. But, on the foregoing Principles, there can be no such thing. For, motion being only an idea, it follows that if it be not perceived it exists not: but the motion of the earth is not perceived by sense.—I answer, That tenet, if rightly understood, will be found to agree with the Principles we have premised: for, the question whether the earth moves or no amounts in reality to no more than this, to wit, whether we have reason to conclude, from what has been observed by astronomers, that if we were placed in such and such circumstances, and such or such a position and distance both from the earth and sun, we should perceive the former to move among the choir of the planets, and appearing in all respects like one of them: and this, by the established rules of nature, which we have no reason to mistrust, is reasonably collected from the phenomena.

59. We may, from the experience we have had of the train and succession of ideas in our minds, often make, I will not say uncertain conjectures, but sure and well-grounded predictions concerning the ideas we shall be affected with pursuant to a great train of actions; and be enabled to pass a right judgment of what would have appeared to us, in case we were placed in circumstances very different from those we are in at present. Herein consists the knowledge of nature, which may preserve its use and certainty very consistently with what hath been said. It will be easy to apply this to whatever objections of the like sort may be drawn from the magnitude of the stars, or any other discoveries in astronomy or nature.

60. In the *eleventh* place, it will be demanded to what purpose serves that curious organization of plants, and the animal mechanism in the parts of animals. Might not vegetables grow, and shoot forth leaves and blossoms.

and animals perform all their motions, as well without as with all that variety of internal parts so elegantly contrived and put together;—which, being ideas, have nothing powerful or operative in them, nor have any *necessary* connexion with the effects ascribed to them? If it be a Spirit that immediately produces every effect by a *fiat*, or act of his will, we must think all that is fine and artificial in the works, whether of man or nature, to be made in vain. By this doctrine, though an artist hath made the spring and wheels, and every movement of a watch, and adjusted them in such a manner as he knew would produce the motions he designed; yet he must think all this done to no purpose, and that it is an Intelligence which directs the index, and points to the hour of the day. If so, why may not the Intelligence do it, without *his* being at the pains of making the movements and putting them together? Why does not an empty case serve as well as another? And how comes it to pass, that whenever there is any fault in the going of a watch, there is some corresponding disorder to be found in the movements, which being mended by a skilful hand all is right again? The like may be said of all the Clockwork of Nature, great part whereof is so wonderfully fine and subtle as scarce to be discerned by the best microscope. In short, it will be asked, how, upon our Principles, any tolerable account can be given, or any final cause assigned of an innumerable multitude of bodies and machines, framed with the most exquisite art, which in the common philosophy have very opposite uses assigned them, and serve to explain abundance of phenomena?

61. To all which I answer, first, that though there were some difficulties relating to the administration of Providence, and the uses by it assigned to the several parts of nature, which I could not solve by the forego-

ing Principles, yet this objection could be of small weight against the truth and certainty of those things which may be proved *a priori,* with the utmost confidence and rigour of demonstration. Secondly, but neither are the received principles free from the like difficulties; for, it may still be demanded to what end God should take those roundabout methods of effecting things by instruments and machines, which no one can deny might have been effected by the mere command of His will, without all that *apparatus.* Nay, if we narrowly consider it, we shall find the objection may be retorted with greater force on those who hold the existence of those machines without the mind; for it has been made evident that solidity, bulk, figure, motion, and the like have no *activity* or *efficacy* in them, so as to be capable of producing any one effect in nature. See sect. 25. Whoever therefore supposes them to exist (allowing the supposition possible) when they are not perceived does it manifestly to no purpose; since the only use that is assigned to them, as they exist unperceived, is that they produce those perceivable effects which in truth cannot be ascribed to anything but Spirit.

62. But, to come nigher the difficulty, it must be observed that though the fabrication of all those parts and organs be not absolutely necessary to the producing any effect, yet it is necessary to the producing of things in a constant regular way, according to the laws of nature. There are certain general laws that run through the whole chain of natural effects: these are learned by the observation and study of nature, and are by men applied, as well to the framing artificial things for the use and ornament of life as to the explaining the various phenomena. Which explication consists only in shewing the conformity any particular phenomenon hath to the general laws of nature, or, which is the same thing, in

discovering the *uniformity* there is in the production of natural effects; as will be evident to whoever shall attend to the several instances wherein philosophers pretend to account for appearances. That there is a great and conspicuous *use* in these regular constant methods of working observed by the Supreme Agent hath been shewn in sect. 31. And it is no less visible that a particular size, figure, motion, and disposition of parts are necessary, though not absolutely to the producing any effect, yet to the producing it according to the standing mechanical laws of nature. Thus, for instance, it cannot be denied that God, or the Intelligence that sustains and rules the ordinary course of things, might if He were minded to produce a miracle, cause all the motions on the dial-plate of a watch, though nobody had ever made the movements and put them in it. But yet, if He will act agreeably to the rules of mechanism, by Him for wise ends established and maintained in the creation, it is necessary that those actions of the watchmaker, whereby *he* makes the movements and rightly adjusts them, precede the production of the aforesaid motions; as also that any disorder in them be attended with the perception of some corresponding disorder in the movements, which being once corrected all is right again.

63. It may indeed on some occasions be necessary that the Author of nature display His overruling power in producing some appearance out of the ordinary series of things. Such exceptions from the general rules of nature are proper to surprise and awe men into an acknowledgment of the Divine Being; but then they are to be used but seldom, otherwise there is a plain reason why they should fail of that effect. Besides, God seems to choose the convincing our reason of His attributes by the works of nature, which discover so much harmony and contrivance in their make, and are such plain

indications of wisdom and beneficence in their Author, rather than to astonish us into a belief of His Being by anomalous and surprising events.

64. To set this matter in a yet clearer light, I shall observe that what has been objected in sect. 60 amounts in reality to no more than this:—*ideas* are not anyhow and at random produced, there being a certain order and connexion between them, like to that of cause and effect: there are also several combinations of them, made in a very regular and artificial manner, which seem like so many instruments in the hand of nature that, being hid as it were behind the scenes, have a secret operation in producing those appearances which are seen on the theatre of the world, being themselves discernible only to the curious eye of the philosopher. But, since one idea cannot be the cause of another, to what purpose is that connexion? And since those instruments, being barely *inefficacious* perceptions in the mind, are not subservient to the production of natural effects, it is demanded why they are made; or, in other words, what reason can be assigned why God should make us, upon a close inspection into His works, behold so great variety of ideas, so artfully laid together, and so much according to rule; it not being credible that He would be at the expense (if one may so speak) of all that art and regularity to no purpose?

65. To all which my answer is, first, that the connexion of ideas does not imply the relation of *cause* and *effect*, but only of a mark or *sign* with the *thing signified*. The fire which I see is not the cause of the pain I suffer upon my approaching it, but the mark that forewarns me of it. In like manner the noise that I hear is not the effect of this or that motion or collision of the ambient bodies, but the sign thereof. Secondly, the reason why ideas are formed into machines,

that is, artificial and regular combinations, is the same with that for combining letters into words. That a few original ideas may be made to signify a great number of effects and actions, it is necessary they be variously combined together. And to the end their use be permanent and universal, these combinations must be made by *rule,* and with *wise contrivance.* By this means abundance of information is conveyed unto us, concerning what we are to expect from such and such actions, and what methods are proper to be taken for the exciting such and such ideas. Which in effect is all that I conceive to be distinctly meant when it is said that, by discerning the figure, texture, and mechanism of the inward parts of bodies, whether natural or artificial, we may attain to know the several uses and properties depending thereon, or the nature of the thing.

66. Hence, it is evident that those things which, under the notion of a cause co-operating or concurring to the production of effects, are altogether inexplicable and run us into great absurdities, may be very naturally explained, and have a proper and obvious use assigned to them, when they are considered only as marks or signs for *our* information. And it is the searching after and endeavouring to understand this Language (if I may so call it) of the Author of Nature, that ought to be the employment of the natural philosopher; and not the pretending to explain things by *corporeal* causes, which doctrine seems to have too much estranged the minds of men from that Active Principle, that supreme and wise Spirit 'in whom we live, move, and have our being.'

67. In the *twelfth* place, it may perhaps be objected that—though it be clear from what has been said that there can be no such thing as an inert, senseless, extended, solid, figured, moveable Substance, existing with-

out the mind, such as philosophers describe Matter; yet, if any man shall leave out of his idea of Matter the positive ideas of extension, figure, solidity and motion, and say that he means only by that word an inert, senseless substance, that exists without the mind, or unperceived, which is the *occasion* of our ideas, or at the presence whereof God is pleased to excite ideas in us—it doth not appear but that Matter taken in this sense may possibly exist.—In answer to which I say, first, that it seems no less absurd to suppose a substance without accidents, than it is to suppose accidents without a substance. But secondly, though we should grant this unknown substance may possibly exist, yet where can it be supposed to be? That it exists not in the mind is agreed; and that it exists not in place is no less certain, since all place or extension exists only in the mind, as hath been already proved. It remains therefore that it exists nowhere at all.

68. Let us examine a little the description that is here given us of Matter. It neither acts, nor perceives, nor is perceived: for this is all that is meant by saying it is an inert, senseless, unknown substance; which is a definition entirely made up of negatives, excepting only the relative notion of its standing under or supporting. But then it must be observed that it supports nothing at all, and how nearly this comes to the description of a *nonentity* I desire may be considered. But, say you, it is the *unknown occasion,* at the presence of which ideas are excited in us by the will of God. Now, I would fain know how anything can be present to us, which is neither perceivable by sense nor reflexion, nor capable of producing any idea in our minds, nor is at all extended, nor hath any form, nor exists in any place. The words 'to be present,' when thus applied, must needs be taken

in some abstract and strange meaning, and which I am not able to comprehend.

69. Again, let us examine what is meant by *occasion*. So far as I can gather from the common use of language, that word signifies either the agent which produces any effect, or else something that is observed to accompany or go before it, in the ordinary course of things. But, when it is applied to Matter, as above described, it can be taken in neither of those senses; for Matter is said to be passive and inert, and so cannot be an agent or efficient cause. It is also unperceivable, as being devoid of all sensible qualities, and so cannot be the occasion of our perceptions in the latter sense; as when the burning my finger is said to be the occasion of the pain that attends it. What therefore can be meant by calling *matter* an *occasion?* This term is either used in no sense at all, or else in some very distant from its received signification.

70. You will perhaps say that Matter, though it be not perceived by us, is nevertheless perceived by God, to whom it is the occasion of exciting ideas in our minds. For, say you, since we observe our sensations to be imprinted in an orderly and constant manner, it is but reasonable to suppose there are certain constant and regular occasions of their being produced. That is to say, that there are certain permanent and distinct parcels of Matter, corresponding to our ideas, which, though they do not excite them in our minds, or anywise immediately affect us, as being altogether passive, and unperceivable to us, they are nevertheless to God, by whom they *are* perceived, as it were so many occasions to remind Him when and what ideas to imprint on our minds: that so things may go on in a constant uniform manner.

71. In answer to this, I observe that, as the notion of Matter is here stated, the question is no longer concern-

ing the existence of a thing distinct from *Spirit* and *idea,* from perceiving and being perceived; but whether there are not certain Ideas (of I know not what sort) in the mind of God, which are so many marks or notes that direct Him how to produce sensations in our minds in a constant and regular method: much after the same manner as a musician is directed by the notes of music to produce that harmonious train and composition of sound which is called a tune; though they who hear the music do not perceive the notes, and may be entirely ignorant of them. But this notion of Matter (which after all is the only intelligible one that I can pick from what is said of unknown occasions) seems too extravagant to deserve a confutation. Besides, it is in effect no objection against what we have advanced, viz. that there is no senseless unperceived substance.

72. If we follow the light of reason, we shall, from the constant uniform method of our sensations, collect the goodness and wisdom of the Spirit who excites them in our minds; but this is all that I can see reasonably concluded from thence. To me, I say, it is evident that the being of a Spirit—infinitely wise, good, and powerful—is abundantly sufficient to explain all the appearances of nature. But, as for *inert, senseless Matter,* nothing that I perceive has any the least connexion with it, or leads to the thoughts of it. And I would fain see any one explain any the meanest phenomenon in nature by it, or shew any manner of reason, though in the lowest rank of probability, that he can have for its existence; or even make any tolerable sense or meaning of that supposition. For, as to its being an occasion, we have, I think, evidently shewn that with regard to us it is no occasion. It remains therefore that it must be, if at all, the occasion to God of exciting ideas in us; and what this amounts to we have just now seen.

73. It is worth while to reflect a little on the motives which induced men to suppose the existence of *material substance;* that so having observed the gradual ceasing and expiration of those motives or reasons, we may proportionably withdraw the assent that was grounded on them. First, therefore, it was thought that colour, figure, motion, and the rest of the sensible qualities or accidents, did really exist without the mind; and for this reason it seemed needful to suppose some unthinking *substratum* or substance wherein they did exist, since they could not be conceived to exist by themselves. Afterwards, in process of time, men being convinced that colours, sounds, and the rest of the sensible, secondary qualities had no existence without the mind, they stripped this *substratum* or material substance of *those* qualities, leaving only the primary ones, figure, motion, and suchlike; which they still conceived to exist without the mind, and consequently to stand in need of a material support. But, it having been shewn that none even of these can possibly exist otherwise than in a Spirit or Mind which perceives them, it follows that we have no longer any reason to suppose the being of Matter, nay, that it is utterly impossible there should be any such thing;—so long as that word is taken to denote an *unthinking substratum* of qualities or accidents, wherein they exist without the mind.

74. But—though it be allowed by the materialists themselves that Matter was thought of only for the sake of supporting accidents, and, the reason entirely ceasing, one might expect the mind should naturally, and without any reluctance at all, quit the belief of what was solely grounded thereon: yet the prejudice is riveted so deeply in our thoughts that we can scarce tell how to part with it, and are therefore inclined, since the *thing* itself is indefensible, at least to retain the *name;* which we apply

to I know not what abstracted and indefinite notions of *being*, or *occasion*, though without any shew of reason, at least so far as I can see. For, what is there on our part, or what do we perceive, amongst all the ideas, sensations, notions which are imprinted on our minds, either by sense or reflexion, from whence may be inferred the existence of an inert, thoughtless, unperceived occasion? and, on the other hand, on the part of an All-sufficient Spirit, what can there be that should make us believe or even suspect He is directed by an inert occasion to excite ideas in our minds?

75. It is a very extraordinary instance of the force of prejudice, and much to be lamented, that the mind of man retains so great a fondness, against all the evidence of reason, for a stupid thoughtless *Somewhat*, by the interposition whereof it would as it were screen itself from the Providence of God, and remove it farther off from the affairs of the world. But, though we do the utmost we can to secure the belief of Matter; though, when reason forsakes us, we endeavour to support our opinion on the bare possibility of the thing, and though we indulge ourselves in the full scope of an imagination not regulated by reason to make out that poor possibility; yet the upshot of all is—that there are certain *unknown* Ideas in the mind of God; for this, if anything, is all that I conceive to be meant by *occasion* with regard to God. And this at the bottom is no longer contending for the thing, but for the name.

76. Whether therefore there are such Ideas in the mind of God, and whether *they* may be called by the name *Matter*, I shall not dispute. But, if you stick to the notion of an unthinking substance or support of extension, motion, and other sensible qualities, then to me it is most evidently impossible there should be any such thing; since it is a plain repugnancy that those

qualities should exist in, or be supported by, an unperceiving substance.

77. But, say you, although it be granted that there is no thoughtless support of extension, and the other qualities or accidents which we perceive, yet there may perhaps be some inert, unperceiving substance or *substratum* of some other qualities, as incomprehensible to us as colours are to a man born blind, because we have not a sense adapted to them. But, if we had a new sense, we should possibly no more doubt of *their* existence than a blind man made to see does of the existence of light and colours.—I answer, first, if what you mean by the word *Matter* be only the unknown support of unknown qualities, it is no matter whether there is such a thing or no, since it no way concerns us. And I do not see the advantage there is in disputing about what we know not *what,* and we know not *why.*

78. But, secondly, if we had a new sense, it could only furnish us with new ideas or sensations; and then we should have the same reason against *their* existing in an unperceiving substance that has been already offered with relation to figure, motion, colour, and the like. *Qualities,* as hath been shewn, are nothing else but *sensations* or *ideas,* which exist only in a mind perceiving them; and this is true not only of the ideas we are acquainted with at present, but likewise of all possible ideas whatever.

79. But you will insist, What if I have no reason to believe the existence of Matter? what if I cannot assign any use to it, or explain anything by it, or even conceive what is meant by that word? yet still it is no contradiction to say that Matter *exists,* and that this Matter is *in general* a *substance,* or *occasion of ideas;* though indeed to go about to unfold the meaning, or adhere to any

particular explication of those words may be attended
with great difficulties.—I answer, when words are used
without a meaning, you may put them together as you
please, without danger of running into a contradiction.
You may say, for example, that *twice two* is equal to
seven; so long as you declare you do not take the words
of that proposition in their usual acceptation, but for
marks of you know not what. And, by the same reason, you may say there is an inert thoughtless substance
without accidents, which is the occasion of our ideas.
And we shall understand just as much by one proposition as the other.

80. In the *last* place, you will say, What if we give
up the cause of material Substance, and stand to it that
Matter is an unknown *Somewhat*—neither substance nor
accident, spirit nor idea—inert, thoughtless, indivisible,
immovable, unextended, existing in no place? For, say
you, whatever may be urged against *substance* or *occasion,* or any other positive or relative notion of Matter,
hath no place at all, so long as this negative definition of
Matter is adhered to.—I answer, You may, if so it shall
seem good, use the word *matter* in the same sense as
other men use *nothing,* and so make those terms con-
vertible in your style. For, after all, this is what appears to me to be the result of that definition; the parts
whereof, when I consider with attention, either collec-
tively or separate from each other, I do not find that
there is any kind of effect or impression made on my
mind, different from what is excited by the term *nothing.*

81. You will reply, perhaps, that in the foresaid
definition is included what doth sufficiently distinguish
it from nothing—the positive abstract idea of *quiddity,
entity,* or *existence.* I own, indeed, that those who pretend to the faculty of framing abstract general ideas

do talk as if they had such an idea, which is, say they, the most abstract and general notion of all: that is to me the most incomprehensible of all others. That there are a great variety of spirits of different orders and capacities, whose faculties, both in number and extent, are far exceeding those the Author of my being has bestowed on me, I see no reason to deny. And for me to pretend to determine, by my own few, stinted, narrow inlets of perception, what ideas the inexhaustible power of the Supreme Spirit may imprint upon them, were certainly the utmost folly and presumption. Since there may be, for aught that I know, innumerable sorts of ideas or sensations, as different from one another, and from all that I have perceived, as colours are from sounds. But, how ready soever I may be to acknowledge the scantiness of my comprehension, with regard to the endless variety of spirits and ideas that may possibly exist, yet for any one to pretend to a *notion* of Entity or Existence, *abstracted* from *spirit* and *idea,* from perceived and being perceived, is, I suspect, a downright repugnancy and trifling with words.

It remains that we consider the objections which may possibly be made on the part of Religion.

82. Some there are who think that, though the arguments for the real existence of bodies which are drawn from Reason be allowed not to amount to demonstration, yet the Holy Scriptures are so clear in the point, as will sufficiently convince every good Christian, that bodies do really exist, and are something more than mere ideas; there being in Holy Writ innumerable facts related which evidently suppose the reality of timber and stone, mountains and rivers, and cities, and human bodies—To which I answer that no sort of writings whatever, sacred or profane, which use those and the like words in the

vulgar acceptation, or so as to have a meaning in them, are in danger of having their truth called in question by our doctrine. That all those things do really exist; that there are bodies, even corporeal substances, when taken in the vulgar sense, has been shewn to be agreeable to our principles: and the difference betwixt *things* and *ideas, realities* and *chimeras,* has been distinctly explained. See sect. 29, 30, 33, 36, &c. And I do not think that either what philosophers call *Matter,* or the existence of objects without the mind, is anywhere mentioned in Scripture.

83. Again, whether there be or be not external things, it is agreed on all hands that the proper use of words is the marking *our* conceptions, or things only as they are known and perceived by us: whence it plainly follows, that in the tenets we have laid down there is nothing inconsistent with the right use and significancy of language, and that discourse, of what kind soever, so far as it is intelligible, remains undisturbed. But all this seems so very manifest, from what has been largely set forth in the premises, that it is needless to insist any farther on it.

84. But, it will be urged that miracles do, at least, lose much of their stress and import by our principles. What must we think of Moses' rod? was it not *really* turned into a serpent? or was there only a change of *ideas* in the minds of the spectators? And, can it be supposed that our Saviour did no more at the marriage-feast in Cana than impose on the sight, and smell, and taste of the guests, so as to create in them the appearance or idea only of wine? The same may be said of all other miracles: which, in consequence of the foregoing principles, must be looked upon only as so many cheats, or illusions of fancy.—To this I reply, that the rod was changed into a real serpent, and the water into

real wine. That this does not in the least contradict what I have elsewhere said will be evident from sect. 34 and 35. But this business of *real* and *imaginary* has been already so plainly and fully explained, and so often referred to, and the difficulties about it are so easily answered from what has gone before, that it were an affront to the reader's understanding to resume the explication of it in this place. I shall only observe that if at table all who were present should see, and smell, and taste, and drink wine, and find the effects of it, with me there could be no doubt of its reality. So that at bottom the scruple concerning real miracles has no place at all on ours, but only on the received principles, and consequently makes rather for than against what has been said.

85. Having done with the Objections, which I endeavoured to propose in the clearest light, and gave them all the force and weight I could, we proceed in the next place to take a view of our tenets in their Consequences. Some of these appear at first sight—as that several difficult and obscure questions, on which abundance of speculation has been thrown away, are entirely banished from philosophy. Whether corporeal substance can think? Whether Matter be infinitely divisible? And how it operates on spirit?—these and the like inquiries have given infinite amusement to philosophers in all ages. But, depending on the existence of Matter, they have no longer any place on our Principles. Many other advantages there are, as well with regard to religion as the sciences, which it is easy for any one to deduce from what has been premised. But this will appear more plainly in the sequel.

86. From the Principles we have laid down it follows human knowledge may naturally be reduced to two heads

—that of *ideas* and that of *Spirits*. Of each of these I shall treat in order.

And First as to *ideas, or unthinking things.* Our knowledge of these has been very much obscured and confounded, and we have been led into very dangerous errors, by supposing a two-fold existence of sense—the one *intelligible* or in the mind, the other *real* and without the mind. Whereby unthinking things are thought to have a natural subsistence of their own, distinct from being perceived by spirits. This, which, if I mistake not, hath been shewn to be a most groundless and absurd notion, is the very root of Scepticism; for, so long as men thought that real things subsisted without the mind, and that their knowledge was only so far forth *real* as it was *conformable to real things,* it follows they could not be certain that they had any real knowledge at all. For how can it be known that the things which are perceived are conformable to those which are not perceived, or exist without the mind?

87. Colour, figure, motion, extension, and the like, considered only as so many *sensations* in the mind, are perfectly known; there being nothing in them which is not perceived. But, if they are looked on as notes or images, referred to *things* or *archetypes existing without the mind,* then are we involved all in scepticism. We see only the appearances, and not the real qualities of things. What may be the extension, figure, or motion of anything really and absolutely, or in itself, it is impossible for us to know, but only the proportion or relation they bear to our senses. Things remaining the same, our ideas vary; and which of them, or even whether any of them at all, represent the true quality really existing in the thing, it is out of our reach to determine. So that, for aught we know, all we see, hear, and feel, may be only

phantom and vain chimera, and not at all agree with the real things existing in *rerum natura*. All this scepticism follows from our supposing a difference between *things* and *ideas,* and that the former have a subsistence without the mind, or unperceived. It were easy to dilate on this subject, and shew how the arguments urged by sceptics in all ages depend on the supposition of external objects. [But this is too obvious to need being insisted on.]

88. So long as we attribute a real existence to unthinking things, distinct from their being perceived, it is not only impossible for us to know with evidence the nature of any real unthinking being, but even that it exists. Hence it is that we see philosophers distrust their senses, and doubt of the existence of heaven and earth, of everything they see or feel, even of their own bodies. And after all their labouring and struggle of thought, they are forced to own we cannot attain to any self-evident or demonstrative knowledge of the existence of sensible things. But, all this doubtfulness, which so bewilders and confounds the mind and makes philosophy ridiculous in the eyes of the world, vanishes if we annex a meaning to our words, and do not amuse ourselves with the terms *absolute, external, exist,* and such like, signifying we know not what. I can as well doubt of my own being as of the being of those things which I actually perceive by sense: it being a manifest contradiction that any sensible object should be immediately perceived by sight or touch, and at the same time have no existence in nature; since the very existence of an *unthinking being* consists in *being perceived*.

89. Nothing seems of more importance towards erecting a firm system of sound and real knowledge, which may be proof against the assaults of Scepticism, than to lay the beginning in a distinct explication of *what is*

meant by *thing, reality, existence;* for in vain shall we dispute concerning the real existence of things, or pretend to any knowledge thereof, so long as we have not fixed the meaning of those words. *Thing* or *being* is the most general name of all: it comprehends under it two kinds, entirely distinct and heterogeneous, and which have nothing common but the name, viz. *spirits* and *ideas.* The former are active, indivisible, [incorruptible] substances: the latter are inert, fleeting, [perishable passions,] or dependent beings; which subsist not by themselves, but are supported by, or exist in, minds or spiritual substances.

[We comprehend our own existence by inward feeling or reflection, and that of other spirits by reason. We may be said to have some knowledge or *notion* of our own minds, of spirits and active beings; whereof in a strict sense we have not *ideas.* In like manner, we know and have a *notion* of relations between things or ideas; which relations are distinct from the ideas or things related, inasmuch as the latter may be perceived by us without our perceiving the former. To me it seems that *ideas, spirits,* and *relations* are all in their respective kinds the object of human knowledge and subject of discourse; and that the term *idea* would be improperly extended to signify *everything* we know or have any notion of.]

90. Ideas imprinted on the senses are *real* things, or do really exist: this we do not deny; but we deny they *can* subsist without the minds which perceive them, or that they are resemblances of any archetypes existing without the mind; since the very being of a sensation or idea consists in being perceived, and an idea can be like nothing but an idea. Again, the things perceived by sense may be termed *external,* with regard to their

origin; in that they are not generated from within by the mind itself, but imprinted by a Spirit distinct from that which perceives them. Sensible objects may likewise be said to be 'without the mind' in another sense, namely when they exist in some other mind. Thus, when I shut my eyes, the things I saw may still exist; but it must be in another mind.

91. It were a mistake to think that what is here said derogates in the least from the reality of things. It is acknowledged, on the received principles, that extension, motion, and in a word all sensible qualities, have need of a support, as not being able to subsist by themselves. But the objects perceived by sense are allowed to be nothing but combinations of those qualities, and consequently cannot subsist by themselves. Thus far it is agreed on all hands. So that in denying the things perceived by sense an existence independent of a substance or support wherein they may exist, we detract nothing from the received opinion of their *reality*, and are guilty of no innovation in that respect. All the difference is that, according to us, the unthinking beings perceived by sense have no existence distinct from being perceived, and cannot therefore exist in any other substance than those unextended indivisible substances, or *spirits*, which act, and think and perceive them. Whereas philosophers vulgarly hold that the sensible qualities do exist in an inert, extended, unperceiving Substance, which they call *Matter*, to which they attribute a natural subsistence, exterior to all thinking beings, or distinct from being perceived by any mind whatsoever, even the Eternal Mind of the Creator; wherein they suppose only Ideas of the corporeal substances created by Him: if indeed they allow them to be at all *created*.

92. For, as we have shewn the doctrine of **Matter** or Corporeal Substance to have been the main pillar and support of Scepticism, so likewise upon the same foundation have been raised all the impious schemes of Atheism and Irreligion. Nay, so great a difficulty has it been thought to conceive Matter produced out of nothing, that the most celebrated among the ancient philosophers, even of those who maintained the being of a God, have thought Matter to be uncreated and co-eternal with Him. How great a friend *material substance* has been to Atheists in all ages were needless to relate. All their monstrous systems have so visible and necessary a dependence on it, that when this corner-stone is once removed, the whole fabric cannot choose but fall to the ground; insomuch that it is no longer worth while to bestow a particular consideration on the absurdities of every wretched sect of Atheists.

93. That impious and profane persons should readily fall in with those systems which favour their inclinations, by deriding *immaterial substance,* and supposing the soul to be divisible, and subject to corruption as the body; which exclude all freedom, intelligence, and design from the formation of things, and instead thereof make a self-existent, stupid, unthinking substance the root and origin of all beings; that they should hearken to those who deny a Providence, or inspection of a Superior Mind, over the affairs of the world, attributing the whole series of events either to blind chance or fatal necessity, arising from the impulse of one body on another—all this is very natural. And, on the other hand, when men of better principles observe the enemies of religion lay so great a stress on *unthinking Matter,* and all of them use so much industry and artifice to reduce everything to it; methinks they should rejoice to see them deprived of their grand support, and driven

from that only fortress, without which your Epicureans,. Hobbists, and the like, have not even the shadow of a pretence, but become the most cheap and easy triumph in the world.

94. The existence of Matter, or bodies unperceived, has not only been the main support of Atheists and Fatalists, but on the same principle doth Idolatry likewise in all its various forms depend. Did men but consider that the sun, moon, and stars, and every other object of the senses, are only so many sensations in their minds, which have no other existence but barely being perceived, doubtless they would never fall down and worship *their own ideas;* but rather address their homage to that Eternal Invisible Mind which produces and sustains all things.

95. The same absurd principle, by mingling itself with the articles of our faith, hath occasioned no small difficulties to Christians. For example, about the Resurrection, how many scruples and objections have been raised by Socinians and others? But do not the most plausible of them depend on the supposition that a body is denominated the *same,* with regard not to the form, or that which is perceived by sense, but the material substance, which remains the same under several forms? Take away this *material substance*—about the identity whereof all the dispute is—and mean by *body* what every plain ordinary person means by that word, to wit, that which is immediately seen and felt, which is only a combination of sensible qualities or ideas: and then their most unanswerable objections come to nothing.

96. Matter being once expelled out of nature drags with it so many sceptical and impious notions, such an incredible number of disputes and puzzling questions, which have been thorns in the sides of divines as well as philosophers, and made so much fruitless work for

mankind, that if the arguments we have produced against it are not found equal to demonstration (as to me they evidently seem), yet I am sure all friends to knowledge, peace, and religion have reason to wish they were.

97. Beside the external existence of the objects of perception, another great source of errors and difficulties with regard to ideal knowledge is the doctrine of *abstract ideas,* such as it hath been set forth in the Introduction. The plainest things in the world, those we are most intimately acquainted with and perfectly know, when they are considered in an abstract way, appear strangely difficult and incomprehensible. Time, place, and motion, taken in particular or concrete, are what everybody knows; but, having passed through the hands of a metaphysician, they become too abstract and fine to be apprehended by men of ordinary sense. Bid your servant meet you at such a *time,* in such a *place,* and he shall never stay to deliberate on the meaning of those words. In conceiving that particular time and place, or the motion by which he is to get thither, he finds not the least difficulty. But if *time* be taken exclusive of all those particular actions and ideas that diversify the day, merely for the continuation of existence or duration in abstract, then it will perhaps gravel even a philosopher to comprehend it.

98. For my own part, whenever I attempt to frame a simple idea of *time,* abstracted from the succession of ideas in my mind, which flows uniformly, and is participated by all beings, I am lost and embrangled in inextricable difficulties. I have no notion of it at all: only I hear others say it is infinitely divisible, and speak of it in such a manner as leads me to harbour odd thoughts of my existence: since that doctrine lays one under an absolute necessity of thinking, either that he

passes away innumerable ages without a thought, or else that he is annihilated every moment of his life: both which seem equally absurd. Time therefore being nothing, abstracted from the succession of ideas in our minds, it follows that the duration of any finite spirit must be estimated by the number of ideas or actions succeeding each other in that same spirit of mind. Hence, it is a plain consequence that the soul always thinks. And in truth whoever shall go about to divide in his thoughts or abstract the *existence* of a spirit from its *cogitation,* will, I believe, find it no easy task.

99. So likewise when we attempt to abstract *extension* and *motion* from all other qualities, and consider them by themselves, we presently lose sight of them, and run into great extravagances. [Hence spring those odd paradoxes, that the fire is not hot, nor the wall white; or that heat and colour are in the objects nothing but figure and motion.] All which depend on a two-fold abstraction: first, it is supposed that extension, for example, may be abstracted from all other sensible qualities; and, secondly, that the entity of extension may be abstracted from its being perceived. But, whoever shall reflect, and take care to understand what he says, will, if I mistake not, acknowledge that all sensible qualities are alike *sensations,* and alike *real;* that where the extension is, there is the colour too, to wit, in his mind, and that their archetypes can exist only in some other *mind:* and that the objects of sense are nothing but those sensations, combined, blended, or (if one may so speak) concreted together; none of all which can be supposed to exist unperceived. [And that consequently the wall is as truly white as it is extended, and in the same sense.]

100. What it is for a man to be happy, or an object good, every one may think he knows. But to frame

an abstract idea of happiness, prescinded from all particular pleasure, or of goodness from everything that is good, this is what few can pretend to. So likewise a man may be just and virtuous without having precise ideas of justice and virtue. The opinion that those and the like words stand for general notions, abstracted from all particular persons and actions, seems to have rendered morality difficult, and the study thereof of less use to mankind. [And in effect one may make a great progress in school-ethics without ever being the wiser or better man for it, or knowing how to behave himself in the affairs of life more to the advantage of himself or his neighbours than he did before.] And in effect the doctrine of *abstraction* has not a little contributed towards spoiling the most useful parts of knowledge.

101. The two great provinces of speculative science conversant about ideas received from sense and their relations, are Natural Philosophy and Mathematics. With regard to each of these I shall make some observations.

And first I shall say somewhat of Natural Philosophy. On this subject it is that the sceptics triumph. All that stock of arguments they produce to depreciate our faculties and make mankind appear ignorant and low, are drawn principally from this head, namely, that we are under an invincible blindness as to the *true* and *real* nature of things. This they exaggerate, and love to enlarge on. We are miserably bantered, say they, by our senses, and amused only with the outside and shew of things. The real essence, the internal qualities and constitution of even the meanest object, is hid from our view: something there is in every drop of water, every grain of sand, which it is beyond the power of human understanding to fathom or comprehend. But, it is evident from what has been shewn that all this complaint is groundless, and that we are influenced by false principles to that degree as to mistrust our senses, and think we know nothing of those things which we perfectly comprehend.

102. One great inducement to our pronouncing ourselves ignorant of the nature of things is, the current opinion that every thing includes *within itself* the cause of its properties: or that there is in each object an inward essence, which is the source whence its discernible qualties flow, and whereon they depend. Some have pretended to account for appearances by occult qualities; but of late they are mostly resolved into mechanical causes, to wit, the figure, motion, weight, and suchlike qualities, of insensible particles: whereas, in truth, there is no other agent or efficient cause than *spirit* it being evident that motion, as well as all other *ideas,* is perfectly inert. See sect. 25. Hence, to endeavour to explain the production of colours or sounds, by figure, motion, magnitude, and the like, must needs be labour in vain. And accordingly we see the attempts of that kind are not at all satisfactory. Which may be said in general of those instances wherein one idea or quality is assigned for the cause of another. I need not say how many hypotheses and speculations are left out, and how much the study of nature is abridged by this doctrine.

103. The great mechanical principle now in vogue is *attraction.* That a stone falls to the earth, or the sea swells towards the moon, may to some appear sufficiently explained thereby. But how are we enlightened by being told this is done by attraction? Is it that that word signifies the manner of the tendency, and that it is by the mutual drawing of bodies instead of their being im-

pelled or protruded towards each other? But nothing is determined of the manner or action, and it may as truly (for aught we know) be termed *impulse*, or *protrusion*, as *attraction*. Again, the parts of steel we see cohere firmly together, and this also is accounted for by attraction; but, in this, as in the other instances, I do not perceive that anything is signified besides the effect itself; for as to the manner of the action whereby it is produced, or the cause which produces it, these are not so much as aimed at.

104. Indeed, if we take a view of the several phenomena, and compare them together, we may observe some likeness and conformity between them. For example, in the falling of a stone to the ground, in the rising of the sea towards the moon, in cohesion and crystallization, there is something alike; namely, an union or mutual approach of bodies. So that any one of these or the like phenomena may not seem strange or surprising to a man who has nicely observed and compared the effects of nature. For that only is thought so which is uncommon, or a thing by itself, and out of the ordinary course of our observation. That bodies should tend towards the centre of the earth is not thought strange, because it is what we perceive every moment of our lives. But that they should have a like gravitation towards the centre of the moon may seem odd and unaccountable to most men, because it is discerned only in the tides. But a philosopher, whose thoughts take in a larger compass of nature, having observed a certain similitude of appearances, as well in the heavens as the earth, that argue innumerable bodies to have a mutual tendency towards each other, which he denotes by the general name *attraction*, whatever can be reduced to that, he thinks justly accounted for. Thus he explains the tides by the attraction of the terraqueous globe to-

wards the moon; which to him doth not appear odd or
anomalous, but only a particular example of a general
rule or law of nature.

105. If therefore we consider the difference there is
betwixt natural philosophers and other men, with regard
to their knowledge of the phenomena, we shall find it
consists, not in an exacter knowledge of the efficient
cause that produces them—for that can be no other than
the *will of a spirit*—but only in a greater largeness of
comprehension, whereby analogies, harmonies, and agreements are discovered in the works of nature, and the
particular effects explained, that is, reduced to general
rules, see sect. 62: which rules, grounded on the analogy
and uniformness observed in the production of natural
effects, are most agreeable and sought after by the
mind; for that they extend our prospect beyond what
is present and near to us, and enable us to make very
probable conjectures touching things that may have
happened at very great distances of time and place, as
well as to predict things to come: which sort of endeavour towards Omniscience is much affected by the
mind.

106. But we should proceed warily in such things: for
we are apt to lay too great a stress on analogies, and, to
the prejudice of truth, humour that eagerness of the
mind, whereby it is carried to extend its knowledge into
general theorems. For example, gravitation or mutual
attraction, because it appears in many instances, some
are straightway for pronouncing *universal;* and that to
attract and be attracted by every other body is an essential quality inherent in all bodies whatsoever. Whereas
it is evident the fixed stars have no such tendency towards each other; and, so far is that gravitation from
being *essential* to bodies that in some instances a quite
contrary principle seems to shew itself; as in the per-

pendicular growth of plants, and the elasticity of the air. There is nothing necessary or essential in the case; but it depends entirely on the will of the Governing Spirit, who causes certain bodies to cleave together or tend towards each other according to various laws, whilst He keeps others at a fixed distance; and to some He gives a quite contrary tendency to fly asunder, just as He sees convenient.

107. After what has been premised, I think we may lay down the following conclusions. First, it is plain philosophers amuse themselves in vain, when they enquire for any natural efficient cause, distinct from a *mind* or *spirit*. Secondly, considering the whole creation is the workmanship of a *wise and good Agent,* it should seem to become philosophers to employ their thoughts (contrary to what some hold) about the final causes of things. [For, besides that this would prove a very pleasing entertainment to the mind, it might be of great advantage, in that it not only discovers to us the attributes of the Creator, but may also direct us in several instances to the proper uses and applications of things.] And I must confess I see no reason why pointing out the various ends to which natural things are adapted, and for which they were originally with unspeakable wisdom contrived, should not be thought one good way of accounting for them, and altogether worthy a philosopher. Thirdly, from what has been premised, no reason can be drawn why the history of nature should not still be studied, and observations and experiments made; which, that they are of use to mankind, and enable us to draw any general conclusions, is not the result of any immutable habitudes or relations between things themselves, but only of God's goodness and kindness to men in the administration of the world. See sects. 30 and 31. Fourthly, by a diligent observation of the phe-

nomena within our view, we may discover the general laws of nature, and from them deduce other phenomena. I do not say *demonstrate;* for all deductions of that kind depend on a supposition that the Author of Nature always operates uniformly, and in a constant observance of those rules *we* take for principles, which we cannot evidently know.

108. [It appears from sect. 66, &c. that the steady consistent methods of nature may not unfitly be styled the Language of its Author, whereby He discovers His attributes to our view and directs us how to act for the convenience and felicity of life.] Those men who frame general rules from the phenomena, and afterwards derive the phenomena from those rules, seem to consider signs rather than causes. A man may well understand natural signs without knowing their analogy, or being able to say by what rule a thing is so or so. And, as it is very possible to write improperly, through too strict an observance of general grammar-rules; so, in arguing from general laws of nature, it is not impossible we may extend the analogy too far, and by that means run into mistakes.

109. [To carry on the resemblance.] As in reading other books a wise man will choose to fix his thoughts on the sense and apply it to use, rather than lay them out in grammatical remarks on the language; so, in perusing the volume of nature, methinks it is beneath the dignity of the mind to affect an exactness in reducing each particular phenomenon to general rules, or shewing how it follows from them. We should propose to ourselves nobler views, such as to recreate and exalt the mind with a prospect of the beauty, order, extent, and variety of natural things: hence, by proper inferences. to enlarge our notions of the grandeur, wisdom, and beneficence of the Creator: and lastly, to make the

several parts of the creation, so far as in us lies, subservient to the ends they were designed for—God's
glory, and the sustentation and comfort of ourselves
and fellow-creatures.

110. [The best key for the aforesaid analogy, or
natural Science, will be easily acknowledged to be a
certain celebrated Treatise of *Mechanics*.[1]] In the entrance of which justly admired treatise, Time, Space, and
Motion are distinguished into *absolute* and *relative, true*
and *apparent, mathematical* and *vulgar:* which distinction, as it is at large explained by the author, does suppose those quantities to have an existence without the
mind: and that they are ordinarily conceived with
relation to sensible things, to which nevertheless in their
own nature they bear no relation at all.

111. As for *Time,* as it is there taken in an absolute,
or abstracted sense, for the duration or perseverance of
the existence of things, I have nothing more to add concerning it after what has been already said on that
subject. Sects. 97 and 98. For the rest, this celebrated
author holds there is an *absolute Space,* which, being
unperceivable to sense, remains in itself similar and
immoveable; and relative space to be the measure thereof, which, being moveable and defined by its situation
in respect of sensible bodies, is vulgarly taken for

---

[1] In the first edition, the section begins as follows: "The best
grammar of the kind we are speaking of will be easily
acknowledged to be a treatise of *Mechanics,* demonstrated
and applied to Nature, by a philosopher of a neighbouring
nation, whom all the world admire. I shall not take upon me
to make remarks on the performance of that extraordinary
person: only some things he has advanced so directly opposite to the doctrine we have hitherto laid down, that we should
be wanting in the regard due to the authority of so great a
man did we not take some notice of them." The reference is
to Newton whose *Principia* was published in 1787.

Immoveable space. *Place* he defines to be that part
of space which is occupied by any body: and according
as the space is absolute or relative so also is the place.
Absolute Motion is said to be the translation of a body
from absolute place to absolute place, as relative motion
is from one relative place to another. And because the
parts of absolute space do not fall under our senses,
instead of them we are obliged to use their sensible
measures; and so define both place and motion with respect to bodies which we regard as immoveable. But it
is said, in philosophical matters we must abstract from
our senses; since it may be that none of those bodies
which seem to be quiescent are truly so; and the same
thing which is moved relatively may be really at rest.
As likewise one and the same body may be in relative
rest and motion, or even moved with contrary relative
motions at the same time, according as its place is variously defined. All which ambiguity is to be found in
the apparent motions; but not at all in the true or absolute, which should therefore be alone regarded in philosophy. And the true we are told are distinguished from
apparent or relative motions by the following properties.
First, in true or absolute motion, all parts which preserve the same position with respect of the whole,
partake of the motions of the whole. Secondly, the
place being moved, that which is placed therein is also
moved: so that a body moving in a place which is in
motion doth participate the motion of its place. Thirdly,
true motion is never generated or changed otherwise
than by force impressed on the body itself. Fourthly,
true motion is always changed by force impressed on
the body moved. Fifthly, in circular motion, barely
relative, there is no centrifugal force, which nevertheless, in that which is true or absolute, is proportional
to the quantity of motion.

112. But, notwithstanding what hath been said, I must confess it does not appear to me that there can be any motion other than *relative:* so that to conceive motion there must be conceived at least two bodies; whereof the distance or position in regard to each other is varied. Hence, if there was one only body in being it could not possibly be moved. This seems evident, in that the idea I have of motion doth necessarily include relation.—[Whether others can conceive it otherwise, a little attention may satisfy them.]

113. But, though in every motion it be necessary to conceive more bodies than one, yet it may be that one only is moved, namely, that on which the force causing the change in the distance or situation of the bodies is impressed. For, however some may define relative motion, so as to term that body *moved* which changes its distance from some other body whether the force [or action] causing that change were impressed on it or no, yet, as relative motion is that which is perceived by sense, and regarded in the ordinary affairs of life, it follows that every man of common sense knows what it is as well as the best philosopher. Now, I ask any one whether, in his sense of motion as he walks along the streets, the stones he passes over may be said to *move,* because they change distance with his feet? To me it appears that though motion includes a relation of one thing to another, yet it is not necessary that each term of the relation be denominated from it. As a man may think of somewhat which does not think, so a body may be moved to or from another body which is not therefore itself in motion, [I mean relative motion, for other I am not able to conceive.]

114. As the place happens to be variously defined, the motion which is related to it varies. A man in a ship may be said to be quiescent with relation to the sides of

the vessel, and yet move with relation to the land. Or he may move eastward in respect of the one, and westward in respect of the other. In the common affairs of life, men never go beyond the Earth to define the place of any body; and what is quiescent in respect of *that* is accounted *absolutely* to be so. But philosophers, who have a greater extent of thought, and juster notions of the system of things, discover even the Earth itself to be moved. In order therefore to fix their notions, they seem to conceive the Corporeal World as finite, and the utmost unmoved walls or shell thereof to be the place whereby they estimate true motions. If we sound our own conceptions, I believe we may find all the absolute motion we can frame an idea of to be at bottom no other than relative motion thus defined. For, as has been already observed, absolute motion, exclusive of *all* external relation, is incomprehensible: and to this kind of relative motion all the above-mentioned properties, causes, and effects ascribed to absolute motion will, if I mistake not, be found to agree. As to what is said of the centrifugal force, that it does not at all belong to circular relative motion, I do not see how this follows from the experiment which is brought to prove it. See Newton's *Philosophiae Naturalis Principia Mathematica, in Schol. Def. VIII.* For the water in the vessel, at that time wheren it is said to have the greatest relative circular motion, hath, I think, no motion at all: as is plain from the foregoing section.

115. For, to denominate a body *moved,* it is requisite, first, that it change its distance or situation with regard to some other body: and secondly, that the force occasioning that change be applied to it. If either of these be wanting, I do not think that, agreeably to the sense of mankind, or the propriety of language, a body can be said to be in motion. I grant indeed that it is pos-

sible for us to think a body, which we see change its
distance from some other, to be moved, though it have
no force applied to it (in which sense there may be
apparent motion); but then it is because the force causing the change of distance is imagined by us to be
[applied or] impressed on that body thought to move.
Which indeed shews we are capable of mistaking a thing
to be in motion which is not, and that is all. [But it
does not prove that, in the common acceptation of motion,
a body is moved merely because it changes distance from
another; since as soon as we are undeceived, and find
that the moving force was not communicated to it, we no
longer hold it to be moved. So, on the other hand, when
one only body (the parts whereof preserve a given
position between themselves) is imagined to exist, some
there are who think that it can be moved all manner of
ways, though without any change of distance or situation to any other bodies; which we should not deny, if
they meant only that it might have an impressed force,
which, upon the bare creation of other bodies, would
produce a motion of some certain quantity and determination. But that an actual motion (distinct from the
impressed force, or power, productive of change of place
in case there were bodies present whereby to define it)
can exist in such a single body, I must confess I am not
able to comprehend.]

116. From what has been said, it follows that the
philosophic consideration of motion doth not imply the
being of an *absolute Space,* distinct from that which is
perceived by sense, and related to bodies: which that
it cannot exist without the mind is clear upon the same
principles that demonstrate the like of all other objects
of sense. And perhaps, if we inquire narrowly, we shall
find we cannot even frame an idea of *pure Space exclusive of all body.* This I must confess seems impossible,

as being a most abstract idea. When I excite a motion in some part of my body, if it be free or without resistance, I say there is *Space*. But if I find a resistance, then I say there is *Body*: and in proportion as the resistance to motion is lesser or greater, I say the space is more or less *pure*. So that when I speak of pure or empty space, it is not to be supposed that the word *space* stands for an idea distinct from, or conceivable without, body and motion. Though indeed we are apt to think every noun substantive stands for a distinct idea that may be separated from all others; which hath occasioned infinite mistakes. When, therefore, supposing all the world to be annihilated besides my own body, I say there still remains *pure Space;* thereby nothing else is meant but only that I conceive it possible for the limbs of my body to be moved on all sides without the least resistance: but if that too were annihilated then there could be no motion, and consequently no Space. Some, perhaps, may think the sense of seeing doth furnish them with the idea of pure space; but it is plain from what we have elsewhere shewn, that the ideas of space and distance are not obtained by that sense. See the *Essay concerning Vision.*

117. What is here laid down seems to put an end to all those disputes and difficulties that have sprung up amongst the learned concerning the nature of *pure Space.* But the chief advantage arising from it is that we are freed from that dangerous dilemma, to which several who have employed their thoughts on that subject imagine themselves reduced, viz. of thinking either that Real Space is God, or else that there is something beside God which is eternal, uncreated, infinite, indivisible, immutable. Both which may justly be thought pernicious and absurd notions. It is certain that not a few divines, as well as philosophers of great note,

have, from the difficulty they found in conceiving either limits or annihilation of space, concluded it must be *divine*. And some of late have set themselves particularly to shew that the incommunicable attributes of God agree to it. Which doctrine, how unworthy soever it may seem of the Divine Nature, yet I must confess I do not see how we can get clear of it, so long as we adhere to the received opinions.

118. Hitherto of Natural Philosophy. We come now to make some inquiry concerning that other great branch of speculative knowledge, to wit, Mathematics. These, how celebrated soever they may be for their clearness and certainty of demonstration, which is hardly anywhere else to be found, cannot nevertheless be supposed altogether free from mistakes, if in their principles there lurks some secret error which is common to the professors of those sciences with the rest of mankind. Mathematicians, though they deduce their theorems from a great height of evidence, yet their first principles are limited by the consideration of Quantity. And they do not ascend into any inquiry concerning those transcendental maxims which influence all the particular sciences; each part whereof, Mathematics not excepted, doth consequently participate of the errors involved in them. That the principles laid down by mathematicians are true, and their way of deduction from those principles clear and incontestible, we do not deny. But we hold there may be certain erroneous maxims of greater extent than the object of Mathematics, and for that reason not expressly mentioned, though tacitly supposed, throughout the whole progress of that science; and that the ill effects of those secret unexamined errors are diffused through all the branches thereof. To be plain, we suspect the mathematicians are no less deeply con-

cerned than other men in the errors arising from the doctrine of abstract general ideas, and the existence of objects without the mind.

119. Arithmetic hath been thought to have for its object abstract ideas of *number*. Of which to understand the properties and mutual habitudes, is supposed no mean part of speculative knowledge. The opinion of the pure and intellectual nature of numbers in abstract has made them in esteem with those philosophers who seem to have affected an uncommon fineness and elevation of thought. It hath set a price on the most trifling numerical speculations, which in practice are of no use, but serve only for amusement; and hath heretofore so far infected the minds of some, that they have dreamed of mighty *mysteries* involved in numbers, and attempted the explication of natural things by them. But, if we narrowly inquire into our own thoughts, and consider what has been premised, we may perhaps entertain a low opinion of those high flights and abstractions, and look on all inquiries about numbers only as so many *difficiles nugae,* so far as they are not subservient to practice, and promote the benefit of life.

120. Unity in abstract we have before considered in sect. 13; from which, and what has been said in the Introduction, it plainly follows there is not any such idea. But, number being defined a *collection of units,* we may conclude that, if there be no such thing as unity, or unit in abstract, there are no *ideas* of number in abstract, denoted by the numeral names and figures. The theories therefore in Arithmetic, if they are abstracted from the names and figures, as likewise from all use and practice, as well as from the particular things numbered, can be supposed to have nothing at all for their object. Hence we may see how entirely the science of numbers is subordinate to practice, and how

je͟ ͟ne and trifling it becomes when considered as a matter of mere speculation.

121. However, since there may be some who, deluded by the specious show of discovering abstracted verities, waste their time in arithmetical theorems and problems which have not any use, it will not be amiss if we more fully consider and expose the vanity of that pretence. And this will plainly appear by taking a view of Arithmetic in its infancy, and observing what it was that originally put men on the study of that science, and to what scope they directed it. It is natural to think that at first, men, for ease of memory and help of computation, made use of counters, or in writing of single strokes, points, or the like, each whereof was made to signify an unit, *i.e.* some one thing of whatever kind they had occasion to reckon. Afterwards they found out the more compendious ways of making one character stand in place of several strokes or points. And, lastly, the notation of the Arabians or Indians came into use; wherein, by the repetition of a few characters or figures, and varying the signification of each figure according to the place it obtains, all numbers may be most aptly expressed. Which seems to have been done in imitation of language, so that an exact analogy is observed betwixt the notation by figures and names, the nine simple figures answering the nine first numeral names and places in the former, corresponding to denominations in the latter. And agreeably to those conditions of the simple and local value of figures, were contrived methods of finding, from the given figures or marks of the parts, what figures and how placed are proper to denote the whole, or *vice versa*. And having found the sought figures, the same rule or analogy being observed throughout, it is easy to read them into words; and so the number becomes per-

fectly known. For then the number of any particular
things is said to be known, when we know the name or
figures (with their due arrangement) that according to
the standing analogy belong to them. For, these signs
being known, we can by the operations of arithmetic
know the signs of any part of the particular sums signified by them; and thus computing in signs, (because
of the connexion established betwixt them and the distinct multitudes of things, whereof one is taken for an
unit), we may be able rightly to sum up, divide, and
proportion the things themselves that we intend to
number.

122. In Arithmetic, therefore, we regard not the
things but the *signs;* which nevertheless are not regarded
for their own sake, but because they direct us how to
act with relation to things, and dispose rightly of them.
Now, agreeably to what we have before observed of
Words in general (sect. 19, Introd.), it happens here
likewise, that abstract ideas are thought to be signified
by numeral names or characters, while they do not
suggest ideas of particular things to our minds. I shall
not at present enter into a more particular dissertation
on this subject; but only observe that it is evident from
what has been said, those things which pass for abstract
truths and theorems concerning numbers, are in reality
conversant about no object distinct from particular
numerable things; except only names and characters,
which originally came to be considered on no other
account but their being *signs,* or capable to represent
aptly whatever particular things men had need to compute. Whence it follows that to study them for their
own sake would be just as wise, and to as good purpose,
as if a man, neglecting the true use or original intention
and subserviency of language, should spend his time in

impertinent criticisms upon words, or reasonings and controversies purely verbal.

123. From numbers we proceed to speak of *extension,* which, considered as relative, is the object of Geometry. The *infinite* divisibility of *finite* extension, though it is not expressly laid down either as an axiom or theorem in the elements of that science, yet is throughout the same everywhere supposed, and thought to have so inseparable and essential a connexion with the principles and demonstrations in Geometry that mathematicians never admit it into doubt, or make the least question of it. And as this notion is the source from whence do spring all those amusing geometrical paradoxes which have such a direct repugnancy to the plain common sense of mankind, and are admitted with so much reluctance into a mind not yet debauched by learning; so is it the principal occasion of all that nice and extreme subtilty, which renders the study of Mathematics so very difficult and tedious. Hence, if we can make it appear that no *finite* extension contains innumerable parts, or is infinitely divisible, it follows that we shall at once clear the science of Geometry from a great number of difficulties and contradictions which have ever been esteemed a reproach to human reason, and withal make the attainment thereof a business of much less time and pains than it hitherto hath been.

124. Every particular finite extension which may possibly be the object of our thought is an *idea* existing only in the mind; and consequently each part thereof must be perceived. If, therefore, I cannot *perceive* innumerable parts in any finite extension that I consider, it is certain they are not contained in it. But it is evident that I cannot distinguish innumerable parts in any particular line, surface, or solid, which I either perceive by sense, or figure to myself in my mind.

Wherefore I conclude they are not contained in it. Nothing can be plainer to me than that the extensions I have in view are no other than my own ideas; and it is no less plain that I cannot resolve any one of my ideas into an infinite number of other ideas; that is, that they are not infinitely divisible. If by *finite extension* be meant something distinct from a finite idea, I declare I do not know what that is, and so cannot affirm or deny anything of it. But if the terms *extension, parts,* and the like, are taken in any sense conceivable—that is, for *ideas,*—then to say a finite quantity or extension consists of parts infinite in number is so manifest and glaring a contradiction, that every one at first sight acknowledges it to be so. And it is impossible it should ever gain the assent of any reasonable creature who is not brought to it by gentle and slow degrees, as a converted Gentile to the belief of transubstantiation. Ancient and rooted prejudices do often pass into principles. And those propositions which once obtain the force and credit of a *principle,* are not only themselves, but likewise whatever is deducible from them, thought privileged from all examination. And there is no absurdity so gross, which, by this means, the mind of man may not be prepared to swallow.

125. He whose understanding is prepossessed with the doctrine of abstract general ideas may be persuaded that (whatever be thought of the ideas of sense) *extension in abstract* is infinitely divisible. And one who thinks the objects of sense exist without the mind will perhaps, in virtue thereof, be brought to admit that a line but an inch long may contain innumerable parts really existing, though too small to be discerned. These errors are grafted as well in the minds of geometricians as of other men, and have a like influence on their reasonings; and it were no difficult thing to shew how

the arguments from Geometry made use of to support the infinite divisibility of extension are bottomed on them. [But this, if it be thought necessary, we may hereafter find a proper place to treat of in a particular manner.] At present we shall only observe in general whence it is the mathematicians are all so fond and tenacious of that doctrine.

126. It has been observed in another place that the theorems and demonstrations in Geometry are conversant about universal ideas (sect. 15, Introd.): where it is explained in what sense this ought to be understood, to wit, the particular lines and figures included in the diagram are supposed to stand for innumerable others of different sizes; or, in other words, the geometer considers them abstracting from their magnitude: which doth not imply that he forms an abstract idea, but only that he cares not what the particular magnitude is, whether great or small, but looks on that as a thing indifferent to the demonstration. Hence it follows that a line in the scheme but an inch long must be spoken of as though it contained ten thousand parts, since it is regarded not in itself, but as it is universal; and it is universal only in its signification, whereby it *represents* innumerable lines greater than itself, in which may be distinguished ten thousand parts or more, though there may not be above an inch in *it*. After this manner, the properties of the lines signified are (by a very usual figure) transferred to the sign; and thence, through mistake, thought to appertain to it considered in its own nature.

127. Because there is no number of parts so great but it is possible there may be a line containing more, the inch-line is said to contain parts more than any assignable number; which is true, not of the inch taken absolutely, but only for the things signified by it. But

men, not retaining that distinction in their thoughts, slide into a belief that the small particular line described on paper contains in itself parts innumerable. There is no such thing as the ten thousandth part of an inch; but there is of a mile or diameter of the earth, which may be signified by that inch. When therefore I delineate a triangle on paper, and take one side, not above an inch for example in length, to be the radius, this I consider as divided into 10,000 or 100,000 parts, or more. For, though the ten thousandth part of that line considered in itself, is nothing at all, and consequently may be neglected without any error or inconveniency, yet these described lines, being only marks standing for greater quantities, whereof it may be the ten thousandth part is very considerable, it follows that, to prevent notable errors in practice, the radius must be taken of 10,000 parts, or more.

128. From what has been said the reason is plain why, to the end any theorem may become universal in its use, it is necessary we speak of the lines described on paper as though they contained parts which really they do not. In doing of which, if we examine the matter thoroughly, we shall perhaps discover that we cannot conceive an inch itself as consisting of, or being divisible into, a thousand parts, but only some other line which is far greater than an inch, and represented by it; and that when we say a line is *infinitely divisible,* we must mean *a line which is infinitely great.* What we have here observed seems to be the chief cause, why to suppose the *infinite* divisibility of *finite extension* has been thought necessary in geometry.

129. The several absurdities and contradictions which flowed from this false principle might, one would think, have been esteemed so many demonstrations against it. But, by I know not what logic, it is held that proofs

a posteriori are not to be admitted against propositions relating to Infinity. As though it were not impossible even for an Infinite Mind to reconcile contradictions; or as if anything absurd and repugnant could have a necessary connexion with truth, or flow from it. But whoever considers the weakness of this pretence, will think it was contrived on purpose to humour the laziness of the mind, which had rather acquiesce in an indolent scepticism than be at the pains to go through with a severe examination of those principles it has ever embraced for true.

130. Of late the speculations about Infinites have run so high, and grown to such strange notions, as have occasioned no small scruples and disputes among the geometers of the present age. Some there are of great note who, not content with holding that finite lines may be divided into an infinite number of parts, do yet farther maintain, that each of those Infinitesimals is itself subdivisible into an infinity of other parts, or Infinitesimals of a second order, and so on *ad infinitum*. These, I say, assert there are Infinitesimals of Infinitesimals of Infinitesimals, without ever coming to an end. So that according to them an inch does not barely contain an infinite number of parts, but an infinity of an infinity of an infinity *ad infinitum* of parts. Others there be who hold all orders of Infinitesimals below the first to be nothing at all; thinking it with good reason absurd to imagine there is any positive quantity or part of extension which, though multiplied infinitely, can ever equal the smallest given extension. And yet on the other hand it seems no less absurd to think the square, cube, or other power of a positive real root, should itself be nothing at all; which they who hold Infinitesimals of the first order, denying all of the subsequent orders, are obliged to maintain.

131. Have we not therefore reason to conclude they are *both* in the wrong, and that there is in effect no such thing as parts infinitely small, or an infinite number of parts contained in any finite quantity? But you will say that if this doctrine obtains it will follow the very foundations of Geometry are destroyed, and those great men who have raised that science to so astonishing a height, have been all the while building a castle in the air. To this it may be replied, that whatever is useful in geometry, and promotes the benefit of human life, does still remain firm and unshaken on our Principles; that science considered as practical will rather receive advantage than any prejudice from what has been said. But to set this in a due light, [and shew how lines and figures may be measured, and their properties investigated, without supposing finite extension to be infinitely divisible,] may be the proper business of another place. For the rest, though it should follow that some of the more intricate and subtle parts of Speculative Mathematics may be pared off without any prejudice to truth, yet I do not see what damage will be thence derived to mankind. On the contrary, I think it were highly to be wished that men of great abilities and obstinate application would draw off their thoughts from those amusements, and employ them in the study of such things as lie nearer the concerns of life, or have a more direct influence on the manners.

132. If it be said that several theorems, undoubtedly true, are discovered by methods in which Infinitesimals are made use of, which could never have been if their existence included a contradiction in it:—I answer that upon a thorough examination it will not be found that in any instance it is necessary to make use of or conceive *infinitesimal* parts of *finite* lines, or even quantities less than the *minimum sensible*: nay, it will be evident

this is never done, it being impossible. [And whatever mathematicians may think of Fluxions, or the Differential Calculus, and the like, a little reflexion will shew them that, in working by those methods, they do not conceive or imagine lines or surfaces less than what are perceivable to sense. They may indeed call those little and almost insensible quantities Infinitesimals, or Infinitesimals of Infinitesimals, if they please. But at bottom this is all, they being in truth finite; nor does the solution of problems require the supposing any other. But this will be more clearly made out hereafter.]

133. By what we have hitherto said, it is plain that very numerous and important errors have taken their rise from those false Principles which were impugned in the foregoing parts of this Treatise; and the opposites of those erroneous tenets at the same time appear to be most fruitful Principles, from whence do flow innumerable consequences, highly advantageous to true philosophy as well as to religion. Particularly *Matter,* or *the absolute existence of corporeal objects,* hath been shewn to be that wherein the most avowed and pernicious enemies of all knowledge, whether human or divine, have ever placed their chief strength and confidence. And surely if by distinguishing the real existence of unthinking things from their being perceived, and allowing them a subsistence of their own, out of the minds of spirits, no one thing is explained in nature, but on the contrary a great many inexplicable difficulties arise; if the supposition of Matter is barely precarious, as not being grounded on so much as one single reason; if its consequences cannot endure the light of examination and free inquiry, but screen themselves under the dark and general pretence of *infinites being incomprehensible;* if withal the removal of *this* Matter be not attended with

the least evil consequence; if it be not even missed in the world, but everything as well, nay much easier conceived without it; if, lastly, both Sceptics and Atheists are for ever silenced upon supposing only spirits and ideas, and this scheme of things is perfectly agreeable both to Reason and Religion: methinks we may expect it should be admitted and firmly embraced, though it were proposed only as an *hypothesis*, and the existence of Matter had been allowed possible: which yet I think we have evidently demonstrated that it is not.

134. True it is that, in consequence of the foregoing Principles, several disputes and speculations which are esteemed no mean parts of learning are rejected as useless [and in effect conversant about nothing at all]. But how great a prejudice soever against our notions this may give to those who have already been deeply engaged, and made large advances in studies of that nature, yet by others we hope it will not be thought any just ground of dislike to the principles and tenets herein laid down, that they abridge the labour of study, and make human sciences more clear, compendious, and attainable than they were before.

135. Having despatched what we intended to say concerning the knowledge of *ideas*, the method we proposed leads us in the next place to treat of *spirits;* with regard to which, perhaps, human knowledge is not so deficient as is vulgarly imagined. The great reason that is assigned for our being thought ignorant of the nature of Spirits is our not having an *idea* of it. But, surely it ought not to be looked on as a defect in a human understanding that it does not perceive the idea of Spirit, if it is manifestly impossible there should be any such idea. And this if I mistake not has been demonstrated in section 27. To which I shall here add that a Spirit has

been shewn to be the only substance **or support** wherein unthinking beings or ideas can exist: but that this *substance* which supports or perceives ideas should itself be an idea, or like an idea, is evidently absurd.

136. It will perhaps be said that we want a *sense* (as some have imagined) proper to know substances withal; which, if we had, we might know our own soul as we do a triangle. To this I answer, that in case we had a new sense bestowed upon us, we could only receive thereby some new *sensations* or *ideas of sense.* But I believe nobody will say that what he means by the terms *soul* and *substance* is only some particular sort of idea or sensation. We may therefore infer that, all things duly considered, it is not more reasonable to think our faculties defective, in that they do not furnish us with an *idea* of Spirit, or active thinking substance, than it would be if we should blame them for not being able to comprehend a *round square.*

137. From the opinion that Spirits are to be known after the manner of an idea or sensation have risen many absurd and heterodox tenets, and much scepticism about the nature of the soul. It is even probable that this opinion may have produced a doubt in some whether they had any soul at all distinct from their body; since upon inquiry they could not find they had an idea of it. That an *idea,* which is inactive, and the existence whereof consists in being perceived, should be the image or likeness of an agent subsisting by itself, seems to need no other refutation than barely attending to what is meant by those words. But perhaps you will say that though an idea cannot resemble a Spirit in its thinking, acting, or subsisting by itself, yet it may in some other respects; and it is not necessary that an idea or image be in all respects like the original.

138. I answer, If it does not in those mentioned, it is

impossible it should represent it in any other thing. Do but leave out the power of willing, thinking, and perceiving ideas, and there remains nothing else wherein the idea can be like a spirit. For, by the word *spirit* we mean only that which thinks, wills, and perceives; this, and this alone, constitutes the signification of that term. If therefore it is impossible that any degree of those powers should be represented in an idea [or notion], it is evident there can be no idea [or notion] of a Spirit.

139. But it will be objected that, if there is no *idea* signified by the terms, *soul, spirit,* and *substance,* they are wholly insignificant, or have no meaning in them. I answer, those words do mean or signify a real thing; which is neither an idea nor like an idea, but that which perceives ideas, and wills, and reasons about them. What I am *myself,* that which I denote by the term *I,* is the same with what is meant by *soul,* or *spiritual substance.* [But if I should say that *I* was nothing, or that *I* was an *idea* or *notion,* nothing could be more evidently absurd than either of these propositions.] If it be said that this is only quarrelling at a word, and that, since the immediate significations of other names are by common consent called *ideas,* no reason can be assigned why that which is signified by the name *spirit* or *soul* may not partake in the same appellation. I answer, all the unthinking objects of the mind agree in that they are entirely passive, and their existence consists only in being perceived: whereas a *soul* or *spirit* is an active being, whose existence consists, not in being perceived, but in perceiving ideas and thinking. It is therefore necessary, in order to prevent equivocation and confounding natures perfectly disagreeing and unlike, that we distinguish between *spirit* and *idea.* See sect. 27.

140. In a large sense indeed, we may be said to have

an idea [or rather a notion] of *spirit*. That is, we understand the meaning of the word, otherwise we could not affirm or deny anything of it. Moreover, as we conceive the ideas that are in the minds of other spirits by means of our own, which we suppose to be resemblances of them, so we know other spirits by means of our own soul: which in that sense is the image or idea of them; it having a like respect to other spirits that blueness or heat by me perceived has to those ideas perceived by another.

141. [The natural immortality of the soul is a necessary consequence of the foregoing doctrine. But before we attempt to prove this, it is fit that we explain the meaning of that tenet.] It must not be supposed that they who assert the natural immortality of the soul are of opinion that it is absolutely incapable of annihilation even by the infinite power of the Creator who first gave it being, but only that it is not liable to be broken or dissolved by the ordinary laws of nature or motion. They indeed who hold the soul of man to be only a thin vital flame, or system of animal spirits, make it perishing and corruptible as the body; since there is nothing more easily dissipated than such a being, which it is naturally impossible should survive the ruin of the tabernacle wherein it is inclosed. And this notion hath been greedily embraced and cherished by the worst part of mankind, as the most effectual antidote against all impressions of virtue and religion. But it hath been made evident that bodies, of what frame or texture soever, are barely passive ideas in the mind, which is more distant and heterogeneous from them than light is from darkness. We have shewn that the soul is indivisible, incorporeal, unextended; and it is consequently incorruptible. Nothing can be plainer than that the motions,

changes, decays, and dissolutions which we hourly see befal natural bodies (and which is what we mean by the *course of nature*) cannot possibly affect an active, simple, uncompounded substance: such a being therefore is indissoluble by the force of nature; that is to say, *the soul of man is naturally immortal.*

142. After what has been said, it is, I suppose, plain that our souls are not to be known in the same manner as senseless, inactive objects, or by way of *idea*. *Spirits* and *ideas* are things so wholly different, that when we say 'they exist,' 'they are known,' or the like, these words must not be thought to signify anything common to both natures. There is nothing alike or common in them; and to expect that by any multiplication or enlargement of our faculties, we may be enabled to know a spirit as we do a triangle, seems as absurd as if we should hope to *see a sound*. This is inculcated because I imagine it may be of moment towards clearing several important questions, and preventing some very dangerous errors concerning the nature of the soul.

[We may not, I think, strictly be said to have an *idea* of an active being, or of an action; although we may be said to have a *notion* of them. I have some knowledge or notion of *my mind,* and its acts about ideas; inasmuch as I know or understand what is meant by these words. What I know, that I have some notion of. I will not say that the terms *idea* and *notion* may not be used convertibly, if the world will have it so. But yet it conduceth to clearness and propriety, that we distinguish things very different by different names. It is also to be remarked that, all *relations* including an act of the mind, we cannot so properly be said to have an idea, but rather a notion, of the relations and habitudes between things. But if, in the modern way, the word *idea* is extended to *spirits,* and *relations,* and *acts,* this is, after all, an affair of verbal concern.]

143. It will not be amiss to add, that the doctrine of *abstract ideas* has had no small share in rendering those sciences intricate and obscure which are particularly conversant about spiritual things. Men have imagined they could frame abstract notions of the *powers* and *acts* of the mind, and consider them prescinded as well from the mind or spirit itself, as from their respective objects and effects. Hence a great number of dark and ambiguous terms, presumed to stand for abstract notions, have been introduced into metaphysics and morality; and from these have grown infinite distractions and disputes amongst the learned.

144. But, nothing seems more to have contributed towards engaging men in controversies and mistakes with regard to the nature and operations of the mind, than the being used to speak of those things in terms borrowed from sensible ideas. For example, the will is termed the *motion* of the soul: this infuses a belief that the mind of man is as a ball in motion, impelled and determined by the objects of sense, as necessarily as that is by the stroke of a racket. Hence arise endless scruples and errors of dangerous consequence in morality. All which, I doubt not, may be cleared, and truth appear plain, uniform, and consistent, could but philosophers be prevailed on to [depart from some received prejudices and modes of speech, and] retire into themselves, and attentively consider their own meaning. [But the difficulties arising on this head demands a more particular disquisition than suits with the design of this treatise.]

145. From what hath been said, it is plain that we cannot know the existence of *other spirits* otherwise than

by their operations, or the ideas by them, excited in us. I perceive several motions, changes, and combinations of ideas, that inform me there are certain particular agents, like myself, which accompany them, and concur in their production. Hence, the knowledge I have of other spirits is not immediate, as is the knowledge of my ideas; but depending on the intervention of ideas, by me referred to agents or spirits distinct from myself, as effects or concomitant signs.

146. But, though there be some things which convince us human agents are concerned in producing them, yet it is evident to every one that those things which are called the Works of Nature, that is, the far greater part of the ideas or sensations perceived by us, are *not* produced by, or dependent on, the wills of *men*. There is therefore some other Spirit that causes them; since it is repugnant that they should subsist by themselves. See sect. 29. But, if we attentively consider the constant regularity, order, and concatenation of natural things, the surprising magnificence, beauty and perfection of the larger, and the exquisite contrivance of the smaller parts of the creation, together with the exact harmony and correspondence of the whole, but above all the never-enough-admired laws of pain and pleasure, and the instincts or natural inclinations, appetites, and passions of animals;—I say if we consider all these things, and at the same time attend to the meaning and import of the attributes One, Eternal, Infinitely Wise, Good, and Perfect, we shall clearly perceive that they belong to the aforesaid Spirit, 'who works all in all' and 'by whom all things consist.'

147. Hence, it is evident that God is known as certainly and immediately as any other mind or spirit whatsoever, distinct from ourselves. We may even assert that the existence of God is far more evidently perceived

than the existence of men; because the effects of Nature are infinitely more numerous and considerable than those ascribed to human agents.   There is not any one mark that denotes a man, or effect produced by him, which does not more strongly evince the being of that Spirit who is the Author of Nature.   For it is evident that, in affecting other persons, the will of man hath no other object than barely the motion of the limbs of his body; but that such a motion should be attended by, or excite any idea in the mind of another, depends wholly on the will of the Creator.   He alone it is who, 'upholding all things by the word of His power,' maintains that intercourse between spirits whereby they are able to perceive the existence of each other.   And yet this pure and clear Light which enlightens everyone is itself invisible [to the greatest part of mankind].

148. It seems to be a general pretence of the unthinking herd that they cannot *see* God.   Could we but see Him, say they, as we see a man, we should believe that He is, and believing obey His commands.   But alas, we need only open our eyes to see the Sovereign Lord of all things, with a *more* full and clear view than we do any one of our fellow-creatures.   Not that I imagine we see God (as some will have it) by a direct and immediate view; or see corporeal things, not by themselves, but by seeing that which represents them in the essence of God; which doctrine is, I must confess, to me incomprehensible.   But I shall explain my meaning.   A human spirit or person is not perceived by sense, as not being an idea.   When therefore we see the colour, size, figure, and motions of a man, we perceive only certain sensations or ideas excited in our own minds; and these being exhibited to our view in sundry distinct collections, serve to mark out unto us the existence of finite and created spirits like ourselves.   Hence it is plain we do not see a

man, if by *man* is meant, that which lives, moves, perceives, and thinks as we do: but only such a certain collection of ideas, as directs us to think there is a distinct principle of thought and motion, like to ourselves, accompanying and represented by it. And after the same manner we see God: all the difference is that, whereas some one finite and narrow assemblage of ideas denotes a particular human mind, whithersoever we direct our view we do at all times and in all places perceive manifest tokens of the Divinity; everything we see, hear, feel, or anywise perceive by sense, being a sign or affect of the power of God; as is our perception of those very motions which are produced by men.

149. It is therefore plain that nothing can be more evident to any one that is capable of the least reflexion than the existence of God, or a Spirit who is intimately present to our minds, producing in them all that variety of ideas or sensations which continually affect us, on whom we have an absolute and entire dependence, in short 'in whom we live, and move, and have our being.' That the discovery of this great truth, which lies so near and obvious to the mind, should be attained to by the reason of so very few, is a sad instance of the stupidity and inattention of men, who, though they are surrounded with such clear manifestations of the Deity, are yet so little affected by them that they seem, as it were, blinded with excess of light.

150. But you will say—Hath Nature no share in the production of natural things, and must they be all ascribed to the immediate and sole operation of God? I answer, If by *Nature* is meant only the *visible series* of effects or sensations imprinted on our minds according to certain fixed and general laws, then it is plain that Nature, taken in this sense, cannot produce anything at all. But if by *Nature* is meant some being distinct from

God, as well as from the laws of nature and things perceived by sense, I must confess that word is to me an empty sound, without any intelligible meaning annexed to it. Nature, in this acceptation. is a vain chimera, introduced by those heathens who had not just notions of the omnipresence and infinite perfection of God. But it is more unaccountable that it should be received among Christians, professing belief in the Holy Scriptures, which constantly ascribe those effects to the immediate hand of God that heathen philosophers are wont to impute to Nature. 'The Lord, He causeth the vapours to ascend; He maketh lightnings with rain; He bringeth forth the wind out of His treasures.' Jerem. x. 13. 'He turneth the shadow of death into the morning, and maketh the day dark with night.' Amos. v. 8. 'He visiteth the earth, and maketh it soft with showers: He blesseth the springing thereof, and crowneth the year with His goodness; so that the pastures are clothed with flocks, and the valleys are covered over with corn.' See Psal. lxv. But, notwithstanding that this is the constant language of Scripture, yet we have I know not what aversion from believing that God concerns Himself so nearly in our affairs. Fain would we suppose Him at a great distance off, and substitute some blind, unthinking deputy in His stead; though (if we may believe Saint Paul) 'He be not far from every one of us.'

151. It will, I doubt not, be objected that the slow, gradual, and roundabout methods observed in the production of natural things do not seem to have for their cause the *immediate* hand of an Almighty Agent: besides, monsters, untimely births, fruits blasted in the blossom, rains falling in desert places, miseries incident to human life, and the like, are so many arguments that the whole frame of nature is not immediately actuated and superintended by a Spirit of infinite wisdom and

goodness. But the answer to this objection is in a good measure plain from sect. 62; it being visible that the aforesaid methods of nature are absolutely necessary in order to working by the most simple and general rules, and after a steady and consistent manner; which argues both the wisdom and goodness of God. [For, it doth hence follow that the finger of God is not so conspicuous to the resolved and careless sinner; which gives him an opportunity to harden in his impiety and grow ripe for vengeance. (Vid. sect. 57.)] Such is the artificial contrivance of this mighty machine of Nature that, whilst its motions and various phenomena strike on our senses, the Hand which actuates the whole is itself unperceivable to men of flesh and blood. 'Verily' (saith the prophet) 'thou art a God that hidest thyself.' Isaiah xlv. 15. But, though the Lord conceal Himself from the eyes of the sensual and lazy, who will not be at the least expense of thought, yet to an unbiassed and attentive mind, nothing can be more plainly legible than the intimate presence of an All-wise Spirit, who fashions, regulates, and sustains the whole system of Being. It is clear, from what we have elsewhere observed, that the operating according to general and stated laws is so necessary for our guidance in the affairs of life, and letting us into the secret of nature, that without it all reach and compass of thought, all human sagacity and design, could serve to no manner of purpose. It were even impossible there should be any such faculties or powers in the mind. See sect. 31. Which one consideration abundantly outbalances whatever particular inconveniences may thence arise.

152. We should further consider, that the very blemishes and defects of nature are not without their use, in that they make an agreeable sort of variety, and augment the beauty of the rest of the creation, as shades

in a picture serve to set off the brighter and more enlightened parts. We would likewise do well to examine, whether our taxing the waste of seeds and embryos, and accidental destruction of plants and animals before they come to full maturity, as an imprudence in the Author of nature, be not the effect of prejudice contracted by our familiarity with impotent and saving mortals. In *man* indeed a thrifty management of those things which he cannot procure without much pains and industry may be esteemed wisdom. But we must not imagine that the inexplicably fine machine of an animal or vegetable costs the great Creator any more pains or trouble in its production than a pebble does; nothing being more evident than that an Omnipotent Spirit can indifferently produce everything by a mere *fiat* or act of his will. Hence it is plain that the splendid profusion of natural things should not be interpreted weakness or prodigality in the Agent who produces them, but rather be looked on as an argument of the riches of His power.

153. As for the mixture of pain or uneasiness which is in the world, pursuant to the general laws of Nature, and the actions of finite, imperfect Spirits, this, in the state we are in at present, is indispensably necessary to our well-being. But our prospects are too narrow. We take, for instance, the idea of some one particular pain into our thoughts, and account it *evil*. Whereas, if we enlarge our view, so as to comprehend the various ends, connexions, and dependencies of things, on what occasions and in what proportions we are affected with pain and pleasure, the nature of human freedom, and the design with which we are put into the world; we shall be forced to acknowledge that those particular things which, considered in themselves, appear to be evil, have the nature of good, when considered as linked with the whole system of beings.

154. From what hath been said, it will be manifest to any considering person, that it is merely for want of attention and comprehensiveness of mind that there are any favourers of Atheism or the Manichean Heresy to be found. Little and unreflecting souls may indeed burlesque the works of Providence; the beauty and order whereof they have not capacity, or will not be at the pains, to comprehend. But those who are masters of any justness and extent of thought, and are withal used to reflect, can never sufficiently admire the divine traces of Wisdom and Goodness that shine throughout the economy of Nature. But what truth is there which glares so strongly on the mind that, by an aversion of thought, a wilful shutting of the eyes, we may not escape seeing it? Is it therefore to be wondered at, if the generality of men, who are ever intent on business or pleasure, and little used to fix or open the eye of their mind, should not have all that conviction and evidence of the Being of God which might be expected in reasonable creatures?

155. We should rather wonder that men can be found so stupid as to neglect, than that neglecting they should be unconvinced of such an evident and momentous truth. And yet it is to be feared that too many of parts and leisure, who live in Christian countries, are, merely through a supine and dreadful negligence, sunk into a sort of Atheism. [They cannot say there is not a God, but neither are they convinced that there is. For what else can it be but some lurking infidelity, some secret misgivings of mind with regard to the existence and attributes of God, which permits sinners to grow and harden in impiety?] Since it is downright impossible that a soul pierced and enlightened with a thorough sense of the omnipresence, holiness, and justice of that Almighty Spirit, should persist in a remorseless viola-

tion of His laws. We ought, therefore, earnestly to meditate and dwell on those important points; that so we may attain conviction without all scruple 'that the eyes of the Lord are in every place, beholding the evil and the good; that He is with us and keepeth us in all places whither we go, and giveth us bread to eat and raiment to put on;' that He is present and conscious to our innermost thoughts; and, that we have a most absolute and immediate dependence on Him. A clear view of which great truths cannot choose but fill our hearts with an awful circumspection and holy fear, which is the strongest incentive to Virtue, and the best guard against Vice.

156. For, after all, what deserves the first place in our studies is, the consideration of GOD and our DUTY; which to promote, as it was the main drift and design of my labours, so shall I esteem them altogether useless and ineffectual if, by what I have said, I cannot inspire my readers with a pious sense of the Presence of God; and, having shewn the falseness or vanity of those barren speculations which make the chief employment of learned men, the better dispose them to reverence and embrace the salutary truths of the Gospel; which to know and to practise is the highest perfection of human nature.

THREE DIALOGUES

BETWEEN

HYLAS AND PHILONOUS

THE DESIGN OF WHICH IS PLAINLY TO DEMON-STRATE THE REALITY AND PERFECTION OF

HUMAN KNOWLEDGE

THE INCORPOREAL NATURE OF THE

SOUL

AND THE IMMEDIATE PROVIDENCE OF A

DEITY

IN OPPOSITION TO

SCEPTICS AND ATHEISTS

ALSO TO OPEN A METHOD FOR RENDERING THE SCIENCES MORE EASY, USEFUL, AND COMPENDIOUS

My Lord,

The virtue, learning, and good sense which are acknowledged to distinguish your character, would tempt me to indulge myself the pleasure men naturally take in giving applause to those whom they esteem and honour: and it should seem of importance to the subjects of Great Britain that they knew the eminent share you enjoy in the favour of your sovereign, and the honours she has conferred upon you, have not been owing to any application from your lordship, but entirely to her majesty's own thought, arising from a sense of your personal merit, and an inclination to reward it. But, as your name is prefixed to this treatise with an intention to do honour to myself alone, I shall only say that I am encouraged by the favour you have treated me with to address these papers to your lordship. And I was the more ambitious of doing this, because a Philosophical Treatise could not so properly be addressed to any one as to a person of your lordship's character, who, to your other valuable distinctions, have added the knowledge and relish of Philosophy.

I am, with the greatest respect,
My Lord,
Your lordship's most obedient and
most humble servant,
GEORGE BERKELEY.

[THE PREFACE]

[Though it seems the general opinion of the world, no less than the design of nature and providence, that the end of speculation be Practice, or the improvement and regulation of our lives and actions; yet those who are most addicted to speculative studies, seem as generally of another mind. And indeed if we consider the pains that have been taken to perplex the plainest things, that distrust of the senses, those doubts and scruples, those abstractions and refinements that occur in the very entrance of the sciences; it will not seem strange that men of leisure and curiosity should lay themselves out in fruitless disquisitions, without descending to the practical parts of life, or informing themselves in the more necessary and important parts of knowledge.

Upon the common principles of philosophers, we are not assured of the existence of things from their being perceived. And we are taught to distinguish their *real* nature from that which falls under our senses. Hence arise scepticism and paradoxes. It is not enough that we see and feel, that we taste and smell a thing: its true nature, its absolute external entity, is still concealed. For, though it be the fiction of our own brain, we have made it inaccessible to all our faculties. Sense is fallacious, reason defective. We spend our lives in doubting of those things which other men evidently know, and believing those things which they laugh at and despise.

In order, therefore, to divert the busy mind of man from vain researches, it seemed necessary to inquire into the source of its perplexities; and, if possible, to lay down such Principles as, by an easy solution of them, together with their own native evidence, may at once recommend themselves for genuine to the mind, and rescue it from those endless pursuits it is engaged in. Which, with a plain demonstration of the Immediate Providence of an all-seeing God, and the natural Immortality of the soul, should seem the readiest preparation, as well as the strongest motive, to the study and practice of virtue.

This design I proposed in the First Part of a treatise concerning the *Principles of Human Knowledge,* published in the year 1710. But, before I proceed to publish the Second Part,[1] I thought it requisite to treat more clearly and fully of certain Principles laid down in the First, and to place them in a new light. Which is the business of the following *Dialogues.*

In this Treatise, which does not presuppose in the reader any knowledge of what was contained in the former, it has been my aim to introduce the notions I advance into the mind in the most easy and familiar manner; especially because they carry with them a great opposition to the prejudices of philosophers, which have so far prevailed against the common sense and natural notions of mankind.

If the Principles which I here endeavour to propagate are admitted for true, the consequences which, I think, evidently flow from thence are, that Atheism and Scepticism will be utterly destroyed, many intricate points made plain, great difficulties solved, several useless parts of science retrenched, speculation referred to practice, and men reduced from paradoxes to common sense.

And although it may, perhaps, seem an uneasy reflex-

[1] The Second Part of the *Principles* was never published, indeed never completed.

ion to some, that when they have taken a circuit through so many refined and unvulgar notions, they should at last come to think like other men; yet, methinks, this return to the simple dictates of nature, after having wandered through the wild mazes of philosophy, is not unpleasant. It is like coming home from a long voyage: a man reflects with pleasure on the many difficulties and perplexities he has passed through, sets his heart at ease, and enjoys himself with more satisfaction for the future.

As it was my intention to convince Sceptics and Infidels by reason, so it has been my endeavour strictly to observe the most rigid laws of reasoning. And, to an impartial reader, I hope it will be manifest that the sublime notion of a God, and the comfortable expectation of Immortality, do naturally arise from a close and methodical application of thought: whatever may be the result of that loose, rambling way, not altogether improperly termed Free-thinking by certain libertines in thought, who can no more endure the restraints of logic than those of religion or government.

It will perhaps be objected to my design that, so far as it tends to ease the mind of difficult and useless inquiries, it can affect only a few speculative persons. But if, by their speculations rightly placed, the study of morality and the law of nature were brought more into fashion among men of parts and genius, the discouragements that draw to Scepticism removed, the measures of right and wrong accurately defined, and the principles of Natural Religion reduced into regular systems, as artfully disposed and clearly connected as those of some other sciences; there are grounds to think these effects would not only have a gradual influence in repairing the too much defaced sense of virtue in the world, but also, by shewing that such parts of revelation as lie within the reach of human inquiry are most agreeable to right reason, would dispose all prudent, unprejudiced persons to a modest and wary treatment of those sacred mysteries which are above the comprehension of our faculties.

It remains that I desire the reader to withhold his censure of these *Dialogues* till he has read them through. Otherwise, he may lay them aside in a mistake of their design, or on account of difficulties or objections which he would find answered in the sequel. A Treatise of this nature would require to be once read over coherently, in order to comprehend its design, the proofs, solution of difficulties, and the connexion and disposition of its parts. If it be thought to deserve a second reading, this, I imagine, will make the entire scheme very plain. Especially if recourse be had to an Essay I wrote some years since upon *Vision,* and the Treatise concerning the *Principles of Human Knowledge;* wherein divers notions advanced in these *Dialogues* are farther pursued, or placed in different lights, and other points handled which naturally tend to confirm and illustrate them.]

THREE DIALOGUES

HYLAS AND PHILONOUS, IN OPPOSITION TO SCEPTICS AND ATHEISTS

THE FIRST DIALOGUE

Philonous. Good morrow, Hylas: I did not expect to find you abroad so early.

Hylas. It is indeed something unusual; but my thoughts were so taken up with a subject I was discoursing of last night, that finding I could not sleep, I resolved to rise and take a turn in the garden.

Phil. It happened well, to let you see what innocent and agreeable pleasures you lose every morning. Can there be a pleasanter time of the day, or a more delightful season of the year? That purple sky, those wild but sweet notes of birds, the fragrant bloom upon the trees and flowers, the gentle influence of the rising sun, these and a thousand nameless beauties of nature inspire the soul with secret transports; its faculties too being at this time fresh and lively, are fit for those meditations, which the solitude of a garden and tranquillity of the morning naturally dispose us to. But I am afraid I interrupt your thoughts: for you seemed very intent on something.

Hyl. It is true, I was, and shall be obliged to you if

you will permit me to go on in the same vein; not that I would by any means deprive myself of your company, for my thoughts always flow more easily in conversation with a friend, than when I am alone: but my request is, that you would suffer me to impart my reflexions to you.

Phil. With all my heart, it is what I should have requested myself if you had not prevented me.

Hyl. I was considering the odd fate of those men who have in all ages, through an affectation of being distinguished from the vulgar, or some unaccountable turn of thought, pretended either to believe nothing at all, or to believe the most extravagant things in the world. This however might be borne, if their paradoxes and scepticism did not draw after them some consequences of general disadvantage to mankind. But the mischief lieth here; that when men of less leisure see them who are supposed to have spent their whole time in the pursuits of knowledge professing an entire ignorance of all things, or advancing such notions as are repugnant to plain and commonly received principles, they will be tempted to entertain suspicions concerning the most important truths, which they had hitherto held sacred and unquestionable.

Phil. I entirely agree with you, as to the ill tendency of the affected doubts of some philosophers, and fantastical conceits of others. I am even so far gone of late in this way of thinking, that I have quitted several of the sublime notions I had got in their schools for vulgar opinions. And I give it you on my word; since this revolt from metaphysical notions to the plain dictates of nature and common sense, I find my understanding strangely enlightened, so that I can now easily comprehend a great many things which before were all mystery and riddle.

Hyl. I am glad to find there was nothing in the accounts I heard of you.

Phil. Pray, what were those?

Hyl. You were represented, in last night's conversation, as one who maintained the most extravagant opinion that ever entered into the mind of man, to wit, that there is no such thing as *material substance* in the world.

Phil. That there is no such thing as what *philosophers* call *material substance,* I am seriously persuaded: but, if I were made to see anything absurd or sceptical in this, I should then have the same reason to renounce this that I imagine I have now to reject the contrary opinion.

Hyl. What! can anything be more fantastical, more repugnant to Common Sense, or a more manifest piece of Scepticism, than to believe there is no such thing as *matter?*

Phil. Softly, good Hylas. What if it should prove that you, who hold there is, are, by virtue of that opinion, a greater sceptic, and maintain more paradoxes and repugnances to Common Sense, than I who believe no such thing?

Hyl. You may as soon persuade me, the part is greater than the whole, as that, in order to avoid absurdity and Scepticism, I should ever be obliged to give up my opinion in this point.

Phil. Well then, are you content to admit that opinion for true, which upon examination shall appear most agreeable to Common Sense, and remote from Scepticism?

Hyl. With all my heart. Since you are for raising disputes about the plainest things in nature, I am content for once to hear what you have to say.

Phil. Pray, Hylas, what do you mean by a *sceptic?*

Hyl. I mean what all men mean—one that doubts of everything.

Phil. He then who entertains no doubt concerning some particular point, with regard to that point cannot be thought a sceptic.

Hyl. I agree with you.

Phil. Whether doth doubting consist in embracing the affirmative or negative side of a question?

Hyl. In neither; for whoever understands English cannot but know that *doubting* signifies a suspense between both.

Phil. He then that denies any point, can no more be said to doubt of it, than he who affirmeth it with the same degree of assurance.

Hyl. True.

Phil. And, consequently, for such his denial is no more to be esteemed a sceptic than the other.

Hyl. I acknowledge it.

Phil. How cometh it to pass then, Hylas, that you pronounce me a *sceptic,* because I deny what you affirm, to wit, the existence of Matter? Since, for aught you can tell, I am as peremptory in my denial, as you in your affirmation.

Hyl. Hold, Philonous, I have been a little out in my definition; but every false step a man makes in discourse is not to be insisted on. I said indeed that a *sceptic* was one who doubted of everything; but I should have added, or who denies the reality and truth of things.

Phil. What things? Do you mean the principles and theorems of sciences? But these you know are universal intellectual notions, and consequently independent of Matter. The denial therefore of this doth not imply the denying them.

Hyl. I grant it. But are there no other things? What think you of distrusting the senses, of denying the real existence of sensible things, or pretending to know nothing of them. Is not this sufficient to denominate a man a *sceptic*?

Phil. Shall we therefore examine which of us it is that denies the reality of sensible things, or professes the greatest ignorance of them; since, if I take you rightly, he is to be esteemed the greatest *sceptic*?

Hyl. That is what I desire.

Phil. What mean you by Sensible Things?

Hyl. Those things which are perceived by the senses. Can you imagine that I mean anything else?

Phil. Pardon me, Hylas, if I am desirous clearly to apprehend your notions, since this may much shorten our inquiry. Suffer me then to ask you this farther question. Are those things only perceived by the senses which are perceived immediately? Or, may those things properly be said to be *sensible* which are perceived mediately, or not without the intervention of others?

Hyl. I do not sufficiently understand you.

Phil. In reading a book, what I immediately perceive are the letters; but mediately, or by means of these, are suggested to my mind the notions of God, virtue, truth, &c. Now, that the letters are truly sensible things, or perceived by sense, there is no doubt: but I would know whether you take the things suggested by them to be so too.

Hyl. No, certainly: it were absurd to think *God* or *virtue* sensible things; though they may be signified and suggested to the mind by sensible marks, with which they have an arbitrary connexion.

Phil. It seems then, that by *sensible things* you mean those only which can be perceived *immediately* by sense?

Hyl. Right.

Phil. Doth it not follow from this, that though I see

one part of the sky red, and another blue, and that my reason doth thence evidently conclude there must be some cause of that diversity of colours, yet that cause cannot be said to be a sensible thing, or perceived by the sense of seeing?

Hyl. It doth.

Phil. In like manner, though I hear variety of sounds, yet I cannot be said to hear the causes of those sounds?

Hyl. You cannot.

Phil. And when by my touch I perceive a thing to be hot and heavy, I cannot say, with any truth or propriety, that I feel the cause of its heat or weight?

Hyl. To prevent any more questions of this kind, I tell you once for all, that by *sensible things* I mean those only which are perceived by sense; and that in truth the senses perceive nothing which they do not perceive *immediately:* for they make no inferences. The deducing therefore of causes or occasions from effects and appearances, which alone are perceived by sense, entirely relates to reason.

Phil. This point then is agreed between us—That *sensible things are those only which are immediately perceived by sense.* You will farther inform me, whether we immediately perceive by sight anything beside light, and colours, and figures; or by hearing, anything but sounds; by the palate, anything beside taste; by the smell, beside odours; or by the touch, more than tangible qualities.

Hyl. We do not.

Phil. It seems, therefore, that if you take away all sensible qualities, there remains nothing sensible?

Hyl. I grant it.

Phil. Sensible things therefore are nothing else but so many sensible qualities, or combinations of sensible qualities?

Hyl. Nothing else.

Phil. *Heat* then is a sensible thing?

Hyl. Certainly.

Phil. Doth the *reality* of sensible things consist in being perceived? or, is it something distinct from their being perceived, and that bears no relation to the mind?

Hyl. To *exist* is one thing, and to be *perceived* is another.

Phil. I speak with regard to sensible things only. And of these I ask, whether by their real existence you mean a subsistence exterior to the mind, and distinct from their being perceived?

Hyl. I mean a real absolute being, distinct from, and without any relation to, their being perceived.

Phil. Heat therefore, if it be allowed a real being, must exist without the mind?

Hyl. It must.

Phil. Tell me, Hylas, is this real existence equally compatible to all degrees of heat, which we perceive; or is there any reason why we should attribute it to some, and deny it to others? And if there be, pray let me know that reason.

Hyl. Whatever degree of heat we perceive by sense, we may be sure the same exists in the object that occasions it.

Phil. What! the greatest as well as the least?

Hyl. I tell you, the reason is plainly the same in respect of both. They are both perceived by sense; nay, the greater degree of heat is more sensibly perceived; and consequently, if there is any difference, we are more certain of its real existence than we can be of the reality of a lesser degree.

Phil. But is not the most vehement and intense degree of heat a very great pain?

Hyl. No one can deny it.

Phil. And is any unperceiving thing capable of pain or pleasure?

Hyl. No, certainly.

Phil. Is your material substance a senseless being, or a being endowed with sense and perception?

Hyl. It is senseless without doubt.

Phil. It cannot therefore be the subject of pain?

Hyl. By no means.

Phil. Nor consequently of the greatest heat perceived by sense, since you acknowledge this to be no small pain?

Hyl. I grant it.

Phil. What shall we say then of your external object; is it a material Substance, or no?

Hyl. It is a material substance with the sensible qualities inhering in it.

Phil. How then can a great heat exist in it, since you own it cannot in a material substance? I desire you would clear this point.

Hyl. Hold, Philonous, I fear I was out in yielding intense heat to be a pain. It should seem rather, that pain is something distinct from heat, and the consequence or effect of it.

Phil. Upon putting your hand near the fire, do you perceive one simple uniform sensation, or two distinct sensations?

Hyl. But one simple sensation.

Phil. Is not the heat immediately perceived?

Hyl. It is.

Phil. And the pain?

Hyl. True.

Phil. Seeing therefore they are both immediately perceived at the same time, and the fire affects you only with one simple or uncompounded idea, it follows that this same simple idea is both the intense heat immediately perceived, and the pain; and, consequently, that the intense heat immediately perceived is nothing distinct from a particular sort of pain.

Hyl. It seems so.

Phil. Again, try in your thoughts, Hylas, if you can conceive a vehement sensation to be without pain or pleasure.

Hyl. I cannot.

Phil. Or can you frame to yourself an idea of sensible pain or pleasure in general, abstracted from every particular idea of heat, cold, tastes, smells, &c.?

Hyl. I do not find that I can.

Phil. Doth it not therefore follow, that sensible pain is nothing distinct from those sensations or ideas, in an intense degree?

Hyl. It is undeniable; and, to speak the truth, I begin to suspect a very great heat cannot exist but in a mind perceiving it.

Phil. What! are you then in that sceptical state of suspense, between affirming and denying?

Hyl. I think I may be positive in the point. A very violent and painful heat cannot exist without the mind.

Phil. It hath not therefore, according to you, any *real* being?

Hyl. I own it.

Phil. Is it therefore certain, that there is no body in nature really hot?

Hyl. I have not denied there is any real heat in bodies. I only say, there is no such thing as an intense real heat.

Phil. But, did you not say before that all degrees of heat were equally real; or, if there was any difference, that the greater were more undoubtedly real than the lesser?

Hyl. True: but it was because I did not then consider

the ground there is for distinguishing between them, which I now plainly see. And it is this: because intense heat is nothing else but a particular kind of painful sensation; and pain cannot exist but in a perceiving being; it follows that no intense heat can really exist in an unperceiving corporeal substance. But this is no reason why we should deny heat in an inferior degree to exist in such a substance.

Phil. But how shall we be able to discern those degrees of heat which exist only in the mind from those which exist without it?

Hyl. That is no difficult matter. You know the least pain cannot exist unperceived; whatever, therefore, degree of heat is a pain exists only in the mind. But, as for all other degrees of heat, nothing obliges us to think the same of them.

Phil. I think you granted before that no unperceiving being was capable of pleasure, any more than of pain.

Hyl. I did.

Phil. And is not warmth, or a more gentle degree of heat than what causes uneasiness, a pleasure?

Hyl. What then?

Phil. Consequently, it cannot exist without the mind in an unperceiving substance, or body.

Hyl. So it seems.

Phil. Since, therefore, as well those degrees of heat that are not painful, as those that are, can exist only in a thinking substance; may we not conclude that external bodies are absolutely incapable of any degree of heat whatsoever?

Hyl. On second thoughts, I do not think it so evident that warmth is a pleasure as that a great degree of heat is a pain.

Phil. I do not pretend that warmth is as great a

pleasure as heat is a pain. But, if you grant it to be even a small pleasure, it serves to make good my conclusion.

Hyl. I could rather call it an *indolence.* It seems to be nothing more than a privation of both pain and pleasure. And that such a quality or state as this may agree to an unthinking substance, I hope you will not deny.

Phil. If you are resolved to maintain that warmth, or a gentle degree of heat, is no pleasure, I know not how to convince you otherwise than by appealing to your own sense. But what think you of cold?

Hyl. The same that I do of heat. An intense degree of cold is a pain; for to feel a very great cold, is to perceive a great uneasiness: it cannot therefore exist without the mind; but a lesser degree of cold may, as well as a lesser degree of heat.

Phil. Those bodies, therefore, upon whose application to our own, we perceive a moderate degree of heat, must be concluded to have a moderate degree of heat or warmth in them; and those, upon whose application we feel a like degree of cold, must be thought to have cold in them.

Hyl. They must.

Phil. Can any doctrine be true that necessarily leads a man into an absurdity?

Hyl. Without doubt it cannot.

Phil. Is it not an absurdity to think that the same thing should be at the same time both cold and warm?

Hyl. It is.

Phil. Suppose now one of your hands hot, and the other cold, and that they are both at once put into the same vessel of water, in an intermediate state; will not the water seem cold to one hand, and warm to the other?

Hyl. It will.

Phil. Ought we not therefore, by your principles, to conclude it is really both cold and warm at the same time, that is, according to your own concession, to believe an absurdity?

Hyl. I confess it seems so.

Phil. Consequently, the principles themselves are false, since you have granted that no true principle leads to an absurdity.

Hyl. But, after all, can anything be more absurd than to say, *there is no heat in the fire?*

Phil. To make the point still clearer; tell me whether, in two cases exactly alike, we ought not to make the same judgment?

Hyl. We ought.

Phil. When a pin pricks your finger, doth it not rend and divide the fibres of your flesh?

Hyl. It doth.

Phil. And when a coal burns your finger, doth it any more?

Hyl. It doth not.

Phil. Since, therefore, you neither judge the sensation itself occasioned by the pin, nor anything like it to be in the pin; you should not, conformably to what you have now granted, judge the sensation occasioned by the fire, or anything like it, to be in the fire.

Hyl. Well, since it must be so, I am content to yield this point, and acknowledge that heat and cold are only sensations existing in our minds. But there still remain qualities enough to secure the reality of external things.

Phil. But what will you say, Hylas, if it shall appear that the case is the same with regard to all other sensible qualities, and that they can no more be supposed to exist without the mind, than heat and cold?

Hyl. Then indeed you will have done something to the purpose; but that is what I despair of seeing proved.

Phil. Let us examine them in order. What think you of *tastes*—do they exist without the mind, or no?

Hyl. Can any man in his senses doubt whether sugar is sweet, or wormwood bitter?

Phil. Inform me, Hylas. Is a sweet taste a particular kind of pleasure or pleasant sensation, or is it not?

Hyl. It is.

Phil. And is not bitterness some kind of uneasiness or pain?

Hyl. I grant it.

Phil. If therefore sugar and wormwood are unthinking corporeal substances existing without the mind, how can sweetness and bitterness, that is, pleasure and pain, agree to them?

Hyl. Hold, Philonous, I now see what it was deluded me all this time. You asked whether heat and cold, sweetness and bitterness, were not particular sorts of pleasure and pain; to which I answered simply, that they were. Whereas I should have thus distinguished: —those qualities, as perceived by us, are pleasures or pains; but not as existing in the external objects. We must not therefore conclude absolutely, that there is no heat in the fire, or sweetness in the sugar, but only that heat or sweetness, as perceived by us, are not in the fire or sugar. What say you to this?

Phil. I say it is nothing to the purpose. Our discourse proceeded altogether concerning sensible things, which you defined to be, *the things we immediately perceive by our senses*. Whatever other qualities, therefore, you speak of, as distinct from these, I know nothing of them, neither do they at all belong to the point in dispute. You may, indeed, pretend to have discovered certain qualities which you do not perceive, and assert those insensible qualities exist in fire and sugar. But what use can be made of this to your present purpose,

I am at a loss to conceive. Tell me then once more, do you acknowledge that heat and cold, sweetness and bitterness (meaning those qualities which are perceived by the senses), do not exist without the mind?

Hyl. I see it is to no purpose to hold out, so I give up the cause as to those mentioned qualities. Though I profess it sounds oddly, to say that sugar is not sweet.

Phil. But, for your farther satisfaction, take this along with you: that which at other times seems sweet, shall, to a distempered palate, appear bitter. And, nothing can be plainer than that divers persons perceive different tastes in the same food; since that which one man delights in, another abhors. And how could this be, if the taste was something really inherent in the food?

Hyl. I acknowledge I know not how.

Phil. In the next place, *odours* are to be considered. And, with regard to these, I would fain know whether what hath been said of tastes doth not exactly agree to them? Are they not so many pleasing or displeasing sensations?

Hyl. They are.

Phil. Can you then conceive it possible that they should exist in an unperceiving thing?

Hyl. I cannot.

Phil. Or, can you imagine that filth and ordure affect those brute animals that feed on them out of choice, with the same smells which we perceive in them?

Hyl. By no means.

Phil. May we not therefore conclude of smells, as of the other forementioned qualities, that they cannot exist in any but a perceiving substance or mind?

Hyl. I think so.

Phil. Then as to *sounds,* what must we think of them: are they accidents really inherent in external bodies, or not?

Hyl. That they inhere not in the sonorous bodies is plain from hence: because a bell struck in the exhausted receiver of an air-pump sends forth no sound. The air, therefore, must be thought the subject of sound.

Phil. What reason is there for that, Hylas?

Hyl. Because, when any motion is raised in the air, we perceive a sound greater or lesser, according to the air's motion; but without some motion in the air, we never hear any sound at all.

Phil. And granting that we never hear a sound but when some motion is produced in the air, yet I do not see how you can infer from thence, that the sound itself is in the air.

Hyl. It is this very motion in the external air that produces in the mind the sensation of *sound*. For, striking on the drum of the ear, it causeth a vibration, which by the auditory nerves being communicated to the brain, the soul is thereupon affected with the sensation called *sound*.

Phil. What! is sound then a sensation?

Hyl. I tell you, as perceived by us, it is a particular sensation in the mind.

Phil. And can any sensation exist without the mind?

Hyl. No, certainly.

Phil. How then can sound, being a sensation, exist in the air, if by the *air* you mean a senseless substance existing without the mind?

Hyl. You must distinguish, Philonous, between sound as it is perceived by us, and as it is in itself; or (which is the same thing) between the sound we immediately perceive, and that which exists without us. The former, indeed, is a particular kind of sensation, but the latter is merely a vibrative or undulatory motion in the air.

Phil. I thought I had already obviated that distinction, by the answer I gave when you were applying it in a

like case before. But, to say no more of that, are you
sure then that sound is really nothing but motion?

Hyl. I am.

Phil. Whatever therefore agrees to real sound, may
with truth be attributed to motion?

Hyl. It may.

Phil. It is then good sense to speak of *motion* as of
a thing that is *loud, sweet, acute, or grave.*

Hyl. I see you are resolved not to understand me. Is
it not evident those accidents or modes belong only to
sensible sound, or *sound* in the common acceptation of
the word, but not to *sound* in the real and philosophic
sense; which, as I just now told you, is nothing but a
certain motion of the air?

Phil. It seems then there are two sorts of sound—the
one vulgar, or that which is heard, the other philosophical and real?

Hyl. Even so.

Phil. And the latter consists in motion?

Hyl. I told you so before.

Phil. Tell me, Hylas, to which of the senses, think
you, the idea of motion belongs? to the hearing?

Hyl. No, certainly; but to the sight and touch.

Phil. It should follow then, that, according to you,
real sounds may possibly be *seen* or *felt,* but never *heard.*

Hyl. Look you, Philonous, you may, if you please,
make a jest of my opinion, but that will not alter the
truth of things. I own, indeed, the inferences you draw
me into sound something oddly; but common language,
you know, is framed by, and for the use of the vulgar:
we must not therefore wonder if expressions adapted to
exact philosophic notions seem uncouth and out of the
way.

Phil. Is it come to that? I assure you, I imagine myself to have gained no small point, since you make so

light of departing from common phrases and opinions;
it being a main part of our inquiry, to examine whose
notions are widest of the common road, and most repugnant to the general sense of the world. But, can
you think it no more than a philosophical paradox, to
say that *real sounds are never heard,* and that the idea
of them is obtained by some other sense? And is there
nothing in this contrary to nature and the truth of
things?

Hyl. To deal ingenuously, I do not like it. And, after
the concessions already made, I had as well grant that
sounds too have no real being without the mind.

Phil. And I hope you will make no difficulty to acknowledge the same of *colours.*

Hyl. Pardon me: the case of colours is very different.
Can anything be plainer than that we see them on the
objects?

Phil. The objects you speak of are, I suppose, corporeal Substances existing without the mind?

Hyl. They are.

Phil. And have true and real colours inhering in them?

Hyl. Each visible object hath that colour which we
see in it.

Phil. How! is there anything visible but what we
perceive by sight?

Hyl. There is not.

Phil. And, do we perceive anything by sense which
we do not perceive immediately?

Hyl. How often must I be obliged to repeat the same
thing? I tell you, we do not.

Phil. Have patience, good Hylas; and tell me once
more, whether there is anything immediately perceived
by the senses, except sensible qualities. I know you asserted there was not; but I would now be informed,
whether you still persist in the same opinion.

Hyl. I do.

Phil. Pray, is your corporeal substance either a sensible quality, or made up of sensible qualities?

Hyl. What a question that is! who ever thought it was?

Phil. My reason for asking was, because in saying, *each visible object hath that colour which we see in it,* you make visible objects to be corporeal substances; which implies either that corporeal substances are sensible qualities, or else that there is something beside sensible qualities perceived by sight: but, as this point was formerly agreed between us, and is still maintained by you, it is a clear consequence, that your *corporeal substance* is nothing distinct from *sensible qualities.*

Hyl. You may draw as many absurd consequences as you please, and endeavour to perplex the plainest things; but you shall never persuade me out of my senses. I clearly understand my own meaning.

Phil. I wish you would make me understand it too. But, since you are unwilling to have your notion of corporeal substance examined, I shall urge that point no farther. Only be pleased to let me know, whether the same colours which we see exist in external bodies, or some other.

Hyl. The very same.

Phil. What! are then the beautiful red and purple we see on yonder clouds really in them? Or do you imagine they have in themselves any other form than that of a dark mist or vapour?

Hyl. I must own, Philonous, those colours are not really in the clouds as they seem to be at this distance. They are only apparent colours.

Phil. Apparent call you them? how shall we distinguish these apparent colours from real?

Hyl. Very easily. Those are to be thought apparent

which, appearing only at a distance, vanish upon a nearer approach.

Phil. And those, I suppose, are to be thought real which are discovered by the most near and exact survey.

Hyl. Right.

Phil. Is the nearest and exactest survey made by the help of a microscope, or by the naked eye?

Hyl. By a microscope, doubtless.

Phil. But a microscope often discovers colours in an object different from those perceived by the unassisted sight. And, in case we had microscopes magnifying to any assigned degree, it is certain that no object whatsoever, viewed through them, would appear in the same colour which it exhibits to the naked eye.

Hyl. And what will you conclude from all this? You cannot argue that there are really and naturally no colours on objects: because by artificial managements they may be altered, or made to vanish.

Phil. I think it may evidently be concluded from your own concessions, that all the colours we see with our naked eyes are only apparent as those on the clouds, since they vanish upon a more close and accurate inspection which is afforded us by a microscope. Then, as to what you say by way of prevention: I ask you whether the real and natural state of an object is better discovered by a very sharp and piercing sight, or by one which is less sharp?

Hyl. By the former without doubt.

Phil. Is it not plain from *Dioptrics* that microscopes make the sight more penetrating, and represent objects as they would appear to the eye in case it were naturally endowed with a most exquisite sharpness?

Hyl. It is.

Phil. Consequently the microscopical representation is to be thought that which best sets forth the real nature

of the thing, or what it is in itself. The colours, therefore, by it perceived are more genuine and real than
those perceived otherwise.

Hyl. I confess there is something in what you say.

Phil. Besides, it is not only possible but manifest,
that there actually are animals whose eyes are by nature
framed to perceive those things which by reason of their
minuteness escape our sight. What think you of those
inconceivably small animals perceived by glasses? must
we suppose they are all stark blind? Or, in case they
see, can it be imagined their sight hath not the same
use in preserving their bodies from injuries, which
appears in that of all other animals? And if it hath,
is it not evident they must see particles less than their
own bodies; which will present them with a far different view in each object from that which strikes our
senses? Even our own eyes do not always represent
objects to us after the same manner. In the jaundice
every one knows that all things seem yellow. Is it not
therefore highly probable those animals in whose eyes
we discern a very different texture from that of ours,
and whose bodies abound with different humours, do not
see the same colours in every object that we do? From
all which, should it not seem to follow that all colours
are equally apparent, and that none of those which we
perceive are really inherent in any outward object?

Hyl. It should.

Phil. The point will be past all doubt, if you consider
that, in case colours were real properties or affections
inherent in external bodies, they could admit of no alteration without some change wrought in the very bodies
themselves: but, is it not evident from what hath been
said that, upon the use of microscopes, upon a change
happening in the humours of the eye, or a variation of
distance, without any manner of real alteration in the

thing itself, the colours of any object are either changed, or totally disappear? Nay, all other circumstances remaining the same, change but the situation of some objects, and they shall present different colours to the eye. The same thing happens upon viewing an object in various degrees of light. And what is more known than that the same bodies appear differently coloured by candlelight from what they do in the open day? Add to these the experiment of a prism which, separating the heterogeneous rays of light, alters the colour of any object, and will cause the whitest to appear of a deep blue or red to the naked eye. And now tell me whether you are still of opinion that every body hath its true real colour inhering in it; and, if you think it hath, I would fain know farther from you, what certain distance and position of the object, what peculiar texture and formation of the eye, what degree or kind of light is necessary for ascertaining that true colour, and distinguishing it from apparent ones.

Hyl. I own myself entirely satisfied, that they are all equally apparent, and that there is no such thing as colour really inhering in external bodies, but that it is altogether in the light. And what confirms me in this opinion is, that in proportion to the light colours are still more or less vivid; and if there be no light, then are there no colours perceived. Besides, allowing there are colours on external objects, yet, how is it possible for us to perceive them? For no external body affects the mind, unless it acts first on our organs of sense. But the only action of bodies is motion; and motion cannot be communicated otherwise than by impulse. A distant object therefore cannot act on the eye; nor consequently make itself or its properties perceivable to the soul. Whence it plainly follows that it is immediately some contiguous substance, which, operating on the eye, occasions a perception of colours: and such is light.

Phil. How! is light then a substance?

Hyl. I tell you, Philonous, external light is nothing but a thin fluid substance, whose minute particles being agitated with a brisk motion, and in various manners reflected from the different surfaces of outward objects to the eyes, communicate different motions to the optic nerves; which, being propagated to the brain, cause therein various impressions; and these are attended with the sensations of red, blue, yellow, &c.

Phil. It seems then the light doth no more than shake the optic nerves.

Hyl. Nothing else.

Phil. And consequent to each particular motion of the nerves, the mind is affected with a sensation, which is some particular colour.

Hyl. Right.

Phil. And these sensations have no existence without the mind.

Hyl. They have not.

Phil. How then do you affirm that colours are in the light; since by *light* you understand a corporeal substance external to the mind?

Hyl. Light and colours, as immediately perceived by us, I grant cannot exist without the mind. But in themselves they are only the motions and configurations of certain insensible particles of matter.

Phil. Colours then, in the vulgar sense, or taken for the immediate objects of sight, cannot agree to any but a perceiving substance.

Hyl. That is what I say.

Phil. Well then, since you give up the point as to those sensible qualities which are alone thought colours by all mankind beside, you may hold what you please with regard to those invisible ones of the philosophers. It is not my business to dispute about *them;* only I would advise you to bethink yourself, whether, considering the inquiry we are upon, it be prudent for you to affirm—*the red and blue which we see are not real colours, but certain unknown motions and figures which no man ever did or can see are truly so.* Are not these shocking notions, and are not they subject to as many ridiculous inferences, as those you were obliged to renounce before in the case of sounds?

Hyl. I frankly own, Philonous, that it is in vain to stand out any longer. Colours, sounds, tastes, in a word all those termed *secondary qualities,* have certainly no existence without the mind. But by this acknowledgment I must not be supposed to derogate anything from the reality of Matter, or external objects; seeing it is no more than several philosophers maintain, who nevertheless are the farthest imaginable from denying Matter. For the clearer understanding of this, you must know sensible qualities are by philosophers divided into *Primary* and *Secondary.* The former are Extension, Figure, Solidity, Gravity, Motion, and Rest; and these they hold exist really in bodies. The latter are those above enumerated; or, briefly, *all sensible qualities beside the Primary;* which they assert are only so many sensations or ideas existing nowhere but in the mind. But all this, I doubt not, you are apprised of. For my part, I have been a long time sensible there was such an opinion current among philosophers, but was never thoroughly convinced of its truth until now.

Phil. You are still then of opinion that *extension* and *figures* are inherent in external unthinking substances?

Hyl. I am.

Phil. But what if the same arguments which are brought against Secondary Qualities will hold good against these also?

Hyl. Why then I shall be obliged to think, they too exist only in the mind.

Phil. Is it your opinion the very figure and extension which you perceive by sense exist in the outward object or material substance?

Hyl. It is.

Phil. Have all other animals as good grounds to think the same of the figure and extension which they see and feel?

Hyl. Without doubt, if they have any thought at all.

Phil. Answer me, Hylas. Think you the senses were bestowed upon all animals for their preservation and well-being in life? or were they given to men alone for this end?

Hyl. I make no question but they have the same use in all other animals.

Phil. If so, is it not necessary they should be enabled by them to perceive their own limbs, and those bodies which are capable of harming them?

Hyl. Certainly.

Phil. A mite therefore must be supposed to see his own foot, and things equal or even less than it, as bodies of some considerable dimension; though at the same time they appear to you scarce discernible, or at best as so many visible points?

Hyl. I cannot deny it.

Phil. And to creatures less than the mite they will seem yet larger?

Hyl. They will.

Phil. Insomuch that what you can hardly discern will to another extremely minute animal appear as some huge mountain?

Hyl. All this I grant.

Phil. Can one and the same thing be at the same time in itself of different dimensions?

Hyl. That were absurd to imagine.

Phil. But, from what you have laid down it follows that both the extension by you perceived, and that perceived by the mite itself, as likewise all those perceived by lesser animals, are each of them the true extension of the mite's foot; that is to say, by your own principles you are led into an absurdity.

Hyl. There seems to be some difficulty in the point.

Phil. Again, have you not acknowledged that no real inherent property of any object can be changed without some change in the thing itself?

Hyl. I have.

Phil. But, as we approach to or recede from an object, the visible extension varies, being at one distance ten or a hundred times greater than at another. Doth it not therefore follow from hence likewise that it is not really inherent in the object?

Hyl. I own I am at a loss what to think.

Phil. Your judgment will soon be determined, if you will venture to think as freely concerning this quality as you have done concerning the rest. Was it not admitted as a good argument, that neither heat nor cold was in the water, because it seemed warm to one hand and cold to the other?

Hyl. It was.

Phil. Is it not the very same reasoning to conclude, there is no extension or figure in an object, because to one eye it shall seem little, smooth, and round, when at the same time it appears to the other, great, uneven, and angular?

Hyl. The very same. But does this latter fact ever happen?

Phil. You may at any time make the experiment, by looking with one eye bare, and with the other through a microscope.

Hyl. I know not how to maintain it; and yet I am loath to give up *extension,* I see so many odd consequences following upon such a concession.

Phil. Odd, say you? After the concessions already made, I hope you will stick at nothing for its oddness. [But, on the other hand, should it not seem very odd, if the general reasoning which includes all other sensible qualities did not also include extension? If it be allowed that no idea, nor anything like an idea, can exist in an unperceiving substance, then surely it follows that no figure, or mode of extension, which we can either perceive, or imagine, or have any idea of, can be really inherent in Matter; not to mention the peculiar difficulty there must be in conceiving a material substance, prior to and distinct from extension, to be the *substratum* of extension. Be the sensible quality what it will—figure, or sound, or colour, it seems alike impossible it should subsist in that which doth not perceive it.]

Hyl. I give up the point for the present, reserving still a right to retract my opinion, in case I shall hereafter discover any false step in my progress to it.

Phil. That is a right you cannot be denied. Figures and extension being despatched, we proceed next to *motion.* Can a real motion in any external body be at the same time both very swift and very slow?

Hyl. It cannot.

Phil. Is not the motion of a body swift in a reciprocal proportion to the time it takes up in describing any given space? Thus a body that describes a mile in an hour moves three times faster than it would in case it described only a mile in three hours.

Hyl. I agree with you.

Phil. And is not time measured by the succession of ideas in our minds?

Hyl. It is.

Phil. And is it not possible ideas should succeed one another twice as fast in your mind as they do in mine, or in that of some spirit of another kind?

Hyl. I own it.

Phil. Consequently the same body may to another seem to perform its motion over any space in half the time that it doth to you. And the same reasoning will hold as to any other proportion: that is to say, according to your principles (since the motions perceived are both really in the object) it is possible one and the same body shall be really moved the same way at once, both very swift and very slow. How is this consistent either with common sense, or with what you just now granted?

Hyl. I have nothing to say to it.

Phil. Then as for *solidity;* either you do not mean any sensible quality by that word, and so it is beside our inquiry: or if you do, it must be either hardness or resistance. But both the one and the other are plainly relative to our senses: it being evident that what seems hard to one animal may appear soft to another, who hath greater force and firmness of limbs. Nor is it less plain that the resistance I feel is not in the body.

Hyl. I own the very *sensation* of resistance, which is all you immediately perceive, is not in the body; but the *cause* of that sensation is.

Phil. But the causes of our sensations are not things immediately perceived, and therefore are not sensible. This point I thought had been already determined.

Hyl. I own it was; but you will pardon me if I seem a little embarrassed: I know not how to quit my old notions.

Phil. To help you out, do but consider that if *exten-*

sion be once acknowledged to have no existence without the mind, the same must necessarily be granted of motion, solidity, and gravity; since they all evidently suppose extension. It is therefore superfluous to inquire particularly concerning each of them. In denying extension, you have denied them all to have any real existence.

Hyl. I wonder, Philonous, if what you say be true, why those philosophers who deny the Secondary Qualities any real existence should yet attribute it to the Primary. If there is no difference between them, how can this be accounted for?

Phil. It is not my business to account for every opinion of the philosophers. But, among other reasons which may be assigned for this, it seems probable that pleasure and pain being rather annexed to the former than the latter may be one. Heat and cold, tastes and smells, have something more vividly pleasing or disagreeable than the ideas of extension, figure, and motion affect us with. And, it being too visibly absurd to hold that pain or pleasure can be in an unperceiving Substance, men are more easily weaned from believing the external existence of the Secondary than the Primary Qualities. You will be satisfied there is something in this, if you recollect the difference you made between an intense and more moderate degree of heat; allowing the one a real existence, while you denied it to the other. But, after all, there is no rational ground for that distinction; for, surely an indifferent sensation is as truly *a sensation* as one more pleasing or painful; and consequently should not any more than they be supposed to exist in an unthinking subject.

Hyl. It is just come into my head, Philonous, that I have somewhere heard of a distinction between absolute and sensible extension. Now, though it be acknowledged that *great* and *small*, consisting merely in the relation which other extended beings have to the parts of our own bodies, do not really inhere in the substances them-selves; yet nothing obliges us to hold the same with regard to *absolute extension*, which is something ab-stracted from *great* and *small*, from this or that par-ticular magnitude or figure. So likewise as to motion; *swift* and *slow* are altogether relative to the succession of ideas in our own minds. But, it doth not follow, because those modifications of motion exist not without the mind, that therefore absolute motion abstracted from them doth not.

Phil. Pray what is it that distinguishes one motion, or one part of extension, from another? Is it not something sensible, as some degree of swiftness or slowness, some certain magnitude or figure peculiar to each?

Hyl. I think so.

Phil. These qualities, therefore, stripped of all sen-sible properties, are without all specific and numerical differences, as the schools call them.

Hyl. They are.

Phil. That is to say, they are extension in general, and motion in general.

Hyl. Let it be so.

Phil. But it is a universally received maxim that *Everything which exists is particular.* How then can motion in general, or extension in general, exist in any corporeal substance?

Hyl. I will take time to solve your difficulty.

Phil. But I think the point may be speedily decided. Without doubt you can tell whether you are able to frame this or that idea. Now I am content to put our dispute on this issue. If you can frame in your thoughts a distinct *abstract idea* of motion or extension, divested of all those sensible modes, as swift and slow, great and small, round and square, and the like, which are acknowledged to exist only in the mind, I will then yield the point you contend for. But if you cannot, it will be unreasonable on your side to insist any longer upon what you have no notion of.

Hyl. To confess ingenuously, I cannot.

Phil. Can you even separate the ideas of extension and motion from the ideas of all those qualities which they who make the distinction term *secondary?*

Hyl. What! is it not an easy matter to consider extension and motion by themselves, abstracted from all other sensible qualities? Pray how do the mathematicians treat of them?

Phil. I acknowledge, Hylas, it is not difficult to form general propositions and reasonings about those qualities, without mentioning any other; and, in this sense, to consider or treat of them abstractedly. But, how doth it follow that, because I can pronounce the word *motion* by itself, I can form the idea of it in my mind exclusive of body? or, because theorems may be great of extension and figures, without any mention of *great* or *small,* or any other sensible mode or quality, that therefore it is possible such an abstract idea of extension, without any particular size or figure, or sensible quality, should be distinctly formed, and apprehended by the mind? Mathematicians treat of quantity, without regarding what other sensible qualities it is attended with, as being altogether indifferent to their demonstrations. But, when laying aside the words, they contemplate the bare ideas, I believe you will find, they are not the pure abstracted ideas of extension.

Hyl. But what say you to *pure intellect?* May not abstracted ideas be framed by that faculty?

Phil. Since I cannot frame abstract ideas at all. it is plain I cannot frame them by the help of *pure intellect;*

whatsoever faculty you understand by those words. Besides, not to inquire into the nature of pure intellect and its spiritual objects, as *virtue, reason, God,* or the like, thus much seems manifest—that sensible things are only to be perceived by sense, or represented by the imagination. Figures, therefore, and extension, being originally perceived by sense, do not belong to pure intellect: but, for your farther satisfaction, try if you can frame the idea of any figure, abstracted from all particularities of size, or even from other sensible qualities.

Hyl. Let me think a little— I do not find that I can.

Phil. And can you think it possible that should really exist in nature which implies a repugnancy in its conception?

Hyl. By no means.

Phil. Since therefore it is impossible even for the mind to disunite the ideas of extension and motion from all other sensible qualities, doth it not follow, that where the one exist there necessarily the other exist likewise?

Hyl. It should seem so.

Phil. Consequently, the very same arguments which you admitted as conclusive against the Secondary Qualities are, without any farther application of force, against the Primary too. Besides, if you will trust your senses, is it not plain all sensible qualities coexist, or to them appear as being in the same place? Do they ever represent a motion, or figure, as being divested of all other visible and tangible qualities?

Hyl. You need say no more on this head. I am free to own, if there be no secret error or oversight in our proceedings hitherto, that *all* sensible qualities are alike to be denied existence without the mind. But, my fear is that I have been too liberal in my former concessions, or overlooked some fallacy or other. In short, I did not take time to think.

Phil. For that matter, Hylas, you may take what time you please in reviewing the progress of our inquiry. You are at liberty to recover any slips you might have made, or offer whatever you have omitted which makes for your first opinion.

Hyl. One great oversight I take to be this—that I did not sufficiently distinguish the *object* from the *sensation*. Now, though this latter may not exist without the mind, yet it will not thence follow that the former cannot.

Phil. What object do you mean? the object of the senses?

Hyl. The same.

Phil. It is then immediately perceived?

Hyl. Right.

Phil. Make me to understand the difference between what is immediately perceived and a sensation.

Hyl. The sensation I take to be an act of the mind perceiving; besides which, there is something perceived; and this I call the *object*. For example, there is red and yellow on that tulip. But then the act of perceiving those colours is in me only, and not in the tulip.

Phil. What tulip do you speak of? Is it that which you see?

Hyl. The same.

Phil. And what do you see beside colour, figure, and extension?

Hyl. Nothing.

Phil. What you would say then is that the red and yellow are coexistent with the extension; is it not?

Hyl. That is not all; I would say they have a real existence without the mind, in some unthinking substance.

Phil. That the colours are really in the tulip which I see is manifest. Neither can it be denied that this tulip may exist independent of your mind or mine; but, that any immediate object of the senses—that is, any idea, or combination of ideas—should exist in an unthinking substance, or exterior to *all* minds, is in itself an evident contradiction. Nor can I imagine how this follows from what you said just now, to wit, that the red and yellow were on the tulip *you saw,* since you do not pretend to *see* that unthinking substance.

Hyl. You have an artful way, Philonous, of diverting our inquiry from the subject.

Phil. I see you have no mind to be pressed that way. To return then to your distinction between *sensation* and *object;* if I take you right, you distinguish in every perception two things, the one an action of the mind, the other not.

Hyl. True.

Phil. And this action cannot exist in, or belong to, any unthinking thing; but, whatever beside is implied in a perception may?

Hyl. That is my meaning.

Phil. So that if there was a perception without any act of the mind, it were possible such a perception should exist in an unthinking substance?

Hyl. I grant it. But it is impossible there should be such a perception.

Phil. When is the mind said to be active?

Hyl. When it produces, puts an end to, or changes, anything.

Phil. Can the mind produce, discontinue, or change anything, but by an act of the will?

Hyl. It cannot.

Phil. The mind therefore is to be accounted *active*

in its perceptions so far forth as *volition* is included in them?

Hyl. It is.

Phil. In plucking this flower I am active; because I do it by the motion of my hand, which was consequent upon my volition; so likewise in applying it to my nose. But is either of these smelling?

Hyl. No.

Phil. I act too in drawing the air through my nose; because my breathing so rather than otherwise is the effect of my volition. But neither can this be called *smelling:* for, if it were, I should smell every time I breathed in that manner?

Hyl. True.

Phil. Smelling then is somewhat consequent to all this?

Hyl. It is.

Phil. But I do not find my will concerned any farther. Whatever more there is—as that I perceive such a particular smell, or any smell at all—this is independent of my will, and therein I am altogether passive. Do you find it otherwise with you, Hylas?

Hyl. No, the very same.

Phil. Then, as to seeing, is it not in your power to open your eyes, or keep them shut; to turn them this or that way?

Hyl. Without doubt.

Phil. But, doth it in like manner depend on *your* will that in looking on this flower you perceive *white* rather than any other colour? Or, directing your open eyes towards yonder part of the heaven, can you avoid seeing the sun? Or is light or darkness the effect of your volition?

Hyl. No, certainly.

Phil. You are then in these respects altogether passive?

Hyl. I am.

Phil. Tell me now, whether *seeing* consists in perceiving light and colours, or in opening and turning the eyes?

Hyl. Without doubt, in the former.

Phil. Since therefore you are in the very perception of light and colours altogether passive, what is become of that action you were speaking of as an ingredient in every sensation? And, doth it not follow from your own concessions, that the perception of light and colours, including no action in it, may exist in an unperceiving substance? And is not this a plain contradiction?

Hyl. I know not what to think of it.

Phil. Besides, since you distinguish the *active* and *passive* in every perception, you must do it in that of pain. But how is it possible that pain, be it as little active as you please, should exist in an unperceiving substance? In short, do but consider the point, and then confess ingenuously, whether light and colours, tastes, sounds, &c. are not all equally passions or sensations in the soul. You may indeed call them *external objects,* and give them in words what subsistence you please. But, examine your own thoughts, and then tell me whether it be not as I say?

Hyl. I acknowledge, Philonous, that, upon a fair observation of what passes in my mind, I can discover nothing else but that I am a thinking being, affected with variety of sensations; neither is it possible to conceive how a sensation should exist in an unperceiving substance.—But then, on the other hand, when I look on sensible things in a different view, considering them as so many modes and qualities, I find it necessary to suppose a *material substratum,* without which they cannot be conceived to exist.

Phil. *Material substratum* call you it? Pray, by which of your senses came you acquainted with that being?

Hyl. It is not itself sensible; its modes and qualities only being perceived by the senses.

Phil. I presume then it was by reflexion and reason you obtained the idea of it?

Hyl. I do not pretend to any proper positive *idea* of it. However, I conclude it exists, because qualities cannot be conceived to exist without a support.

Phil. It seems then you have only a relative *notion* of it, or that you conceive it not otherwise than by conceiving the relation it bears to sensible qualities?

Hyl. Right.

Phil. Be pleased therefore to let me know wherein that relation consists.

Hyl. Is it not sufficiently expressed in the term *substratum,* or *substance?*

Phil. If so, the word *substratum* should import that it is spread under the sensible qualities or accidents?

Hyl. True.

Phil. And consequently under extension?

Hyl. I own it.

Phil. It is therefore somewhat in its own nature entirely distinct from extension?

Hyl. I tell you, extension is only a mode, and Matter is something that supports modes. And is it not evident the thing supported is different from the thing supporting?

Phil. So that something distinct from, and exclusive of, extension is supposed to be the *substratum* of extension?

Hyl. Just so.

Phil. Answer me, Hylas. Can a thing be spread without extension? or is not the idea of extension necessarily included in *spreading?*

Hyl. It is.

Phil. Whatsoever therefore you suppose spread under anything must have in itself an extension distinct from the extension of that thing under which it is spread?

Hyl. It must.

Phil. Consequently, every corporeal substance, being the *substratum* of extension, must have in itself another extension, by which it is qualified to be a *substratum:* and so on to infinity? And I ask whether this be not absurd in itself, and repugnant to what you granted just now, to wit, that the *substratum* was something distinct from and exclusive of extension?

Hyl. Aye but, Philonous, you take me wrong. I do not mean that Matter is *spread* in a gross literal sense under extension. The word *substratum* is used only to express in general the same thing with *substance.*

Phil. Well then, let us examine the relation implied in the term *substance.* Is it not that it stands under accidents?

Hyl. The very same.

Phil. But, that one thing may stand under or support another, must it not be extended?

Hyl. It must.

Phil. Is not therefore this supposition liable to the same absurdity with the former?

Hyl. You still take things in a strict literal sense. That is not fair, Philonous.

Phil. I am not for imposing any sense on your words: you are at liberty to explain them as you please. Only, I beseech you, make me understand something by them.

You tell me Matter supports or stands under accidents. How! is it as your legs support your body?

Hyl. No; that is the literal sense.

Phil. Pray let me know any sense, literal or not literal, that you understand it in.—How long must I wait for an answer, Hylas?

Hyl. I declare I know not what to say. I once thought I understood well enough what was meant by Matter's supporting accidents. But now, the more I think on it the less can I comprehend it: in short I find that I know nothing of it.

Phil. It seems then you have no idea at all, neither relative nor positive, of Matter; you know neither what it is in itself, nor what relation it bears to accidents?

Hyl. I acknowledge it.

Phil. And yet you asserted that you could not conceive how qualities or accidents should really exist, without conceiving at the same time a material support of them?

Hyl. I did.

Phil. That is to say, when you conceive the *real existence of qualities, you do withal conceive Something which you cannot conceive?*

Hyl. It was wrong, I own. But still I fear there is some fallacy or other. Pray what think you of this? It is just come into my head that the ground of all our mistake lies in your treating of each quality by itself. Now, I grant that each quality cannot singly subsist without the mind. Colour cannot without extension, neither can figure without some other sensible quality. But, as the several qualities united or blended together form entire sensible things, nothing hinders why such things may not be supposed to exist without the mind.

Phil. Either, Hylas, you are jesting, or have a very bad memory. Though indeed we went through all the qualities by name one after another, yet my arguments, or rather your concessions, nowhere tend to prove that the Secondary Qualities did not subsist each alone by itself; but, that they were not *at all* without the mind. Indeed, in treating of figure and motion we concluded they could not exist without the mind, because it was impossible even in thought to separate them from all secondary qualities, so as to conceive them existing by themselves. But then this was not the only argument made use of upon that occasion. But (to pass by all that hath been hitherto said, and reckon it for nothing, if you will have it so) I am content to put the whole upon this issue. If you can conceive it possible for any mixture or combination of qualities, or any sensible object whatever, to exist without the mind, then I will grant it actually to be so.

Hyl. If it comes to that the point will soon be decided. What more easy than to conceive a tree or house existing by itself, independent of, and unperceived by, any mind whatsoever? I do at this present time conceive them existing after that manner.

Phil. How say you, Hylas, can you see a thing which is at the same time unseen?

Hyl. No, that were a contradiction.

Phil. Is it not as great a contradiction to talk of *conceiving* a thing which is *unconceived?*

Hyl. It is.

Phil. The tree or house therefore which you think of is conceived by you?

Hyl. How should it be otherwise?

Phil. And what is conceived is surely in the mind?

Hyl. Without question, that which is conceived is in the mind.

Phil. How then came you to say, you conceived a

house or tree existing independent and out of all minds whatsoever?

Hyl. That was I own an oversight; but stay, let me consider what led me into it.—It is a pleasant mistake enough. As I was thinking of a tree in a solitary place, where no one was present to see it, methought that was to conceive a tree as existing unperceived or unthought of; not considering that I myself conceived it all the while. But now I plainly see that all I can do is to frame ideas in my own mind. I may indeed conceive in my own thoughts the idea of a tree, or a house, or a mountain, but that is all. And this is far from proving that I can conceive them *existing out of the minds of all Spirits*.

Phil. You acknowledge then that you cannot possibly conceive how any one corporeal sensible thing should exist otherwise than in a mind?

Hyl. I do.

Phil. And yet you will earnestly contend for the truth of that which you cannot so much as conceive?

Hyl. I profess I know not what to think; but still there are some scruples remain with me. Is it not certain I *see things at a distance?* Do we not perceive the stars and moon, for example, to be a great way off? Is not this, I say, manifest to the senses?

Phil. Do you not in a dream too perceive those or the like objects?

Hyl. I do.

Phil. And have they not then the same appearance of being distant?

Hyl. They have.

Phil. But you do not thence conclude the apparitions in a dream to be without the mind?

Hyl. By no means.

Phil. You ought not therefore to conclude that sensible objects are without the mind, from their appearance, or manner wherein they are perceived.

Hyl. I acknowledge it. But doth not my sense deceive me in those cases?

Phil. By no means. The idea or thing which you immediately perceive, neither sense nor reason informs you that *it* actually exists without the mind. By sense you only know that you are affected with such certain sensations of light and colours, &c. And these you will not say are without the mind.

Hyl. True: but, beside all that, do you not think the sight suggests something of *outness* or *distance*?

Phil. Upon approaching a distant object, do the visible size and figure change perpetually, or do they appear the same at all distances?

Hyl. They are in a continual change.

Phil. Sight therefore doth not suggest, or any way inform you, that the visible object you immediately perceive exists at a distance,[1] or will be perceived when you advance farther onward; there being a continued series of visible objects succeeding each other during the whole time of your approach.

Hyl. It doth not; but still I know, upon seeing an object, what object I shall perceive after having passed over a certain distance: no matter whether it be exactly the same or no: there is still something of distance suggested in the case.

Phil. Good Hylas, do but reflect a little on the point, and then tell me whether there be any more in it than this: From the ideas you actually perceive by sight, you have by experience learned to collect what other ideas you will (according to the standing order of na-

---

[1] [See the *Essay towards a New Theory of Vision*, and its *Vindication*.] Note by Berkeley in the 1734 edition.

ture) be affected with, after such a certain succession of time and motion.

Hyl. Upon the whole, I take it to be nothing else.

Phil. Now, is it not plain that if we suppose a man born blind was on a sudden made to see, he could at first have no experience of what may be *suggested* by sight?

Hyl. It is.

Phil. He would not then, according to you, have any notion of distance annexed to the things he saw; but would take them for a new set of sensations, existing only in his mind?

Hyl. It is undeniable.

Phil. But, to make it still more plain: is not *distance* a line turned endwise to the eye?

Hyl. It is.

Phil. And can a line so situated be perceived by sight?

Hyl. It cannot.

Phil. Doth it not therefore follow that distance is not properly and immediately perceived by sight?

Hyl. It should seem so.

Phil. Again, is it your opinion that colours are at a distance?

Hyl. It must be acknowledged they are only in the mind.

Phil. But do not colours appear to the eye as coexisting in the same place with extension and figures?

Hyl. They do.

Phil. How can you then conclude from sight that figures exist without, when you acknowledge colours do not; the sensible appearance being the very same with regard to both?

Hyl. I know not what to answer.

Phil. But, allowing that distance was truly and immediately perceived by the mind, yet it would not thence follow it existed out of the mind. For, whatever is immediately perceived is an idea: and can any idea exist out of the mind?

Hyl. To suppose that were absurd: but, inform me, Philonous, can we perceive or know nothing beside our ideas?

Phil. As for the rational deducing of causes from effects, that is beside our inquiry. And, by the senses you can best tell whether you perceive anything which is not immediately perceived. And I ask you, whether the things immediately perceived are other than your own sensations or ideas? You have indeed more than once, in the course of this conversation, declared yourself on those points; but you seem, by this last question, to have departed from what you then thought.

Hyl. To speak the truth, Philonous, I think there are two kinds of objects:—the one perceived immediately, which are likewise called *ideas;* the other are real things or external objects, perceived by the mediation of ideas, which are their images and representations. Now, I own ideas do not exist without the mind; but the latter sort of objects do. I am sorry I did not think of this distinction sooner; it would probably have cut short your discourse.

Phil. Are those external objects perceived by sense, or by some other faculty?

Hyl. They are perceived by sense.

Phil. How! Is there anything perceived by sense which is not immediately perceived?

Hyl. Yes, Philonous, in some sort there is. For example, when I look on a picture or statue of Julius Cæsar, I may be said after a manner to perceive him (though not immediately) by my senses.

Phil. It seems then you will have our ideas, which alone are immediately perceived, to be pictures of external things: and that these also are perceived by sense, inasmuch as they have a conformity or resemblance to our ideas?

Hyl. That is my meaning.

Phil. And, in the same way that Julius Cæsar, in himself invisible, is nevertheless perceived by sight; real things, in themselves imperceptible, are perceived by sense.

Hyl. In the very same.

Phil. Tell me, Hylas, when you behold the picture of Julius Cæsar, do you see with your eyes any more than some colours and figures, with a certain symmetry and composition of the whole?

Hyl. Nothing else.

Phil. And would not a man who had never known anything of Julius Cæsar see as much?

Hyl. He would.

Phil. Consequently he hath his sight, and the use of it, in as perfect a degree as you?

Hyl. I agree with you.

Phil. Whence comes it then that your thoughts are directed to the Roman emperor, and his are not? This cannot proceed from the sensations or ideas of sense by you then perceived; since you acknowledge you have no advantage over him in that respect. It should seem therefore to proceed from reason and memory: should it not?

Hyl. It should.

Phil. Consequently, it will not follow from that instance that anything is perceived by sense which is not immediately perceived. Though I grant we may, in one acceptation, be said to perceive sensible things mediately by sense: that is, when, from a frequently perceived connexion, the immediate perception of ideas by one sense *suggests* to the mind others, perhaps belonging to another sense, which are wont to be connected with them. For instance, when I hear a coach drive along the streets, immediately I perceive only the sound; but, from the experience I have had that such a sound is connected with a coach, I am said to hear the coach. It is nevertheless evident that, in truth and strictness, nothing can be *heard* but *sound;* and the coach is not then properly perceived by sense, but suggested from experience. So likewise when we are said to see a red-hot bar of iron; the solidity and heat of the iron are not the objects of sight, but suggested to the imagination by the colour and figure which are properly perceived by that sense. In short, those things alone are actually and strictly perceived by any sense, which would have been perceived in case that same sense had then been first conferred on us. As for other things, it is plain they are only suggested to the mind by experience, grounded on former conceptions. But, to return to your comparison of Cæsar's picture, it is plain, if you keep to that, you must hold the real things, or archetypes of our ideas, are not perceived by sense, but by some internal faculty of the soul, as reason or memory. I would therefore fain know what arguments you can draw from reason for the existence of what you call *real things* or *material objects.* Or, whether you remember to have seen them formerly as they are in themselves; or, if you have heard or read of any one that did.

Hyl. I see, Philonous, you are disposed to raillery; but that will never convince me.

Phil. My aim is only to learn from you the way to come at the knowledge of *material beings.* Whatever we perceive is perceived immediately or mediately: by sense, or by reason and reflexion. But, as you have excluded sense, pray shew me what reason you have to believe their existence; or what *medium* you can possibly make use of to prove it, either to mine or your own understanding.

Hyl. To deal ingenuously, Philonous, now I consider the point, I do not find I can give you any good reason for it. But, thus much seems pretty plain, that it is at least possible such things may really exist. And, as long as there is no absurdity in supposing them, I am resolved to believe as I did, till you bring good reasons to the contrary.

Phil. What! Is it come to this, that you only *believe* the existence of material objects, and that your belief is founded barely on the possibility of its being true? Then you will have me bring reasons against it: though another would think it reasonable the proof should lie on him who holds the affirmative. And, after all, this very point which you are now resolved to maintain, without any reason, is in effect what you have more than once during this discourse seen good reason to give up. But, to pass over all this; if I understand you rightly, you say our ideas do not exist without the mind, but that they are copies, images, or representations, of certain originals that do?

Hyl. You take me right.

Phil. They are then like external things?

Hyl. They are.

Phil. Have those things a stable and permanent nature, independent of our senses; or are they in a perpetual change, upon our producing any motions in our bodies—suspending, exerting, or altering, our faculties or organs of sense?

Hyl. Real things, it is plain, have a fixed and real nature, which remains the same notwithstanding any change in our senses, or in the posture and motion of our bodies; which indeed may affect the ideas in our minds;

but it were absurd to think they had the same effect on things existing without the mind.

Phil. How then is it possible that things perpetually fleeting and variable as our ideas should be copies or images of anything fixed and constant? Or, in other words, since all sensible qualities, as size, figure, colour, &c., that is, our ideas, are continually changing, upon every alteration in the distance, medium, or instruments of sensation; how can any determinate material objects be properly represented or painted forth by several distinct things, each of which is so different from and unlike the rest? Or, if you say it resembles some one only of our ideas, how shall we be able to distinguish the true copy from all the false ones?

Hyl. I profess, Philonous, I am at a loss. I know not what to say to this.

Phil. But neither is this all. Which are material objects in themselves—perceptible or imperceptible?

Hyl. Properly and immediately nothing can be perceived but ideas. All material things, therefore, are in themselves insensible, and to be perceived only by our ideas.

Phil. Ideas then are sensible, and their archetypes or originals insensible?

Hyl. Right.

Phil. But how can that which is sensible be *like* that which is insensible? Can a real thing, in itself *invisible,* be like a *colour;* or a real thing, which is not *audible,* be like a *sound?* In a word, can anything be like a sensation or idea, but another sensation or idea?

Hyl. I must own, I think not.

Phil. Is it possible there should be any doubt on the point? Do you not perfectly know your own ideas?

Hyl. I know them perfectly; since what I do not perceive or know can be no part of my idea.

Phil. Consider, therefore, and examine them, and then tell me if there be anything in them which can exist without the mind: or if you can conceive anything like them existing without the mind.

Hyl. Upon inquiry, I find it is impossible for me to conceive or understand how anything but an idea can be like an idea. And it is most evident that *no idea can exist without the mind*.

Phil. You are therefore, by your principles, forced to deny the *reality* of sensible things; since you made it to consist in an absolute existence exterior to the mind. That is to say, you are a downright sceptic. So I have gained my point, which was to shew your principles led to Scepticism.

Hyl. For the present I am, if not entirely convinced, at least silenced.

Phil. I would fain know what more you would require in order to a perfect conviction. Have you not had the liberty of explaining yourself all manner of ways? Were any little slips in discourse laid hold and insisted on? Or were you not allowed to retract or reinforce anything you had offered, as best served your purpose? Hath not everything you could say been heard and examined with all the fairness imaginable? In a word, have you not in every point been convinced out of your own mouth? And, if you can at present discover any flaw in any of your former concessions, or think of any remaining subterfuge, any new distinction, colour, or comment whatsoever, why do you not produce it?

Hyl. A little patience, Philonous. I am at present so amazed to see myself ensnared, and as it were imprisoned in the labyrinths you have drawn me into, that on the sudden it cannot be expected I should find my way out. You must give me time to look about me and recollect myself.

Phil. Hark; is not this the college bell?

Hyl. It rings for prayers.

Phil. We will go in then, if you please, and meet here again to-morrow morning. In the meantime, you may employ your thoughts on this morning's discourse, and try if you can find any fallacy in it, or invent any new means to extricate yourself.

Hyl. Agreed.

THE SECOND DIALOGUE

Hylas. I beg your pardon, Philonous, for not meeting you sooner. All this morning my head was so filled with our late conversation that I had not leisure to think of the time of the day, or indeed of anything else.

Philonous. I am glad you were so intent upon it, in hopes if there were any mistakes in your concessions, or fallacies in my reasonings from them, you will now dis-cover them to me.

Hyl. I assure you I have done nothing ever since I saw you but search after mistakes and fallacies, and, with that view, have minutely examined the whole series of yesterday's discourse: but all in vain, for the notions it led me into, upon review, appear still more clear and evident; and, the more I consider them, the more irre-sistibly do they force my assent.

Phil. And is not this, think you, a sign that they are genuine, that they proceed from nature, and are con-formable to right reason? Truth and beauty are in this alike, that the strictest survey sets them both off to advantage; while the false lustre of error and disguise cannot endure being reviewed, or too nearly inspected.

Hyl. I own there is a great deal in what you say. Nor can any one be more entirely satisfied of the truth of those odd consequences, so long as I have in view the reasonings that lead to them. But, when these are out of my thoughts, there seems, on the other hand, something so satisfactory, so natural and intelligible, in the modern way of explaining things that, I profess, I know not how to reject it.

Phil. I know not what way you mean.

Hyl. I mean the way of accounting for our sensations or ideas.

Phil. How is that?

Hyl. It is supposed the soul makes her residence in some part of the brain, from which the nerves take their rise, and are thence extended to all parts of the body; and that outward objects, by the different impressions they make on the organs of sense, communicate certain vibrative motions to the nerves; and these being filled with spirits propagate them to the brain or seat of the soul, which, according to the various impressions or traces thereby made in the brain, is variously affected with ideas.

Phil. And call you this an explication of the manner whereby we are affected with ideas?

Hyl. Why not, Philonous? Have you anything to object against it?

Phil. I would first know whether I rightly understood your hypothesis. You make certain traces in the brain to be the causes or occasions of our ideas. Pray tell me whether by the *brain* you mean any sensible thing.

Hyl. What else think you I could mean?

Phil. Sensible things are all immediately perceivable; and those things which are immediately perceivable are ideas; and these exist only in the mind. Thus much you have, if I mistake not, long since agreed to.

Hyl. I do not deny it.

Phil. The brain therefore you speak of, being a sensible thing, exists only in the mind. Now, I would fain know whether you think it reasonable to suppose that one idea or thing existing in the mind occasions all other ideas. And, if you think so, pray how do you account for the origin of that primary idea or brain itself?

Hyl. I do not explain the origin of our ideas by that brain which is perceivable to sense—this being itself only a combination of sensible ideas—but by another which I imagine.

Phil. But are not things imagined as truly *in the mind* as things perceived?

Hyl. I must confess they are.

Phil. It comes, therefore, to the same thing; and you have been all this while accounting for ideas by certain motions or impressions of the brain; that is, by some alterations in an idea, whether sensible or imaginable it matters not.

Hyl. I begin to suspect my hypothesis.

Phil. Besides spirits, all that we know or conceive are our own ideas. When, therefore, you say all ideas are occasioned by impressions in the brain, do you conceive this brain or no? If you do, then you talk of ideas imprinted in an idea causing that same idea, which is absurd. If you do not conceive it, you talk unintelligibly, instead of forming a reasonable hypothesis.

Hyl. I now clearly see it was a mere dream. There is nothing in it.

Phil. You need not be much concerned at it; for after all, this way of explaining things, as you called it, could never have satisfied any reasonable man. What connexion is there between a motion in the nerves, and the sensations of sound or colour in the mind? Or how is it possible these should be the effect of that?

Hyl. But I could never think it had so little in it as now it seems to have.

Phil. Well then, are you at length satisfied that no sensible things have a real existence; and that you are in truth an arrant sceptic?

Hyl. It is too plain to be denied.

Phil. Look! are not the fields covered with a delightful verdure? Is there not something in the woods and groves, in the rivers and clear springs, that soothes, that delights, that transports the soul? At the prospect of the wide and deep ocean, or some huge mountain whose top is lost in the clouds, or of an old gloomy forest, are not our minds filled with a pleasing horror? Even in rocks and deserts is there not an agreeable wildness? How sincere a pleasure is it to behold the natural beauties of the earth! To preserve and renew our relish for them, is not the veil of night alternately drawn over her face, and doth she not change her dress with the seasons? How aptly are the elements disposed! What variety and use [in the meanest productions of nature!]¹ What delicacy, what beauty, what contrivance, in animal and vegetable bodies! How exquisitely are all things suited, as well to their particular ends, as to constitute opposite parts of the whole! And, while they mutually aid and support, do they not also set off and illustrate each other? Raise now your thoughts from this ball of earth to all those glorious luminaries that adorn the high arch of heaven. The motion and situation of the planets, are they not admirable for use and order? Were those (miscalled *erratic*) globes once known to stray, in their repeated journeys through the pathless void? Do they not measure areas round the sun ever proportioned to the times? So fixed, so immutable are the laws by which the unseen Author of nature actuates the universe. How vivid and radiant is the

¹ The text of the first and of the second edition reads: "in stones and minerals."

lustre of the fixed stars! How magnificent and rich that negligent profusion with which they appear to be scattered throughout the whole azure vault! Yet, if you take the telescope, it brings into your sight a new host of stars that escape the naked eye. Here they seem contiguous and minute, but to a nearer view immense orbs of light are various distances, far sunk in the abyss of space. Now you must call imagination to your aid. The feeble narrow sense cannot descry innumerable worlds revolving round the central fires; and in those worlds the energy of an all-perfect Mind displayed in endless forms. But, neither sense nor imagination are big enough to comprehend the boundless extent, with all its glittering furniture. Though the labouring mind exert and strain each power to its utmost reach, there still stands out ungrasped a surplusage immeasurable. Yet all the vast bodies that compose this mighty frame, how distant and remote soever, are by some secret mechanism, some Divine art and force, linked in a mutual dependence and intercourse with each other; even with this earth, which was almost slipt from my thoughts and lost in the crowd of worlds. Is not the whole system immense, beautiful, glorious beyond expression and beyond thought! What treatment, then, do those philosophers deserve, who would deprive these noble and delightful scenes of all *reality?* How should those Principles be entertained that lead us to think all the visible beauty of the creation a false imaginary glare? To be plain, can you expect this Scepticism of yours will not be thought extravagantly absurd by all men of sense?

Hyl. Other men may think as they please; but for your part you have nothing to reproach me with. My comfort is, you are as much a sceptic as I am.

Phil. There, Hylas, I must beg leave to differ from you.

Hyl. What! Have you all along agreed to the premises, and do you now deny the conclusion, and leave me to maintain those paradoxes by myself which you led me into? This surely is not fair.

Phil. I deny that I agreed with you in those notions that led to Scepticism. You indeed said the *reality of sensible things consisted in an absolute existence out of the minds of spirits,* or distinct from their being perceived. And pursuant to this notion of reality, *you* are obliged to deny sensible things any real existence: that is, according to your own definition, you profess yourself a sceptic. But I neither said nor thought the reality of sensible things was to be defined after that manner. To me it is evident, for the reasons you allow, that sensible things cannot exist otherwise than in a mind or spirit. Whence I conclude, not that they have no real existence, but that, seeing they depend not on my thought, and have an existence distinct from being perceived by me, *there must be some other Mind wherein they exist.* As sure, therefore, as the sensible world really exists, so sure is there an infinite omnipresent Spirit who contains and supports it.

Hyl. What! This is no more than I and all Christians hold; nay, and all others too who believe there is a God, and that He knows and comprehends all things.

Phil. Aye, but here lies the difference. Men commonly believe that all things are known or perceived by God, because they believe the being of a God; whereas I, on the other side, immediately and necessarily conclude the being of a God, because all sensible things must be perceived by Him.

Hyl. But, so long as we all believe the same thing, what matter is it how we come by that belief?

Phil. But neither do we agree in the same opinion. For philosophers, though they acknowledge all corporeal

beings to be perceived by God, yet they attribute to
them an absolute subsistence distinct from their being
perceived by any mind whatever; which I do not. Besides, is there no difference between saying, *There is a
God, therefore He perceives all things;* and saying, *Sensible things do really exist; and, if they really exist,
they are necessarily perceived by an infinite Mind:
therefore there is an infinite Mind, or God?* This furnishes you with a direct and immediate demonstration,
from a most evident principle, of the *being of a God.*
Divines and philosophers had proved beyond all controversy, from the beauty and usefulness of the several
parts of the creation, that it was the workmanship of
God. But that—setting aside all help of astronomy
and natural philosophy, all contemplation of the contrivance, order, and adjustment of things—an infinite
Mind should be necessarily inferred from the bare *existence of the sensible world,* is an advantage to them only
who have made this easy reflexion: That the sensible
world is that which we perceive by our several senses;
and that nothing is perceived by the senses beside ideas;
and that no idea or archetype of an idea can exist otherwise than in a mind. You may now, without any labori-
ous search into the sciences, without any subtlety of reason, or tedious length of discourse, oppose and baffle the
most strenuous advocate for Atheism. Those miserable
refuges, whether in an eternal succession of unthinking
causes and effects, or in a fortuitous concourse of atoms;
those wild imaginations of Vanini, Hobbes, and Spinoza:
in a word, the whole system of Atheism, is it not entirely
overthrown, by this single reflexion on the repugnancy
included in supposing the whole, or any part, even the
most rude and shapeless, of the visible world, to exist
without a Mind? Let any one of those abettors of impiety but look into his own thoughts, and there try if he

can conceive how so much as a rock, a desert, a chaos, or confused jumble of atoms; how anything at all, either sensible or imaginable, can exist independent of a Mind, and he need go no farther to be convinced of his folly. Can anything be fairer than to put a dispute on such an issue, and leave it to a man himself to see if he can conceive, even in thought, what he holds to be true in fact, and from a notional to allow it a real existence?

Hyl. It cannot be denied there is something highly serviceable to religion in what you advance. But do you not think it looks very like a notion entertained by some eminent moderns,[1] of *seeing all things in God?*

Phil. I would gladly know that opinion: pray explain it to me.

Hyl. They conceive that the soul, being immaterial, is incapable of being united with material things, so as to perceive them in themselves; but that she perceives them by her union with the substance of God, which, being spiritual, is therefore purely intelligible, or capable of being the immediate object of a spirit's thought. Besides, the Divine essence contains in it perfections correspondent to each created being; and which are, for that reason, proper to exhibit or represent them to the mind.

Phil. I do not understand how our ideas, which are things altogether passive and inert, can be the essence, or any part (or like any part) of the essence or substance of God, who is an impassive, indivisible, pure, active being. Many more difficulties and objections there are which occur at first view against this hypothesis; but I shall only add, that it is liable to all the absurdities of the common hypothesis, in making a created world exist otherwise than in the mind of a Spirit. Beside all which it hath this peculiar to itself; that it makes that material world serve to no purpose. And, if it pass

[1] The reference is to Malebranche.

for a good argument against other hypotheses in the sciences, that they suppose Nature, or the Divine wisdom, to make something in vain, or do that by tedious roundabout methods which might have been performed in a much more easy and compendious way, what shall we think of that hypothesis which supposes the whole world made in vain?

Hyl. But what say you? Are not you too of opinion that we see all things in God? If I mistake not, what you advance comes near it.

Phil. [Few men think; yet all have opinions. Hence men's opinions are superficial and confused. It is nothing strange that tenets which in themselves are ever so different, should nevertheless be confounded with each other, by those who do not consider them attentively. I shall not therefore be surprised if some men imagine that I run into the enthusiasm of Malebranche; though in truth I am very remote from it. He builds on the most abstract general ideas, which I entirely disclaim. He asserts an absolute external world, which I deny. He maintains that we are deceived by our senses, and know not the real natures or the true forms and figures of extended beings; of all which I hold the direct contrary. So that upon the whole there are no Principles more fundamentally opposite than his and mine. It must be owned that] I entirely agree with what the holy Scripture saith, 'That in God we live and move and have our being.' But that we see things in His essence, after the manner above set forth, I am far from believing. Take here in brief my meaning:—It is evident that the things I perceive are my own ideas, and that no idea can exist unless it be in a mind: nor is it less plain that these ideas or things by me perceived, either themselves or their archetypes, exist independently of *my* mind, since I know myself not to be their author, it being out of my power to determine at pleasure what particular ideas I shall be affected with upon opening my eyes or ears: they must therefore exist in some other Mind, whose Will it is they should be exhibited to me. The things, I say, immediately perceived are ideas or sensations, call them which you will. But how can any idea or sensation exist in, or be produced by, anything but a mind or spirit? This indeed is inconceivable. And to assert that which is inconceivable is to talk nonsense: is it not?

Hyl. Without doubt.

Phil. But, on the other hand, it is very conceivable that they should exist in and be produced by a Spirit; since this is no more than I daily experience in myself, inasmuch as I perceive numberless ideas; and, by an act of my will, can form a great variety of them, and raise them up in my imagination: though, it must be confessed, these creatures of the fancy are not altogether so distinct, so strong, vivid, and permanent, as those perceived by my senses—which latter are called *real things*. From all which I conclude, *there is a Mind which affects me every moment with all the sensible impressions I perceive.* And, from the variety, order, and manner of these, I conclude *the Author of them to be wise, powerful, and good, beyond comprehension.* Mark it well; I do not say, I see things by perceiving that which represents them in the intelligible Substance of God. This I do not understand; but I say, the things by me perceived are known by the understanding, and produced by the will of an infinite Spirit. And is not all this most plain and evident? Is there any more in it than what a little observation in our own minds, and that which passeth in them, not only enables us to conceive, but also obliges us to acknowledge?

Hyl. I think I understand you very clearly; and own the proof you give of a Deity seems no less evident than it is surprising. But, allowing that God is the supreme and universal Cause of all things, yet, may there not be still a Third Nature besides Spirits and Ideas? May we not admit a subordinate and limited cause of our ideas? In a word, may there not for all that be *Matter?*

Phil. How often must I inculcate the same thing? You allow the things immediately perceived by sense to exist nowhere without the mind; but there is nothing perceived by sense which is not perceived immediately: therefore there is nothing sensible that exists without the mind. The Matter, therefore, which you still insist on is something intelligible, I suppose; something that may be discovered by reason, and not by sense.

Hyl. You are in the right.

Phil. Pray let me know what reasoning your belief of Matter is grounded on; and what this Matter is, in your present sense of it.

Hyl. I find myself affected with various ideas, whereof I know I am not the cause; neither are they the cause of themselves, or of one another, or capable of subsisting by themselves, as being altogether inactive, fleeting, dependent beings. They have therefore *some* cause distinct from me and them: of which I pretend to know no more than that it is *the cause of my ideas.* And this thing, whatever it be, I call Matter.

Phil. Tell me, Hylas, hath every one a liberty to change the current proper signification attached to a common name in any language? For example, suppose a traveller should tell you that in a certain country men pass unhurt through the fire; and, upon explaining himself, you found he meant by the word *fire* that which others call *water.* Or, if he should assert that there are trees that walk upon two legs, meaning men by the term *trees.* Would you think this reasonable?

Hyl. No; I should think it very absurd. Common

custom is the standard of propriety in language. And for any man to affect speaking improperly is to pervert the use of speech, and can never serve to a better purpose than to protract and multiply disputes where there is no difference in opinion.

Phil. And doth not *Matter,* in the common current acceptation of the word, signify an extended, solid, moveable, unthinking, inactive Substance?

Hyl. It doth.

Phil. And, hath it not been made evident that no *such* substance can possibly exist? And, though it should be allowed to exist, yet how can that which is *inactive* be a *cause;* or that which is *unthinking* be a *cause of thought?* You may, indeed, if you please, annex to the word *Matter* a contrary meaning to what is vulgarly received; and tell me you understand by it, an unextended, thinking, active being, which is the cause of our ideas. But what else is this than to play with words, and run into that very fault you just now condemned with so much reason? I do by no means find fault with your reasoning, in that you collect *a* cause from the *phenomena:* but I deny that *the* cause deducible by reason can properly be termed Matter.

Hyl. There is indeed something in what you say. But I am afraid you do not thoroughly comprehend my meaning. I would by no means be thought to deny that God, or an infinite Spirit, is the Supreme Cause of all things. All I contend for is, that, subordinate to the Supreme Agent, there is a cause of a limited and inferior nature, which *concurs* in the production of our ideas, not by any act of will, or spiritual efficiency, but by that kind of action which belongs to Matter, viz. *motion.*

Phil. I find you are at every turn relapsing into your old exploded conceit, of a moveable, and consequently an extended, substance, existing without the mind. What!

Have you already forgotten you were convinced; or are you willing I should repeat what has been said on that head? In truth this is not fair dealing in you, still to suppose the being of that which you have so often acknowledged to have no being. But, not to insist farther on what has been so largely handled, I ask whether all your ideas are not perfectly passive and inert, including nothing of action in them.

Hyl. They are.

Phil. And are sensible qualities anything else but ideas?

Hyl. How often have I acknowledged that they are not.

Phil. But is not *motion* a sensible quality?

Hyl. It is.

Phil. Consequently it is no action?

Hyl. I agree with you. And indeed it is very plain that when I stir my finger, it remains passive; but my will which produced the motion is active.

Phil. Now, I desire to know, in the first place, whether, motion being allowed to be no action, you can conceive any action besides volition: and, in the second place, whether to say something and conceive nothing be not to talk nonsense: and, lastly, whether, having considered the premises, you do not perceive that to suppose any efficient or active Cause of our ideas, other than *Spirit,* is highly absurd and unreasonable?

Hyl. I give up the point entirely. But, though Matter may not be a cause, yet what hinders its being an *instrument,* subservient to the supreme Agent in the production of our ideas?

Phil. An instrument say you; pray what may be the figure, springs, wheels, and motions, of that instrument?

Hyl. Those I pretend to determine nothing of, both

the substance and its qualities being entirely unknown to me.

Phil. What? You are then of opinion it is made up of unknown parts, that it hath unknown motions, and an unknown shape?

Hyl. I do not believe that it hath any figure or motion at all, being already convinced, that no sensible qualities can exist in an unperceiving substance.

Phil. But what notion is it possible to frame of an instrument void of all sensible qualities, even extension itself?

Hyl. I do not pretend to have any notion of it.

Phil. And what reason have you to think this unknown, this inconceivable Somewhat doth exist? Is it that you imagine God cannot act as well without it; or that you find by experience the use of some such thing, when you form ideas in your own mind?

Hyl. You are always teasing me for reasons of my belief. Pray what reasons have you not to believe it?

Phil. It is to me a sufficient reason not to believe the existence of anything, if I see no reason for believing it. But, not to insist on reasons for believing, you will not so much as let me know *what it is* you would have me believe; since you say you have no manner of notion of it. After all, let me entreat you to consider whether it be like a philosopher, or even like a man of common sense, to pretend to believe you know not what, and you know not why.

Hyl. Hold, Philonous. When I tell you Matter is an *instrument*, I do not mean altogether nothing. It is true I know not the particular kind of instrument; but, however, I have some notion of *instrument in general*, which I apply to it.

Phil. But what if it should prove that there is something, even in the most general notion of *instrument*, as

taken in a distinct sense from *cause,* which makes the use
of it inconsistent with the Divine attributes?

Hyl. Make that appear and I shall give up the point.

Phil. What mean you by the general nature or notion
of *instrument?*

Hyl. That which is common to all particular instruments composeth the general notion.

Phil. Is it not common to all instruments, that they
are applied to the doing those things only which cannot
be performed by the mere act of our wills? Thus, for
instance, I never use an instrument to move my finger,
because it is done by a volition. But I should use one
if I were to remove part of a rock, or tear up a tree by
the roots. Are you of the same mind? Or, can you
shew any example where an instrument is made use of
in producing an effect *immediately* depending on the will
of the agent?

Hyl. I own I cannot.

Phil. How therefore can you suppose that an All-
perfect Spirit, on whose Will all things have an absolute
and immediate dependence, should need an instrument
in his operations, or, not needing it, make use of it?
Thus it seems to me that you are obliged to own the use
of a lifeless inactive instrument to be incompatible with
the infinite perfection of God; that is, by your own
confession, to give up the point.

Hyl. It doth not readily occur what I can answer you.

Phil. But, methinks you should be ready to own the
truth, when it has been fairly proved to you. We indeed,
who are beings of finite powers, are forced to make use
of instruments. And the use of an instrument sheweth
the agent to be limited by rules of another's prescription,
and that he cannot obtain his end but in such a way, and
by such conditions. Whence it seems a clear consequence, that the supreme unlimited Agent useth no tool

or instrument at all. The will of an Omnipotent Spirit is no sooner exerted than executed, without the application of means; which, if they are employed by inferior agents, it is not upon account of any real efficacy that is in them, or necessary aptitude to produce any effect, but merely in compliance with the laws of nature, or those conditions prescribed to them by the First Cause, who is Himself above all limitation or prescription whatsoever.

Hyl. I will no longer maintain that Matter is an instrument. However, I would not be understood to give up its existence neither; since, notwithstanding what hath been said, it may still be an *occasion.*

Phil. How many shapes is your Matter to take? Or, how often must it be proved not to exist, before you are content to part with it? But, to say no more of this (though by all the laws of disputation I may justly blame you for so frequently changing the signification of the principal term)—I would fain know what you mean by affirming that matter is an occasion, having already denied it to be a cause. And, when you have shewn in what sense you understand *occasion,* pray, in the next place, be pleased to shew me what reason induceth you to believe there is such an occasion of our ideas?

Hyl. As to the first point: by *occasion* I mean an inactive unthinking being, at the presence whereof God excites ideas in our minds.

Phil. And what may be the nature of that inactive unthinking being?

Hyl. I know nothing of its nature.

Phil. Proceed then to the second point, and assign some reason why we should allow an existence to this inactive, unthinking, unknown thing.

Hyl. When we see ideas produced in our minds, after

an orderly and constant manner, it is natural to think they have some fixed and regular occasions, at the presence of which they are excited.

Phil. You acknowledge then God alone to be the cause of our ideas, and that He causes them at the presence of those occasions?

Hyl. That is my opinion.

Phil. Those things which you say are present to God, without doubt He perceives.

Hyl. Certainly; otherwise they could not be to Him an occasion of acting.

Phil. Not to insist now on your making sense of this hypothesis, or answering all the puzzling questions and difficulties it is liable to: I only ask whether the order and regularity observable in the series of our ideas, or the course of nature, be not sufficiently accounted for by the wisdom and power of God; and whether it doth not derogate from those attributes, to suppose He is influenced, directed, or put in mind, when and what He is to act, by an unthinking substance? And, lastly, whether, in case I granted all you contend for, it would make anything to your purpose; it not being easy to conceive how the external or absolute existence of an unthinking substance, distinct from its being perceived, can be inferred from my allowing that there are certain things perceived by the mind of God, which are to Him the occasion of producing ideas in us?

Hyl. I am perfectly at a loss what to think, this notion of *occasion* seeming now altogether as groundless as the rest.

Phil. Do you not at length perceive that in all these different acceptations of *Matter,* you have been only supposing you know not what, for no manner of reason, and to no kind of use?

Hyl. I freely own myself less fond of my notions

since they have been so accurately examined. But still, methinks, I have some confused perception that there is such a thing as *Matter*.

Phil. Either you perceive the being of Matter immediately or mediately. If immediately, pray inform me by which of the senses you perceive it. If mediately, let me know by what reasoning it is inferred from those things which you perceive immediately. So much for the perception. Then for the Matter itself, I ask whether it is object, *substratum,* cause, instrument, or occasion? You have already pleaded for each of these, shifting your notions, and making Matter to appear sometimes in one shape, then in another. And what you have offered hath been disapproved and rejected by yourself. If you have anything new to advance I would gladly hear it.

Hyl. I think I have already offered all I had to say on those heads. I am at a loss what more to urge.

Phil. And yet you are loath to part with your old prejudice. But, to make you quit it more easily, I desire that, beside what has been hitherto suggested, you will farther consider whether, upon supposition that Matter exists, you can possibly conceive how you should be affected by it. Or, supposing it did not exist, whether it be not evident you might for all that be affected with the same ideas you now are, and consequently have the very same reasons to believe its existence that you now can have.

Hyl. I acknowledge it is possible we might perceive all things just as we do now, though there was no Matter in the world; neither can I conceive, if there be Matter, how it should produce any idea in our minds. And, I do farther grant you have entirely satisfied me that it is impossible there should be such a thing as Matter in any of the foregoing acceptations. But still I cannot help supposing that there is *Matter* in some sense or other. *What that is* I do not indeed pretend to determine.

Phil. I do not expect you should define exactly the nature of that unknown being. Only be pleased to tell me whether it is a Substance; and if so, whether you can suppose a Substance without accidents; or, in case you suppose it to have accidents or qualities, I desire you will let me know what those qualities are, at least what is meant by Matter's supporting them?

Hyl. We have already argued on those points. I have no more to say to them. But, to prevent any farther questions, let me tell you I at present understand by *Matter* neither substance nor accident, thinking nor extended being, neither cause, instrument, nor occasion, but Something entirely unknown, distinct from all these.

Phil. It seems then you include in your present notion of Matter nothing but the general abstract idea of *entity*.

Hyl. Nothing else; save only that I superadd to this general idea the negation of all those particular things, qualities, or ideas, that I perceive, imagine, or in anywise apprehend.

Phil. Pray where do you suppose this unknown Matter to exist?

Hyl. Oh Philonous! now you think you have entangled me; for, if I say it exists in place, then you will infer that it exists in the mind, since it is agreed that place or extension exists only in the mind. But I am not ashamed to own my ignorance. I know not where it exists; only I am sure it exists not in place. There is a negative answer for you. And you must expect no other to all the questions you put for the future about Matter.

Phil. Since you will not tell me where it exists, be

pleased to inform me after what manner you suppose it to exist, or what you mean by its *existence?*

Hyl. It neither thinks nor acts, neither perceives nor is perceived.

Phil. But what is there positive in your abstracted notion of its existence?

Hyl. Upon a nice observation, I do not find I have any positive notion or meaning at all. I tell you again, I am not ashamed to own my ignorance. I know not what is meant by its *existence,* or how it exists.

Phil. Continue, good Hylas, to act the same ingenuous part, and tell me sincerely whether you can frame a distinct idea of Entity in general, prescinded from and exclusive of all thinking and corporeal beings, all particular things whatsoever.

Hyl. Hold, let me think a little ——I profess, Philonous, I do not find that I can. At first glance, methought I had some dilute and airy notion of Pure Entity in abstract; but, upon closer attention, it hath quite vanished out of sight. The more I think on it, the more am I confirmed in my prudent resolution of giving none but negative answers, and not pretending to the least degree of any positive knowledge or conception of Matter, its *where,* its *how,* its *entity,* or anything belonging to it.

Phil. When, therefore, you speak of the existence of Matter, you have not any notion in your mind?

Hyl. None at all.

Phil. Pray tell me if the case stands not thus:—At first, from a belief of material substance, you would have it that the immediate objects existed without the mind; then that they are archetypes; then causes; next instruments; then occasions: lastly, *something in general,* which being interpreted proves *nothing.* So Matter comes to nothing. What think you, Hylas, is not this a fair summary of your whole proceeding?

Hyl. Be that as it will, yet I still insist upon it, that *our* not being able to conceive a thing is no argument against its existence.

Phil. That from a cause, effect, operation, sign, or other circumstance, there may reasonably be inferred the existence of a thing not immediately perceived; and that it were absurd for any man to argue against the existence of that thing, from his having no direct and positive notion of it, I freely own. But, where there is nothing of all this; where neither reason nor revelation induces us to believe the existence of a thing; where we have not even a relative notion of it; where an abstraction is made from perceiving and being perceived, from Spirit and idea: lastly, where there is not so much as the most inadequate or faint idea pretended to—I will not indeed thence conclude against the reality of any notion, or existence of anything; but my inference shall be, that you mean nothing at all; that you employ words to no manner of purpose, without any design or signification whatsoever. And I leave it to you to consider how mere jargon should be treated.

Hyl. To deal frankly with you, Philonous, your arguments seem in themselves unanswerable; but they have not so great an effect on me as to produce that entire conviction, that hearty acquiescence, which attends demonstration. I find myself still relapsing into an obscure surmise of I know not what, *matter.*

Phil. But, are you not sensible, Hylas, that two things must concur to take away all scruple, and work a plenary assent in the mind? Let a visible object be set in never so clear a light, yet, if there is any imperfection in the sight, or if the eye is not directed towards it, it will not be distinctly seen. And though a demonstration be never so well grounded and fairly proposed, yet, if there is withal a stain of prejudice, or a wrong bias on the understanding, can it be expected on a sudden to perceive clearly, and adhere firmly to the truth? No; there is need of time and pains: the attention must be awakened and detained by a frequent repetition of the same thing placed oft in the same, oft in different lights. I have said it already, and find I must still repeat and inculcate, that it is an unaccountable license you take, in pretending to maintain you know not what, for you know not what reason, to you know not what purpose. Can this be paralleled in any art of science, any sect or profession of men? Or is there anything so bare-facedly groundless and unreasonable to be met with even in the lowest of common conversation? But, per-haps you will still say, Matter may exist; though at the same time you neither know *what is meant* by *Matter,* or by its *existence.* This indeed is surprising, and the more so because it is altogether voluntary [and of your own head], you not being led to it by any one reason; for I challenge you to shew me that thing in nature which needs Matter to explain or account for it.

Hyl. The *reality* of things cannot be maintained with-out supposing the existence of Matter. And is not this, think you, a good reason why I should be earnest in its defence?

Phil. The reality of things! What things? sensible or intelligible?

Hyl. Sensible things.

Phil. My glove for example?

Hyl. That, or any other thing perceived by the senses.

Phil. But to fix on some particular thing. Is it not a sufficient evidence to me of the existence of this *glove,* that J see it, and feel it, and wear it? Or, if this will not do, how is it possible I should be assured of the reality of this thing, which I actually see in this place, by supposing that some unknown thing, which I never did or can see, exists after an unknown manner, in an unknown place, or in no place at all? How can the supposed reality of that which is intangible be a proof that anything tangible really exists? Or, of that which is invisible, that any visible thing, or, in general of anything which is imperceptible, that a perceptible exists? Do but explain this and I shall think nothing too hard for you.

Hyl. Upon the whole, I am content to own the existence of Matter is highly improbable; but the direct and absolute impossibility of it does not appear to me.

Phil. But granting Matter to be possible, yet, upon that account merely, it can have no more claim to existence than a golden mountain, or a centaur.

Hyl. I acknowledge it; but still you do not deny it is possible; and that which is possible, for aught you know, may actually exist.

Phil. I deny it to be possible; and have, if I mistake not, evidently proved, from your own concessions, that it is not. In the common sense of the word *Matter,* is there any more implied than an extended, solid, figured, moveable substance, existing without the mind? And have not you acknowledged, over and over, that you have seen evident reason for denying the possibility of such a substance?

Hyl. True, but that is only one sense of the term *Matter.*

Phil. But is it not the only proper genuine received sense? And, if Matter, in such a sense, be proved impossible, may it not be thought with good grounds absolutely impossible? Else how could anything be proved impossible? Or, indeed, how could there be any proof at all one way or other, to a man who takes the liberty to unsettle and change the common signification of words?

Hyl. I thought philosophers might be allowed to speak more accurately than the vulgar, and were not always confined to the common acceptation of a term.

Phil. But this now mentioned is the common received sense among philosophers themselves. But, not to insist on that, have you not been allowed to take Matter in what sense you pleased? And have you not used this privilege in the utmost extent; sometimes entirely changing, at others leaving out, or putting into the definition of it whatever, for the present, best served your design, contrary to all the known rules of reason and logic? And hath not this shifting, unfair method of yours spun out our dispute to an unnecessary length; Matter having been particularly examined, and by your own confession refuted in each of those senses? And can any more be required to prove the absolute impossibility of a thing, than the proving it impossible in every particular sense that either you or any one else understands it in?

Hyl. But I am not so thoroughly satisfied that you have proved the impossibility of Matter, in the last most obscure abstracted and indefinite sense.

Phil. When is a thing shewn to be impossible?

Hyl. When a repugnancy is demonstrated between the ideas comprehended in its definition.

Phil. But where there are no ideas, there no repugnancy can be demonstrated between ideas?

Hyl. I agree with you.

Phil. Now, in that which you call the obscure indefinite sense of the word *Matter,* it is plain, by your own confession, there was included no idea at all, no sense except an unknown sense; which is the same thing as none. You are not, therefore, to expect I should prove a repugnancy between ideas, where there are no ideas; or the impossibility of Matter taken in an *unknown* sense, that is, no sense at all. My business was only to shew you meant *nothing;* and this you were brought to own. So that, in all your various senses, you have been shewed either to mean nothing at all, or, if anything, an absurdity. And if this be not sufficient to prove the impossibility of a thing, I desire you will let me know what is.

Hyl. I acknowledge you have proved that Matter is impossible; nor do I see what more can be said in defence of it. But, at the same time that I give up this, I suspect all my other notions. For surely none could be more seemingly evident than this once was: and yet it now seems as false and absurd as ever it did true before. But I think we have discussed the point sufficiently for the present. The remaining part of the day I would willingly spend in running over in my thoughts the several heads of this morning's conversation, and to-morrow shall be glad to meet you here again about the same time.

Phil. I will not fail to attend you.

THE THIRD DIALOGUE

Philonous. Tell me, Hylas, what are the fruits of yesterday's meditation? Has it confirmed you in the same mind you were in at parting? or have you since seen cause to change your opinion?

Hylas. Truly my opinion is that all our opinions are alike vain and uncertain. What we approve to-day, we condemn to-morrow. We keep a stir about knowledge, and spend our lives in the pursuit of it, when, alas! we know nothing all the while: nor do I think it possible for us ever to know anything in this life. Our faculties are too narrow and too few. Nature certainly never intended us for speculation.

Phil. What! Say you we can know nothing, Hylas?

Hyl. There is not that single thing in the world whereof we can know the real nature, or what it is in itself.

Phil. Will you tell me I do not really know what fire or water is?

Hyl. You may indeed know that fire appears hot, and water fluid; but this is no more than knowing what sensations are produced in your own mind, upon the application of fire and water to your organs of sense. Their internal constitution, their true and real nature, you are utterly in the dark as to *that*.

Phil. Do I not know this to be a real stone that I stand on, and that which I see before my eyes to be a real tree?

Hyl. Know? No, it is impossible you or any man alive should know it. All you know is, that you have such a certain idea or appearance in your own mind. But what is this to the real tree or stone? I tell you that colour, figure, and hardness, which you perceive, are not the real natures of those things, or in the least like them. The same may be said of all other real things, or corporeal substances, which compose the world. They have none of them anything of themselves, like those sensible qualities by us perceived. We should not therefore pretend to affirm or know anything of them, as they are in their own nature.

Phil. But surely, Hylas, I can distinguish gold, for example, from iron: and how could this be, if I knew not what either truly was?

Hyl. Believe me, Philonous, you can only distinguish between your own ideas. That yellowness, that

weight, and other sensible qualities, think you they are
really in the gold? They are only relative to the senses,
and have no absolute existence in nature. And in pretending to distinguish the species of real things, by the
appearances in your mind, you may perhaps act as
wisely as he that should conclude two men were of a
different species, because their clothes were not of the
same colour.

Phil. It seems, then, we are altogether put off with
the appearance of things, and those false ones too. The
very meat I eat, and the cloth I wear, have nothing in
them like what I see and feel.

Hyl. Even so.

Phil. But is it not strange the whole world should be
thus imposed on, and so foolish as to believe their
senses? And yet I know not how it is, but men eat,
and drink, and sleep, and perform all the offices of life,
as comfortably and conveniently as if they really knew
the things they are conversant about.

Hyl. They do so: but you know ordinary practice
does not require a nicety of speculative knowledge.
Hence the vulgar retain their mistakes, and for all that
make a shift to bustle through the affairs of life. But
philosophers know better things.

Phil. You mean, they *know* that they *know nothing.*

Hyl. That is the very top and perfection of human
knowledge.

Phil. But are you all this while in earnest, Hylas;
and are you seriously persuaded that you know nothing
real in the world? Suppose you are going to write,
would you not call for pen, ink, and paper, like another
man; and do you not know what it is you call for?

Hyl. How often must I tell you, that I know not the
real nature of any one thing in the universe? I may
indeed upon occasion make use of pen, ink, and paper.

But what any one of them is in its own true nature, I declare positively I know not. And the same is true with regard to every other corporeal thing. And, what is more, we are not only ignorant of the true and real nature of things, but even of their existence. It cannot be denied that we perceive such certain appearances or ideas; but it cannot be concluded from thence that bodies really exist. Nay, now I think on it, I must, agreeably to my former concessions, farther declare that it is impossible any *real* corporeal thing should exist in nature.

Phil. You amaze me. Was ever anything more wild and extravagant than the notions you now maintain: and is it not evident you are led into all these extravagances by the belief of *material substance?* This makes you dream of those unknown natures in everything. It is this occasions your distinguishing between the reality and sensible appearances of things. It is to this you are indebted for being ignorant of what everybody else knows perfectly well. Nor is this all: you are not only ignorant of the true nature of everything, but you know not whether anything really exists, or whether there are any true natures at all; forasmuch as you attribute to your material beings an absolute or external existence, wherein you suppose their reality consists. And, as you are forced in the end to acknowledge such an existence means either a direct repugnancy, or nothing at all, it follows that you are obliged to pull down your own hypothesis of material Substance, and positively to deny the real existence of any part of the universe. And so you are plunged into the deepest and most deplorable scepticism that ever man was. Tell me, Hylas, is it not as I say?

Hyl. I agree with you. *Material substance* was no more than an hypothesis; and a false and groundless one too. I will no longer spend my breath in defence of it.

But whatever hypothesis you advance, or whatsoever scheme of things you introduce in its stead, I doubt not it will appear every whit as false: let me but be allowed to question you upon it. That is, suffer me to serve you in your own kind, and I warrant it shall conduct you through as many perplexities and contradictions, to the very same state of scepticism that I myself am in at present.

Phil. I assure you, Hylas, I do not pretend to frame any hypothesis at all. I am of a vulgar cast, simple enough to believe my senses, and leave things as I find them. To be plain, it is my opinion that the real things are those very things I see, and feel, and perceive by my senses. These I know; and, finding they answer all the necessities and purposes of life, have no reason to be solicitous about any other unknown beings. A piece of sensible bread, for instance, would stay my stomach better than ten thousand times as much of that insensible, unintelligible, real bread you speak of. It is likewise my opinion that colours and other sensible qualities are on the objects. I cannot for my life help thinking that snow is white, and fire hot. You indeed, who by *snow* and *fire* mean certain external, unperceived, unperceiving substances, are in the right to deny whiteness or heat to be affections inherent in *them*. But I, who understand by those words the things I see and feel, am obliged to think like other folks. And, as I am no sceptic with regard to the nature of things, so neither am I as to their existence. That a thing should be really perceived by my senses, and at the same time not really exist, is to me a plain contradiction; since I cannot prescind or abstract, even in thought, the existence of a sensible thing from its being perceived. Wood, stones, fire, water, flesh, iron, and the like things, which I name and discourse of, are things that I know. And I should not have known them but that I perceived them by my senses; and things perceived by the senses are immediately perceived; and things immediately perceived are ideas; and ideas cannot exist without the mind; their existence therefore consist in being perceived; when, therefore, they are actually perceived there can be no doubt of their existence. Away then with all that scepticism, all those ridiculous philosophical doubts. What a jest is it for a philosopher to question the existence of sensible things, till he hath it proved to him from the veracity of God; or to pretend our knowledge in this point falls short of intuition or demonstration! I might as well doubt of my own being, as of the being of those things I actually see and feel.

Hyl. Not so fast, Philonous: you say you cannot conceive how sensible things should exist without the mind. Do you not?

Phil. I do.

Hyl. Supposing you were annihilated, cannot you conceive it possible that things perceivable by sense may still exist?

Phil. I can; but then it must be in another mind. When I deny sensible things an existence out of the mind, I do not mean my mind in particular, but all minds. Now, it is plain they have an existence exterior to my mind; since I find them by experience to be independent of it. There is therefore some other Mind wherein they exist, during the intervals between the times of my perceiving them: as likewise they did before my birth, and would do after my supposed annihilation. And, as the same is true with regard to all other finite created spirits, it necessarily follows there is an *omnipresent eternal Mind,* which knows and comprehends all things, and exhibits them to our view in such a manner, and according to such rules, as He Himself hath ordained, and are by us termed the *laws of nature.*

Hyl. Answer me, Philonous. Are all our ideas perfectly inert beings? Or have they any agency included in them?

Phil. They are altogether passive and inert.

Hyl. And is not God an agent, a being purely active?

Phil. I acknowledge it.

Hyl. No idea therefore can be like unto, or represent the nature of God?

Phil. It cannot.

Hyl. Since therefore you have no *idea* of the mind of God, how can you conceive it possible that things should exist in His mind? Or, if you can conceive the mind of God, without having an idea of it, why may not I be allowed to conceive the existence of Matter, notwithstanding I have no idea of it?

Phil. As to your first question: I own I have properly no *idea,* either of God or any other spirit; for these being active, cannot be represented by things perfectly inert, as our ideas are. I do nevertheless know that I, who am a spirit or thinking substance, exist as certainly as I know my ideas exist. Farther, I know what I mean by the terms *I* and *myself;* and I know this immediately or intuitively, though I do not perceive it as I perceive a triangle, a colour, or a sound. The Mind, Spirit, or Soul is that indivisible unextended thing which thinks, acts, and perceives. I say *indivisible,* because unextended; and *unextended,* because extended, figured, moveable things are ideas; and that which perceives ideas, which thinks and wills, is plainly itself no idea, nor like an idea. Ideas are things inactive, and perceived. And Spirits a sort of beings altogether different from them. I do not therefore say my soul is an idea, or like an idea. However, taking the word *idea* in a large sense, my soul may be said to furnish me with an idea, that is, an image or likeness of God—though indeed extremely inadequate. For, all the notion I have of God is obtained by reflecting on my own soul, heightening its powers, and removing its imperfections. I have, therefore, though not an inactive idea, yet in *myself* some sort of an active thinking image of the Deity. And, though I perceive Him not by sense, yet I have a notion of Him, or know Him by reflexion and reasoning. My own mind and my own ideas I have an immediate knowledge of; and, by the help of these, do mediately apprehend the possibility of the existence of other spirits and ideas. Farther, from my own being, and from the dependency I find in myself and my ideas, I do, by an act of reason, necessarily infer the existence of a God, and of all created things in the mind of God. So much for your first question. For the second: I suppose by this time you can answer it yourself. For you neither perceive Matter objectively, as you do an inactive being or idea; nor know it, as you do yourself, by a reflex act; neither do you mediately apprehend it by similitude of the one or the other; nor yet collect it by reasoning from that which you know immediately. All which makes the case of *Matter* widely different from that of the *Deity*.

[*Hyl.* You say your own soul supplies you with some sort of an idea or image of God. But, at the same time, you acknowledge you have, properly speaking, no *idea* of your own soul. You even affirm that spirits are a sort of beings altogether different from ideas. Consequently that no idea can be like a spirit. We have therefore no idea of any spirit. You admit nevertheless that there is spiritual Substance, although you have no idea of it; while you deny there can be such a thing as material Substance, because you have no notion or idea of it.

Is this fair dealing? To act consistently, you must either admit Matter or reject Spirit. What say you to this?

Phil. I say, in the first place, that I do not deny the existence of material substance, merely because I have no notion of it, but because the notion of it is inconsistent; or, in other words, because it is repugnant that there should be a notion of it. Many things, for aught I know, may exist, whereof neither I nor any other man hath or can have any idea or notion whatsoever. But then those things must be possible, that is, nothing inconsistent must be included in their definition. I say, secondly, that, although we believe things to exist which we do not perceive, yet we may not believe that any particular thing exists, without some reason for such belief: but I have no reason for believing the existence of Matter. I have no immediate intuition thereof: neither can I immediately from my sensations, ideas, notions, actions, or passions, infer an unthinking, unperceiving, inactive Substance—either by probable deduction, or necessary consequence. Whereas the being of my Self, that is, my own soul, mind, or thinking principle, I evidently know by reflexion. You will forgive me if I repeat the same things in answer to the same objections. In the very notion or definition of *material Substance,* there is included a manifest repugnance and inconsistency. But this cannot be said of the notion of Spirit. That ideas should exist in what doth not perceive, or be produced by what doth not act, is repugnant. But, it is no repugnancy to say that a perceiving thing should be the subject of ideas, or an active thing the cause of them. It is granted we have neither an immediate evidence nor a demonstrative knowledge of the existence of other finite spirits; but it will not thence follow that such spirits are on a foot with material substances: if to suppose the one be inconsistent, and it be not inconsistent to suppose the other; if the one can be inferred by no argument, and there is a probability for the other; if we see signs and effects indicating distinct finite agents like ourselves, and see no sign or symptom whatever that leads to a rational belief of Matter. I say, lastly, that I have a notion of Spirit, though I have not, strictly speaking, an idea of it. I do not perceive it as an idea, or by means of an idea, but know it by reflexion.

Hyl. Notwithstanding all you have said, to me it seems that, according to your own way of thinking, and in consequence of your own principles, it should follow that *you* are only a system of floating ideas, without any substance to support them. Words are not to be used without a meaning. And, as there is no more meaning in *spiritual Substance* than in *material Substance,* the one is to be exploded as well as the other.

Phil. How often must I repeat, that I know or am conscious of my own being; and that *I myself* am not my ideas, but somewhat else, a thinking, active principle that perceives, knows, wills, and operates about ideas. I know that I, one and the same self, perceive both colours and sounds: that a colour cannot perceive a sound, nor a sound a colour: that I am therefore one individual principle, distinct from colour and sound; and, for the same reason, from all other sensible things and inert ideas. But, I am not in like manner conscious either of the existence or essense of Matter. On the contrary, I know that nothing inconsistent can exist, and that the existence of Matter implies an inconsistency. Farther, I know what I mean when I affirm that there is a spiritual substance or support of ideas, that is, that a spirit knows and perceives ideas. But, I do not know what is meant when it is said that an unperceiving

substance hath inherent in it and supports either ideas
or the archetypes of ideas. There is therefore upon the
whole no parity of case between Spirit and Matter.]

Hyl. I own myself satisfied in this point. But, do you
in earnest think the real existence of sensible things consists in their being actually perceived? If so; how comes
it that all mankind distinguish between them? Ask the
first man you meet, and he shall tell you, *to be perceived*
is one thing, and *to exist* is another.

Phil. I am content, Hylas, to appeal to the common
sense of the world for the truth of my notion. Ask the
gardener why he thinks yonder cherry-tree exists in the
garden, and he shall tell you, because he sees and feels
it; in a word, because he perceives it by his senses. Ask
him why he thinks an orange-tree not to be there, and he
shall tell you, because he does not perceive it. What he
perceives by sense, that he terms a real being, and saith
it *is* or *exists;* but, that which is not perceivable, the
same, he saith, hath no being.

Hyl. Yes, Philonous, I grant the existence of a sensible thing consists in being perceivable, but not in being
actually perceived.

Phil. And what is perceivable but an idea? And can
an idea exist without being actually perceived? These
are points long since agreed between us.

Hyl. But, be your opinion never so true, yet surely
you will not deny it is shocking, and contrary to the
common sense of men. Ask the fellow whether yonder
tree hath an existence out of his mind: what answer
think you he would make?

Phil. The same that I should myself, to wit, that it
doth exist out of his mind. But then to a Christian it
cannot surely be shocking to say, the real tree, existing
without his mind, is truly known and comprehended by

(that is *exists in*) the infinite mind of God. Probably
he may not at first glance be aware of the direct and
immediate proof there is of this; inasmuch as the very
being of a tree, or any other sensible thing, implies
a mind wherein it is. But the point itself he cannot
deny. The question between the Materialists and me
is not, whether things have a *real* existence out of the
mind of this or that person, but, whether they have an
absolute existence, distinct from being perceived by God,
and exterior to *all* minds. This indeed some heathens
and philosophers have affirmed, but whoever entertains
notions of the Deity suitable to the Holy Scriptures will
be of another opinion.

Hyl. But, according to your notions, what difference
is there between real things, and chimeras formed by
the imagination, or the visions of a dream—since they
are all equally in the mind?

Phil. The ideas formed by the imagination are faint
and indistinct; they have, besides, an entire dependence
on the will. But the ideas perceived by sense, that is,
real things, are more vivid and clear; and, being imprinted on the mind by a spirit distinct from us, have
not the like dependence on our will. There is therefore
no danger of confounding these with the foregoing: and
there is as little of confounding them with the visions
of a dream, which are dim, irregular, and confused.
And, though they should happen to be never so lively
and natural, yet, by their not being connected, and of a
piece with the preceding and subsequent transactions
of our lives, they might easily be distinguished from
realities. In short, by whatever method you distinguish
things from *chimeras* on your scheme, the same, it is
evident, will hold also upon mine. For, it must be, I
presume, by some perceived difference; and I am not
for depriving you of any one thing that you perceive.

Hyl. But still, Philonous, you hold, there is nothing in the world but spirits and ideas. And this, you must needs acknowledge, sounds very oddly.

Phil. I own the word *idea,* not being commonly used for *thing,* sounds something out of the way. My reason for using it was, because a necessary relation to the mind is understood to be implied by that term; and it is now commonly used by philosophers to denote the immediate objects of the understanding. But, however oddly the proposition may sound in words, yet it includes nothing so very strange or shocking in its sense; which in effect amounts to no more than this, to wit, that there are only things perceiving, and things perceived; or that every unthinking being is necessarily, and from the very nature of its existence, perceived by some mind; if not by a finite created mind, yet certainly by the infinite mind of God, in whom 'we live, and move, and have our being.' Is this as strange as to say, the sensible qualities are not on the objects: or that we cannot be sure of the existence of things, or know anything of their real natures— though we both see and feel them, and perceive them by all our senses?

Hyl. And, in consequence of this, must we not think there are no such things as physical or corporeal causes; but that a Spirit is the immediate cause of all the phenomena in nature? Can there be anything more extravagant than this?

Phil. Yes, it is infinitely more extravagant to say— a thing which is inert operates on the mind, and which is unperceiving is the cause of our perceptions, [without any regard either to consistency, or the old known axiom, *Nothing can give to another that which it hath not itself*]. Besides, that which to you, I know not for what reason, seems so extravagant is no more than the Holy Scriptures assert in a hundred places. In them God is represented as the sole and immediate Author of all those effects which some heathens and philosophers are wont to ascribe to Nature, Matter, Fate, or the like unthinking principle. This is so much the constant language of Scripture that it were needless to confirm it by citations.

Hyl. You are not aware, Philonous, that, in making God the immediate Author of all the motions in nature, you make Him the Author of murder, sacrilege, adultery, and the like heinous sins.

Phil. In answer to that, I observe, first, that the imputation of guilt is the same, whether a person commits an action with or without an instrument. In case therefore you suppose God to act by the mediation of an instrument, or occasion, called *Matter,* you as truly make Him the author of sin as I, who think Him the immediate agent in all those operations vulgarly ascribed to Nature. I farther observe that sin or moral turpitude doth not consist in the outward physical action, or motion, but in the internal deviation of the will from the laws of reason and religion. This is plain, in that the killing an enemy in a battle, or putting a criminal legally to death, is not thought sinful; though the outward act be the very same with that in the case of murder. Since, therefore, sin doth not consist in the physical action, the making God an immediate cause of all such actions is not making Him the Author of sin. Lastly, I have nowhere said that God is the only agent who produces all the motions in bodies. It is true I have denied there are any other agents besides spirits; but this is very consistent with allowing to thinking rational beings, in the production of motions, the use of limited powers, ultimately indeed derived from God, but immediately under the direction of their own wills, which is sufficient to entitle them to all the guilt of their actions.

Hyl. But the denying Matter, Philonous, or corporeal Substance; there is the point. You can never persuade me that this is not repugnant to the universal sense of mankind. Were our dispute to be determined by most voices, I am confident you would give up the point, without gathering the votes.

Phil. I wish both our opinions were fairly stated and submitted to the judgment of men who had plain common sense, without the prejudices of a learned education. Let me be represented as one who trusts his senses, who thinks he knows the things he sees and feels, and entertains no doubts of their existence; and you fairly set forth with all your doubts, your paradoxes, and your scepticism about you, and I shall willingly acquiesce in the determination of any indifferent person. That there is no substance wherein ideas can exist beside spirit is to me evident. And that the objects immediately perceived are ideas, is on all hands agreed. And that sensible qualities are objects immediately perceived no one can deny. It is therefore evident there can be no *substratum* of those qualities but spirit; *in* which they exist, not by way of mode or property, but as a thing perceived in that which perceives it. I deny therefore that there is any unthinking *substratum* of the objects of sense, and *in that acceptation* that there is any material substance. But if by *material substance* is meant only *sensible body*—that which is seen and felt (and the unphilosophical part of the world, I dare say, mean no more)—then I am more certain of matter's existence than you or any other philosopher pretend to be. If there be anything which makes the generality of mankind averse from the notions I espouse: it is a misapprehension that I deny the reality of sensible things. But, as it is you who are guilty of that, and not I, it follows that in truth their aversion is against your

notions and not mine. I do therefore assert that I am
as certain as of my own being, that there are bodies or
corporeal substances (meaning the things I perceive by
my senses); and that, granting this, the bulk of mankind will take no thought about, nor think themselves at
all concerned in the fate of those unknown natures, and
philosophical quiddities, which some men are so fond of.

Hyl. What say you to this? Since, according to you,
men judge of the reality of things by their senses, how
can a man be mistaken in thinking the moon a plain lucid
surface, about a foot in diameter; or a square tower,
seen at a distance, round; or an oar, with one end in the
water, crooked?

Phil. He is not mistaken with regard to the ideas he
actually perceives, but in the inferences he makes from
his present perceptions. Thus, in the case of the oar,
what he immediately perceives by sight is certainly
crooked; and so far he is in the right. But if he thence
conclude that upon taking the oar out of the water he
shall perceive the same crookedness; or that it would
affect his touch as crooked things are wont to do: in that
he is mistaken. In like manner, if he shall conclude from
what he perceives in one station, that, in case he advances towards the moon or tower, he should still be
affected with the like ideas, he is mistaken. But his
mistake lies not in what he perceives immediately, and
at present, (it being a manifest contradiction to suppose
he should err in respect of that) but in the wrong judgment he makes concerning the ideas he apprehends to be
connected with those immediately perceived; or, concerning the ideas that, from what he perceives at present, he imagines would be perceived in other circumstances. The case is the same with regard to the
Copernican system. We do not here perceive any motion
of the earth: but it were erroneous thence to conclude,

that, in case we were placed at as great a distance from that as we are now from the other planets, we should not then perceive its motion.

Hyl. I understand you; and must needs own you say things plausible enough. But, give me leave to put you in mind of one thing. Pray, Philonous, were you not formerly as positive that Matter existed, as you are now that it does not?

Phil. I was. But here lies the difference. Before, my positiveness was founded, without examination, upon prejudice; but now, after inquiry, upon evidence.

Hyl. After all, it seems our dispute is rather about words than things. We agree in the thing, but differ in the name. That we are affected with ideas *from without* is evident; and it is no less evident that there must be (I will not say archetypes, but) Powers without the mind, corresponding to those ideas. And, as these Powers cannot subsist by themselves, there is some subject of them necessarily to be admitted; which I call *Matter,* and you call *Spirit.* This is all the difference.

Phil. Pray, Hylas, is that powerful Being, or subject of powers, extended?

Hyl. It hath not extension; but it hath the power to raise in you the idea of extension.

Phil. It is therefore itself unextended?

Hyl. I grant it.

Phil. Is it not also active?

Hyl. Without doubt. Otherwise, how could we attribute powers to it?

Phil. Now let me ask you two questions: *First,* Whether it be agreeable to the usage either of philosophers or others to give the name *Matter* to an unextended active being? And, *Secondly,* Whether it be not ridiculously absurd to misapply names contrary to the common use of language?

Hyl. Well then, let it not be called Matter, since you will have it so, but some *Third Nature* distinct from Matter and Spirit. For what reason is there why you should call it Spirit? Does not the notion of spirit imply that it is thinking, as well as active and un-extended?

Phil. My reason is this: because I have a mind to have some notion of meaning in what I say: but I have no notion of any action distinct from volition, neither can I conceive volition to be anywhere but in a spirit: therefore, when I speak of an active being, I am obliged to mean a Spirit. Beside, what can be plainer than that a thing which hath no ideas in itself cannot impart them to me; and, if it hath ideas, surely it must be a Spirit. To make you comprehend the point still more clearly if it be possible. I assert as well as you that, since we are affected from without, we must allow Powers to be without, in a Being distinct from ourselves. So far we are agreed. But then we differ as to the kind of this powerful Being. I will have it to be Spirit, you Matter, or I know not what (I may add too, you know not what) Third Nature. Thus I prove it to be Spirit. From the effects I see produced, I conclude there are actions; and, because actions, volitions; and, because there are volitions, there must be a *will*. Again, the things I perceive must have an existence, they or their archetypes, out of *my* mind: but, being ideas, neither they nor their archetypes can exist otherwise than in an understanding; there is therefore an *understanding*. But will and understanding constitute in the strictest sense a mind or spirit. The powerful cause, therefore, of my ideas is in strict propriety of speech a *Spirit*.

Hyl. And now I warrant you think you have made the point very clear, little suspecting that what you advance leads directly to a contradiction. Is it not an absurdity to imagine any imperfection in God?

Phil. Without a doubt.

Hyl. To suffer pain is an imperfection?

Phil. It is.

Hyl. Are we not sometimes affected with pain and uneasiness by some other Being?

Phil. We are.

Hyl. And have you not said that Being is a Spirit, and is not that Spirit God?

Phil. I grant it.

Hyl. But you have asserted that whatever ideas we perceive from without are in the mind which affects us. The ideas, therefore, of pain and uneasiness are in God; or, in other words, God suffers pain: that is to say, there is an imperfection in the Divine nature: which, you acknowledged, was absurd. So you are caught in a plain contradiction.

Phil. That God knows or understands all things, and that He knows, among other things, what pain is, even every sort of painful sensation, and what it is for His creatures to suffer pain, I make no question. But, that God, though He knows and sometimes causes painful sensations in us, can Himself suffer pain, I positively deny. We, who are limited and dependent spirits, are liable to impressions of sense, the effects of an external Agent, which, being produced against our wills, are sometimes painful and uneasy. But God, whom no external being can affect, who perceives nothing by sense as we do; whose will is absolute and independent, causing all things, and liable to be thwarted or resisted by nothing: it is evident, such a Being as this can suffer nothing, nor be affected with any painful sensation, or indeed any sensation at all. We are chained to a body: that is to say, our perceptions are connected with corporeal motions. By the law of our nature, we are affected upon every alteration in the nervous parts of our sensible body; which sensible body, rightly considered, is nothing but a complexion of such qualities or ideas as have no existence distinct from being perceived by a mind. So that this connexion of sensations with corporeal motions means no more than a correspondence in the order of nature, between two sets of ideas, or things immediately perceivable. But God is a Pure Spirit, disengaged from all such sympathy, or natural ties. No corporeal motions are attended with the sensations of pain or pleasure in His mind. To know everything knowable, is certainly a perfection; but to endure, or suffer, or feel anything by sense, is an imperfection. The former, I say, agrees to God, but not the latter. God knows, or hath ideas; but His ideas are not conveyed to Him by sense, as ours are. Your not distinguishing, where there is so manifest a difference, makes you fancy you see an absurdity where there is none.

Hyl. But, all this while you have not considered that the quantity of Matter has been demonstrated to be proportioned to the gravity of bodies. And what can withstand demonstration?

Phil. Let me see how you demonstrate that point.

Hyl. I lay it down for a principle, that the moments or quantities of motion in bodies are in a direct compounded reason of the velocities and quantities of Matter contained in them. Hence, where the velocities are equal, it follows the moments are directly as the quantity of Matter in each. But it is found by experience that all bodies (bating the small inequalities, arising from the resistance of the air) descend with an equal velocity; the motion therefore of descending bodies, and consequently their gravity, which is the cause or principle of that motion, is proportional to the quantity of Matter; which was to be demonstrated.

Phil. You lay it down as a self-evident principle that the quantity of motion in any body is proportional to the velocity and *Matter* taken together; and this is made use of to prove a proposition from whence the existence of *Matter* is inferred. Pray is not this arguing in a circle?

Hyl. In the premise I only mean that the motion is proportional to the velocity, jointly with the extension and solidity.

Phil. But, allowing this to be true, yet it will not thence follow that gravity is proportional to *Matter,* in your philosophic sense of the word; except you take it for granted that unknown *substratum,* or whatever else you call it, is proportional to those sensible qualities; which to suppose is plainly begging the question. That there is magnitude and solidity, or resistance, perceived by sense, I readily grant; as likewise, that gravity may be proportional to those qualities I will not dispute. But that either these qualities as perceived by us, or the powers producing them, do exist in a *material substratum;* this is what I deny, and you indeed affirm, but, notwithstanding your demonstration, have not yet proved.

Hyl. I shall insist no longer on that point. Do you think, however, you shall persuade me the natural philosophers have been dreaming all this while? Pray what becomes of all their hypotheses and explications of the phenomena, which suppose the existence of Matter?

Phil. What mean you, Hylas, by the *phenomena?*

Hyl. I mean the appearances which I perceive by my senses.

Phil. And the appearances perceived by sense, are they not ideas?

Hyl. I have told you so a hundred times.

Phil. Therefore, to explain the phenomena is, to shew how we come to be affected with ideas, in that manner and order wherein they are imprinted on our senses. Is it not?

Hyl. It is.

Phil. Now, if you can prove that any philosopher has explained the production of any one idea in our minds by the help of *Matter,* I shall for ever acquiesce, and look on all that hath been said against it as nothing; but, if you cannot, it is vain to urge the explication of phenomena. That a Being endowed with knowledge and will should produce or exhibit ideas is easily understood. But that a Being which is utterly destitute of these faculties should be able to produce ideas, or in any sort to affect an intelligence, this I can never understand. This I say, though we had some positive conception of Matter, though we knew its qualities, and could comprehend its existence, would yet be so far from explaining things, that it is itself the most inexplicable thing in the world. And yet, for all this, it will not follow that philosophers have been doing nothing; for, by observing and reasoning upon the connexion of ideas, they discover the laws and methods of nature, which is a part of knowledge both useful and entertaining.

Hyl. After all, can it be supposed God would deceive all mankind? Do you imagine He would have induced the whole world to believe the being of Matter, if there was no such thing?

Phil. That every epidemical opinion, arising from prejudice, or passion, or thoughtlessness, may be imputed to God, as the Author of it, I believe you will not affirm. Whatsoever opinion we father on Him, it must be either because He has discovered it to us by supernatural revelation; or because it is so evident to our natural faculties, which were framed and given us by

God, that it is impossible we should withhold our assent from it. But where is the revelation? or where is the evidence that extorts the belief of Matter? Nay, how does it appear, that Matter, *taken for something distinct from what we perceive by our senses,* is thought to exist by all mankind; or, indeed, by any except a few philosophers, who do not know what they would be at? Your question supposes these points are clear; and, when you have cleared them, I shall think myself obliged to give you another answer. In the meantime, let it suffice that I tell you, I do not suppose God has deceived mankind at all.

Hyl. But the novelty, Philonous, the novelty! There lies the danger. New notions should always be discountenanced; they unsettle men's minds, and nobody knows where they will end.

Phil. Why the rejecting a notion that has no foundation, either in sense, or in reason, or in Divine authority, should be thought to unsettle the belief of such opinions as are grounded on all or any of these, I cannot imagine. That innovations in government and religion are dangerous, and ought to be discountenanced, I freely own. But is there the like reason why they should be discouraged in philosophy? The making anything known which was unknown before is an innovation in knowledge: and, if all such innovations had been forbidden, men would have made a notable progress in the arts and sciences. But it is none of my business to plead for novelties and paradoxes. That the qualities we perceive are not on the objects: that we must not believe our senses: that we know nothing of the real nature of things, and can never be assured even of their existence: that real colours and sounds are nothing but certain unknown figures and motions: that motions are in themselves neither swift nor slow: that there are in bodies absolute extensions, without any particular magnitude or figure: that a thing stupid, thoughtless, and inactive, operates on a spirit: that the least particle of a body contains innumerable extended parts:—these are the novelties, these are the strange notions which shock the genuine uncorrupted judgment of all mankind; and being once admitted, embarrass the mind with endless doubts and difficulties. And it is against these and the like innovations I endeavour to vindicate Common Sense. It is true, in doing this, I may perhaps be obliged to use some *ambages,* and ways of speech not common. But, if my notions are once thoroughly understood, that which is most singular in them will, in effect, be found to amount to no more than this:—that it is absolutely impossible, and a plain contradiction, to suppose any unthinking Being should exist without being perceived by a Mind. And, if this notion be singular, it is a shame it should be so, at this time of day, and in a Christian country.

Hyl. As for the difficulties other opinions may be liable to, those are out of the question. It is your business to defend your own opinion. Can anything be plainer than that you are for changing all things into ideas? You, I say, who are not ashamed to charge me with *scepticism.* This is so plain, there is no denying it.

Phil. You mistake me. I am not for changing things into ideas, but rather ideas into things; since those immediate objects of perception, which, according to you, are only appearances of things, I take to be the real things themselves.

Hyl. Things! You may pretend what you please; but it is certain you leave us nothing but the empty forms of things, the outside only which strikes the senses.

Phil. What you call the empty forms and outside of things seem to me the very things themselves. Nor are they empty or incomplete, otherwise than upon your supposition—that Matter is an essential part of all corporeal things. We both, therefore, agree in this, that we perceive only sensible forms: but herein we differ— you will have them to be empty appearances, I real beings. In short, you do not trust your senses, I do.

Hyl. You say you believe your senses; and seem to applaud yourself that in this you agree with the vulgar. According to you, therefore, the true nature of a thing is discovered by the senses. If so, whence comes that disagreement? Why is not the same figure, and other sensible qualities, perceived all manner of ways? and why should we use a microscope the better to discover the true nature of a body, if it were discoverable to the naked eye?

Phil. Strictly speaking, Hylas, we do not see the same object that we feel; neither is the same object perceived by the microscope which was by the naked eye. But, in case every variation was thought sufficient to constitute a new kind or individual, the endless number or confusion of names would render language impracticable. Therefore, to avoid this, as well as other inconveniences which are obvious upon a little thought, men combine together several ideas, apprehended by divers senses, or by the same sense at different times, or in different circumstances, but observed, however, to have some connexion in nature, either with respect to co-existence or succession; all which they refer to one name, and consider as one thing. Hence it follows that when I examine, by my other senses, a thing I have seen, it is not in order to understand better the same object which I had perceived by sight, the object of one sense not being perceived by the other senses. And, when I look through a microscope, it is not that I may perceive more clearly what I perceived already with my bare eyes; the object perceived by the glass being quite different from the former. But, in both cases, my aim is only to know what ideas are connected together; and the more a man knows of the connexion of ideas, the more he is said to know of the nature of things. What, therefore, if our ideas are variable; what if our senses are not in all circumstances affected with the same appearances? It will not thence follow they are not to be trusted; or that they are inconsistent either with themselves or anything else: except it be with your preconceived notion of (I know not what) one single, unchanged, unperceivable, real Nature, marked by each name. Which prejudice seems to have taken its rise from not rightly understanding the common language of men, speaking of several distinct ideas as united into one thing by the mind. And, indeed, there is cause to suspect several erroneous conceits of the philosophers are owing to the same original: while they began to build their schemes not so much on notions as on words, which were framed by the vulgar, merely for conveniency and dispatch in the common actions of life, without any regard to speculation.

Hyl. Methinks I apprehend your meaning.

Phil. It is your opinion the ideas we perceive by our senses are not real things, but images or copies of them. Our knowledge, therefore, is no farther real than as our ideas are the true *representations* of those *originals*. But, as they supposed originals are in themselves unknown, it is impossible to know how far our ideas resemble them; or whether they resemble them at all. We cannot, therefore, be sure we have any real knowledge. Farther, as our ideas are perpetually varied, without any change in the supposed real things, it necessarily follows they cannot all be true copies of them: or, if some are and others are not, it is impossible to distinguish the former from the latter. And this plunges us yet deeper in uncertainty. Again, when we consider the point, we cannot conceive how any idea, or anything like an idea, should have an absolute existence out of a mind: nor consequently, according to you, how there should be any real thing in nature. The result of all which is that we are thrown into the most hopeless and abandoned scepticism. Now, give me leave to ask you, First, Whether your referring ideas to certain absolutely existing unperceived substances, as their originals, be not the source of all this scepticism? Secondly, whether you are informed, either by sense or reason, of the existence of those unknown originals? And, in case you are not, whether it be not absurd to suppose them? Thirdly, Whether, upon inquiry, you find there is anything distinctly conceived or meant by the *absolute or external existence of unperceiving substances*? Lastly, Whether, the premises considered, it be not the wisest way to follow nature, trust your senses, and, laying aside all anxious thought about unknown natures or substances, admit with the vulgar those for real things which are perceived by the senses?

Hyl. For the present, I have no inclination to the answering part. I would much rather see how you can get over what follows. Pray are not the objects perceived by the *senses* of one, likewise perceivable to others present? If there were a hundred more here, they would all see the garden, the trees, and flowers, as I see them. But they are not in the same manner affected with the ideas I frame in my *imagination*. Does not this make a difference between the former sort of objects and the latter?

Phil. I grant it does. Nor have I ever denied a difference between the objects of sense and those of

imagination. But what would you infer from thence?
You cannot say that sensible objects exist unperceived,
because they are perceived by many.

Hyl. I own I can make nothing of that objection: but
it hath led me into another. Is it not your opinion that
by our senses we perceive only the ideas existing in our
minds?

Phil. It is.

Hyl. But the *same* idea which is in my mind cannot be
in yours, or in any other mind. Doth it not therefore
follow, from your principles, that no two can see the
same thing? And is not this highly absurd?

Phil. If the term *same* be taken in the vulgar acceptation, it is certain (and not at all repugnant to the principles I maintain) that different persons may perceive
the same thing; or the same thing or idea exist in different minds. Words are of arbitrary imposition; and,
since men are used to apply the word *same* where no
distinction or variety is perceived, and I do not pretend
to alter their perceptions, it follows that, as men have
said before, *several saw the same thing,* so they may,
upon like occasions, still continue to use the same phrase,
without any deviation either from propriety of language,
or the truth of things. But, if the term *same* be used in
the acceptation of philosophers, who pretend to an abstracted notion of identity, then, according to their
sundry definitions of this notion (for it is not yet agreed
wherein that philosophic identity consists), it may or
may not be possible for divers persons to perceive the
same thing. But whether philosophers shall think fit to
call a thing the *same* or no, is, I conceive, of small importance. Let us suppose several men together, all
endued with the same faculties, and consequently affected
in like sort by their senses, and who had yet never
known the use of language; they would, without ques-

tion, agree in their perceptions. Though perhaps, when they came to the use of speech, some regarding the uniformness of what was perceived, might call it the *same* thing: others, especially regarding the diversity of persons who perceived, might choose the denomination of *different* things. But who sees not that all the dispute is about a word? to wit, whether what is perceived by different persons may yet have the term *same* applied to it? Or, suppose a house, whose walls or outward shell remaining unaltered, the chambers are all pulled down, and new ones built in their place; and that you should call this the *same*, and I should say it was not the *same* house:—would we not, for all this, perfectly agree in our thoughts of the house, considered in itself? And would not all the difference consist in a sound? If you should say, We differed in our notions; for that you superadded to your idea of the house the simple abstracted idea of identity, whereas I did not; I would tell you, I know not what you mean by the *abstracted idea of identity;* and should desire you to look into your own thoughts, and be sure you understood yourself.——Why so silent, Hylas? Are you not yet satisfied men may dispute about identity and diversity, without any real difference in their thoughts and opinions, abstracted from names? Take this farther reflexion with you—that whether Matter be allowed to exist or no, the case is exactly the same as to the point in hand. For the Materialists themselves acknowledge what we immediately perceive by our senses to be our own ideas. Your difficulty, therefore, that no two see the same thing, makes equally against the Materialists and me.

Hyl. [Ay, Philonous,] But they suppose an external archetype, to which referring their several ideas they may truly be said to perceive the same thing.

Phil. And (not to mention your having discarded those

archetypes) so may you suppose an external archetype
on my principles;—*external, I mean, to your own mind:*
though indeed it must be supposed to exist in that Mind
which comprehends all things; but then, this serves all
the ends of *identity,* as well as if it existed out of a mind.
And I am sure you yourself will not say it is less intelligible.

Hyl. You have indeed clearly satisfied me—either
that there is no difficulty at bottom in this point; or, if
there be, that it makes equally against both opinions.

Phil. But that which makes equally against two contradictory opinions can be a proof against neither.

Hyl. I acknowledge it.

But, after all, Philonous, when I consider the substance of what you advance against *Scepticism,* it
amounts to no more than this:—We are sure that we
really see, hear, feel; in a word, that we are affected
with sensible impressions.

Phil. And how are *we* concerned any farther? I see
this cherry, I feel it, I taste it: and I am sure *nothing*
cannot be seen, or felt, or tasted: it is therefore *real.*
Take away the sensations of softness, moisture, redness,
tartness, and you take away the cherry, since it is not
a being distinct from sensations. A cherry, I say, is
nothing but a congeries of sensible impressions, or ideas
perceived by various senses: which ideas are united into
one thing (or have one name given them) by the mind,
because they are observed to attend each other. Thus,
when the palate is affected with such a particular taste,
the sight is affected with a red colour, the touch with
roundness, softness, &c. Hence, when I see, and feel,
and taste, in such sundry certain manners, I am sure
the cherry exists, or is real; its reality being in my
opinion nothing abstracted from those sensations. But

if by the word *cherry* you mean an unknown nature,
distinct from all those sensible qualities, and by its
existence something distinct from its being perceived;
then, indeed, I own, neither you nor I, nor any one else,
can be sure it exists.

Hyl. But, what would you say, Philonous, if I should
bring the very same reasons against the existence of
sensible things *in a mind,* which you have offered against
their existing *in a material substratum?*

Phil. When I see your reasons, you shall hear what
I have to say to them.

Hyl. Is the mind extended or unextended?

Phil. Unextended, without doubt.

Hyl. Do you say the things you perceive are in your
mind?

Phil. They are.

Hyl. Again, have I not heard you speak of sensible
impressions?

Phil. I believe you may.

Hyl. Explain to me now, O Philonous! how it is possible there should be room for all those trees and houses
to exist in your mind. Can extended things be contained
in that which is unextended? Or, are we to imagine
impressions made on a thing void of all solidity? You
cannot say objects are in your mind, as books in your
study: or that things are imprinted on it, as the figure
of a seal upon wax. In what sense, therefore, are we
to understand those expressions? Explain me this if
you can: and I shall then be able to answer all those
queries you formerly put to me about my *substratum.*

Phil. Look you, Hylas, when I speak of objects as
existing in the mind, or imprinted on the senses, I would
not be understood in the gross literal sense; as when
bodies are said to exist in a place, or a seal to make an
impression upon wax. My meaning is only that the mind

comprehends or perceives them; and that it is affected from without, or by some being distinct from itself. This is my explication of your difficulty; and how it can serve to make your tenet of an unperceiving material *substratum* intelligible, I would fain know.

Hyl. Nay, if that be all, I confess I do not see what use can be made of it. But are you not guilty of some abuse of language in this?

Phil. None at all. It is no more than common custom, which you know is the rule of language, hath authorised: nothing being more usual, than for philosophers to speak of the immediate objects of the understanding as things existing in the mind. Nor is there anything in this but what is comfortable to the general analogy of language; most part of the mental operations being signified by words borrowed from sensible things; as is plain in the terms *comprehend, reflect, discourse, &c.*, which, being applied to the mind, must not be taken in their gross, original sense.

Hyl. You have, I own, satisfied me in this point. But there still remains one great difficulty, which I know not how you will get over. And, indeed, it is of such importance that if you could solve all others, without being able to find a solution for this, you must never expect to make me a proselyte to your principles.

Phil. Let me know this mighty difficulty.

Hyl. The Scripture account of the creation is what appears to me utterly irreconcilable with your notions. Moses tells us of a creation: a creation of what? of ideas? No, certainly, but of things, of real things, solid corporeal substances. Bring your principles to agree with this, and I shall perhaps agree with you.

Phil. Moses mentions the sun, moon, and stars, earth and sea, plants and animals. That all these do really exist, and were in the beginning created by God, I make no question. If by *ideas* you mean fictions and fancies of the mind, then these are no ideas. If by *ideas* you mean immediate objects of the understanding, or sensible things, which cannot exist unperceived, or out of a mind, then these things are ideas. But whether you do or do not call them *ideas*, it matters little. The difference is only about a name. And, whether that name be retained or rejected, the sense, the truth, and reality of things continues the same. In common talk, the objects of our senses are not termed *ideas*, but *things*. Call them so still: provided you do not attribute to them any absolute external existence, and I shall never quarrel with you for a word. The creation, therefore, I allow to have been a creation of things, of *real* things. Neither is this in the least inconsistent with my principles, as is evident from what I have now said; and would have been evident to you without this, if you had not forgotten what had been so often said before. But as for solid corporeal substances, I desire you to shew where Moses makes any mention of them; and, if they should be mentioned by him, or any other inspired writer, it would still be incumbent on you to shew those words were not taken in the vulgar acceptation, for things falling under our senses, but in the philosophic acceptation, for Matter, or *an unknown quiddity, with an absolute existence*. When you have proved these points, then (and not till then) may you bring the authority of Moses into our dispute.

Hyl. It is in vain to dispute about a point so clear. I am content to refer it to your own conscience. Are you not satisfied there is some peculiar repugnancy between the Mosaic account of the creation and your notions?

Phil. If all possible sense which can be put on the first chapter of Genesis may be conceived as consistently with my principles as any other, then it has no peculiar repugnancy with them. But there is no sense you may not as well conceive, believing as I do. Since, besides spirits, all you conceive are ideas; and the existence of these I do not deny. Neither do you pretend they exist without the mind.

Hyl. Pray let me see any sense you can understand it in.

Phil. Why, I imagine that if I had been present at the creation, I should have seen things produced into being —that is become perceptible—in the order prescribed by the sacred historian. I ever before believed the Mosaic account of the creation, and now find no alteration in my manner of believing it. When things are said to begin or end their existence, we do not mean this with regard to God, but His creatures. All objects are eternally known by God, or, which is the same thing, have an eternal existence in His mind: but when things, before imperceptible to creatures, are, by a decree of God, perceptible to them, then are they said to begin a relative existence, with respect to created minds. Upon reading therefore the Mosaic account of the creation, I understand that the several parts of the world became gradually perceivable to finite spirits, endowed with proper faculties; so that, whoever such were present, they were in truth perceived by them. This is the literal obvious sense suggested to me by the words of the Holy Scripture: in which is included no mention, or no thought, either of *substratum,* instrument, occasion, or absolute existence. And, upon inquiry, I doubt not it will be found that most plain honest men, who believe the creation, never think of those things any more than I. What metaphysical sense you may understand it in, you only can tell.

Hyl. But, Philonous, you do not seem to be aware

that you allow created things, in the beginning, only a relative, and consequently hypothetical being: that is to say, upon supposition there were *men* to perceive them; without which they have no actuality of absolute existence, wherein creation might terminate.   Is it not, therefore, according to you, plainly impossible the creation of any inanimate creatures should precede that of man?   And is not this directly contrary to the Mosaic account?

Phil. In answer to that, I say, first, created beings might begin to exist in the mind of other created intelligences, beside men.   You will not therefore be able to prove any contradiction between Moses and my notions, unless you first shew there was no other order of finite created spirits in being, before man.   I say, farther, in case we conceive the creation, as we should at this time, a parcel of plants or vegetables of all sorts produced, by an invisible Power, in a desert where nobody was present—that this way of explaining or conceiving it is consistent with my principles, since they deprive you of nothing, either sensible or imaginable; that it exactly suits with the common, natural, and undebauched notions of mankind; that it manifests the dependence of all things on God; and consequently hath all the good effect or influence, which it is possible that important article of our faith should have in making men humble, thankful, and resigned to their [great] Creator.   I say, moreover, that, in this naked conception of things, divested of words, there will not be found any notion of what you call the *actuality of absolute existence*. You may indeed raise a dust with those terms, and so lengthen our dispute to no purpose.   But I entreat you calmly to look into your own thoughts, and then tell me if they are not a useless and unintelligible jargon.

Hyl. I own I have no very clear notion annexed to

them. But what say you to this? Do you not make the
existence of sensible things consist in their being in a
mind? And were not all things eternally in the mind of
God? Did they not therefore exist from all eternity,
according to you? And how could that which was eternal be created in time? Can anything be clearer or
better connected than this?

Phil. And are not you too of opinion, that God knew
all things from eternity?

Hyl. I am.

Phil. Consequently they always had a being in the
Divine intellect.

Hyl. This I acknowledge.

Phil. By your own confession, therefore, nothing is
new, or begins to be, in respect of the mind of God.
So we are agreed in that point.

Hyl. What shall we make then of the creation?

Phil. May we not understand it to have been entirely
in respect of finite spirits; so that things, with regard to
us, may properly be said to begin their existence, or be
created, when God decreed they should become perceptible to intelligent creatures, in that order and manner
which He then established, and we now call the laws
of nature? You may call this a *relative,* or *hypothetical
existence* if you please. But, so long as it supplies us
with the most natural, obvious, and literal sense of the
Mosaic history of the creation; so long as it answers all
the religious ends of that great article; in a word, so
long as you can assign no other sense or meaning in its
stead; why should we reject this? Is it to comply with
a ridiculous sceptical humour of making everything nonsense and unintelligible? I am sure you cannot say it is
for the glory of God. For, allowing it to be a thing
possible and conceivable that the corporeal world should
have an absolute existence extrinsical to the mind of

God, as well as to the minds of all created spirits; yet how could this set forth either the immensity or omniscience of the Deity, or the necessary and immediate dependence of all things on Him? Nay, would it not rather seem to derogate from those attributes?

Hyl. Well, but as to this decree of God's, for making things perceptible, what say you, Philonous? Is it not plain, God did either execute that decree from all eternity, or at some certain time began to will what He had not actually willed before, but only designed to will? If the former, then there could be no creation, or beginning of existence, in finite things. If the latter, then we must acknowledge something new to befall the Deity; which implies a sort of change: and all change argues imperfection.

Phil. Pray consider what you are doing. Is it not evident this objection concludes equally against a creation in any sense; nay, against every other act of the Deity, discoverable by the light of nature? None of which can *we* conceive, otherwise than as performed in time, and having a beginning. God is a Being of transcendent and unlimited perfections: His nature, therefore, is incomprehensible to finite spirits. It is not, therefore, to be expected, that any man, whether Materialist or Immaterialist, should have exactly just notions of the Deity, His attributes, and ways of operation. If then you would infer anything against me, your difficulty must not be drawn from the inadequateness of our conceptions of the Divine nature, which is unavoidable on any scheme; but from the denial of Matter, of which there is not one word, directly or indirectly, in what you have now objected.

Hyl. I must acknowledge the difficulties you are concerned to clear are such only as arise from the nonexistence of Matter, and are peculiar to that notion.

So far you are in the right. But I cannot by any means bring myself to think there is no such peculiar repugnancy between the creation and your opinion; though indeed where to fix it, I do not distinctly know.

Phil. What would you have? Do I not acknowledge a twofold state of things—the one ectypal or natural, the other archetypal and eternal? The former was created in time; the latter existed from everlasting in the mind of God. Is not this agreeable to the common notions of divines? or, is any more than this necessary in order to conceive the creation? But you suspect some peculiar repugnancy, though you know not where it lies. To take away all possibility of scruple in the case, do but consider this one point. Either you are not able to conceive the creation on any hypothesis whatsoever; and, if so, there is no ground for dislike or complaint against any particular opinion on that score: or you are able to conceive it; and, if so, why not on my Principles, since thereby nothing conceivable is taken away? You have all along been allowed the full scope of sense, imagination, and reason. Whatever, therefore, you could before apprehend, either immediately or mediately by your senses, or by ratiocination from your senses; whatever you could perceive, imagine, or understand, remains still with you. If, therefore, the notion you have of the creation by other Principles be intelligible, you have it still upon mine; if it be not intelligible, I conceive it to be no notion at all; and so there is no loss of it. And indeed it seems to me very plain that the supposition of Matter, that is a thing perfectly unknown and inconceivable, cannot serve to make us conceive anything. And, I hope it need not be proved to you that if the existence of Matter doth not make the creation conceivable, the creation's being without it inconceivable can be no objection against its non-existence.

Hyl. I confess, Philonous, you have almost satisfied me in this point of the creation.

Phil. I would fain know why you are not quite satisfied. You tell me indeed of a repugnancy between the Mosaic history and Immaterialism: but you know not where it lies. Is this reasonable, Hylas? Can you expect I should solve a difficulty without knowing what it is? But, to pass by all that, would not a man think you were assured there is no repugnancy between the received notions of Materialists and the inspired writings?

Hyl. And so I am.

Phil. Ought the historical part of Scripture to be understood in a plain obvious sense, or in a sense which is metaphysical and out of the way?

Hyl. In the plain sense, doubtless.

Phil. When Moses speaks of herbs, earth, water, &c. as having been created by God; think you not the sensible things commonly signified by those words are suggested to every unphilosophical reader?

Hyl. I cannot help thinking so.

Phil. And are not all ideas, or things perceived by sense, to be denied a real existence by the doctrine of the Materialist?

Hyl. This I have already acknowledged.

Phil. The creation, therefore, according to them, was not the creation of things sensible, which have only a relative being, but of certain unknown natures, which have an absolute being, wherein creation might terminate?

Hyl. True.

Phil. Is it not therefore evident the assertors of Matter destroy the plain obvious sense of Moses, with which their notions are utterly inconsistent; and instead of it obtrude on us I know not what; something equally unintelligible to themselves and me?

Hyl. I cannot contradict you.

Phil. Moses tells us of a creation. A creation of what? of unknown quiddities, of occasions, or *substratum*? No, certainly; but of things obvious to the senses. You must first reconcile this with your notions, if you expect I should be reconciled to them.

Hyl. I see you can assault me with my own weapons.

Phil. Then as to *absolute existence;* was there ever known a more jejune notion than that? Something it is so abstracted and unintelligible that you have frankly owned you could not conceive it, much less explain anything by it. But allowing Matter to exist, and the notion of absolute existence to be as clear as light; yet, was this ever known to make the creation more credible? Nay, hath it not furnished the atheists and infidels of all ages with the most plausible arguments against a creation? That a corporeal substance, which hath an absolute existence without the minds of spirits, should be produced out of nothing, by the mere will of a Spirit, hath been looked upon as a thing so contrary to all reason, so impossible and absurd, that not only the most celebrated among the ancients, but even divers modern and Christian philosophers have thought Matter co-eternal with the Deity. Lay these things together, and then judge you whether Materialism disposes men to believe the creation of things.

Hyl. I own, Philonous, I think it does not. This of the *creation* is the last objection I can think of; and I must needs own it hath been sufficiently answered as well as the rest. Nothing now remains to be overcome but a sort of unaccountable backwardness that I find in myself towards your notions.

Phil. When a man is swayed, he knows not why, to

one side of the question, can this, think you, be anything else but the effect of prejudice, which never fails to attend old and rooted notions? And indeed in this respect I cannot deny the belief of Matter to have very much the advantage over the contrary opinion, with men of a learned education.

Hyl. I confess it seems to be as you say.

Phil. As a balance, therefore, to this weight of prejudice, let us throw into the scale the great advantages that arise from the belief of Immaterialism, both in regard to religion and human learning. The being of a God, and incorruptibility of the soul, those great articles of religion, are they not proved with the clearest and most immediate evidence? When I say the being of a God, I do not mean an obscure general Cause of things, whereof we have no conception, but God, in the strict and proper sense of the word. A Being whose spirituality, omnipresence, providence, omniscience, infinite power and goodness, are as conspicuous as the existence of sensible things, of which (notwithstanding the fallacious pretences and affected scruples of Sceptics) there is no more reason to doubt than of our own being.— Then, with relation to human sciences. In Natural Philosophy, what intricacies, what obscurities, what contradictions hath the belief of Matter led men into! To say nothing of the numberless disputes about its extent, continuity, homogeneity, gravity, divisibility, &c.—do they not pretend to explain all things by bodies operating on bodies, according to the laws of motion? and yet, are they able to comprehend how one body should move another? Nay, admitting there was no difficulty in reconciling the notion of an inert being with a cause, or in conceiving how an accident might pass from one body to another; yet, by all their strained thoughts and extravagant suppositions, have they been able to reach

the *mechanical* production of any one animal or vegetable body? Can they account, by the laws of motion,
for sounds, tastes, smells, or colours; or for the regular
course of things? Have they accounted, by physical
principles, for the aptitude and contrivance even of the
most inconsiderable parts of the universe? But, laying
aside Matter and corporeal causes, and admitting only
the efficiency of an All-perfect Mind, are not all the
effects of nature easy and intelligible? If the *phenomena* are nothing else but *ideas;* God is a *spirit,* but Matter an unintelligent, unperceiving being. If they demonstrate an unlimited power in their cause; God is active
and omnipotent, but Matter an inert mass. If the order,
regularity, and usefulness of them can never be sufficiently admired; God is infinitely wise and provident,
but Matter destitute of all contrivance and design.
These surely are great advantages in *Physics.* Not to
mention that the apprehension of a distant Deity naturally disposes men to a negligence in their moral
actions; which they would be more cautious of, in case
they thought Him immediately present, and acting on
their minds, without the interposition of Matter, or unthinking second causes.—Then in *Metaphysics:* what
difficulties concerning entity in abstract, substantial
forms, hylarchic principles, plastic natures, substance
and accident, principle of individuation, possibility of
Matter's thinking, origin of ideas, the manner how two
independent substances so widely different as *Spirit* and
Matter, should mutually operate on each other? what
difficulties, I say, and endless disquisitions, concerning
these and innumerable other the like points, do we escape, by supposing only Spirits and ideas?—Even the
Mathematics themselves, if we take away the absolute
existence of extended things, becomes much more clear
and easy; the most shocking paradoxes and intricate

speculations in those sciences depending on the infinite divisibility of finite extension; which depends on that supposition.—But what need is there to insist on the particular sciences? Is not that opposition to all science whatsoever, that frenzy of the ancient and modern Sceptics, built on the same foundation? Or can you produce so much as one argument against the reality of corporeal things, or in behalf of that avowed utter ignorance of their natures, which doth not suppose their reality to consist in an external absolute existence? Upon this supposition, indeed, the objections from the change of colours in a pigeon's neck, or the appearance of the broken oar in the water, must be allowed to have weight. But these and the like objections vanish, if we do not maintain the being of absolute external originals, but place the reality of things in ideas, fleeting indeed, and changeable;—however, not changed at random, but according to the fixed order of nature. For, herein consists that constancy and truth of things which secures all the concerns of life, and distinguishes that which is *real* from the *irregular visions* of the fancy.

Hyl. I agree to all you have now said, and must own that nothing can incline me to embrace your opinion more than the advantages I see it is attended with. I am by nature lazy; and this would be a mighty abridgment in knowledge. What doubts, what hypotheses, what labyrinths of amusement, what fields of disputation, what an ocean of false learning, may be avoided by that single notion of *Immaterialism!*

Phil. After all, is there anything farther remaining to be done? You may remember you promised to embrace that opinion which upon examination should appear most agreeable to Common Sense and remote from Scepticism. This, by your own confession, is that which denies Matter, or the *absolute* existence of corporeal things. Nor is this all; the same notion has been proved several ways, viewed in different lights, pursued in its consequences, and all objections against it cleared. Can there be a greater evidence of its truth? or is it possible it should have all the marks of a true opinion and yet be false?

Hyl. I own myself entirely satisfied for the present in all respects. But, what security can I have that I shall still continue the same full assent to your opinion, and that no unthought-of objection or difficulty will occur hereafter?

Phil. Pray, Hylas, do you in other cases, when a point is once evidently proved, withhold your consent on account of objections or difficulties it may be liable to? Are the difficulties that attend the doctrine of incommensurable quantities, of the angle of contact, of the asymptotes to curves, or the like, sufficient to make you hold out against mathematical demonstration? Or will you disbelieve the Providence of God, because there may be some particular things which *you* know not how to reconcile with it? If there are difficulties attending *Immaterialism,* there are at the same time direct and evident proofs of it. But for the existence of Matter there is not one proof, and far more numerous and insurmountable objections lie against it. But where are those mighty difficulties you insist on? Alas! you know not where or what they are; something which may possibly occur hereafter. If this be a sufficient pretence for withholding your full assent, you should never yield it to any proposition, how free soever from exceptions, how clearly and solidly soever demonstrated.

Hyl. You have satisfied me, Philonous.

Phil. But, to arm you against all future objections, do but consider: That which bears equally hard on two contradictory opinions can be proof against neither. Whenever, therefore, any difficulty occurs, try if you can find a solution for it on the hypothesis of the *Materialists*. Be not deceived by words; but sound your own thoughts. And in case you cannot conceive it easier by the help of *Materialism,* it is plain it can be no objection against *Immaterialism*. Had you proceeded all along by this rule, you would probably have spared yourself abundance of trouble in objecting; since of all your difficulties I challenge you to shew one that is explained by Matter: nay, which is not more unintelligible with than without that supposition; and consequently makes rather *against* than *for* it. You should consider, in each particular, whether the difficulty arises from the *non-existence of Matter*. If it doth not, you might as well argue from the infinite divisibility of extension against the Divine prescience, as from such a difficulty against *Immaterialism*. And yet, upon recollection, I believe you will find this to have been often, if not always, the case. You should likewise take heed not to argue on a *petitio principii*. One is apt to say— The unknown substances ought to be esteemed real things, rather than the ideas in our minds: and who can tell but the unthinking external substance may concur, as a cause or instrument, in the production of our ideas? But is not this proceeding on a supposition that there are such external substances? And to suppose this, is it not begging the question? But, above all things, you should beware of imposing on yourself by that vulgar sophism which is called *ignoratio elenchi*. You talked often as if you thought I maintained the non-existence of Sensible Things. Whereas in truth no one can be more thoroughly assured of their existence than I am. And it is you who doubt; I should have said, positively deny it. Everything that is seen, felt, heard, or any way perceived by the senses, is, on the principles I embrace, a real being; but not on yours. Remember, the Matter you contend for is an Unknown Somewhat (if indeed it may be termed *somewhat*), which is quite stripped of all sensible qualities, and can neither be perceived by sense, nor apprehended by the mind. Remember, I say, that it is not any object which is hard or soft, hot or cold, blue or white, round or square, &c. For all these things I affirm do exist. Though indeed I deny they have an existence distinct from being perceived; or that they exist out of all minds whatsoever. Think on these points; let them be attentively considered and still kept in view. Otherwise you will not comprehend the state of the question; without which your objections will always be wide of the mark, and, instead of mine, may possibly be directed (as more than once they have been) against your own notions.

Hyl. I must needs own, Philonous, nothing seems to have kept me from agreeing with you more than this same *mistaking the question*. In denying Matter, at first glimpse I am tempted to imagine you deny the things we see and feel: but, upon reflexion, find there is no ground for it. What think you, therefore, of retaining the name *Matter*, and applying it to *sensible things?* This may be done without any change in your sentiments: and, believe me, it would be a means of reconciling them to some persons who may be more shocked at an innovation in words than in opinion.

Phil. With all my heart: retain the word *Matter*, and apply it to the objects of sense, if you please; provided you do not attribute to them any subsistence distinct from their being perceived. I shall never quarrel with you for an expression. *Matter*, or *material substance*, are terms introduced by philosophers; and, as used by them, imply a sort of independency, or a subsistence distinct from being perceived by a mind: but are never used by common people; or, if ever, it is to signify the immediate objects of sense. One would think, therefore, so long as the names of all particular things, with the terms *sensible, substance, body, stuff,* and the like, are retained, the word *Matter* should be never missed in common talk. And in philosophical discourses it seems the best way to leave it quite out: since there is not, perhaps, any one thing that hath more favoured and strengthened the depraved bent of the mind towards Atheism than the use of that general confused term.

Hyl. Well but, Philonous, since I am content to give up the notion of an unthinking substance exterior to the mind, I think you ought not to deny me the privilege of using the word *Matter* as I please, and annexing it to a collection of sensible qualities subsisting only in the mind. I freely own there is no other substance, in a strict sense, than *Spirit.* But I have been so long accustomed to the *term Matter* that I know not how to part with it: to say, there is no *Matter* in the world, is still shocking to me. Whereas to say—There is no *Matter,* if by that term be meant an unthinking substance existing without the mind; but if by *Matter* is meant some sensible thing, whose existence consists in being perceived, then there is *Matter:*—this distinction gives it quite another term; and men will come into your notions with small difficulty, when they are proposed in that manner. For, after all, the controversy about *Matter* in the strict acceptation of it, lies altogether between you and the philosophers: whose principles, I acknowledge, are not near so natural, or so agreeable to the common sense of mankind, and Holy Scripture, as yours. There is nothing we either desire or shun but as it makes, or is apprehended to make, some part of our happiness or misery. But what hath happiness or misery, joy or grief, pleasure or pain, to do with Absolute Existence; or with unknown entities, *abstracted from all relation to us?* It is evident, things regard us only as they are pleasing or displeasing: and they can please or displease only so far forth as they are perceived. Farther, therefore, we are not concerned; and thus far you leave things as you found them. Yet still there is something new in this doctrine. It is plain, I do not now think with the philosophers; nor yet altogether with the vulgar. I would know how the case stands in that respect; precisely, what you have added to, or altered in my former notions.

Phil. I do not pretend to be a setter-up of new notions. My endeavours tend only to unite, and place in a clearer light, that truth which was before shared between the vulgar and the philosophers:—the former being of opinion, that *those things they immediately perceive are the real things;* and the latter, that *the things immediately perceived are ideas, which exist only in the mind.* Which two notions put together, do, in effect, constitute the substance of what I advance.

Hyl. I have been a long time distrusting my senses: methought I saw things by a dim light and through false glasses. Now the glasses are removed and a new light breaks in upon my understanding. I am clearly convinced that I see things in their native forms, and am no longer in pain about their *unknown natures* or *absolute existence.* This is the state I find myself in at present; though, indeed, the course that brought me to it I do not yet thoroughly comprehend. You set out upon the same principles that Academics, Cartesians, and the like sects usually do; and for a long time it looked as if you were advancing their philosophical Scepticism: but, in the end, your conclusions are directly opposite to theirs.

Phil. You see, Hylas, the water of yonder fountain, how it is forced upwards, in a round column, to a certain height; at which it breaks, and falls back into the basin from whence it rose: its ascent, as well as descent, proceeding from the same uniform law or principle of gravitation. Just so, the same Principles which, at first view, lead to Scepticism, pursued to a certain point, bring men back to Common Sense.

ALCIPHRON

OR THE MINUTE PHILOSOPHER

IN SEVEN DIALOGUES

CONTAINING AN APOLOGY FOR THE CHRISTIAN RELIGION AGAINST THOSE WHO ARE CALLED FREE-THINKERS

They have forsaken me the Fountain of living waters, and hewed them out cisterns, broken cisterns, that can hold no water.—Jer. ii. 13.

Sin mortuus, ut quidam Minuti Philosophi censent, nihil sentiam, non vereor ne hunc errorem meum mortui philosophi irrideant.—Cicero.

ALCIPHRON

OR

THE MINUTE PHILOSOPHER

THE FIRST DIALOGUE.

1. I FLATTERED myself, Theages, that before this time I might have been able to have sent you an agreeable account of the success of the affair which brought me into this remote corner of the country. But, instead of this, I should now give you the detail of its miscarriage, if I did not rather choose to entertain you with some amusing incidents, which have helped to make me easy under a circumstance I could neither obviate nor foresee . . . For several months past, I have enjoyed . . . liberty and leisure in this distant retreat, far beyond the verge of that great whirlpool of business, faction, and pleasure, which is called *the world*. And a retreat in itself agreeable, after a long scene of trouble and disquiet, was made much more so by the conversation and good qualities of my host, Euphranor, who units in his own person the philosopher and the farmer, two characters not so inconsistent in nature as by custom they seem to be.

Euphranor, from the time he left the university, hath lived in this small town, where he is possessed of a con-

venient house with a hundred acres of land adjoining to
it; which, being improved by his own labour, yield him
a plentiful subsistence.   He hath a good collection,
chiefly of old books, left him by a clergyman his uncle,
under whose care he was brought up. And the business
of his farm doth not hinder him from making good use
of it. He hath read much, and thought more; his health
and strength of body enabling him the better to bear
fatigue of mind. He is of opinion that he could not
carry on his studies with more advantage in the closet
than the field, where his mind is seldom idle while he
prunes the trees, follows the plough, or looks after his
flocks.

In the house of this honest friend I became acquainted
with Crito, a neighbouring gentleman of distinguished
merit and estate, who lives in great friendship with
Euphranor.

Last summer, Crito, whose parish-church is in our
town, dining on a Sunday at Euphranor's, I happened to
inquire after his guests, whom we had seen at church
with him the Sunday before. They are both well, said
Crito, but, having once occasionally conformed, to see
what sort of assembly our parish could afford, they had
no further curiosity to gratify at church, and so chose to
stay at home. How, said *Euphranor,* are they then dis-
senters?   No, replied *Crito,* they are *free-thinkers.*
Euphranor, who had never met with any of this species
or sect of men, and but little of their writings, shewed
a great desire to know their principles or system. That
is more, said *Crito,* than I will undertake to tell you.
Their writers are of different opinions. Some go farther,
and explain themselves more freely than others. But the
current general notions of the sect are best learned from
conversation with those who profess themselves of it.
Your curiosity may now be satisfied, if you and Dion

would spend a week at my house with these gentlemen, who seem very ready to declare and propagate their opinions. Alciphron is above forty, and no stranger either to men or books. . . . The young gentleman, Lysicles, is a near kinsman of mine, one of lively parts and a general insight into letters, who, after having passed the forms of education, and seen a little of the world, fell into an intimacy with men of pleasure and free-thinkers, I am afraid much to the damage of his constitution and his fortune. . . . They are both men of fashion, and would be agreeable enough, if they did not fancy themselves free-thinkers. But this, to speak the truth, has given them a certain air and manner, which a little too visibly declare they think themselves wiser than the rest of the world. I should therefore be not at all displeased if my guests met with their match, where they least expected it—in a country farmer. I shall not, replied *Euphranor*, pretend to any more than barely to inform myself of their principles and opinions. For this end I propose to-morrow to set a week's task to my labourers, and accept your invitation, if Dion thinks good. To which I gave consent. . . .

Next morning Euphranor rose early, and spent the forenoon in ordering his affairs. After dinner we took our walk to Crito's, which lay through half a dozen pleasant fields planted round with plane-trees, that are very common in this part of the country. We walked under the delicious shade of these trees for about an hour before we came to Crito's house, which stands in the middle of a small park, beautified with two fine groves of oak and walnut, and a winding stream of sweet and clear water. We met a servant at the door with a small basket of fruit, which he was carrying into a grove, where he said his master was with the two strangers. We found them all three sitting under a shade. And after the usual forms at first meeting, Euphranor and I sat down by them.

* * * * * * *

THE FOURTH DIALOGUE

1. EARLY the next morning, as I looked out of my window, I saw Alciphron walking in the garden with all the signs of a man in deep thought. Upon which I went down to him.

Alciphron, said I, this early and profound meditation puts me in no small fright. How so? Because I should be sorry to be convinced there was no God. The thought of anarchy in nature, is to me more shocking than in civil life: inasmuch as natural concerns are more important than civil, and the basis of all others.

I grant, replied *Alciphron,* that some inconvenience may possibly follow from disproving a God: but as to what you say of fright and shocking, all that is nothing but mere prejudice. Men frame an idea or chimera in their own minds, and then fall down and worship it. Notions govern mankind: but of all notions that of God's governing the world hath taken the deepest root and spread the farthest. It is therefore in philosophy an heroical achievement to dispossess this imaginary monarch of his government, and banish all those fears and spectres which the light of reason alone can dispel:

> Non radii solis, non lucida tela diei
> Discutiunt, sed naturae species ratioque.[1]

My part, said I, shall be to stand by, as I have hitherto done, and take notes of all that passeth during this memorable event; while a minute philosopher, not six

[1] [Lucretius.]—BERKELEY.

feet high, attempts to dethrone the Monarch of the Universe.

Alas! replied *Alciphron,* arguments are not to be measured by feet and inches. One man may see more than a million; and a short argument, managed by a freethinker, may be sufficient to overthrow the most gigantic chimera.

As we were engaged in this discourse, Crito and Euphranor joined us.

I find you have been beforehand with us to-day, said *Crito* to Alciphron, and taken the advantage of solitude and early hours, while Euphranor and I were asleep in our beds. We may, therefore, expect to see atheism placed in the best light, and supported by the strongest arguments.

2. *Alc.* The being of a God is a subject upon which there has been a world of commonplace, which it is needless to repeat. Give me leave therefore to lay down certain rules and limitations, in order to shorten our present conference. For, as the end of debating is to persuade, all those things which are foreign to this end should be left out of our debate.

First then, let me tell you I am not to be persuaded by metaphysical arguments; such, for instance, as are drawn from the idea of an all-perfect being, or the absurdity of an infinite progression of causes.[1] This sort of arguments I have always found dry and jejune; and, as they are not suited to my way of thinking, they may perhaps puzzle, but never will convince me. Secondly, I am not to be persuaded by the authority either of past or present ages, of mankind in general, or of particular wise men, all which passeth for little or nothing with a man of sound argument and free thought. Thirdly, all

[1] Cf. the *Meditations* of Descartes.

proofs drawn from utility or convenience are foreign to the purpose. They may prove indeed the usefulness of the notion, but not the existence of the thing. Whatever legislators or statesmen may think, truth and convenience are very different things to the rigorous eye of a philosopher.

And now, that I may not seem partial, I will limit myself also not to object, in the first place, from anything that may seem irregular or unaccountable in the works of nature, against a cause of infinite power and wisdom; because I already know the answer you will make, to wit, that no one can judge of the symmetry and use of the parts of an infinite machine, which are all relative to each other, and to the whole, without being able to comprehend the entire machine, or the whole universe. And, in the second place, I shall engage myself not to object against the justice and providence of a supreme Being from the evil that befals good men and the prosperity which is often the portion of wicked men in this life; because I know that, instead of admitting this to be an objection against a Deity, you would make it an argument for a future state, in which there shall be such a retribution of rewards and punishments as may vindicate the Divine attributes, and set all things right in the end. Now, these answers, though they should be admitted for good ones, are in truth no proofs of the being of God, but only solutions of certain difficulties which might be objected, supposing it already proved by proper arguments. Thus much I thought fit to premise, in order to save time and trouble both to you and myself.

Cri. I think that as the proper end of our conference ought to be supposed the discovery and defence of truth, so truth may be justified, not only by persuading its adversaries, but, where that cannot be done, by shewing them to be unreasonable. Arguments, therefore, which carry light have their effect, even against an opponent who shuts his eyes, because they shew him to be obstinate and prejudiced. Besides, this distinction between arguments that puzzle and that convince, is least of all observed by minute philosophers, and need not therefore be observed by others in their favour.—But, perhaps, Euphranor may be willing to encounter you on your own terms, in which case I have nothing further to say.

3. *Euph.* Alciphron acts like a skilful general, who is bent upon gaining the advantage of the ground, and alluring the enemy out of their trenches. We who believe a God are entrenched within tradition, custom, authority, and law. And, nevertheless, instead of attempting to force us, he proposes that he should voluntarily abandon these intrenchments, and make the attack; when we may act on the defensive with much security and ease, leaving him the trouble to dispossess us of what we need not resign. Those reasons (continued he, addressing himself to Alciphron) which you have mustered up in this morning's meditation, if they do not weaken, must establish our belief of a God; for the utmost is to be expected from so great a master in his profession, when he sets his strength to a point.

Alc. I hold the confused notion of a Deity, or some invisible power, to be of all prejudices the most unconquerable. When half-a-dozen ingenious men are got together over a glass of wine, by a cheerful fire, in a room well lighted, we banish with ease all the spectres of fancy and education, and are very clear in our decisions. But, as I was taking a solitary walk before it was broad daylight in yonder grove, methought the point was not quite so clear; nor could I readily recollect the force of those arguments which used to appear so conclusive at other times. I had I know not what awe upon my mind, and seemed haunted by a sort of panic, which I cannot otherwise account for than by supposing it the effect of prejudice: for, you must know that I, like the rest of the world, was once upon a time catechised and tutored into the belief of a God or Spirit. There is no surer mark of prejudice than the believing a thing without reason. What necessity then can there be that I should set myself the difficult task of proving a negative, when it is sufficient to observe that there is no proof of the affirmative, and that the admitting it without proof is unreasonable? Prove therefore your opinion; or, if you cannot, you may indeed remain in possession of it, but you will only be possessed of a prejudice.

Euph. O Alciphron, to content you we must prove, it seems, and we must prove upon your own terms. But, in the first place, let us see what sort of proof you expect.

Alc. Perhaps I may not expect it, but I will tell you what sort of proof I would have: and that is, in short— such proof as every man of sense requires of a matter of fact, or the existence of any other particular thing. For instance, should a man ask why I believe there is a king of Great Britain? I might answer—Because I had seen him. Or a king of Spain? Because I had seen those who saw him. But as for this King of kings, I neither saw Him myself, or any one else that ever did see Him. Surely, if there be such a thing as God, it is very strange that He should leave Himself without a witness; that men should still dispute His being; and that there should be no one evident, sensible, plain proof of it, without recourse to philosophy or metaphysics. A matter of fact is not to be proved by notions, but by facts. This is clear and full to the point. You see what I would be at.   Upon these principles I defy superstition.

Euph. You believe then as far as you can see?

Alc. That is my rule of faith.

Euph. How! will you not believe the existence of things which you hear, unless you also see them?

Alc. I will not say so neither.   When I insisted on *seeing,* I would be understood to mean perceiving in general.   Outward objects make very different impressions upon the animal spirits, all which are comprised under the common name of *sense.*   And whatever we can perceive by any sense we may be sure of.

4. *Euph.* What! do you believe then that there are such things as animal spirits?

Alc. Doubtless.

Euph. By what sense do you perceive them?

Alc. I do not perceive them immediately by any of my senses.   I am nevertheless persuaded of their existence, because I can collect it from their effects and operations.   They are the messengers which, running to and fro in the nerves, preserve a communication between the soul and outward objects.

Euph. You admit then the being of a soul?

Alc. Provided I do not admit an immaterial substance, I see no inconvenience in admitting there may be such a thing as a soul.   And this may be no more than a thin fine texture of subtile parts or spirits residing in the brain.

Euph. I do not ask about its nature.   I only ask whether you admit that there is a principle of thought and action, and whether it be perceivable by sense.

Alc. I grant that there is such a principle, and that it is not the object of sense itself, but inferred from appearances which are perceived by sense.

Euph. If I understand you rightly, from animal func-
tions and motions you infer the existence of animal
spirits, and from reasonable acts you infer the existence
of a reasonable soul. Is it not so?

Alc. It is.

Euph. It should seem, therefore, that the being of
things imperceptible to sense may be collected from
effects and signs, or sensible tokens.

Alc. It may.

Euph. Tell me, Alciphron, is not the soul that which
makes the principal distinction between a real person
and a shadow, a living man and a carcass?

Alc. I grant it is.

Euph. I cannot, therefore, know that *you,* for instance,
are a distinct thinking individual, or a living real man,
by surer or other signs than those from which it can
be inferred that you have a soul?

Alc. You cannot.

Euph. Pray tell me, are not all acts immediately and
properly perceived by sense reducible to motion?

Alc. They are.

Euph. From motions, therefore, you infer a mover or
cause; and from reasonable motions (or such as appear
calculated for a reasonable end) a rational cause, soul
or spirit?

Alc. Even so.

5. *Euph.* The soul of man actuates but a small body,
an insignificant particle, in respect of the great masses
of nature, the elements, and heavenly bodies, and system of the world. And the wisdom that appears in
those motions which are the effect of human reason is
incomparably less than that which discovers itself in the
structure and use of organised natural bodies, animal or
vegetable. A man with his hand can make no machine

so admirable as the hand itself; nor can any of those
motions by which we trace out human reason approach
the skill and contrivance of those wonderful motions of
the heart, and brain, and other vital parts, which do
not depend on the will of man.

Alc. All this is true.

Euph. Doth it not follow, then, that from natural
motions, independent of man's will, may be inferred
both power and wisdom incomparably greater than that
of the human soul?

Alc. It should seem so.

Euph. Further, is there not in natural productions
and effects a visible unity of counsel and design? Are
not the rules fixed and immoveable? Do not the same
laws of motion obtain throughout? The same in China
and here, the same two thousand years ago and at this
day?

Alc. All this I do not deny.

Euph. Is there not also a connexion or relation between animals and vegetables, between both and the elements, between the elements and heavenly bodies; so
that, from their mutual respects, influences, subordina-
tions, and uses, they may be collected to be parts of one
whole, conspiring to one and the same end, and fulfilling
the same design?

Alc. Supposing all this to be true.

Euph. Will it not then follow that this vastly great,
or infinite power and wisdom must be supposed in one
and the same Agent, Spirit, or Mind; and that we have
at least as clear, full, and immediate certainty of the being of this infinitely wise and powerful Spirit, as of any
one human soul whatsoever besides our own?

Alc. Let me consider: I suspect we proceed too has-
tily. What! Do you pretend you can have the same
assurance of the being of a God that you can have of

mine, whom you actually see stand before you and talk to you?

Euph. The very same, if not greater.

Alc. How do you make this appear?

Euph. By the person Alciphron is meant an individual thinking thing, and not the hair, skin, or visible surface, or any part of the outward form, colour, or shape, of Alciphron.

Alc. This I grant.

Euph. And, in granting this, you grant that, in a strict sense, I do not see Alciphron, i.e. that individual thinking thing, but only such visible signs and tokens as suggest and infer the being of that invisible thinking principle or soul. Even so, in the self-same manner, it seems to me that, though I cannot with eyes of flesh behold the invisible God, yet I do in the strictest sense behold and perceive by all my senses such signs and tokens, such effects and operations, as suggest, indicate, and demonstrate an invisible God—as certainly, and with the same evidence, at least, as any other signs, perceived by sense, do suggest to me the existence of your soul, spirit, or thinking principle; which I am convinced of only by a few signs or effects, and the motions of one small organised body: whereas I do at all times and all places perceive sensible signs which evince the being of God. The point, therefore, doubted or denied by you at the beginning now seems manifestly to follow from the premises. Throughout this whole inquiry, have we not considered every step with care, and made not the least advance without clear evidence? You and I examined and assented singly to each foregoing proposition: what shall we do then with the conclusion? For my part, if you do not help me out, I find myself under an absolute necessity of admitting it for true. You must therefore be content henceforward to bear the blame, if I live and die in the belief of a God.

6. *Alc.* It must be confessed, I do not readily find an answer. There seems to be some foundation for what you say. But, on the other hand, if the point was so clear as you pretend, I cannot conceive how so many sagacious men of our sect should be so much in the dark as not to know or believe one syllable of it.

Euph. O Alciphron, it is not our present business to account for the oversights, or vindicate the honour, of those great men the free-thinkers, when their very existence is in danger of being called in question.

Alc. How so?

Euph. Be pleased to recollect the concessions you have made, and then shew me, if the arguments for a Deity be not conclusive, by what better arguments you can prove the existence of that thinking thing which in strictness constitutes the free-thinker.

As soon as Euphranor had uttered these words, *Alciphron* stopped short, and stood in a posture of meditation, while the rest of us continued our walk and took two or three turns, after which he joined us again with a smiling countenance, like one who had made some discovery. I have found, said he, what may clear up the point in dispute, and give Euphranor entire satisfaction; I would say an argument which will prove the existence of a free-thinker, the like whereof cannot be applied to prove the existence of God. You must know then that your notion of our perceiving the existence of God, as certainly and immediately as we do that of a human person, I could by no means digest, though I must own it puzzled me, till I had considered the matter. At first methought a particular structure, shape, or motion was a most certain proof of a thinking reasonable soul. But a little attention satisfied me that these things have no necessary connexion with reason, knowledge, and wisdom; and that, allowing them to be certain proofs of a living soul, they cannot be so of a thinking and reasonable one. Upon second thoughts, therefore, and a minute examination of this point, I have found that nothing so much convinces me of the existence of another person as *his speaking to me.* It is my hearing you talk that, in strict and philosophical truth, is to me the best argument for your being. And this is a peculiar argument, inapplicable to your purpose; for, you will not, I suppose, pretend that God speaks to man in the same clear and sensible manner as one man doth to another?

7. *Euph.* How! is then the impression of sound so much more evident than that of other senses? Or, if it be, is the voice of man louder than that of thunder?

Alc. Alas! you mistake the point. What I mean is not the sound of speech merely as such, but the arbitrary use of sensible signs, which have no similitude or necessary connexion with the things signified; so as by the apposite management of them to suggest and exhibit to my mind an endless variety of things, differing in nature, time, and place; thereby informing me, entertaining me, and directing me how to act, not only with regard to things near and present, but also with regard to things distant and future. No matter whether these signs are pronounced or written; whether they enter by the eye or ear: they have the same use, and are equally proofs of an intelligent, thinking, designing cause.

Euph. But what if it should appear that God really speaks to man; would this content you?

Alc. I am for admitting no inward speech, no holy instincts, or suggestions of light or spirit. All that, you must know, passeth with men of sense for nothing.

If you do not make it plain to me that God speaks of men by outward sensible signs, of such sort and in such manner as I have defined, you do nothing.

Euph. But if it shall appear plainly that God speaks to men by the intervention and use of arbitrary, outward, sensible signs, having no resemblance or necessary connexion with the things they stand for and suggest: if it shall appear that, by innumerable combinations of these signs, an endless variety of things is discovered and made known to us; and that we are thereby instructed or informed in their different natures; that we are taught and admonished what to shun, and what to pursue; and are directed how to regulate our motions, and how to act with respect to things distant from us, as well in time as place, will this content you?

Alc. It is the very thing I would have you make out; for therein consists the force, and use, and nature of language.

8. *Euph.* Look, Alciphron, do you not see the castle upon yonder hill?

Alc. I do.

Euph. Is it not at a great distance from you?

Alc. It is.

Euph. Tell me, Alciphron, is not distance a line turned end-wise to the eye?

Alc. Doubtless.

Euph. And can a line, in that situation, project more than one single point on the bottom of the eye?

Alc. It cannot.

Euph. Therefore the appearance of a long and of a short distance is of the same magnitude, or rather of no magnitude at all—being in all cases one single point.

Alc. It seems so.

Euph. Should it not follow from hence that distance is not immediately perceived by the eye?

Alc. It should.

Euph. Must it not then be perceived by the mediation of some other thing?

Alc. It must.

Euph. To discover what this is, let us examine what alteration there may be in the appearance of the same object, placed at different distances from the eye. Now, I find by experience that when an object is removed still farther and farther off in a direct line from the eye, its visible appearance still grows lesser and fainter; and this change of appearance, being proportional and universal, seems to me to be that by which we apprehend the various degrees of distance.

Alc. I have nothing to object to this.

Euph. But littleness or faintness, in their own nature, seem to have no necessary connexion with greater length of distance?

Alc. I admit this to be true.

Euph. Will it not follow then that they could never suggest it but from experience?

Alc. It will.

Euph. That is to say—we perceive distance, not immediately, but by mediation of a sign, which hath no likeness to it, or necessary connexion with it, but only suggests it from repeated experience, as words do things.

Alc. Hold, Euphranor: now I think of it, the writers in optics tell us of an angle made by the two optic axes, where they meet in the visible point or object; which angle, the obtuser it is the nearer it shews the object to be, and by how much the acuter, by so much the farther off; and this from a necessary demonstrable connexion.

Euph. The mind then finds out the distance of things by geometry?

Alc. It doth.

Euph. Should it not follow, therefore, that nobody could see but those who had learned geometry, and knew something of lines and angles?

Alc. There is a sort of natural geometry which is got without learning.

Euph. Pray inform me, Alciphron, in order to frame a proof of any kind, or deduce one point from another, is it not necessary that I perceive the connexion of the terms in the premises, and the connexion of the premises with the conclusion; and, in general, to know one thing by means of another, must I not first know that other thing? When I perceive your meaning by your words, must I not first perceive the words themselves? and must I not know the premises before I infer the conclusion?

Alc. All this is true.

Euph. Whoever, therefore, collects a nearer distance from a wider angle, or a farther distance from an acuter angle, must first perceive the angles themselves. And he who doth not perceive those angles can infer nothing from them. Is it so or not?

Alc. It is as you say.

Euph. Ask now the first man you meet whether he perceives or knows anything of those optic angles? or whether he ever thinks about them, or makes any inferences from them, either by natural or artificial geometry? What answer do you think he would make?

Alc. To speak the truth, I believe his answer would be, that he knew nothing of these matters.

Euph. It cannot therefore be that men judge of distance by angles: nor, consequently, can there be any force in the argument you drew from thence, to prove that distance is perceived by means of something which hath a necessary connexion with it.

Alc. I agree with you.

9. *Euph.* To me it seems that a man may know whether he perceives a thing or no; and, if he perceives it, whether it be immediately or mediately: and, if mediately, whether by means of something like or unlike, necessarily or arbitrarily connected with it.

Alc. It seems so.

Euph. And is it not certain that distance is perceived only by experience, if it be neither perceived immediately by itself, nor by means of any image, nor of any lines and angles which are like it, or have a necessary connexion with it?

Alc. It is.

Euph. Doth it not seem to follow, from what hath been said and allowed by you, that before all experience a man would not imagine the things he saw were at any distance from him?

Alc. How! let me see.

Euph. The littleness or faintness of appearance, or any other idea or sensation not necessarily connected with or resembling distance, can no more suggest different degrees of distance, or any distance at all, to the mind which hath not experienced a connexion of the things signifying and signified, than words can suggest notions before a man hath learned the language.

Alc. I allow this to be true.

Euph. Will it not thence follow that a man born blind, and made to see, would, upon first receiving his sight, take the things he saw not to be at any distance from him, but in his eye, or rather in his mind?

Alc. I must own it seems so. And yet, on the other hand, I can hardly persuade myself that, if I were in such a state, I should think those objects which I now see at so great distance to be at no distance at all.

Euph. It seems, then, that you now think the objects of sight are at a distance from you?

Alc. Doubtless I do. Can any one question but yonder castle is at a great distance?

Euph. Tell, me Alciphron, can you discern the doors, windows, and battlements of that same castle?

Alc. I cannot. At this distance it seems only a small round tower.

Euph. But I, who have been at it, know that it is no small round tower, but a large square building with battlements and turrets, which it seems you do not see.

Alc. What will you infer from thence?

Euph. I would infer that the very object which you strictly and properly perceive by sight is not that thing which is several miles distant.

Alc. Why so?

Euph. Because a little round object is one thing, and a great square object is another. Is it not?

Alc. I cannot deny it.

Euph. Tell me, is not the visible appearance alone the proper object of sight?

Alc. It is.

What think you now (said *Euphranor*, pointing towards the heavens) of the visible appearance of yonder planet? Is it not a round luminous flat, no bigger than a six-pence?

Alc. What then?

Euph. Tell me then, what you think of the planet itself. Do you not conceive it to be a vast opaque globe, with several unequal risings and valleys?

Alc. I do.

Euph. How can you therefore conclude that the proper object of your sight exists at a distance?

Alc. I confess I know not.

Euph. For your further conviction, do but consider that crimson cloud. Think you that, if you were in the very place where it is, you would perceive anything like what you now see?

Alc. By no means. I should perceive only a dark mist.

Euph. Is it not plain, therefore, that neither the castle, the planet, nor the cloud, which you see here, are those real ones which you suppose exist at a distance?

10. *Alc.* What am I to think then? Do we see anything at all, or is it altogether fancy and illusion?

Euph. Upon the whole, it seems the proper objects of sight are light and colours, with their several shades and degrees; all which, being infinitely diversified and combined, do form a language wonderfully adapted to suggest and exhibit to us the distances, figures, situations, dimensions, and various qualities of tangible objects—not by similitude, nor yet by inference of necessary connexion, but by the arbitrary imposition of Providence, just as words suggest the things signified by them.

Alc. How! Do we not, strictly speaking, perceive by sight such things as trees, houses, men, rivers, and the like?

Euph. We do, indeed, perceive or apprehend those things by the faculty of sight. But, will it follow from thence that they are the proper and immediate objects of sight, any more than that all those things are the proper and immediate objects of hearing which are signified by the help of words or sounds?

Alc. You would have us think, then, that light, shades, and colours, variously combined, answer to the several articulations of sound in language; and that, by means thereof, all sorts of objects are suggested to the mind through the eye, in the same manner as they are suggested by words or sounds through the ear: that is, neither from necessary deduction to the judgment, nor from similitude to the fancy, but purely and solely from experience, custom, and habit.

Euph. I would not have you think anything more than the nature of things obligeth you to think, nor submit in the least to my judgment, but only to the force of truth: which is an imposition that I suppose the freest thinkers will not pretend to be exempt from.

Alc. You have led me, it seems, step by step, till I am got I know not where. But I shall try to get out again, if not by the way I came, yet by some other of my own finding.

Here *Alciphron,* having made a short pause, proceeded as follows—

11. Answer me, Euphranor, should it not follow from these principles that a man born blind, and made to see, would, at first sight, not only not perceive their distance, but also not so much as know the very things themselves which he saw, for instance, men or trees? which surely to suppose must be absurd.

Euph. I grant, in consequence of those principles, which both you and I have admitted, that such a one would never think of men, trees, or any other objects that he had been accustomed to perceive by touch, upon having his mind filled with new sensations of light and colours, whose various combinations he doth not yet understand, or know the meaning of; no more than a Chinese, upon first hearing the words *man* and *tree* would think of the things signified by them. In both cases, there must be time and experience, by repeated acts, to acquire a habit of knowing the connexion between the signs and things signified; that is to say, of understanding the language, whether of the eyes or of the ears. And I conceive no absurdity in all this.

Alc. I see, therefore, in strict philosophical truth, that rock only in the same sense that I may be said to hear it, when the word *rock* is pronounced.

Euph. In the very same.

Alc. How comes it to pass then that every one shall say he sees, for instance, a rock or a house, when those things are before his eyes; but nobody will say he hears a rock or a house, but only the words or sounds themselves by which those things are said to be signified or suggested but not heard? Besides, if vision be only a language speaking to the eyes, it may be asked, when did men learn this language? To acquire the knowledge of so many signs as go to the making up a language is a work of some difficulty. But, will any man say he hath spent time, or been at pains, to learn this Language of Vision?

Euph. No wonder; we cannot assign a time beyond our remotest memory. If we have been all practising this language, ever since our first entrance into the world: if the Author of Nature constantly speaks to the eyes of all mankind, even in their earliest infancy, whenever the eyes are open in the light, whether alone or in company: it does not seem to me at all strange that men should not be aware they had ever learned a language begun so early, and practised so constantly, as this of Vision. And, if we also consider that it is the same throughout the whole world, and not, like other languages, differing in different places, it will not seem unaccountable that men should mistake the connexion between the proper objects of sight and the things signified by them to be founded in necessary relation or likeness; or, that they should even take them for the same things. Hence it seems easy to conceive why men who do not think should confound in this language of vision the signs with the things signified, otherwise than they are wont to do in the various particular languages formed by the several nations of men.

12. It may be also worth while to observe that signs, being little considered in themselves, or for their own sake, but only in their relative capacity, and for the sake of those things whereof they are signs, it comes to pass that the mind overlooks them, so as to carry its attention immediately on to the things signified. Thus, for example, in reading we run over the characters with the slightest regard, and pass on to the meaning. Hence it is frequent for men to say, they see words, and notions, and things in reading of a book; whereas in strictness they see only the characters which suggest words, notions, and things. And, by parity of reason, may we not suppose that men, not resting in, but overlooking the immediate and proper objects of sight, as in their own nature of small moment, carry their attention onward to the very things signified, and talk as if they saw the secondary objects? which, in truth and strictness, are not seen, but only suggested and apprehended by means of the proper objects of sight, which alone are seen.

Alc. To speak my mind freely, this dissertation grows tedious, and runs into points too dry and minute for a gentleman's attention.

I thought, said *Crito,* we had been told that minute philosophers loved to consider things closely and minutely.

Alc. That is true, but in so polite an age who would be a mere philosopher? There is a certain scholastic accuracy which ill suits the freedom and ease of a well-bred man. But, to cut short this chicane, I propound it fairly to your own conscience, whether you really think that God Himself speaks every day and in every place to the eyes of all men.

Euph. That is really and in truth my opinion; and it should be yours too, if you are consistent with yourself, and abide by your own definition of language. Since you cannot deny that the great Mover and Author of nature constantly explaineth Himself to the eyes of men by the sensible intervention of arbitrary signs, which have no similitude or connexion with the things signified; so as, by compounding and disposing them, to suggest and exhibit an endless variety of objects, differing in nature, time, and place; thereby informing and directing men how to act with respect to things distant and future, as well as near and present. In consequence, I say, of your own sentiments and concessions, you have as much reason to think the Universal Agent or God speaks to your eyes, as you can have for thinking any particular person speaks to your ears.

Alc. I cannot help thinking that some fallacy runs throughout this whole ratiocination, though perhaps I may not readily point it out. Hold! let me see. In language the signs are arbitrary, are they not?

Euph. They are.

Alc. And, consequently, they do not always suggest real matters of fact. Whereas this Natural Language, as you call it, or these visible signs, do always suggest things in the same uniform way, and have the same constant regular connexion with matters of fact: whence it should seem the connexion was neccessary; and, therefore, according to the definition premised, it can be no language. How do you solve this objection?

Euph. You may solve it yourself by the help of a picture or looking-glass.

Alc. You are in the right. I see there is nothing in it. I know not what else to say to this opinion, more than that it is so odd and contrary to my way of thinking that I shall never assent to it.

13. *Euph.* Be pleased to recollect your own lectures upon prejudice, and apply them in the present case. Perhaps they may help you to follow where reason leads, and to suspect notions which are strongly rivetted, without having been ever examined.

Alc. I disdain the suspicion of prejudice. And I do not speak only for myself. I know a club of most ingenious men, the freest from prejudice of any men alive, who abhor the notion of a God, and I doubt not would be very able to untie this knot.

Upon which words of Alciphron, I, who had acted the part of an indifferent stander-by, observed to him—That it misbecame his character and repeated professions, to own an attachment to the judgment, or build upon the presumed abilities of other men, how ingenious soever; and that this proceeding might encourage his adversaries to have recourse to authority, in which perhaps they would find their account more than he.

Oh! said *Crito,* I have often observed the conduct of minute philosophers. When one of them has got a ring of disciples round him, his method is to exclaim against prejudice, and recommend thinking and reasoning, giving to understand that himself is a man of deep researches and close argument, one who examines impartially, and concludes warily. The same man, in other company, if he chance to be pressed with reason, shall laugh at logic, and assume the lazy supine airs of a fine gentleman, a wit, a *railleur,* to avoid the dryness of a regular and exact inquiry. This double face of the minute philosopher is of no small use to propagate and maintain his notions. Though to me it seems a plain case that if a fine gentleman will shake off authority, and appeal from religion to reason, unto reason he must go: and, if he cannot go without leading-strings, surely he had better be led by the authority of the public than by that of any knot of minute philosophers.

Alc. Gentlemen, this discourse is very irksome, and needless. For my part, I am a friend to inquiry. I am willing reason should have its full and free scope. I build on no man's authority. For my part, I have no interest in denying a God. Any man may believe or not believe a God, as he pleases, for me. But, after all, Euphranor must allow me to stare a little at his conclusions.

Euph. The conclusions are yours as much as mine, for you were led to them by your own concessions.

14. You, it seems, stare to find that God is not far from every one of us; and that in Him we live, and move, and have our being. You, who, in the beginning of this morning's conference, thought it strange that God should leave Himself without a witness, do now think it strange the witness should be so full and clear.

Alc. I must own I do. I was aware, indeed, of a certain metaphysical hypothesis of our seeing all things in God by the union of the human soul with the intelligible substance of the Deity, which neither I, nor any one else could make sense of. But I never imagined it could be pretended that we saw God with our fleshy eyes as plain as we see any human person whatsoever, and that He daily speaks to our senses in a manifest and clear dialect.

Cri. [As for that metaphysical hypothesis, I can make no more of it than you. But I think it plain] this Optic Language hath a necessary connexion with knowledge, wisdom, and goodness. It is equivalent to a constant creation, betokening an immediate act of power and providence. It cannot be accounted for by mechanical principles, by atoms, attractions, or effluvia. The instantaneous production and reproduction of so many signs, combined, dissolved, transposed, diversified, and adapted to such an endless variety of purposes, ever shifting with the occasions and suited to them, being utterly inexplicable and unaccountable by the laws of motion, by chance, by fate, or the like blind principles, doth set forth and testify the immediate operation of a spirit or thinking being; and not merely of a spirit, which every motion or gravitation may possibly infer, but of one wise, good, and provident Spirit, which directs and rules and governs the world. Some philos ophers, being convinced of the wisdom and power of the Creator, from the make and contrivance of organised bodies and orderly system of the world, did nevertheless imagine that he left this system with all its parts and contents well adjusted and put in motion, as an artist leaves a clock, to go thenceforward of itself for a certain period. But this Visual Language proves not a Creator merely, but a provident Governor, actually and intimately present, and attentive to all our interests and motions, who watches over our conduct, and takes care of our minutest actions and designs throughout the whole course of our lives, informing, admonishing, and directing incessantly, in a most evident and sensible manner. This is truly wonderful.

Euph. And is it not so, that men should be encompassed by such a wonder, without reflecting on it?

15. Something there is of Divine and admirable in this Language, addressed to our eyes, that may well awaken the mind, and deserve its utmost attention:—it is learned

with so little pains: it expresseth the differences of things so clearly and aptly: it instructs with such facility and despatch, by one glance of the eye conveying a greater variety of advices, and a more distinct knowledge of things, than could be got by a discourse of several hours. And, while it informs, it amuses and entertains the mind with such singular pleasure and delight. It is of such excellent use in giving a stability and permanency to human discourse, in recording sounds and bestowing life on dead languages, enabling us to converse with men of remote ages and countries. And it answers so apposite to the uses and necessities of mankind, informing us more distinctly of those objects whose nearness and magnitude qualify them to be of greatest detriment or benefit to our bodies, and less exactly in proportion as their littleness or distance makes them of less concern to us.

Alc. And yet these strange things affect men but little.

Euph. But they are not strange, they are familiar; and that makes them be overlooked. Things which rarely happen strike; whereas frequency lessens the admiration of things, though in themselves ever so admirable. Hence, a common man, who is not used to think and make reflexions, would probably be more convinced of the being of a God by one single sentence heard once in his life from the sky than by all the experience he has had of this Visual Language, contrived with such exquisite skill, so constantly addressed to his eyes, and so plainly declaring the nearness, wisdom, and providence of Him with whom we have to do.

Alc. After all, I cannot satisfy myself how men should be so little surprised or amazed about this visive faculty, if it was really of a nature so surprising and amazing.

Euph. But let us suppose a nation of men blind from their infancy, among whom a stranger arrives, the only man who can see in all the country; let us suppose this stranger travelling with some of the natives, and that one while he foretels to them that, in case they walk straight forward, in half a hour they shall meet men or cattle, or come to a house; that, if they turn to the right and proceed, they shall in a few minutes be in danger of falling down a precipice; that, shaping their course to the left, they will in such a time arrive at a river, a wood, or a mountain. What think you? Must they not be infinitely surprised that one who had never been in their country before should know it so much better than themselves? And would not those predictions seem to them as unaccountable and incredible as Prophecy to a minute philosopher?

Alc. I cannot deny it.

Euph. But it seems to require intense thought to be able to unravel a prejudice that has been so long forming; to get over the vulgar errors or ideas common to both senses; and so to distinguish between the objects of sight and touch, which have grown (if I may so say), blended together in our fancy, as to be able to suppose ourselves exactly in the state that one of those men would be in, if he were made to see. And yet this I believe is possible, and might seem worth the pains of a little thinking, especially to those men whose proper employment and profession it is to think, and unravel prejudices, and confute mistakes.

Alc. I frankly own I cannot find my way out of this maze, and should gladly be set right by those who see better than myself.

Cri. The pursuing this subject in their own thoughts would possibly open a new scene to those speculative gentlemen of the minute philosophy. It puts me in mind of a passage in the Psalmist, where he represents God to be covered with light as with a garment, and

would methinks be no ill comment on that ancient notion
of some eastern sages—that God had light for His body,
and truth for His soul.

This conversation lasted till a servant came to tell us
the tea was ready: upon which we walked in, and found
Lysicles at the tea-table.

16. As soon as we sat down, I am glad, said *Alciphron,* that I have here found my second, a fresh man
to maintain our common cause, which, I doubt, Lysicles
will think hath suffered by his absence.

Lys. Why so?

Alc. I have been drawn into some concessions you will
not like.

Lys. Let me know what they are.

Alc. Why, that there is such a thing as a God, and
that His existence is very certain.

Lys. Bless me! How came you to entertain so wild
a notion?

Alc. You know we profess to follow reason wherever
it leads. And in short I have been reasoned into it.

Lys. Reasoned! You should say, amused with words,
bewildered with sophistry.

Euph. Have you a mind to hear the same reasoning
that led Alciphron and me step by step, that we may
examine whether it be sophistry or no?

Lys. As to that I am very easy. I guess all that can
be said on that head. It shall be my business to help
my friend out, whatever arguments drew him in.

Euph. Will you admit the premises and deny the conclusions?

Lys. What if I admit the conclusion?

Euph. How! will you grant there is a God?

Lys. Perhaps I may.

Euph. Then we are agreed.

Lys. Perhaps not.

Euph. O Lysicles, you are a subtle adversary. I know not what you would be at.

Lys. You must know then that at bottom the *being* of a God is a point in itself of small consequence, and a man may make this concession without yielding much. The great point is *what sense the word God is to be taken in.* The very Epicureans allowed the being of gods; but then they were indolent gods, unconcerned with human affairs. Hobbes allowed a corporeal God: and Spinosa held the universe to be God. And yet nobody doubts they were staunch free-thinkers. I could wish indeed the word God were quite omitted; because in most minds it is coupled with a sort of superstitious awe, the very root of all religion. I shall not, nevertheless, be much disturbed, though the name be retained, and the being of a God allowed in any sense but in that of a Mind which knows all things, and beholds human actions, like some judge or magistrate, with infinite observation and intelligence. The belief of a God in this sense fills a man's mind with scruples, lays him under constraints, and embitters his very being: but in another sense it may be attended with no great ill consequence. This I know was the opinion of our great Diagoras,[1] who told me he would never have been at the pains to find out a demonstration that there was no God, if the received notion of God had been the same with that of some Fathers and Schoolmen.

Euph. Pray what was that?

17. *Lys.* You must know, Diagoras, a man of much reading and inquiry, had discovered that once upon a time the most profound and speculative divines, finding it impossible to reconcile the attributes of God, taken

[1] This 'demonstration' is attributed to Anthony Collins. (FRASER.)

in the common sense, or in any known sense, with human
reason, and the appearances of things, taught that the
words *knowledge, wisdom, goodness,* and such like, when
spoken of the Deity, must be understood in a quite different sense from what they signify in the vulgar acceptation, or from anything that we can form a notion of
or conceive. Hence, whatever objections might be made
against the attributes of God they easily solved—by
denying those attributes belonged to God, in this, or
that, or any known particular sense or notion; which was
the same thing as to deny they belonged to Him at all.
And thus denying the attributes of God, they in effect
denied His being, though perhaps they were not aware
of it.

Suppose, for instance, a man should object that future
contingencies were inconsistent with the Foreknowledge
of God, because it is repugnant that certain knowledge
should be of an uncertain thing: it was a ready and an
easy answer to say that this may be true with respect
to knowledge taken in the common sense, or in any sense
that we can possibly form any notion of; but that there
would not appear the same inconsistency between the
contingent nature of things and Divine Foreknowledge,
taken to signify somewhat that we know nothing of,
which in God supplies the place of what we understand
by knowledge; from which it differs not in quantity or
degree of perfection, but altogether, and in kind, as light
doth from sound;—and even more, since these agree
in that they are both sensations; whereas knowledge in
God hath no sort of resemblance or agreement with any
notion that man can frame of knowledge. The like may
be said of all the other attributes, which indeed may by
this means be equally reconciled with everything or with
nothing. But all men who think must needs see this is
cutting knots and not untying them. For, how are things

reconciled with the Divine attributes when these attributes themselves are in every intelligible sense denied; and, consequently, the very notion of God taken away, and nothing left but the name, without any meaning annexed to it? In short, the belief that there is an unknown subject of attributes absolutely unknown is a very innocent doctrine; which the acute Diagoras well saw, and was therefore wonderfully delighted with this system.

18. For, said he, if this could once make its way and obtain in the world, there would be an end of all natural or rational religion, which is the basis both of the Jewish and the Christian: for he who comes to God, or enters himself in the church of God, must first believe that there is a God in some intelligible sense; and not only that there is *something in general,* without any proper notion, though never so inadequate, of any of its qualities or attributes: for this may be fate, or chaos, or plastic nature, or anything else as well as God. Nor will it avail to say—There is something in this unknown being *analogous* to knowledge and goodness; that is to say, which produceth those effects which we could not conceive to be produced by men, in any degree, without knowledge and goodness. For, this is in fact to give up the point in dispute between theists and atheists—the question having always been, not whether there was a Principle (which point was allowed by all philosophers, as well before as since Anaxagoras), but whether this Principle was a *νοῦς*, a thinking intelligent being: that is to say, whether that order, and beauty, and use, visible in natural effects, could be produced by anything but a Mind or Intelligence, in the proper sense of the word? And whether there must not be true, real, and proper knowledge, in the First Cause? We will, there-

fore, acknowledge that all those natural effects which
are vulgarly ascribed to knowledge and wisdom proceed
from a being in which there is, properly speaking, no
knowledge or wisdom at all, but only something else,
which in reality is the cause of those things which men,
for want of knowing better, ascribe to what they call
knowledge and wisdom and understanding. You wonder
perhaps to hear a man of pleasure, who diverts himself
as I do, philosophize at this rate. But you should consider that much is to be got by conversing with ingenious men, which is a short way to knowledge, that saves
a man the drudgery of reading and thinking.

And, now we have granted to you that there is a God
in this indefinite sense, I would fain see what use you
can make of this concession. You cannot argue from
unknown attributes, or, which is the same thing, from
attributes in an unknown sense. You cannot prove that
God is to be loved for His goodness, or feared for His
justice, or respected for His knowledge: all which consequences, we own, would follow from those attributes
admitted in an intelligible sense. But we deny that
those or any other consequences can be drawn from
attributes admitted in no particular sense, or in a sense
which none of us understand. Since, therefore, nothing
can be inferred from such an account of God, about
conscience, or worship or religion, you may even make
the best of it. And, not to be singular, we will use the
name too, and so at once there is an end of atheism.

Euph. This account of a Deity is new to me. I do
not like it, and therefore shall leave it to be maintained
by those who do.

19. *Cri.* It is not new to me. I remember not long
since to have heard a minute philosopher triumph upon
this very point; which put me on inquiring what founda-

tion there was for it in the Fathers or Schoolmen. And,
for aught that I can find, it owes its original to those
writings which have been published under the name of
Dionysius the Areopagite. The author of which, it must
be owned, hath written upon the Divine attributes in
a very singular style. In his treatise of the Celestial
Hierarchy,[1] he saith that God is something above all
essence and life, ὑπὲρ πᾶσαν οὐσίαν καὶ ζωήν; and again, in
his treatise of the Divine Names [2] that He is above all
wisdom and understanding, ὑπὲρ πᾶσαν σοφίαν καὶ σύνεσιν,
ineffable and innominable, ἄρρητος καὶ ἀνώνυμος; the wisdom
of God he terms an unreasonable, unintelligent, and
foolish wisdom; τὴν ἄλογον, καὶ ἄνουν, καὶ μωρὰν σοφίαν.
But then the reason he gives for expressing himself in
this strange manner is, that the Divine wisdom is the
cause of all reason, wisdom, and understanding, and
therein are contained the treasures of all wisdom and
knowledge. He calls God ὑπέρσοφος and ὑπέζως; as if
wisdom and life were words not worthy to express the
Divine perfections: and he adds that the attributes unintelligent and unperceiving must be ascribed to the Divinity, not κατ᾽ἔλλειψιν, by way of defect, but καθ᾽ὑπεροχήν,
by way of eminency; which he explains by our giving
the name of darkness to light inaccessible. And, notwithstanding the harshness of his expressions in some
places, he affirms over and over in others—that God
knows all things; not that He is beholden to the creatures
for His knowledge, but by knowing Himself, from
whom they all derive their being, and in whom they are
contained as in their cause. It was late before these
writings appear to have been known in the world; and,
although they obtained credit during the age of the
Schoolmen, yet, since critical learning hath been culti-

[1] [De Hierarch. Cœlest, cap. 2.]—BERKELEY.
[2] [De Nom. Div. cap. 7.]—BERKELEY.

vated, they have lost that credit, and are at this day given up for spurious, as containing several evident marks of a much later date than the age of Dionysius. Upon the whole, although this method of growing in expression and dwindling in notion, of clearing up doubts by nonsense, and avoiding difficulties by running into affected contradictions, may perhaps proceed from a well-meant zeal, yet it appears not to be according to knowledge; and, instead of reconciling atheists to the truth, hath, I doubt, a tendency to confirm them in their own persuasion. It should seem, therefore, very weak and rash in a Christian to adopt this harsh language of an apocryphal writer preferably to that of the Holy Scriptures. I remember, indeed, to have read of a certain philosopher, who lived some centuries ago, that used to say—if these supposed works of Dionysius had been known to the primitive Fathers, they would have furnished them admirable weapons against the heretics, and would have saved a world of pains. But the event since their discovery hath by no means confirmed his opinion.

It must be owned, the celebrated Picus of Mirandula, among his nine hundred conclusions (which that prince, being very young, proposed to maintain by public disputation at Rome), hath this for one—to wit, that it is more improper to say of God, He is an intellect or intelligent Being, than to say of a reasonable soul that it is an angel: which doctrine it seems was not relished. And Picus, when he comes to defend it, supports himself altogether by the example and authority of Dionysius, and in effect explains it away into a mere verbal difference—affirming that neither Dionysius nor himself ever meant to deprive God of knowledge, or to deny that He knows all things; but that, as reason is of kind peculiar to man, so by intellection he understands a kind or manner of knowing peculiar to angels; and that the knowledge which is in God is more above the intellection of angels than angel is above man. He adds that, as his tenet consists with admitting the most perfect knowledge in God, so he would by no means be understood to exclude from the Deity intellection itself, taken in the common or general sense, but only that peculiar sort of intellection proper to angels, which he thinks ought not to be attributed to God any more than human reason. Picus,[1] therefore, though he speaks as the apocryphal Dionysius, yet, when he explains himself, it is evident he speaks like other men. And, although the forementioned books of the Celestial Hierarchy and of the Divine Names, being attributed to a saint and martyr of the apostolical age, were respected by the Schoolmen, yet it is certain they rejected or softened his harsh expressions, and explained away or reduced his doctrine to the received notions taken from Holy Scripture and the light of nature.

20. Thomas Aquinas expresseth his sense of this point in the following manner. All perfections, saith he, derived from God to the creatures are in a certain higher sense, or (as the Schoolmen term it) eminently in God. Whenever therefore a name borrowed from any perfection in the creature is attributed to God, we must exclude from its signification everything that belongs to the imperfect manner wherein that attribute is found in the creature. Whence he concludes that knowledge in God is not a habit but a pure act.[2] And again, the same Doctor observes that our intellect gets its notions of all

---

[1] [*Pic. Mirand. in Apolog.* p. 155, ed. Bas.]—BERKELEY.

[2] [*Sum. Theolog.* Part I. quest. xiv. art i.]—BERKELEY.

sorts of perfections from the creatures, and that as it apprehends those perfections so it signifies them by names. Therefore, saith he, in attributing these names to God we are to consider two things: first the perfections themselves, as goodness, life, and the like, which are properly in God; and secondly, the manner which is peculiar to the creature, and cannot, strictly and properly speaking, be said to agree to the Creator.[1]

And although Suarez, with other Schoolmen, teacheth that the mind of man conceiveth knowledge and will to be in God as faculties or operations, by analogy only to created beings, yet he gives it plainly as his opinion that when knowledge is said not to be properly in God it must be understood in a sense including imperfection, such as discursive knowledge, or the like imperfect kind found in the creatures: and that, none of those imperfections in the knowledge of men or angels belonging to the formal notion of knowledge, or to knowledge as such, it will not thence follow that knowledge, in its proper formal sense, may not be attributed to God. And of knowledge taken in general for the clear evident understanding of all truth, he expressly affirms that it is in God, and that this was never denied by any philosopher who believed a God.[2] It was, indeed, a current opinion in the schools that even Being itself should be attributed analogically to God and the creatures. That is, they held that God, the supreme, independent, self-originate cause and source of all beings, must not be supposed to *exist* in the same sense with created beings; not that He exists less truly, properly, or formally than they, but only because He exists in a more eminent and perfect manner.

[1] [*Ibid.* quest. xiii. art. iii.]—BERKELEY.
[2] [*Suaez, Dis. Metaph.* tom. II. disp. xxx. sect. 15.]—BERKELEY.

21. But, to prevent any man's being led, by mistaking the scholastic use of the terms *analogy* and *analogical,* into an opinion that we cannot frame in any degree a true and proper notion of attributes applied by analogy, or, in the school phrase, predicated analogically, it may not be amiss to inquire into the true sense and meaning of those words. Every one knows that *analogy* is a Greek word used by mathematicians to signify a similitude of proportions. For instance, when we observe that two is to six as three is to nine, this similitude or equality of proportion is termed analogy. And, although proportion strictly signifies the habitude or relation of one quantity to another, yet, in a looser and translated sense, it hath been applied to signify every other habitude; and, consequently, the term analogy comes to signify all similitude of relations or habitudes whatsoever. Hence the Schoolmen tell us there is analogy between intellect and sight; forasmuch as intellect is to the mind what sight is to the body, and that he who governs the state is analogous to him who steers a ship. Hence a a prince is analogically styled a pilot, being to the state as a pilot is to his vessel [1].

For the further clearing of this point, it is to be observed that a twofold analogy is distinguished by the Schoolmen—metaphorical and proper. Of the first kind there are frequent instances in Holy Scripture, attributing human parts and passions to God. When He is represented as having a finger, an eye, or an ear; when He is said to repent, to be angry, or grieved; every one sees that analogy is metaphorical. Because those parts and passions, taken in the proper signification, must in every degree necessarily, and from the formal nature of the thing, include imperfection. When, therefore, it is said—the finger of God appears in this or that event,

[1] [Vide *Cajetan. de Nom. Analog.* cap. 3.]—BERKELEY.

men of common sense mean no more but that it is as truly
ascribed to God as the works wrought by human fingers
are to man: and so of the rest. But the case is different
when wisdom and knowledge are attributed to God.
Passions and senses, as such, imply defect; but in knowledge simply, or as such, there is no defect. Knowledge,
therefore, in the proper formal meaning of the word,
may be attributed to God *proportionably,* that is, preserving a proportion to the infinite nature of God. We
may say, therefore, that as God is infinitely above man,
so is the knowledge of God infinitely above the knowledge of man, and this is what Cajetan calls *analogia
proprie facta.* And after this same analogy we must
understand all those attributes to belong to the Deity
which in themselves simply, and as such, denote perfection. We may, therefore, consistently with what hath
been premised, affirm that all sorts of perfection which
we can conceive in a finite spirit are in God, but without
any of that allay which is found in the creatures. This
doctrine, therefore, of analogical perfections in God,
or our knowing God by analogy, seems very much mis-
understood and misapplied by those who would infer
from thence that we cannot frame any direct or proper
notion, though never so inadequate, of knowledge or wisdom, as they are in the Deity; or understand any more
of them than one born blind can of light and colours.

22. And now, gentlemen, it may be expected I should
ask your pardon for having dwelt so long on a point of
metaphysics, and introduced such unpolished and un-
fashionable writers as the Schoolmen into good company:
but, as Lysicles gave the occasion, I leave him to answer
for it.

Lys. I never dreamt of this dry dissertation. But, if
I have been the occasion of discussing these scholastic

points, by my unluckily mentioning the Schoolmen, it
was my first fault of the kind, and I promise it shall be
the last. The meddling with crabbed authors of any
sort is none of my taste. I grant one meets now and
then with a good notion in what we call dry writers,
such a one for example as this I was speaking of, which
I must own struck my fancy. But then, for these we
have such as Prodicus or Diagoras, who look into obso-
lete books, and save the rest of us that trouble.

Cri. So you pin your faith upon them?

Lys. It is only for some odd opinions, and matters of
fact, and critical points. Besides, we know the men
to whom we give credit: they are judicious and honest,
and have no end to serve but truth. And I am confident some author or other has maintained the forementioned notion in the same sense as Diagoras related it.

Cri. That may be. But it never was a received notion,
and never will, so long as men believe a God: the same
arguments that prove a first cause proving an intelligent
cause;—intelligent, I say, in the proper sense; wise and
good in the true and formal acceptation of the words.
Otherwise, it is evident that every syllogism brought to
prove those attributes, or, which is the same thing, to
prove the being of a God, will be found to consist of
four terms, and consequently can conclude nothing.
But for your part, Alciphron, you have been fully convinced that God is a thinking intelligent being, in the
same sense with other spirits; though not in the same
imperfect manner or degree.

23. *Alc.* And yet I am not without my scruples: for,
with knowledge you infer wisdom, and with wisdom goodness. [Though I cannot see that it is either wise or
good to enact such laws as can never be obeyed.]

Cri. Doth any one find fault with the exactness of

geometrical rules, because no one in practice can attain to it? The perfection of a rule is useful, even though it is not reached. Many approach what all may fall short of.

Alc. But how is it possible to conceive God so good and man so wicked? It may, perhaps, with some colour be alleged that a little soft shadowing of evil sets off the bright and luminous parts of the creation, and so contributes to the beauty of the whole piece; but for blots so large and so black it is impossible to account by that principle. That there should be so much vice, and so little virtue upon earth, and that the laws of God's kingdom should be so ill observed by His subjects, is what can never be reconciled with that surpassing wisdom and goodness of the supreme Monarch.

Euph. Tell me, Alciphron, would you argue that a state was ill administered, or judge of the manners of its citizens, by the disorders committed in the jail or dungeon?

Alc. I would not.

Euph. And, for aught we know, this spot, with the few sinners on it, bears no greater proportion to the universe of intelligences than a dungeon doth to a kingdom. It seems we are led not only by revelation, but by common sense, observing and inferring from the analogy of visible things, to conclude there are innumerable orders of intelligent beings more happy and more perfect than man; whose life is but a span, and whose place, this earthly globe, is but a point, in respect of the whole system of God's creation. We are dazzled, indeed, with the glory and grandeur of things here below, because we know no better. But, I am apt to think, if we knew what it was to be an angel for one hour, we should return to this world, though it were to sit on the brightest throne in it, with vastly more loathing and re-

luctance than we would now descend into a loathsome
dungeon or sepulchre.

24. *Cri.* To me it seems natural that such a weak,
passionate, and short-sighted creature as man should be
ever liable to scruples of one kind or other. But, as this
same creature is apt to be over-positive in judging, and
over-hasty in concluding, it falls out that these difficulties and scruples about God's conduct are made objections to His being. And so men come to argue from
their own defects against the Divine perfections. And,
as the views and humours of men are different and often
opposite, you may sometimes see them deduce the same
atheistical conclusions from contrary premises. I knew
an instance of this in two minute philosophers of my
acquaintance, who used to argue each from his own
temper against a Providence. One of them, a man of
a choleric and vindictive spirit, said he could not believe
a Providence, because London was not swallowed up or
consumed by fire from heaven; the streets being, as he
said, full of people who shew no other belief or worship of God but perpetually praying that He would
damn, rot, sink, and confound them. The other, being
of an indolent easy temper, concluded there could be no
such thing as Providence; for that a being of consum-
mate wisdom must needs employ himself better than in
minding the prayers and actions and little interests of
mankind.

Alc. After all, if God have no passions, how can it
be true that vengeance is His? Or how can He be said
to be jealous of His glory?

Cri. We believe that God executes vengeance without
revenge, and is jealous without weakness, just as the
mind of man sees without eyes, and apprehends without
hands.

25. *Alc.* To put a period to this discourse, we will grant there is a God in this dispassionate sense: but what then? What hath this to do with Religion or Divine worship? To what purpose are all these prayers, and praises, and thanksgivings, and singing of psalms, which the foolish vulgar call serving God? What sense, or use, or end is there in all these things?

Cri. We worship God, we praise and pray to Him: not because we think that He is proud of our worship, or fond of our praise or prayers, and affected with them as mankind are; or that all our service can contribute in the least degree to His happiness or good: but because it is good for us to be so disposed towards God: because it is just and right, and suitable to the nature of things, and becoming the relation we stand in to our supreme Lord and Governor.

Alc. If it be good for us to worship God, it should seem that the Christian Religion, which pretends to teach men the knowledge and worship of God, was of some use and benefit to mankind.

Cri. Doubtless.

Alc. If this can be made appear, I shall own myself very much mistaken.

Cri. It is now near dinner-time. Wherefore, if you please, we will put an end to this conversation for the present, and to-morrow morning resume our subject.

* * * * * * *

THE SEVENTH DIALOGUE

* * * * * * *

16. *Alc.* I will allow, Euphranor, this reasoning of yours to have all the force you meant it should have. I freely own there may be mysteries; that we may believe where we do not understand; and that faith may be of

use, although its object is not distinctly apprehended. In a word, I grant there may be faith and mysteries in other things, but not in religion: and that for this plain reason, because it is absurd to suppose there should be any such thing as religion; and, if there be no religion, it follows there cannot be religious faith or mysteries. Religion, it is evident, implies the worship of a God, which worship supposeth rewards and punishments, which suppose merits and demerits, actions good and evil, and these suppose *human liberty,* a thing impossible: and, consequently, religion, a thing built thereon, must be an unreasonable absurd thing. There can be no rational hopes or fears where there is no guilt; nor any guilt where there is nothing done but what unavoidably follows from the structure of the world and the laws of motion. Corporeal objects strike on the organs of sense, whence ensues a vibration in the nerves, which, being communicated to the soul or animal spirit in the brain or root of the nerves, produceth therein that motion called volition: and this produceth a new determination in the spirits, causing them to flow into such nerves as must necessarily by the laws of mechanism produce such certain actions. This being the case, it follows that those things which vulgarly pass for human actions are to be esteemed mechanical, and that they are falsely ascribed to a free principle. There is therefore no foundation for praise or blame, fear or hope, reward or punishment; nor consequently for religion, which, as I observed before, is built upon and supposeth those things.

Euph. You imagine, Alciphron, if I rightly understand you, that man is a sort of organ played on by outward objects, which, according to the different shape and texture of the nerves, produce different motions and effects therein.

Alc. Man may, indeed, be fitly compared to an organ: but a puppet is the very thing. You must know that certain particles, issuing forth in right lines from all sensible objects, compose so many rays, or filaments, which drive, draw, and actuate every part of the soul and body of man, just as threads or wires do the joints of that little wooden machine vulgarly called a *puppet:* with this only difference, that the latter are gross, and visible to common eyes, whereas the former are too fine and subtle to be discerned by any but a sagacious free-thinker. This admirably accounts for all those operations which we have been taught to ascribe to a thinking principle within us.

Euph. This is an ingenious thought, and must be of great use in freeing men from all anxiety about moral notions; as it transfers the principle of action from the human soul to things outward and foreign. But I have my scruples about it. For you suppose the mind in a literal sense to be moved, and its volitions to be mere motions. Now, if another should affirm, as it is not impossible some or other may, that the soul is incorporeal, and that motion is one thing and volition another, I would fain know how you could make your point clear to such a one. It must be owned very clear to those who admit the soul to be corporeal, and all her acts to be but so many motions. Upon this supposition, indeed, the light wherein you place human nature is no less true than it is fine and new. But, let any one deny this supposition, which is easily done, and the whole superstructure falls to the ground. If we grant the above-mentioned points, I will not deny a fatal necessity must ensue. But I see no reason for granting them. On the contrary, it seems plain that motion and thought are two things as really and as manifestly distinct as a triangle and a sound. It seems, therefore, that, in order to prove the necessity of human actions, you suppose what wants proof as much as the very point to be proved.

17. *Alc.* But, supposing the mind incorporeal, I shall, nevertheless, be able to prove my point. Not to amuse you with far-fetched arguments, I shall only desire you to look into your own breast and observe how things pass there, when an object offers itself to the mind. First, the understanding considers it: in the next place, the judgment decrees about it, as a thing to be chosen or rejected, to be omitted or done, in this or that manner: and this decree of the judgment doth necessarily determine the will, whose office is merely to execute what is ordained by another faculty: consequently, there is no such thing as freedom of the will. For, that which is necessary cannot be free. In freedom there should be an indifference to either side of the question, a power to act or not to act, without prescription or control: and without this indifference and this power, it is evident the will cannot be free. But it is no less evident that the will is not indifferent in its actions, being absolutely determined and governed by the judgment. Now, whatever moves the judgment, whether the greatest present uneasiness, or the greatest apparent good, or whatever else it be, it is all one to the point in hand. The will, being ever concluded and controlled by the judgment, is in all cases alike under necessity. There is, indeed, throughout the whole of human nature, nothing like a principle of freedom, every faculty being determined in all its acts by something foreign to it. The understanding, for instance, cannot alter its idea, but must necessarily see it such as it presents itself. The appetites by a natural necessity are carried towards their respective objects. Reason cannot infer indifferently anything from anything, but is limited by the nature and

connexion of things, and the eternal rules of reasoning. And, as this is confessedly the case of all other faculties, so it equally holds with respect to the will itself, as hath been already shewn. And, if we may credit the divine Characteriser of our times, this above all others must be allowed the most slavish faculty. 'Appetite (saith that noble writer [1]), which is elder brother to Reason, being the lad of stronger growth, is sure, on every contest, to take the advantage of drawing all to his own side. And Will, so highly boasted, is but at best a foot-ball or top between these youngsters, who prove very unfortunately matched; till the youngest, instead of now and then a kick or lash bestowed to little purpose, forsakes the ball or top itself, and begins to lay about his elder brother.'

Cri. This beautiful parable for style and manner might equal those of a known English writer in low life, renowned for allegory, were it not a little incorrect, making the weaker lad find his account in laying about the stronger.

Alc. This is helped up by supposing the stronger lad the greater coward. But, be that as it will, so far as it relates to the point in hand, this is a clear state of the case.

The same point may be also proved from the prescience of God. That which is certainly foreknown will certainly be. And what is certain is necessary. And necessary actions cannot be the effect of free-will. Thus you have this fundamental point of our free-thinking philosophy demonstrated different ways.

Euph. Tell me, Alciphron, do you think it implies a contradiction that God should make a man free?

Alc. I do not.

Euph. It is then possible there may be such a thing?

Alc. This I do not deny.

[1] Shaftesbury. See *Characteristics*, vol. I.

Euph. You can therefore conceive and suppose such a free agent?

Alc. Admitting that I can; what then?

Euph. Would not such a one think that he acted?

Alc. He would.

Euph. And condemn himself for some actions, and approve himself for others?

Alc. This too I grant.

Euph. Would he not think he deserved reward or punishment?

Alc. He would.

Euph. And are not all these characters actually found in man?

Alc. They are.

Euph. Tell me now, what other character of your supposed free agent may not actually be found in man? For, if there is none such, we must conclude that man hath all the marks of a free agent.

Alc. Let me see! I was certainly overseen in granting it possible, even for Almighty power, to make such a thing as a free agent. I wonder how I came to make such an absurd concession, after what had been, as I observed before, demonstrated so many different ways.

Euph. [Certainly whatever is possible may be supposed: and whatever doth not imply a contradiction is possible to an Infinite Power: therefore, if a natural agent implieth no contradiction, such a being may be supposed. Perhaps, from this supposition, I might infer man to be free. But I will not suppose him that free agent; since, it seems, you pretend to have demonstrated the contrary.] O Alciphron! it is vulgarly observed that men judge of others by themselves. But, in judging of me by this rule, you may be mistaken. Many things are plain to one of your sagacity, which are not so to me, who am often bewildered rather than enlight-

ened by those very proofs that with you pass for clear
and evident. And, indeed, be the inference never so
just, yet, so long as the premises are not clear, I cannot
be thoroughly convinced. You must give me leave therefore to propose some questions, the solution of which
may perhaps shew what at present I am not able to
discern.

Alc. I shall leave what hath been said with you, to
consider and ruminate upon. It is now time to set out
on our journey: there is, therefore, no room for a long
string of question and answer.

18. *Euph.* I shall then only beg leave, in a summary
manner, to make a remark or two on what you have
advanced. In the first place, I observe you take that for
granted which I cannot grant, when you assert whatever
is certain the same to be necessary. To me, certain and
necessary seem very different; there being nothing in the
former notion that implies constraint, nor consequently
which may not consist with a man's being accountable
for his actions. If it is foreseen that such an action
shall be done, may it not also be foreseen that it shall
be an effect of human choice and liberty? In the next
place, I observe that you very nicely abstract and distinguish the actions of the mind, judgment, and will:
that you make use of such terms as power, faculty, act,
determination, indifference, freedom, necessity, and the
like, as if they stood for distinct abstract ideas: and
that this supposition seems to ensnare the mind into the
same perplexities and errors, which, in all other instances, are observed to attend the doctrine of abstraction. It is self-evident that there is such a thing as
motion: and yet there have been found philosophers,
who, by refined reasoning, would undertake to prove
that there was no such thing. *Walking before them* was

thought the proper way to confute those ingenious men.
It is no less evident that man is a free agent: and
though, by abstracted reasonings, you would puzzle
me, and seem to prove the contrary, yet, so long as
I am conscious of my own actions, this inward evidence
of plain fact will bear me up against all your reasonings, however subtle and refined. The confuting plain
points by obscure ones may perhaps convince me of the
ability of your philosophers, but never of their tenets.
I cannot conceive why the acute Cratylus [1] should suppose a power of acting in the appetite and reason, and
none at all in the will? Allowing, I say, the distinction
of three such beings in the mind, I do not see how this
could be true. But, if I cannot abstract and distinguish
so many beings in the soul of man so accurately as you
do, I do not find it necessary; since it is evident to me,
in the gross and concrete, that I am a free agent. Nor
will it avail to say, the will is governed by the judgment, or determined by the object, while, in every sudden
common cause, I cannot discern nor abstract the decree
of the judgment from the command of the will; while I
know the sensible object to be absolutely inert: and
lastly, while I am conscious that I am an active being,
who can and do determine myself. If I should suppose
things spiritual to be corporeal, or refine things actual
and real into general abstracted notions, or by metaphysical skill split things simple and individual into
manifold parts, I do not know what may follow. But, if
I take things as they are, and ask any plain untutored
man, whether he acts or is free in this or that particular
action, he readily assents, and I as readily believe him—
from what I find within. And thus, by an induction
of particulars, I may conclude man to be a free agent,
although I may be puzzled to define or conceive a notion

[1] Shaftesbury.

of freedom in general and abstract. And if man be
free, he is plainly accountable. But, if you shall define,
abstract, suppose, and it shall follow that, according
to your definitions, abstractions, and suppositions, there
can be no freedom in man, and you shall thence infer
that he is not accountable, I shall make bold to depart
from your metaphysical Abstracted Sense, and appeal to
the Common Sense of mankind.

19. If we consider the notions that obtain in the
world of guilt and merit, praise and blame, accountable
and unaccountable, we shall find the common question,
in order to applaud or censure, acquit or condemn a man,
is, whether *he* did such an action? and whether he was
himself when he did it? which comes to the same thing.
It should seem, therefore, that, in the ordinary commerce
of mankind, any person is esteemed accountable simply
as he is an agent. And, though you should tell me that
man is inactive, and that the sensible objects act upon
him, yet my own experience assures me of the contrary.
I know I act: and what I act I am accountable for.
And, if this be true, the foundation of religion and
morality remains unshaken. Religion, I say, is concerned no further than that man should be accountable:
and this he is, according to my sense, and the common
sense of the world, if he acts; and that he doth act is
self-evident. The grounds, therefore, and ends of religion are secured, whether your philosophic notion of
liberty agrees with man's actions or no; and whether his
actions are certain or contingent: the question being not
whether he did it with a free will? or what determined
his will? not, whether it was certain or foreknown that
he would do it? but only, whether he did it *wilfully?*
as what must entitle him to the guilt or merit of it.

Alc. But still, the question recurs, whether man be free?

Euph. To determine this question, ought we not at first to determine what is meant by the word *free?*

Alc. We ought.

Euph. In my opinion, a man is said to be free, so far forth as he can do what he will. Is this so, or is it not?

Alc. It seems so.

Euph. Man, therefore, acting according to his will, is to be accounted free.

Alc. This I admit to be true in the vulgar sense. But a philosopher goes higher, and inquires whether man be free to will?

Euph. That is, whether he can will as he wills? I know not how philosophical it may be to ask this question, but it seems very unintelligible. The notions of guilt and merit, justice and reward, are in the minds of men antecedent to all metaphysical disquisitions; and, according to those received natural notions, it is not doubted that man is accountable, that he acts, and is self-determined.

* * * * * * *

[SIRIS]

A CHAIN OF

PHILOSOPHICAL REFLEXIONS AND INQUIRIES

CONCERNING

THE VIRTUES OF TAR-WATER

AND DIVERS OTHER SUBJECTS CONNECTED TOGETHER AND ARISING ONE FROM ANOTHER

As we have opportunity, let us do good unto
all men.—GAL. vi. 10.
Hoc opus, hoc studium, parvi properemus et ampli.—HOR.

[CONTENTS]

[S I R I S :]

A CHAIN OF PHILOSOPHICAL REFLEXIONS
AND INQUIRIES, &c.

For Introduction to the following piece, I assure the reader that nothing could, in my present situation, have induced me to be at the pains of writing it, but a firm belief that it would prove a valuable present to the public. What entertainment soever the reasoning or notional part may afford the Mind, I will venture to say, the other part seemeth so surely calculated to do good to the Body that both must be gainers. For, if the lute be not well tuned, the musician fails of his harmony. And, in our present state, the operations of the mind so far depend on the right tone or good condition of its instrument, that anything which greatly contributes to preserve or recover the health of the Body is well worth the attention of the Mind. These considerations have moved me to communicate to the public the salutary virtues of Tar-water; to which I thought myself indispensably obliged by the duty every man owes to mankind. And, as effects are linked with their causes, my thoughts on this low but useful theme led to farther inquiries, and those on to others; remote perhaps and speculative, but I hope not altogether useless or unentertaining.

---

1. In certain parts of America, Tar-water is made by putting a quart of cold water to a quart of tar, and

stirring them well together in a vessel, which is left standing till the tar sinks to the bottom. A glass of clear water, being poured off for a draught, is replaced by the same quantity of fresh water, the vessel being shaken and left to stand as before. And this is repeated for every glass, so long as the tar continues to impregnate the water sufficiently, which appears by the smell and taste. But, as this method produceth tar-water of a nauseous kind, and different degrees of strength, I choose to make it in the following manner: Pour a gallon of cold water on a quart of tar, and stir, work, and mix them thoroughly together, with a wooden ladle or flat stick, for the space of five or six minutes; after which the vessel must stand close covered and unmoved three days and nights, that the tar may have full time to subside; and then the clear water, having been first carefully skimmed without shaking the vessel, is to be poured off, and kept in bottles well stopped for use, no more being made from the same tar, which may still serve for common uses.

* * * * * *

72. To suppose that all distempers, arising from very different, and it may be from contrary causes, can be cured by one and the same medicine must seem chimerical. But it may with truth be affirmed, that the virtue of tar-water extends to a surprising variety of cases, very distant and unlike (sect. 3, 4, 5, 6, 21, &c.). This I have experienced in my neighbours, my family, and myself. And, as I live in a remote corner, among poor neighbours, who for want of a regular physician have often recourse to me, I have had frequent opportunities of trial, which convince me it is of so just a temperament as to be an enemy to all extremes. I have known it to do great good in a cold, watery constitution,

as a cardiac and stomachic: and at the same time allay heat and feverish thirst in another. I have known it correct costive habits in some, and the contrary habit in others. Nor will this seem incredible if it be considered that middle qualities naturally reduce the extreme. Warm water, for instance, mixed with hot and cold, will lessen the heat in that, and the cold in this.

* * * * * * *

82. The great force of tar-water to correct the acrimony of the blood appears in nothing more than in the cure of a gangrene from an internal cause; which was performed on a servant of my own, by prescribing the copious and constant use of tar-water for a few weeks. From my representing tar-water as good for so many things, some perhaps may conclude it is good for nothing. But charity obligeth me to say what I know, and what I think, howsoever it may be taken. Men may censure and object as they please, but I appeal to time and experiment. Effects misimputed, cases wrong told, circumstances overlooked, perhaps, too, prejudices and partialities against truth, may for a time prevail, and keep her at the bottom of her well, from whence nevertheless she emergeth sooner or later, and strikes the eyes of all those who do not keep them shut.

* * * * * * *

120. In the distilling of turpentine and other balsams by a gentle heat, it hath been observed that there riseth first an acid spirit (sect. 7) that will mix with water; which spirit, except the fire be very gentle, is lost. This grateful acid spirit that first comes over is, as a learned chemist and physician informs us, highly refrigeratory, diuretic, sudorific, balsamic, or preservative from putre-

faction, excellent in nephritic cases, and for quenching
thirst—all which virtues are contained in the cold infu-
sion which draws forth from tar only its fine flower or
quintessence, if I may so say, or the native vegetable
spirit, together with a little volatile oil.

121. The distinguishing principle of all vegetables—
that whereon their peculiar smell, taste, and specific
properties depend—seems to be some extremely fine and
subtle spirit, whose immediate vehicle is an exceeding
thin volatile oil; which is itself detained in a grosser
and more viscid resin or balsam, lodged in proper
cells in the bark and seeds, and most abounding in au-
tumn or winter, after the crude juices have been thoroughly concocted, ripened, and impregnated with solar
light. The spirit itself is by some supposed to be an
oil highly subtilized, so as to mix with water. But such
volatile oil is not the spirit, but only its vehicle. Since
aromatic oils being long exposed to air will lose their
specific smell and taste, which fly off with the spirit or
vegetable salt, without any sensible diminution of the
oil.

*   *   *   *   *   *   *

137. These native spirits or vegetable souls are all
breathed or exhaled into the Air, which seems the re-
ceptacle as well as source of all sublunary forms, the
great mass or chaos which imparts and receives them.
The air or atmosphere that surrounds our earth contains a mixture of all the active volatile parts of the
whole habitable world, that is, of all vegetables, minerals, and animals. Whatever perspires, corrupts, or
exhales, impregnates the air; which, being acted upon
by the solar fire, produceth within itself all sorts of
chemical operations, dispensing again those salts and

spirits in new generations, which it had received from putrefactions.

* * * * * * *

147. Upon the whole, it is manifest that air is no distinct element, but a mass or mixture of things the most heterogeneous and even opposite to each other (sect. 137, 145), which become air by acquiring an elasticity and volatility from the attraction of some active subtle substance, whether it be called fire, æther, light, or the vital spirit of the world; in like manner as the particles of antimony, of themselves not volatile, are carried off in sublimation, and rendered volatile by cohering with the particles of sal ammoniac. But action and reaction being equal, the spring of this ethereal spirit is diminished by being imparted. Its velocity and subtlety are also less from its being mixed with grosser particles. Hence sound moves slower than light, as mud than water.

* * * * * * *

151. Æther, fire, or spirit, being attracted and clogged by heterogeneous particles, becometh less active; and the particles cohering with those of æther become more active than before. Air therefore is a mass of various particles, abraded and sublimated from wet and dry bodies of all sorts, cohering with particles of æther; the whole permeated by pure æther, or light, or fire: for these words are used promiscuously by ancient philosophers.

152. This Æther or pure invisible Fire, the most subtle and elastic of all bodies, seems to pervade and expand itself throug¹ ⌐ut the whole universe. If air be the immediate agent or instrument in natural things, it

is the pure invisible fire that is the first natural mover or spring from whence the air derives its power (sect. 139, 149, 151). This mighty agent is everywhere at hand, ready to break forth into action, if not restrained and governed with the greatest wisdom. Being always restless and in motion, it actuates and enlivens the whole visible mass, is equally fitted to produce and to destroy, distinguishes the various stages of nature, and keeps up the perpetual round of generations and corruptions, pregnant with forms which it constantly sends forth and resorbs. So quick in its motions, so subtle and penetrating in its nature, so extensive in its effects, it seemeth no other than the Vegetative Soul or Vital Spirit of the World.

153. The animal spirit in man is the instrumental or physical cause both of sense and motion. To suppose sense in the world would be gross and unwarranted. But locomotive faculties are evident in all its parts. The Pythagoreans, Platonists, and Stoics held the world to be an animal; though some of them have chosen to consider it as a vegetable. However, the phænomena and effects do plainly shew there is a Spirit that moves, and a Mind or Providence that presides. This Providence, Plutarch saith, was thought to be in regard to the world what the soul is in regard to man.

154. The order and course of things, and the experiments we daily make, shew there is a Mind that governs and actuates this mundane system, as the proper real agent and cause; and that the inferior instrumental cause is pure æther, fire, or the substance of light (sect. 29, 37, 136, 149), which is applied and determined by an Infinite Mind in the macrocosm or universe, with unlimited power, and according to stated rules, as it is in

the microcosm with limited power and skill by the human mind. We have no proof, either from experiment or reason, of any other Agent, or efficient cause, than Mind or Spirit. When, therefore, we speak of corporeal agents, or corporeal causes, this is to be understood in a different, subordinate, and improper sense.

* * * * * * *

160. The mind of man acts by an instrument *necessarily*. The τὸ ἡγεμονικόν, or Mind presiding in the world, acts by an instrument *freely*. Without instrumental and second causes, there could be no regular course of nature. And without a regular course, nature could never be understood; mankind must always be at a loss, not knowing what to expect, or how to govern themselves, or direct their actions for the obtaining of any end. Therefore in the government of the world physical agents, improperly so called, or mechanical, or second causes, or natural causes, or instruments, are necessary to assist, not the governor, but the governed.

161. In the human body the mind orders and moves the limbs: but the animal spirit is supposed the immediate physical cause of their motion. So likewise in the mundane system, a mind presides: but the immediate, mechanical, or instrumental cause, that moves or animates all its parts, is the pure elementary fire or spirit of the world. The more fine and subtle part or spirit is supposed to receive the impressions of the First Mover, and communicate them to the grosser sensible parts of this world. Motion, though in metaphysical rigour and truth a passion or mere effect, yet in physics passeth for an action. And by this action all effects are supposed to be produced. Hence the various com-

munications, determinations, accelerations of motion, constitute the laws of nature.

* * * * * * *

251. It passeth with many, I know not how, that mechanical principles give a clear solution of the phænomena. The Democritic hypothesis, saith Dr. Cudworth, doth much more handsomely and intelligibly solve the phænomena, than that of Aristotle and Plato. But, things rightly considered, perhaps it will be found not to solve any phænomenon at all: for all phænomena are, to speak truly, appearances in the soul or mind; and it hath never been explained, nor can it be explained, how external bodies, figures, and motions, should produce an appearance in the mind. These principles, therefore, do not solve, if by solving is meant assigning the real, either efficient or final, cause of appearances; but only reduce them to general rules.

252. There is a certain analogy, constancy, and uniformity in the phænomena or appearances of nature, which are a foundation for general rules: and these are a grammar for the understanding of nature, or that series of effects in the visible world whereby we are enabled to foresee what will come to pass in the natural course of things. Plotinus observes, in his third Ennead, that the art of presaging is in some sort the reading of natural letters denoting order, and that so far forth as analogy obtains in the universe, there may be vaticination. And in reality, he that foretells the motions of the planets, or the effects of medicines, or the results of chemical or mechanical experiments, may be said to do it by *natural vaticination*.

253. We know a thing when we understand it; and we understand it when we can interpret or tell what it

signifies. Strictly, the sense knows nothing. We perceive indeed sounds by hearing, and characters by sight. But we are not therefore said to understand them. After the same manner, the phænomena of nature are alike visible to all: but all have not alike learned the connexion of natural things, or understand what they signify, or know how to vaticinate by them. There is no question, saith Socrates in Theæteto, concerning that which *is* agreeable to each person; but concerning what will in time to come be agreeable, of which all men are not equally judges. He who foreknoweth what will be in every kind is the wisest. According to Socrates, you and the cook may judge of a dish on the table equally well; but while the dish is making, the cook can better foretell what will ensue from this or that manner of composing it. Nor is this manner of reasoning confined only to morals or politics, but extends also to natural science.

254. As the natural connexion of *signs* with *the things signified* is regular and constant, it forms a sort of rational discourse (sect. 152), and is therefore the immediate effect of an Intelligent Cause. This is agreeable to the philosophy of Plato, and other ancients. Plotinus indeed saith, that which acts naturally is not intellection, but a certain power of moving matter, which doth not know but only do. And it must be owned that, as faculties are multiplied by philosophers according to their operations, the *will* may be distinguished from the *intellect*. But it will not therefore follow that the Will which operates in the course of nature is not conducted and applied by intellect, although it be granted that neither will understands, nor intellect wills. Therefore, the phænomena of nature, which strike on the senses and are understood by the mind, do form not only a magnificent spectacle, but also a most coherent, enter-

taining, and instructive Discourse; and to effect this, they are conducted, adjusted, and ranged by the greatest wisdom. This Language or Discourse is studied with different attention, and interpreted with different degrees of skill. But so far as men have studied and remarked its rules, and can interpret right, so far they may be said to be knowing in nature. A beast is like a man who hears a strange tongue but understands nothing.

* * * * * * *

263. It cannot be denied that, with respect to the Universe of things, we in this mortal state are like men educated in Plato's cave, looking on shadows with our backs turned to the light. But though our light be dim, and our situation bad, yet if the best use be made of both, perhaps something may be seen. Proclus, in his Commentary on the Theology of Plato, observes there are two sorts of philosophers. The one placed Body first in the order of beings, and made the faculty of thinking depend thereupon, supposing that the principles of all things are corporeal: that Body most really or principally exists, and all other things in a secondary sense, and by virtue of that. Others, making all corporeal things to be dependent upon Soul or Mind, think this to exist in the first place and primary sense, and the being of Bodies to be altogether derived from, and presuppose that of the Mind.

264. Sense and experience acquaint us with the course and analogy of appearances or natural effects. Thought, reason, intellect introduce us into the knowledge of their causes. Sensible appearances, though of a flowing, unstable, and uncertain nature, yet having first occupied the mind, they do by an early prevention render the aftertask of thought more difficult; and, as they amuse

the eyes and ears, and are more suited to vulgar uses and the mechanic arts of life, they easily obtain a preference, in the opinion of most men, to those superior principles, which are the later growth of the human mind arrived to maturity and perfection; but, not affecting the corporeal sense, are thought to be so far deficient in point of solidity and reality, *sensible* and *real,* to common apprehensions, being the same thing. Although it be certain that the *principles* of science are neither objects of sense nor imagination; and that intellect and reason are alone the sure guides to truth.

* * * * * * *

285. Naturalists, whose proper province it is to consider phænomena, experiments, mechanical organs and motions, principally regard the visible frame of things or corporeal world; supposing soul to be contained in body. And this hypothesis may be tolerated in physics, as it is not necessary in the arts of dialling or navigation to mention the true system or earth's motion. But those who, not content with sensible appearances, would penetrate into the real and true causes (the object of theology, metaphysics, or the *philosophia prima*), will rectify this error, and speak of the world as contained by the soul, and not the soul by the world.

286. Aristotle hath observed there were indeed some who thought so grossly as to suppose the universe to be one only corporeal and extended nature: but in the first book of his *Metaphysics* he justly remarks they were guilty of a great mistake; forasmuch as they took into their account the elements of corporeal beings alone, whereas there are incorporeal beings also in the universe; and while they attempted to assign the causes of generation and corruption, and account for the nature

of all things, they did at the same time destroy the very cause of motion.

287. It is a doctrine among other speculations contained in the Hermaic writings—that all things are One. And it is not improbable that Orpheus, Parmenides, and others among the Greeks, might have derived their notion of Τὸ Ἕν, THE ONE, from Egypt. Though that subtle metaphysician Parmenides, in his doctrine of ἓν ἕστως, seems to have added something of his own. If we suppose that one and the same Mind is the Universal Principle of order and harmony throughout the world, containing and connecting all its parts, and giving unity to the system, there seems to be nothing atheistical or impious in this supposition.

288. Number is no object of sense: it is an act of the mind. The same thing in a different conception is one or many. Comprehending God and the creatures in one general notion, we may say that all things together make one universe, or τὸ πᾶν. But if we should say that all things make one God, this would, indeed, be an erroneous notion of God; but would not amount to Atheism, so long as Mind or Intellect was admitted to be the τὸ ἡγεμονικόν, the governing part. It is, nevertheless, more respectful, and consequently the truer notion of God, to suppose him neither made up of parts, nor to be himself a part of any whole whatsoever.

289. All those who conceived the Universe to be an Animal must, in consequence of that notion, suppose all things to be One. But to conceive God to be the sentient soul of an animal is altogether unworthy and absurd. There is no sense nor sensory, nor any thing like a sense or sensory, in God. Sense implies an impression from some other being, and denotes a dependence in the soul which hath it. Sense is a passion: and passions imply imperfection. God knoweth all things, as pure mind or

intellect; but nothing by sense, nor in nor through a sensory. Therefore to suppose a sensory of any kind— whether space or any other—in God, would be very wrong, and lead us into false conceptions of His nature. The presuming there was such a thing as real, absolute, uncreated space seems to have occasioned that modern mistake. But this presumption was without grounds.

290. Body is opposite to spirit or mind. We have a notion of spirit from thought and action. We have a notion of body from resistance. So far forth as there is real power, there is spirit. So far forth, as there is resistance, there is inability or want of power: that is, there is a negation of spirit. We are embodied, that is, we are clogged by weight, and hindered by resistance. But in respect of a perfect spirit, there is nothing hard or impenetrable: there is no resistance to the Deity: nor hath he any body: nor is the Supreme Being united to the world as the soul of an animal is to its body; which necessarily implieth defect, both as an instrument, and as a constant weight and impediment.

291. Thus much it consists with piety to say—that a Divine Agent doth by his virtue permeate and govern the elementary fire or light (sect. 157, 172), which serves as animal spirit to enliven and actuate the whole mass, and all the members of this visible world. Nor is this doctrine less philosophical than pious. We see all nature alive or in motion. We see water turned into air, and air rarefied and made elastic (sect. 149, 152, 200) by the attraction of another medium, more pure indeed, more subtle, and more volatile, than air. But still, as this is a moveable, extended, and consequently a corporeal being (sect. 207), it cannot be itself the principle of motion, but leads us naturally and necessarily to an incorporeal spirit or agent. We are conscious that a spirit can begin, alter, or determine motion;

but nothing of this appears in body. Nay, the contrary is evident, both to experiment and reflexion.

292. Natural phænomena are only natural appearances. They are, therefore, such as we see and perceive them. Their real and objective natures are, therefore, the same: passive without anything active; fluent and changing without anything permanent in them. However, as these make the first impressions, and the mind takes her first flight and spring, as it were, by resting her foot on these objects, they are not only first considered by all men, but most considered by most men. They and the phantoms that result from those appearances—the children of imagination grafted upon sense—such for example as pure space (sect. 270), are thought by many the very first in existence and stability, and to embrace and comprehend all other beings.

293. Now, although such phantoms as *corporeal forces, absolute motions,* and *real spaces* do pass in physics for causes and principles (sect. 220, 249, 250), yet are they in truth but hypotheses; nor can they be the objects of real science. They pass nevertheless in physics, conversant about things of Sense, and confined to experiments and mechanics. But when we enter the province of the *philosophia prima,* we discover another order of beings—Mind and its acts; permanent being; not dependent on corporeal things; nor resulting, nor connected, nor contained, but containing, connecting, enlivening the whole frame; and imparting those motions, forms, qualities, and that order and symmetry, to all those transient phænomena, which we term the Course of Nature.

294. It is with our faculties as with our affections: what first seizes holds fast (sect. 264). It is a vulgar theme, that man is a compound of contrarieties, which breed a restless struggle in his nature, between flesh

and spirit, the beast and the angel, earth and heaven, ever weighed down and ever bearing up. During which conflict the character fluctuates: when either side prevails, it is then fixed for vice or virtue. And life from different principles takes a different issue. It is the same in regard to our faculties. Sense at first besets and overbears the mind. The sensible appearances are all in all: our reasonings are employed about them: our desires terminate in them: we look no farther for realities or causes; till Intellect begins to dawn, and cast a ray on this shadowy scene. We then perceive the true principle of unity, identity, and existence. Those things that before seemed to constitute the whole of Being, upon taking an intellectual view of things, prove to be but fleeting phantoms.

295. From the outward form of gross masses which occupy the vulgar, a curious inquirer proceeds to examine the inward structure and minute parts, and, from observing the motions in nature, to discover the laws of those motions. By the way he frames his hypotheses, and suits his language to this natural philosophy. And these fit the occasion and answer the end of a maker of experiments or mechanic; who means only to apply the powers of nature, and reduce the phænomena to rules. But if, proceeding still in his analysis and inquiry, he ascends from the sensible into the intellectual world, and beholds things in a new light and a new order, he will then change his system, and perceive that what he took for substances and causes are but fleeting shadows: that the Mind contains all, and acts all, and is to all created beings the source of unity and identity, harmony and order, existence and stability.

296. It is neither acid, nor salt, nor sulphur, nor air, nor æther, nor visible corporeal fire (sect. 155), much less the phantom Fate or Necessity, that is the real

agent, but, by a certain analysis, a regular connexion and climax, we ascend through all those mediums to a glimpse of the First Mover, invisible, incorporeal, unextended, intellectual source of life and being. There is, it must be owned, a mixture of obscurity and prejudice in human speech and reasonings. This is unavoidable, since the veils of prejudice and error are slowly and singly taken off one by one. But, if there are many links in the Chain which connects the two extremes of what is grossly sensible and purely intelligible, and it seems a tedious work, by the slow helps of memory, imagination, and reason, oppressed and overwhelmed, as we are, by the senses, through erroneous principles, and long ambages of words and notions, to struggle upwards into the light of truth; yet, as this gradually dawns, farther discoveries still correct the style and clear up the notions.

297. The Mind her acts and faculties, furnish a new and distinct class of objects (sect. 163, 266), from the contemplation whereof arise certain other notions, principles, and verities, so remote from, and even so repugnant to, the first prejudices which surprise the sense of mankind that they may well be excluded from vulgar speech and books, as *abstract* from sensible matters, and more fit for the speculation of truth, the labour and aim of a few, than for the practice of the world, or the subjects of experimental or mechanical inquiry. Nevertheless, though, perhaps, it may not be relished by some modern readers, yet the treating in physical books concerning metaphysical and divine matters can be justified by great authorities among the ancients: not to mention that he who professedly delivers the elements of a science is more obliged to method and system, and

tied down to more rigorous laws, than a mere essay writer. It may, therefore, be pardoned if this rude Essay doth, by insensible transitions, draw the reader into remote inquiries and speculations, that were not, [perhaps,] thought of either by him or by the author at first setting out.

* * * * * * *

307. Aristotle maketh a threefold distinction of objects, according to the three speculative sciences. Physics he supposeth to be conversant about such things as have a principle of motion in themselves; Mathematics about things permanent but not abstracted; and Theology about Being abstracted and immoveable; which distinction may be seen in the ninth book of his *Metaphysics*. Where by abstracted, χωριστόν, he understands separable from corporeal beings and sensible qualities.

308. That philosopher held that the mind of man was a *tabula rasa,* and that there were no innate ideas. Plato, on the contrary, held original ideas in the mind; that is, notions which never were or can be in the sense, such as being, beauty, goodness, likeness, parity. Some, perhaps, may think the truth to be this: that there are properly no *ideas*, or passive objects, in the mind but what were derived from sense: but that there are also besides these her own acts or operations; such are *notions.*

309. It is a maxim of the Platonic philosophy, that the soul of man was originally furnished with native inbred notions, and stands in need of sensible occasions, not absolutely for producing them, but only for awakening, rousing, or exciting into act what was already preexistent, dormant, and latent in the soul; as things are said to be laid up in the memory, though not actually

perceived until they happen to be called forth and
brought into view by other objects. This notion seemeth somewhat different from that of innate ideas, as
understood by those moderns who have attempted to
explode them.[1] To understand and to be are, according
to Parmenides, the same thing. And Plato in his seventh
Letter makes no difference between νοῦς and ἐπιστήμη,
mind and knowledge. Whence it follows that mind,
knowledge, and notions, either in habit or in act, always
go together.

310. And albeit Aristotle considered the soul in its
original state as a blank paper, yet he held it to be the
proper place of forms—τὴν ψυχὴν εἶναι τόπον εἴδων (sect.
269). Which doctrine, first maintained by others, he
admits, under this restriction, that it is not to be understood of the whole soul, but only of the νοητική; as is to
be seen in his third book *De Anima*. Whence, according
to Themistius in his commentary on that treatise, it may
be inferred that all beings are in the soul. For, saith
he, the forms are the beings. By the form every thing
is what it is. And he adds, it is the soul that im-
parteth forms to matter; τὴν ὕλην μορφῶσα ποικίλαις μορφαῖς.
Therefore they are first in the soul. He farther adds
that the mind is all things, taking the forms of all things
it becomes all things by intellect and sense. Alexander
Aphrodisæus saith as much, affirming the mind to be all
things, κατά τε τὸ νοεῖν καὶ τὸ αἰσθάνεσθαι. And this in fact
is Aristotle's own doctrine, in his third book *De Anima*,
where he also asserts, with Plato, that actual knowledge
and the thing known are all one. Τὸ δ᾽ αὐτό ἐστιν ἡ κατ᾽
ἐνέργειαν ἐπιστήμη τῷ πράγματι. Whence it follows, that
the things are where the knowledge is, that is to say, in
the mind. Or, as it is otherwise expressed, that the soul

[1] Cf. Locke, *Essay concerning Human Understanding*,
Book I.

is all things. More might be said to explain Aristotle's notion, but it would lead too far.

311. As to an absolute actual existence of sensible or corporeal things (sect. 264, 292, 294), it doth not seem to have been admitted either by Plato or Aristotle. In the *Theætetus* we are told that if any one saith a thing is, or is made, he must withal say, for what, or of what, or in respect of what, it is, or is made; for, that any thing should exist in itself or absolutely is absurd. Agreeably to which doctrine it is also farther affirmed by Plato, that it is impossible a thing should be sweet and sweet to nobody. It must, nevertheless, be owned with regard to Aristotle, that even in his *Metaphysics* there are some expressions which seem to favour the absolute existence of corporeal things. For instance, in the eleventh book, speaking of corporeal sensible things, what wonder, saith he, if they never appear to us the same, no more than to sick men; since we are always changing and never remain the same ourselves? And again, he saith, sensible things, although they receive no change in themselves, do nevertheless in sick persons produce different sensations and not the same. These passages would seem to imply a distinct and absolute existence of the objects of sense.

312. But it must be observed, that Aristotle distinguisheth a twofold existence—potential and actual. It will not therefore follow that, according to Aristotle, because a thing is, it must actually exist.

* * * * * * *

330. These disquisitions will probably seem dry and useless to such readers as are accustomed to consider only sensible objects. The employment of the mind on things purely intellectual is to most men irksome; whereas the sensitive powers, by constant use, acquire

strength. Hence, the objects of sense more forcibly affect us (sect. 264, 294), and are too often counted the chief good. For these things men fight, cheat, and scramble. Therefore, in order to tame mankind, and introduce a sense of virtue, the best human means is to exercise their understanding, to give them a glimpse of another world, superior to the sensible, and, while they take pains to cherish and maintain the animal life, to teach them not to neglect the intellectual.

* * * * * * *

346. According to the Platonic philosophy, *ens* and *unum* are the same. And consequently our minds participate so far of existence as they do of unity. But it should seem that Personality is the indivisible centre of the soul or mind; which is a monad so far forth as she is a person. Therefore Person is really that which exists; inasmuch as it participates the Divine Unity. In man the monad or indivisible is the αὐτὸ τὸ αὐτό, the self-same self, or very self; a thing in the opinion of Socrates, much and narrowly to be inquired into and discussed, to the end that, knowing ourselves, we may know what belongs to ourselves and to our happiness.

347. Upon mature reflexion, the person or mind of all created beings seemeth alone indivisible, and to partake most of unity. But sensible things are rather considered as one than truly so, they being in a perpetual flux or succession, ever differing and various. Nevertheless, all things together may be considered as one universe (sect. 287, 288); one by the connexion, relation, and order of its parts, which is the work of mind, whose unit is, by Platonics, supposed a participation of the first τὸ Ἕν.

348. Socrates, in the *Theætetus* of Plato, speaketh of two parties of philosophers—the ῥέοντες, and οἱ τοῦ ὅλου στασιῶται: the flowing philosophers, who held all things

to be in a perpetual flux, always generating and never existing; and those others who maintained the universe to be fixed and immoveable. The difference seems to have been this, that Heraclitus, Protagoras, Empedocles, and in general those of the former sect, considered things sensible and natural; whereas Parmenides and his party considered τὸ πᾶν, not as the sensible but as the intelligible world (sect. 293, 294, 295), abstracted from all sensible things.

349. In effect, if we mean by *things* the *sensible* objects, these, it is evident, are always flowing; but if we mean things purely *intelligible,* then we may say on the other hand, with equal truth, that they are immoveable and unchangeable. So that those who thought the Whole, or τὸ Πᾶν, to be Ἓν ἑστώς, a fixed or permanent One, seem to have understood the Whole of real beings; which in their sense was only the intellectual world, not allowing reality of being to things not permanent.

* * * * * * *

368. The eye by long use comes to see even in the darkest cavern: and there is no subject so obscure but we may discern some glimpse of truth by long poring on it. Truth is the cry of all, but the game of a few. Certainly, where it is the chief passion, it doth not give way to vulgar cares and views; nor is it contented with a little ardour in the early time of life; active, perhaps, to pursue, but not so fit to weigh and revise. He that would make a real progress in knowledge must dedicate his age as well as youth, the later growth as well as first fruits, at the altar of Truth.

Cujusvis est errare; nullius nisi insipientis in errore perseverare. *Cic.* [*Orat. Philip.* XII. 2.]

PASSIVE OBEDIENCE

OR

THE CHRISTIAN DOCTRINE OF NOT RESIST-ING THE SUPREME POWER, PROVED AND VINDICATED

UPON

THE PRINCIPLES OF THE LAW OF NATURE

IN A DISCOURSE DELIVERED AT THE CHAPEL OF TRINITY COLLEGE, DUBLIN

Nec vero aut per Senatum aut per Populum salvi hac **Lege** possumus.'

CICERO, *Fragment. de Repub.*

PASSIVE OBEDIENCE

Romans, chap. xiii. ver. 2.

'Whosoever resisteth the Power, resisteth the ordinance
of God.'

1. It is not my design to inquire into the particular
nature of the government and constitution of these kingdoms; much less to pretend to determine concerning the
merits of the different parties now reigning in the state.
Those topics I profess to lie out of my sphere, and they
will probably be thought by most men improper to be
treated of in an audience almost wholly made up of
young persons, set apart from the business and noise
of the world, for their more convenient instruction in
learning and piety. But surely it is in no respect
unsuitable to the circumstances of this place to inculcate
and explain every branch of the Law of Nature; or those
virtues and duties which are equally binding in every
kingdom or society of men under heaven. And of this
kind I take to be that Christian Duty of not resisting
the supreme Power, implied in my text—'Whosoever
resisteth the Power, resisteth the ordinance of God.'

In treating on which words I shall observe the following method:—

2. First, I shall endeavour to prove that there is an
absolute unlimited non-resistance, or passive obedience,
due to the supreme civil power, wherever placed in any
nation.

Secondly, I shall inquire into the grounds and reasons of the contrary opinion.

Thirdly, I shall consider the objections drawn from the pretended consequences of non-resistance to the supreme power.

In handling these points I intend not to build on the authority of Holy Scripture, but altogether on the Principles of Reason common to all mankind; and that, because there are some very rational and learned men, who, being verily persuaded an absolute passive subjection to any earthly power is repugnant to right reason, can never bring themselves to admit such an interpretation of Holy Scripture (however natural and obvious from the words) as shall make that a part of Christian religion which seems to them in itself manifestly absurd, and destructive of the original inherent rights of human nature.

3. I do not mean to treat of that submission which men are, either in duty or prudence, obliged to pay inferior or executive powers; neither shall I consider where or in what persons the supreme or legislative power is lodged in this or that government. Only thus much I shall take for granted: that there is in every civil community, somewhere or other, placed a Supreme Power of making laws, and enforcing the observation of them. The fulfilling of those laws, either by a punctual performance of what is enjoined in them, or, if that be inconsistent with reason or conscience, by a patient submission to whatever penalties the supreme power hath annexed to the neglect or transgression of them, is termed *loyalty;* as, on the other hand, the making use of force and open violence, either to withstand the execution of the laws, or ward off the penalties appointed by the supreme power, is properly named *rebellion.*

Now, to make it evident that every degree of rebellion is criminal in the subject, I shall, in the first place, endeavour to prove that Loyalty is a natural or moral duty; and Disloyalty, or Rebellion, in the most strict and proper sense, a vice or breach of the law of nature. And, secondly, I propose to shew that the prohibitions of vice, or negative precepts of the law of nature, as, 'Thou shalt not commit adultery, Thou shalt not forswear thyself, Thou shalt not resist the supreme power,' and the like, ought to be taken in a most absolute, necessary, and immutable sense: insomuch that the attainment of the greatest good, or deliverance from the greatest evil, that can befal any man or number of men in this life, may not justify the least violation of them.

First then, I am to shew that Loyalty is a moral duty, and Disloyalty or Rebellion, in the most strict and proper sense, a vice, or breach of the Law of Nature.

4. Though it be a point agreed amongst all wise men, that there are certain moral rules or laws of nature, which carry with them an eternal and indispensable obligation; yet, concerning the proper methods for discovering those laws, and distinguishing them from others dependent on the humour and discretion of men, there are various opinions. Some direct us to look for them in the Divine Ideas; others in the natural inscriptions on the mind: some derive them from the authority of learned men, and the universal agreement and consent of nations: lastly, others hold that they are only to be discovered by the deductions of reason. The three first methods must be acknowledged to labour under great difficulties; and the last has not, that I know, been anywhere distinctly explained, or treated of so fully as the importance of the subject doth deserve.

I hope therefore it will be pardoned, if, in a discourse of passive obedience, in order to lay the foundation of that duty the deeper, we make some inquiry into the origin, nature, and obligation of moral duties in general, and the criterions whereby they are to be known.

5. Self-love being a principle of all others the most universal, and the most deeply engraven in our hearts, it is natural for us to regard things as they are fitted to augment or impair our own happiness; and accordingly we denominate them *good* or *evil*. Our judgment is ever employed in distinguishing between these two; and it is the whole business of our lives to endeavour, by a proper application of our faculties, to procure the one and avoid the other. At our first coming into the world, we are entirely guided by the impressions of sense; sensible pleasure being the infallible characteristic of present good, as pain is of evil. But, by degrees, as we grow up in our acquaintance with the nature of things, experience informs us that present good is afterwards often attended with a greater evil; and, on the other side, that present evil is not less frequently the occasion of procuring to us a greater future good. Besides, as the nobler faculties of the human soul begin to display themselves, they discover to us goods far more excellent than those which affect the senses. Hence an alteration is wrought in our judgments; we no longer comply with the first solicitations of sense, but stay to consider the remote consequences of an action; what good may be hoped, or what evil feared from it, according to the wonted course of things. This obliges us frequently to overlook present momentary enjoyments, when they come in competition with greater and more lasting goods; though too far off, or of too refined a nature to affect our senses.

6. But, as the whole Earth and the entire duration of those perishing things contained in it is altogether inconsiderable, or, in the prophet's expressive style, 'less than nothing' in respect of Eternity, who sees not that every reasonable man ought so to frame his actions as that they may most effectually contribute to promote his eternal interest? And, since it is a truth, evident by the light of nature, that there is a sovereign omniscient Spirit, who alone can make us for ever happy, or for ever miserable; it plainly follows that a conformity to His will, and not any prospect of temporal advantage, is the sole rule whereby every man who acts up to the principles of reason must govern and square his actions. The same conclusion doth likewise evidently result from the relation which God bears to His creatures. God alone is maker and preserver of all things. He is, therefore, with the most undoubted right, the great legislator of the world; and mankind are, by all the ties of duty, no less than interest, bound to obey His laws.

7. Hence we should above all things endeavour to trace out the Divine will, or the general design of Providence with regard to mankind, and the methods most directly tending to the accomplishment of that design. And this seems the genuine and proper way for discovering the laws of nature. For, laws being rules directive of our actions to the end intended by the legislator, in order to attain the knowledge of God's laws, we ought first to inquire what that end is which He designs should be carried on by human actions. Now, as God is a being of infinite goodness, it is plain the end He proposes is good. But, God enjoying in Himself all possible perfection, it follows that it is not His own good, but that of His creatures. Again, the moral actions of men are entirely terminated within themselves, so as to have no influence on the other orders of intelligences

or reasonable creatures; the end therefore to be procured by them can be no other than the good of men.
But, as nothing in a natural state can entitle one man
more than another to the favour of God, except only
moral goodness; which, consisting in a conformity to
the laws of God, doth presuppose the being of such laws,
and law ever supposing an end, to which it guides our
actions—it follows that, antecedent to the end proposed
by God, no distinction can be conceived between men:
that end therefore itself, or general design of Providence, is not determined or limited by any respect of
persons. It is not therefore the private good of this
or that man, nation, or age, but the general well-being
of all men, of all nations, of all ages of the world,
which God designs should be procured by the concurring
actions of each individual.

Having thus discovered the great end to which all
moral obligations are subordinate, it remains that we
inquire what methods are necessary for the obtaining
that end.

8. The well-being of mankind must necessarily be carried on in one of these two ways:—Either, first, without
the injunction of any certain universal rules of morality;
only by obliging every one, upon each particular occasion, to consult the public good, and always to do that
which to him shall seem, in the present time and circumstances, most to conduce to it: or, secondly, by
enjoining the observation of some determinate, established laws, which, if universally practised, have, from
the nature of things, an essential fitness to procure the
well-being of mankind; though, in their particular application, they are sometimes, through untoward accidents,
and the perverse irregularity of human wills, the occa-

sions of great sufferings and misfortunes, it may be, to very many good men.

Against the former of these methods there lie several strong objections. For brevity I shall mention only two:—

9. First, it will thence follow that the best men, for want of judgment, and the wisest, for want of knowing all the hidden circumstances and consequences of an action, may very often be at a loss how to behave themselves; which they would not be, in case they judged of each action by comparing it with some particular precept, rather than by examining the good or evil which in that single instance it tends to procure: it being far more easy to judge with certainty, whether such or such an action be a transgression of this or that precept, than whether it will be attended with more good or ill consequences. In short, to calculate the events of each particular action is impossible; and, though it were not, would yet take up too much time to be of use in the affairs of life.

Secondly, if that method be observed, it will follow that we can have no sure standard to which, comparing the actions of another, we may pronounce them good or bad, virtues or vices. For, since the measure and rule of every good man's actions is supposed to be nothing else but his own private disinterested opinion of what makes most for the public good at that juncture; and, since this opinion must unavoidably in different men, from their particular views and circumstances, be very different: it is impossible to know, whether any one instance of parricide or perjury, for example, be criminal. The man may have had his reasons for it; and that which in me would have been a heinous sin may be in him a duty. Every man's particular rule is buried in his own breast, invisible to all but himself, who therefore can only tell whether he observes it or no. And, since that rule is fitted to particular occasions, it must ever change as they do: hence it is not only various in different men, but in one and the same man at different times.

10. From all which it follows, there can be no harmony or agreement between the actions of good men: no apparent steadiness or consistency of one man with himself; no adhering to principles: the best actions may be condemned, and the most villainous meet with applause. In a word, there ensues the most horrible confusion of vice and virtue, sin and duty, that can possibly be imagined. It follows, therefore, that the great end to which God requires the concurrence of human actions must of necessity be carried on by the second method proposed, namely, the observation of certain, universal, determinate rules or moral precepts, which, in their own nature, have a necessary tendency to promote the well-being of the sum of mankind, taking in all nations and ages, from the beginning to the end of the world.

11. Hence, upon an equal comprehensive survey of the general nature, the passions, interests, and mutual respects of mankind; whatsoever practical proposition doth to right reason evidently appear to have a necessary connexion with the Universal well-being included in it, is to be looked upon as enjoined by the will of God. For, he that willeth the end doth will the necessary means conducive to that end; but it hath been shewn that God willeth the universal well-being of mankind should be promoted by the concurrence of each particular person; therefore, every such practical proposition necessarily tending thereto is to be esteemed a decree of God, and is consequently a law to man.

12. These propositions are called *laws of nature,* because they are universal, and do not derive their obligation from any civil sanction, but immediately from the

Author of nature himself. They are said to be *stamped on the mind*, to be *engraven on the tables of the heart*, because they are well known to mankind, and suggested and inculcated by conscience. Lastly, they are termed *eternal rules of reason*, because they necessarily result from the nature of things, and may be demonstrated by the infallible deductions of reason.

13. And, notwithstanding that these rules are too often, either by the unhappy concurrence of events, or more especially by the wickedness of perverse men who will not conform to them, made accidental causes of misery to those good men who do, yet this doth not vacate their obligation: they are ever to be esteemed the fixed unalterable standards of moral good and evil; no private interest, no love of friends, no regard to the public good, should make us depart from them. Hence, when any doubt arises concerning the morality of an action, it is plain this cannot be determined by computing the public good which in that particular case it is attended with, but only by comparing it with the Eternal Law of Reason. He who squares his actions by this rule can never do amiss, though thereby he should bring himself to poverty, death, or disgrace: no, not though he should involve his family, his friends, his country, in all those evils which are accounted the greatest and most insupportable to human nature. Tenderness and benevolence of temper are often motives to the best and greatest actions; but we must not make them the sole rule of our actions: they are passions rooted in our nature, and, like all other passions, must be restrained and kept under, otherwise they may possibly betray us into as great enormities as any other unbridled lust. Nay, they are more dangerous than other passions, insomuch as they are more plausible, and apt to dazzle and

corrupt the mind with the appearance of goodness and generosity.

14. For the illustration of what has been said, it will not be amiss, if from the moral we turn our eyes on the natural world. *Homo ortus est* (says Balbus in Cicero) *ad mundum contemplandum, et imitandum.* And, surely, it is not possible for free intellectual agents to propose a nobler pattern for their imitation than Nature; which is nothing else but a series of free actions, produced by the best and wisest Agent. But, it is evident that those actions are not adapted to particular views, but all conformed to certain general rules, which, being collected from observation, are by philosophers termed laws of nature. And these indeed are excellently suited to promote the general well-being of the creation: but, what from casual combinations of events, and what from the voluntary motions of animals, it often falls out, that the natural good not only of private men but of entire cities and nations would be better promoted by a particular suspension, or contradiction, than an exact observation of those laws. Yet, for all that, nature still takes its course; nay, it is plain that plagues, famines, inundations, earthquakes, with an infinite variety of pains and sorrows—in a word, all kinds of calamities public and private, do arise from a uniform steady observation of those General Laws which are once established by the Author of Nature, and which He will not change or deviate from upon any of those accounts, how wise or benevolent soever it may be thought by foolish men to do so. As for the miracles recorded in Scripture, they were always wrought for confirmation of some doctrine or mission from God, and not for the sake of the particular natural goods, as health or life, which some men might have reaped from them. From all which it seems sufficiently plain that we cannot be at a loss which way

to determine, in case we think God's own methods the properest to obtain His ends, and that it is our duty to copy after them, so far as the frailty of our nature will permit.

15. Thus far in general, of the nature and necessity of Moral Rules, and the criterion or mark whereby they may be known.

As for the particulars, from the foregoing discourse, the principal of them may without much difficulty be deduced. It hath been shewn that the Law of Nature is a system of such rules or precepts as that, if they be all of them, at all times, in all places, and by all men observed, they will necessarily promote the well-being of mankind, so far as it is attainable by human actions. Now, let any one who hath the use of reason take but an impartial survey of the general frame and circumstances of human nature, and it will appear plainly to him that the constant observation of truth, for instance, or of justice, and chastity hath a necessary connexion with their universal well-being; that, therefore, they are to be esteemed virtues or duties; and that 'Thou shalt not forswear thyself,' 'Thou shalt not commit adultery,' 'Thou shalt not steal,' are so many unalterable moral rules, which to violate in the least degree is vice or sin. I say, the agreement of these particular practical propositions with the definition or criterion premised doth so clearly result from the nature of things, that it were a needless digression, in this place, to enlarge upon it.

And, from the same principle, by the very same reasoning, it follows that Loyalty is a moral virtue, and 'Thou shalt not resist the Supreme Power' a rule or law of nature, the least breach whereof hath the inherent stain of moral turpitude.

16. The miseries inseparable from a state of anarchy

are easily imagined. So insufficient is the wit or strength of any single man, either to avert the evils, or procure the blessings of life, and so apt are the wills of different persons to contradict and thwart each other, that it is absolutely necessary several independent powers be combined together, under the direction (if I may so speak) of one and the same will—I mean the Law of the Society. Without this there is no politeness, no order, no peace, among men, but the world is one great heap of misery and confusion; the strong as well as the weak, the wise as well as the foolish, standing on all sides exposed to all those calamities which man can be liable to, in a state where he has no other security than the not being possessed of any thing which may raise envy or desire in another. A state by so much more ineligible than that of brutes as a reasonable creature hath a greater reflexion and foresight of miseries than they. From all which it plainly follows, that Loyalty, or submission to the supreme authority, hath, if universally practised in conjunction with all other virtues, a necessary connexion with the well-being of the whole sum of mankind; and, by consequence, if the criterion we have laid down be true, it is, strictly speaking, a moral duty, or branch of natural religion. And, therefore, the least degree of Rebellion is, with the utmost strictness and propriety, a sin: not only in Christians, but also in those who have the light of reason alone for their guide. Nay, upon a thorough and impartial view, this submission will, I think, appear one of the very first and fundamental laws of nature; inasmuch as it is civil government which ordains and marks out the various relations between men, and regulates property; thereby giving scope and laying a foundation for the exercise of all other duties. And, in truth, whoever considers the condition of man will scarce conceive it possible that the practice of any one moral virtue should obtain, in the naked, forlorn state of nature.

17. But, since it must be confessed that in all cases our actions come not within the direction of certain fixed moral rules, it may possibly be still questioned, whether obedience to the Supreme Power be not one of those exempted cases; and consequently to be regulated by the prudence and discretion of every single person rather than adjusted to the rule of absolute non-resistance. I shall therefore endeavour to make it yet more plain, that 'Thou shalt not resist the Supreme Power' is an undoubted precept of morality; as will appear from the following considerations:—

First, then, submission to government is a point important enough to be established by a moral rule. Things of insignificant and trifling concern are, for that very reason, exempted from the rules of morality. But government, on which so much depend the peace, order, and well-being, of mankind, cannot surely be thought of too small importance to be secured and guarded by a moral rule. Government, I say, which is itself the principal source under heaven of those particular advantages for the procurement and conservation whereof several unquestionable moral rules were prescribed to men.

18. Secondly, obedience to government is a case universal enough to fall under the direction of a law of nature. Numberless rules there may be for regulating affairs of great concernment, at certain junctures, and to some particular persons or societies, which, notwithstanding, are not to be esteemed moral or natural laws, but may be either totally abrogated or dispensed with; because the private ends they were intended to promote respect only some particular persons, as engaged in relations not founded in the general nature of men; who, on various occasions, and in different postures of things,

may prosecute their own designs by different measures, as in human prudence shall seem convenient. But what relation is there more extensive and universal than that of *subject* and *law?* This is confined to no particular age or climate, but universally obtains, at all times, and in all places, wherever men live in a state exalted above that of brutes. It is, therefore, evident that the rule forbidding resistance to the Law or Supreme Power is not, upon pretence of any defect in point of universality, to be excluded from the number of the laws of nature.

19. Thirdly, there is another consideration which confirms the necessity of admitting this rule for a moral or natural law: namely, because the case it regards is of too nice and difficult a nature to be left to the judgment and determination of each private person. Some cases there are so plain and obvious to judge of that they may safely be trusted to the prudence of every reasonable man. But in all instances to determine, whether a civil law is fitted to promote the public interest; or whether submission or resistance will prove most advantageous in the consequence; or when it is that the general good of a nation may require an alteration of government, either in its form, or in the hands which administer it;—these are points too arduous and intricate, and which require too great a degree of parts, leisure, and liberal education, as well as disinterestedness and thorough knowledge in the particular state of a kingdom, for every subject to take upon him the determination of them. From which it follows that, upon this account also, Non-resistance, which in the main, nobody can deny to be a most profitable and wholesome duty, ought not to be limited by the judgment of private persons to particular occasions, but esteemed a most sacred law of nature.

20. The foregoing arguments do, I think, make it manifest, that the precept against Rebellion is on a level with other moral rules. Which will yet further appear from this fourth and last consideration. It cannot be denied that right reason doth require some common stated rule or measure, whereby subjects ought to shape their submission to the Supreme Power; since any clashing or disagreement in this point must unavoidably tend to weaken and dissolve the society. And it is unavoidable that there should be great clashing, where it is left to the breast of each individual to suit his fancy with a different measure of obedience. But this common stated measure must be either the general precept forbidding resistance, or else the public good of the whole nation; which last, though it is allowed to be in itself something certain and determinate, yet, forasmuch as men can regulate their conduct only by what appears to them, whether in truth it be what it appears or no; and, since the prospects men form to themselves of a country's public good are commonly as various as its landscapes, which meet the eye in several situations: it clearly follows, that to make the public good the rule of obedience is, in effect, not to establish any determinate, agreed, common measure of loyalty, but to leave every subject to the guidance of his own particular mutable fancy.

21. From all which arguments and considerations it is a most evident conclusion, that the law prohibiting Rebellion is in strict truth a law of nature, universal reason, and morality. But to this it will perhaps be objected by some that, whatever may be concluded with regard to resistance from the tedious deductions of reason, yet there is I know not what turpitude and deformity in some actions, which at first blush shews them to be vicious; but they, not finding themselves

struck with such a sensible and immediate horror at the thought of Rebellion, cannot think it on a level with other crimes against nature. To which I answer:— that it is true, there are certain natural antipathies implanted in the soul, which are ever the most lasting and insurmountable; but, as custom is a second nature, whatever aversions are from our early childhood continually infused into the mind give it so deep a stain as is scarce to be distinguished from natural complexion. And, as it doth hence follow, that to make all the inward horrors of soul pass for infallible marks of sin were the way to establish error and superstition in the world; so, on the other hand, to suppose all actions lawful which are unattended with those starts of nature would prove of the least dangerous consequence to virtue and morality. For, these pertaining to us as men, we must not be directed in respect of them by any emotions in our blood and spirits, but by the dictates of sober and impartial reason. And if there be any who find they have a less abhorrence of Rebellion than of other villainies, all that can be inferred from it is, that this part of their duty was not so much reflected on, or so early and frequently inculcated into their hearts, as it ought to have been. Since without question there are other men who have as thorough an aversion for that as for any other crime.[1]

22. Again, it will probably be objected that submission to government differs from moral duties in that

[1] ['Il disoit ordinairement qu'il avoit un aussi grand éloignement pour ce péché là que pour assassiner le monde, ou pour voler sur les grands chemins, et qu'enfin il n'y avoit rien qui fût plus contraire à son naturel.' He (Mr. Pascal) used to say he had as great an abhorrence of rebellion as of murder, or robbing on the highway, and that there was nothing more shocking to his nature.—*Vide M. Pascal*, p. 44.]—BERKELEY.

ʀɛ is founded in a contract,[1] which, upon the violation
of its conditions, doth of course become void, and in
such case Rebellion is lawful: it hath not therefore the
nature of a sin or crime, which is in itself absolutely
unlawful, and must be committed on no pretext whatsoever. Now, passing over all inquiry and dispute concerning the first obscure rise of government, I observe
its being founded on a contract may be understood in a
twofold sense:—either, first, that several independent
persons, finding the insufferable inconvenience of a state
of anarchy, where every one was governed by his own
will, consented and agreed together to pay an absolute
submission to the decrees of some certain legislative;
which, though sometimes they may bear hard on the
subject, yet must surely prove easier to be governed by
than the violent humours and unsteady opposite wills
of a multitude of savages. And, in case we admit such
a compact to have been the original foundation of civil
government, it must even on that supposition be held
sacred and inviolable.

23. Or, secondly, it is meant that subjects have contracted with their respective sovereigns or legislators
to pay, not an absolute, but conditional and limited,
submission to their laws; that is, upon condition, and
so far forth, as the observation of them shall contribute
to the public good: reserving still to themselves a right
of superintending the laws, and judging whether they
are fitted to promote the public good or no; and (in
case they or any of them think it needful) of resisting
the higher powers, and changing the whole frame of
government by force: which is a right that all mankind, whether single persons or societies, have over those
that are deputed by them. But, in this sense, a contract
cannot be admitted for the ground and measure of civil

[1] Cf. Locke's *Treatise* on *Government*, Bk. II. ch. 8.

obedience, except one of these two things be clearly shewn:—either, first, that such a contract is an express known part of the fundamental constitution of a nation, equally allowed and unquestioned by all as the common law of the land; or, secondly, if it be not express, that it is at least necessarily implied in the very nature or notion of civil polity, which supposes it is a thing manifestly absurd, that a number of men should be obliged to live under an unlimited subjection to civil law, rather than continue wild and independent of each other. But to me it seems most evident that neither of those points will ever be proved.

24. And till they are proved beyond all contradiction, the doctrine built upon them ought to be rejected with detestation. Since, to represent the higher powers as deputies of the people manifestly tends to diminish that awe and reverence which all good men should have for the laws and government of their country. And to speak of a condition, limited loyalty, and I know not what vague and undetermined contracts, is a most effectual means to loosen the bands of civil society; than which nothing can be of more mischievous consequence to mankind. But, after all, if there be any man who either cannot or will not see the absurdity and perniciousness of those notions, he would, I doubt not, be convinced with a witness, in case they should once become current, and every private man take it in his head to believe them true, and put them in practice.

25. But there still remains an objection which hath the appearance of some strength against what has been said. Namely, that, whereas civil polity is a thing entirely of human institution, it seems contrary to reason to make submission to it part of the law of nature, and not rather of the civil law. For, how can it be imagined that nature should dictate or prescribe a natu-

ral law about a thing which depends on the arbitrary humour of men, not only as to its kind or form, which is very various and mutable, but even as to its existence; there being no where to be found a civil government set up by nature.—In answer to this, I observe, first, that most moral precepts do presuppose some voluntary actions, or pacts of men, and are nevertheless esteemed laws of nature. Property is assigned, the signification of words ascertained, and matrimony contracted, by the agreement and consent of mankind; and, for all that, it is not doubted whether theft, falsehood, and adultery be prohibited by the law of nature. Loyalty, therefore, though it should suppose and be the result of human institutions, may, for all that, be of natural obligation.—I say, secondly, that, notwithstanding particular societies are formed by men, and are not in all places alike, as things esteemed natural are wont to be, yet there is implanted in mankind a natural tendency or disposition to a social life. I call it *natural,* because it is universal, and because it necessarily results from the differences which distinguish man from beast; the peculiar wants, appetites, faculties, and capacities of man being exactly calculated and framed for such a state, insomuch that without it it is impossible he should live in a condition in any degree suitable to his nature. And, since the bond and cement of society is a submission to its laws, it plainly follows that this duty hath an equal right with any other to be thought a law of nature. And surely that precept which enjoins obedience to civil laws cannot itself, with any propriety, be accounted a civil law; it must therefore either have no obligation at all on the conscience, or, if it hath, it must be derived from the universal voice of nature and reason.

26. And thus the first point proposed seems clearly made out:—namely, that Loyalty is a virtue or moral

duty; and Disloyalty or Rebellion, in the most strict and proper sense, a vice or crime against the law of nature.

We are now come to the second point, which was to shew that the prohibitions of vice, or negative precepts of morality, are to be taken in a most absolute, necessary, and immutable sense; insomuch that the attainment of the greatest good, or deliverance from the greatest evil, that can befal any man or number of men in this life may not justify the least violation of them.—But, in the first place, I shall explain the reason of distinguishing between positive and negative precepts, the latter only being included in this general proposition. Now, the ground of that distinction may be resolved into this: namely, that very often, either through the difficulty or number of moral actions, or their inconsistence with each other, it is not possible for one man to perform several of them at the same time; whereas it is plainly consistent and possible that any man should, at the same time, abstain from all manner of positive actions whatsoever. Hence it comes to pass that prohibitions or negative precepts must by every one, in all times and places, be all actually observed: whereas those which enjoin the doing of an action allow room for human prudence and discretion in the execution of them: it is for the most part depending on various accidental circumstances; all which ought to be considered, and care taken that duties of less moment do not interfere with, and hinder the fulfilling of those which are more important. And, for this reason, if not the positive laws themselves, at least the exercise of them, admits of suspension, limitation, and diversity of degrees. As to the indispensableness of the negative precepts of the law of nature, I shall in its proof offer two arguments; the first from the nature of the thing, and the second from the imitation of God in His government of the world.

27. First, then, from the nature of the thing it hath been already shewn that the great end of morality can never be carried on, by leaving each particular person to promote the public good in such a manner as *he* shall think most convenient; without prescribing certain determinate universal rules, to be the common measure of moral actions. And, if we allow the necessity of these, and at the same time think it lawful to transgress them whenever the public good shall seem to require it, what is this but in words indeed to enjoin the observation of moral rules, but in effect to leave every one to be guided by his own judgment? Than which nothing can be imagined more pernicious and destructive to mankind, as hath been already proved. Secondly, this same point may be collected from the example set us by the Author of Nature, who, as we have above observed, acts according to certain fixed laws; which He will not transgress upon the account of accidental evils arising from them. Suppose a prince on whose life the welfare of a kingdom depends to fall down a precipice, we have no reason to think that the universal law of gravitation would be suspended in that case. The like may be said of all other laws of nature, which we do not find to admit of exceptions on particular accounts.

28. And as, without such a steadiness in nature, we should soon, instead of this beautiful frame, see nothing but a disorderly and confused chaos; so, if once it become current that the moral actions of men are not to be guided by certain definite inviolable rules, there will be no longer found that beauty, order, and agreement in the system of rational beings, or moral world, which will then be all covered over with darkness and violence.

It is true, he who stands close to a palace can hardly make a right judgment of the architecture and symmetry of its several parts, the nearer ever appearing disproportionably great. And, if we have a mind to take a fair prospect of the order and general well-being which the inflexible laws of nature and morality derive on the world, we must, if I may so say, go out of it, and imagine ourselves to be distant spectators of all that is transacted and contained in it; otherwise we are sure to be deceived by the too near view of the little present interests of ourselves, our friends, or our country.

The right understanding of what hath been said will, I think, afford a clear solution to the following difficulties:—

29. First, it may perhaps seem to some that, in consequence of the foregoing doctrine, men will be left to their own private judgments as much as ever. For, first, the very being of the laws of nature; secondly, the criterion whereby to know them; and, thirdly, the agreement of any particular precept with that criterion, are all to be discovered by reason and argumentation, in which every man doth necessarily judge for himself: hence, upon that supposition, there is place for as great confusion, unsteadiness, and contrariety of opinions and actions as upon any other. I answer, that however men may differ as to what were most proper and beneficial to the public to be done or omitted on particular occasions, when they have for the most part narrow and interested views; yet, in general conclusions, drawn from an equal and enlarged view of things, it is not possible there should be so great, if any, disagreement at all amongst candid rational inquirers after truth.

30. Secondly, the most plausible pretence of all against the doctrine we have premised, concerning a rigid

indispensable observation of moral rules, is that which is founded on the consideration of the public weal.[1] For, since the common good of mankind is confessedly the end which God requires should be promoted by the free actions of men, it may seem to follow that all good men ought ever to have this in view, as the great mark to which all their endeavours should be directed: if, therefore, in any particular case, a strict keeping to the moral rule shall prove manifestly inconsistent with the public good, it may be thought agreeable to the will of God that in that case the rule does restrain an honest disinterested person from acting for that end to which the rule itself was ordained. For, it is an axiom that 'the end is more excellent than the means,' which, deriving their goodness from the end, may not come in competition with it.

31. In answer to this, let it be observed, that nothing is a law merely because it conduceth to the public good, but because it is decreed by the will of God, which alone can give the sanction of a law of nature to any precept; neither is any thing, how expedient or plausible soever, to be esteemed lawful on any other account than its being coincident with, or not repugnant to, the laws promulgated by the voice of nature and reason. It must indeed be allowed that the rational deduction of those laws is founded in the intrinsic tendency they have to promote the well-being of mankind, on condition they are universally and constantly observed. But, though it afterwards comes to pass that they accidentally fail of that end, or even promote the contrary; they are nevertheless binding, as hath been already proved. In short, that whole difficulty may be resolved by the following distinction:—In framing the general laws of nature, it is granted we must be entirely guided by the

[1] Cf. Locke's *Treatise on Government*, Bk. II. ch. 19.

public good of mankind, but not in the ordinary moral actions of our lives. Such a rule, if universally observed, hath, from the nature of things, a necessary fitness to promote the general well-being of mankind: therefore it is a law of nature. This is good reasoning. But if we should say, such an action doth in this instance produce much good, and no harm to mankind; therefore it is lawful: this were wrong. The rule is framed with respect to the good of mankind; but our practice must be always shaped immediately by the rule. They who think the public good of a nation to be the sole measure of the obedience due to the civil power seem not to have considered this distinction.

32. If it be said that some negative precepts, e.g. 'Thou shalt not kill,' do admit of limitation, since otherwise it were unlawful for the magistrate, for a soldier in a battle, or for a man in his own defence, to kill another; I answer, when a duty is expressed in too general terms, as in this instance, in order to a distinct declaration of it, either those terms may be changed for others of a more limited sense, as *kill* for *murder;* or else, from the general proposition remaining in its full latitude, exceptions may be made of those precise cases which, not agreeing with the notion of murder, are not prohibited by the law of nature. In the former case there is a limitation; but it is only of the signification of a single term, too general and improper, by substituting another, more proper and particular, in its place. In the latter case there are exceptions; but then they are not from the law of nature, but from a more general proposition, which, besides that law, includes somewhat more, which must be taken away in order to leave the law by itself clear and determinate. From neither of which concessions will it follow that any negative law of nature is limited to those cases only where its par-

ticular application promotes the public good, or admits
all other cases to be excepted from it wherein its being
actually observed produceth harm to the public. But
of this I shall have occasion to say more in the sequel.

I have now done with the first head, which was to shew
that there is an absolute, unlimited, passive obedience
due to the Supreme Power, wherever placed in any
nation; and come to inquire into the grounds and reasons of the contrary opinion. Which was the second
thing proposed.

33. One great principle which the leaders for resistance make the ground-work of their doctrine is, that
the law of self-preservation is prior to all other en-
gagements, being the very first and fundamental law
of nature. Hence, say they, subjects are obliged by
nature, and it is their duty, to resist the cruel attempts
of tyrants, however authorised by unjust and bloody
laws; which are nothing else but the decrees of men,
and consequently must give way to those of God or
Nature. But perhaps, if we narrowly examine this
notion, it will not be found so just and clear as some
men may imagine, or, indeed, as at first sight it seems
to be. For, we ought to distinguish between a twofold
signification of the terms *law of nature;* which words
do either denote a rule or precept for the direction of
the voluntary actions of reasonable agents; and in that
sense they imply a duty: or else they are used to signify
any general rule which we observe to obtain in the
works of nature, independent of the wills of men; in
which sense no duty is implied. And, in this last acceptation, I grant it is a general law of nature, that in every
animal there be implanted a desire of self-preservation;
which, though it is the earliest, the deepest, and most
lasting of all, whether natural or acquired appetites, yet

cannot with any propriety be termed a moral duty. But if, in the former sense of the words, they mean that self-preservation is the first and most fundamental law of nature, which therefore must take place of all other natural or moral duties, I think that assertion to be manifestly false; for this plain reason, because it would thence follow, a man may lawfully commit any sin whatsoever to preserve his life, than which nothing can be more absurd.

34. It cannot indeed be denied that the law of nature restrains us from doing those things which may injure the life of any man, and consequently our own. But, notwithstanding all that is said of the obligativeness and priority of the law of self-preservation, yet, for aught I can see, there is no particular law which obliges any man to prefer his own temporal good, not even life itself, to that of another man, much less to the observation of any one moral duty. This is what we are too ready to perform of our own accord; and there is more need of a law to curb and restrain, than there is of one to excite and inflame our self-love.

35. But, secondly, though we should grant the duty of self-preservation to be the first and most necessary of all the positive or affirmative laws of nature; yet, forasmuch as it is a maxim allowed by all moralists, that 'evil is never to be committed, to the end good may come of it,' it will thence plainly follow that no negative precept ought to be transgressed for the sake of observing a positive one. And therefore, since we have shewn, 'Thou shalt not resist the supreme power,' to be a negative law of nature, it is a necessary consequence that it may not be transgressed under pretence of fulfilling the positive duty of self-preservation.

36. A second erroneous ground of our adversaries, whereon they lay a main stress, is that they hold the

public good of a particular nation to be the measure of the obedience due from the subject to the civil power, which therefore may be resisted whensoever the public good shall verily seem to require it. But this point hath been already considered; and in truth it can give small difficulty to whoever understands Loyalty to be on the same foot with other moral duties enjoined in negative precepts; all which, though equally calculated to promote the general well-being, may not nevertheless be limited or suspended, under pretext of giving way to the end, as is plain from what hath been premised on that subject.

37. A third reason which they insist on is to this effect:—All civil authority or right is derived originally from the people; but nobody can transfer that to another which he hath not himself; therefore, since no man hath an absolute unlimited right over his own life, the subject cannot transfer such a right to the prince (or supreme power), who consequently hath no such unlimited right to dispose of the lives of his subjects. In case, therefore, a subject resist his prince, who, acting according to law, maketh an unjust, though legal, attempt on his life, he does him no wrong; since wrong it is not, to prevent another from seizing what he hath no right to: whence it should seem to follow that, agreeably to reason, the prince, or supreme power wheresoever placed, may be resisted. Having thus endeavoured to state their argument in its clearest light, I make this answer:— First, it is granted, no civil power hath an unlimited right to dispose of the life of any man. Secondly, in case one man resist another invading that which he hath no right to, it is granted he doth him no wrong. But, in the third place, I deny that it doth thence follow, the supreme power may consonantly to reason be resisted; because that, although such resistance wronged not the

prince or supreme power wheresoever placed, yet it were injurious to the Author of Nature, and a violation of His law, which reason obligeth us to transgress upon no account whatsoever, as hath been demonstrated.

38. A fourth mistake or prejudice which influenceth the impugners of non-resistance arises from the natural dread of slavery, chains, and fetters, which inspires them with an aversion for any thing, which even metaphorically comes under those denominations. Hence they cry out against us that we would deprive them of their natural freedom, that we are making chains for mankind, that we are for enslaving them, and the like. But, how harsh soever the sentence may appear, yet it is most true, that our appetites, even the most natural, as of ease, plenty, or life itself, must be chained and fettered by the laws of nature and reason. This slavery, if they will call it so, or subjection of our passions to the immutable decrees of reason, though it may be galling to the sensual part or the beast, yet sure I am it addeth much to the dignity of that which is peculiarly human in our composition. This leads me to the fifth fundamental error.

39. Namely, the mistaking the object of passive obedience. We should consider that when a subject endures the insolence and oppression of one or more magistrates, armed with the supreme civil power, the object of his submission is, in strict truth, nothing else but right reason; which is the voice of the Author of Nature. Think not we are so senseless as to imagine tyrants cast in a better mould than other men: no, they are the worst and vilest of men, and for their own sakes have not the least right to our obedience. But the laws of God and nature must be obeyed; and our obedience to them is never more acceptable and sincere than when it exposeth us to temporal calamities.

40. A sixth false ground of persuasion to those we argue against is their not distinguishing between the natures of positive and negative duties. For, say they, since our *active* obedience to the supreme civil power is acknowledged to be limited, why may not our duty of *non-resistance* be thought so too? The answer is plain: because positive and negative moral precepts are not of the same nature; the former admitting such limitations and exceptions as the latter are on no account liable to, as hath been already proved. It is very possible that a man, in obeying the commands of his lawful governors, might transgress some law of God contrary to them; which it is not possible for him to do merely by a patient suffering and non-resistance for conscience sake. And this furnishes such a satisfactory and obvious solution of the fore-mentioned difficulty that I am not a little surprised to see it insisted on, by men, otherwise, of good sense and reason. And so much for the grounds and reasons of the adversaries of non-resistance.

I now proceed to the third and last thing proposed, namely, the consideration of the objections drawn from the pretended consequences of non-resistance.

41. First, then, it will be objected that, in consequence of that notion, we must believe that God hath, in several instances, laid the innocent part of mankind under an unavoidable necessity of enduring the greatest sufferings and hardships, without any remedy; which is plainly inconsistent with the Divine wisdom and goodness: and therefore the principle from whence that consequence flows, ought not to be admitted as a law of God or nature. In answer to which I observe, we must carefully distinguish between the necessary and accidental consequences of a moral law. The former kind are those

which the law is in its own nature calculated to produce, and which have an inseparable connexion with the observation of it; and indeed, if these are bad, we may justly conclude the law to be so too; and consequently not from God. But the accidental consequences of a law have no intrinsic natural connexion with, nor do they strictly speaking flow from its observation, but are the genuine result of something foreign and circumstantial, which happens to be joined with it. And these accidental consequences of a very good law may nevertheless be very bad; which badness of theirs is to be charged on their own proper and necessary cause, and not on the law, which hath no essential tendency to produce them. Now, though it must be granted that a lawgiver infinitely wise and good will constitute such laws for the regulation of human actions as have in their own nature a necessary inherent aptness to promote the common good of all mankind, and that in the greatest degree that the present circumstances and capacities of human nature will admit; yet we deny that the wisdom and goodness of the lawgiver are concerned, or may be called in question, on account of the particular evils which arise, necessarily and properly, from the transgression of some one or more good laws, and but accidentally from the observation of others. But it is plain that the several calamities and devastations which oppressive governments bring on the world are not the genuine necessary effects of the law that enjoineth a passive objection to the supreme power, neither are they included in the primary intention thereof, but spring from avarice, ambition, cruelty, revenge, and the like inordinate affections and vices raging in the breasts of governors. They may not therefore argue a defect of wisdom or goodness in God's law, but of righteousness in men.

42. Such is the present state of things, so irregular are the wills, and so unrestrained the passions, of men, that we every day see manifest breaches and violations of the laws of nature, which, being always committed in favour of the wicked, must surely be sometimes attended with heavy disadvantages and miseries on the part of those who by a firm adhesion to His laws endeavour to approve themselves in the eyes of their Creator. There are in short no rules of morality, not excepting the best, but what may subject good men to great sufferings and hardships; which necessarily follows from the wickedness of those they have to deal with, and but accidently from those good rules. And as, on the one hand, it were inconsistent with the wisdom of God, by suffering a retaliation of fraud, perjury, or the like, on the head of offenders, to punish one transgression by another: so, on the other hand, it were inconsistent with His justice to leave the good and innocent a hopeless sacrifice to the wicked. God therefore hath appointed a day of retribution in another life, and in this we have His grace and a good conscience for our support. We should not therefore repine at the Divine laws, or shew a forwardness or impatience of those transient sufferings they accidentally expose us to, which, however grating to flesh and blood, will yet seem of small moment, if we compare the littleness and fleetingness of this present world with the glory and eternity of the next.

43. From what hath been said, I think it is plain that the premised doctrine of non-resistance were safe, though the evils incurred thereby should be allowed never so great. But perhaps, upon a strict examination, they will be found much less than by many they are thought to be. The mischievous effects which are charged on that doctrine may be reduced to these two points:—First, that it is an encouragement for all gov-

ernors to become tyrants, by the prospect it gives them of impunity or non-resistance. Secondly, that it renders the oppression and cruelty of those who are tyrants more insupportable and violent, by cutting off all opposition, and consequently all means of redress. I shall consider each of these distinctly.—As to the first point, either you will suppose the governors to be good or ill men. If they are good, there is no fear of their becoming tyrants. And if they are ill men, that is, such as postpone the observation to God's laws to the satisfying of their own lusts, then it can be no security to them that others will rigidly observe those moral precepts which they find themselves so prone to transgress.

44. It is indeed a breach of the law of nature for a subject, though under the greatest and most unjust sufferings, to lift up his hand against the supreme power. But it is a more heinous and inexcusable violation of it for the persons invested with the supreme power to use that power to the ruin and destruction of the people committed to their charge. What encouragement therefore can any man have to think that others will not be pushed on by the strong implanted appetite of self-preservation, to commit a crime, when he himself commits a more brutish and unnatural crime, perhaps without any provocation at all? Or is it to be imagined that they who daily break God's laws, for the sake of some little profit or transient pleasure, will not be tempted, by the love of property, liberty, or life itself, to transgress that single precept which forbids resistance to the supreme power?

45. But it will be demanded—To what purpose then is this duty of non-resistance preached, and proved, and recommended to our practice, if, in all likelihood, when things come to an extremity, men will never observe it? I answer, to the very same purpose that any other duty

is preached. For, what duty is there which many, too many, upon some consideration or other, may not be prevailed on to transgress? Moralists and divines do not preach the duties of nature and religion with a view of gaining mankind to a perfect observation of them; that they know is not to be done. But, however, our pains are answered, if we can make men less sinners than otherwise they would be; if, by opposing the force of duty to that of present interest and passion, we can get the better of some temptations, and balance others, while the greatest still remain invincible.

46. But, granting those who are invested with the supreme power to have all imaginable security that no cruel and barbarous treatment whatever could provoke their subjects to rebellion, yet I believe it may be justly questioned, whether such security would tempt them to more or greater acts of cruelty than jealousy, distrust, suspicion, and revenge may do in a state less secure.— And so far in consideration of the first point, namely, that the doctrine of non-resistance is an encouragement for governors to become tyrants.

47. The second mischievous effect it was charged with is, that it renders the oppression and cruelty of those who are tyrants more insupportable and violent, by cutting off all opposition, and consequently all means of redress. But, if things are rightly considered, it will appear that redressing the evils of government by force is at best a very hazardous attempt, and what often puts the public in a worse state than it was before. For, either you suppose the power of the rebels to be but small, and easily crushed, and then this is apt to inspire the governors with confidence and cruelty. Or, in case you suppose it more considerable, so as to be a match for the supreme power supported by the public

treasure, forts, and armies, and that the whole nation is engaged in a civil war;—the certain effects of this are, rapine, bloodshed, misery, and confusion to all orders and parties of men, greater and more insupportable by far than are known under any the most absolute and severe tyranny upon earth. And it may be that, after much mutual slaughter, the rebellious party may prevail. And if they do prevail to destroy the government in being, it may be they will substitute a better in its place, or change it into better hands. And may not this come to pass without the expense, and toil, and blood of war? Is not the heart of a prince in the hand of God? May He not therefore give him a right sense of his duty, or may He not call him out of the world by sickness, accident, or the hand of some desperate ruffian, and send a better in his stead? When I speak as of a monarchy, I would be understood to mean all sorts of government, wheresoever the supreme power is lodged. Upon the whole, I think we may close with the heathen philosopher, who thought it the part of a wise man never to attempt the change of government by force, when it could not be mended without the slaughter and banishment of his countrymen: but to sit still, and pray for better times [1]. For, this way may do, and the other may not do; there is uncertainty in both courses. The difference is that in the way of rebellion we are sure to increase the public calamities, for a time at least, though we are not sure of lessening them for the future.

48. But, though it should be acknowledged that, in the

[1] [Plato in Epist. vii.]—BERKELEY. The passage referred to is the following:—Λέγειν μέν, εἰ μὴ καλῶς αὐτῷ φαίνοιτο πολιτεύεσθαι, εἰ μέλλοι μήτε ματαίως ἐρεῖν, μήτε ἀποθανεῖσθαι λέγων, βίαν δὲ πατρίδι πολιτείας μεταβολῆς μὴ προσφέρειν, ὅταν ἄνευ φυγῆς καὶ σφαγῆς ἀνδρῶν μὴ δυνατὸν ᾖ γίγνεσθαι τὴν ἀρίστην, ἡσυχίαν δὲ ἄγοντα εὔχεσθαι τὰ ἀγαθὰ αὐτῷ τε καὶ τῇ πόλει.

main, submission and patience ought to be recommended, yet, men will be still apt to demand, whether extraordinary cases may not require extraordinary measures; and therefore, in case the oppression be insupportable, and the prospect of deliverance sure, whether rebellion may not be allowed of? I answer, by no means. Perjury, or breach of faith, may, in some possible cases, bring great advantage to a nation, by freeing it from conditions inconsistent with its liberty and public welfare. So likewise may adultery, by procuring a domestic heir, prevent a kingdom's falling into the hands of a foreign power, which would in all probability prove its ruin. Yet, will any man say, the extraordinary nature of those cases can take away the guilt of perjury and adultery [1]? This is what I will not suppose. But it

[1] [When I wrote this, I could not think any man would avow the justifying those crimes on any pretext. But I since find that an author (supposed the same who published the book entitled, *The Rights of the Christian Church*), in a *Discourse concerning Obedience to the Supreme Powers*, printed with three other discourses at London, in the year 1706, chap. iv. p. 28, speaking of Divine laws, is not ashamed to assert, 'There is no law which wholly relates to man but ceases to oblige, if, upon the infinite variety of circumstances attending human affairs, it happens to be contrary to the good of man.' So that, according to this writer, parricide, incest, or breach of faith become innocent things, if, in the infinite variety of circumstances, they should happen to promote (or be thought by any private person to promote) the public good. After what has been already said, I hope I need not be at any pains to convince the reader of the absurdity and perniciousness of this notion. I shall only observe, that it appears the author was led into it by a more than ordinary aversion to passive obedience; which put him upon measuring or limiting that duty, and, with equal reason, all others, by the public good, to the entire unhinging of all order and morality among men. And it must be owned the transition was very natural.] —BERKELEY.

This note was added in the third edition. The author referred to is Matthew Tindal.

hath been shewn, that rebellion is as truly a crime against nature and reason as either of the foregoing; it may not therefore be justified upon any account whatever, any more than they.

49. What! must we then submit our necks to the sword? and is there no help, no refuge, against extreme tyranny established by law? In answer to this I say, in the first place, it is not to be feared that men in their wits should seek the destruction of their people, by such cruel and unnatural decrees as some are forward to suppose. I say, secondly, that, in case they should, yet most certainly the subordinate magistrates may not, nay, they ought not, in obedience to those decrees, to act any thing contrary to the express laws of God. And, perhaps, all things considered, it will be thought that representing this limitation of their active obedience, by the laws of God or nature, as a duty to the ministers of the supreme power, may prove in those extravagant supposed cases no less effectual for the peace and safety of a nation than preaching up the power of resistance to the people.

50. Further, it will probably be objected as an absurdity in the doctrine of passive obedience, that it enjoineth subjects a blind implicit submission to the decrees of other men; which is unbecoming the dignity and freedom of reasonable agents; who indeed ought to pay obedience to their superiors, but it should be a rational obedience, such as arises from a knowledge of the equity of their laws, and the tendency they have to promote the public good. To which I answer, that it is not likely a government should suffer much for want of having its laws inspected and amended by those who are not legally entitled to a share in the management of affairs of that nature. And it must be confessed the bulk of mankind are by their circumstances and occupa-

tions so far unqualified to judge of such matters, that they must necessarily pay an implicit deference to some or other. And to whom so properly as to those invested with the supreme power?

51. There is another objection against absolute submission, which I should not have mentioned but that I find it insisted on by men of so great note as Grotius and Puffendorf [1], who think our non-resistance should be measured by the intention of those who first framed the society. Now, say they, if we suppose the question put to them, whether they meant to lay every subject under the necessity of choosing death, rather than in any case to resist the cruelty of his superiors, it cannot be imagined they would answer in the affirmative. For, this were to put themselves in a worse condition than that which they endeavoured to avoid by entering into society. For, although they were before obnoxious to the injuries of many, they had nevertheless the power of resisting them. But now they are bound, without any opposition at all, to endure the greatest injuries from those whom they have armed with their own strength. Which is by so much worse than the former state, as the undergoing an execution is worse than the hazard of a battle. But (passing by all other exceptions which this method of arguing may be liable to), it is evident that a man had better be exposed to the absolute irresistible decrees, even of one single person, whose own and posterity's true interest it is to preserve him in peace and plenty, and protect him from the injuries of all mankind beside, than remain an open prey to the rage and avarice of every wicked man upon earth, who either exceeds him in strength, or takes him at an ad-

[1] [Grotius *De Jure Belli et Pacis*, Lib. I. chap. iv. sect. 7; et Puffendorf *De Jure Naturæ et Gentium*, Lib. VII. cap. vii. sect. 7.]—BERKELEY.

vantage. The truth of this is confirmed, as well by the constant experience of the far greater part of the world, as by what we have already observed concerning anarchy, and the inconsistence of such a state with that manner of life which human nature requires. Hence it is plain the objection last mentioned is built on a false supposition, viz. That men, by quitting the natural state of anarchy for that of absolute non-resisting obedience to government, would put themselves in a worse condition than they were in before.

52. The last objection I shall take notice of is, that, in pursuance of the premised doctrine, where no exceptions, no limitations, are to be allowed of, it should seem to follow men were bound to submit, without making any opposition, to usurpers, or even madmen, possessed of the supreme authority. Which is a notion so absurd, and repugnant to common sense, that the foundation on which it is built may justly be called in question. Now, in order to clear this point, I observe the limitation of moral duties may be understood in a twofold sense—either, first, as a distinction applied to the terms of a proposition, whereby that which was expressed before too generally is limited to a particular acceptation; and this, in truth, is not so properly limiting the duty as defining it. Or, secondly, it may be understood as a suspending the observation of a duty, for avoiding some extraordinary inconvenience, and thereby confining it to certain occasions. And in this last sense only, we have shewn negative duties not to admit of limitation. Having premised this remark, I make the following answer to the objection:—namely, that by virtue of the duty of non-resistance we are not obliged to submit the disposal of our lives and fortunes to the discretion either of madmen, or of all those who by craft or violence invade the supreme power; because

the object of the submission enjoined subjects by the law of nature is, from the reason of the thing, manifestly limited so as to exclude both the one and the other. Which I shall not go about to prove, because I believe nobody has denied it. Nor doth the annexing such limits to the object of our obedience at all limit the duty itself, in the sense we except against.

53. [In morality the eternal rules of action have the same immutable universal truth with propositions in geometry. Neither of them depends on circumstances or accidents, being at all times and in all places, without limitation or exception, true. 'Thou shalt not resist the supreme civil power' is no less constant and unalterable a rule, for modelling the behaviour of a subject toward the government, than 'multiply the height by half the base' is for measuring a triangle. And, as it would not be thought to detract from the universality of this mathematical rule that it did not exactly measure a field which was not an exact triangle, so ought it not to be thought an argument against the universality of the rule prescribing passive obedience, that it does not reach a man's practice in all cases where a government is unhinged, or the supreme power disputed. There must be a triangle, and you must use your senses to know this, before there is room for applying your mathematical rule. And there must be a civil government, and you must know in whose hands it is lodged, before the moral precept takes place. But, where the supreme power is ascertained, we should no more doubt of our submission to it, than we would doubt of the way to measure a figure we know to be a triangle.]

54. In the various changes and fluctuations of government, it is impossible to prevent that controversies should sometimes arise concerning the seat of the supreme power. And in such cases subjects cannot be denied

the liberty of judging for themselves, or of taking part with some, and opposing others, according to the best of their judgments; all which is consistent with an exact observation of their duty, so long as, when the constitution is clear in the point, and the object of their submission undoubted, no pretext of interest, friends, or the public good, can make them depart from it. In short, it is acknowledged that the precept enjoining non-resistance is limited to particular objects, but not to particular occasions. And in this it is like all other moral negative duties, which, considered as general propositions, do admit of limitations and restrictions, in order to a distinct definition of the duty; but what is once known to be a duty of that sort can never become otherwise by any good or ill effect, circumstance, or event whatsoever. And in truth if it were not so, if there were no general inflexible rules, but all negative as well as positive duties might be dispensed with, and warpt to serve particular interests and occasions, there were an end of all morality.

55. It is therefore evident that, as the observation of any other negative moral law is not to be limited to those instances only where it may produce good effects, so neither is the observation of non-resistance limited in such sort as that any man may lawfully transgress it, whensoever in his judgment the public good of his particular country shall require it. And it is with regard to this limitation *by the effects* that I speak of non-resistance as an absolute, unconditioned, unlimited duty. Which must inevitably be granted, unless one of these three things can be proved:—either, first, that non-resistance is no moral duty: or, secondly, that other negative moral duties are limited by the effects: or, lastly, that there is something peculiar in the nature of non-resistance, which necessarily subjects it to such

a limitation as no other negative moral duty can admit. The contrary to each of which points, if I mistake not, hath been clearly made out.

56. I have now briefly gone through the objections drawn from the consequences of non-resistance, which was the last general head I proposed to treat of. In handling this and the other points, I have endeavoured to be as full and clear as the usual length of these discourses would permit, and throughout to consider the argument with the same indifference as I should any other part of general knowledge; being verily persuaded that men as Christians are obliged to the practice of no one moral duty which may not abide the severest test of Reason.

THE QUERIST

CONTAINING SEVERAL QUERIES

PROPOSED

TO THE CONSIDERATION OF THE PUBLIC

'I the Lord have brought down the high Tree, have exalted the low Tree, have dried up the green Tree, and have made the dry Tree to flourish.'—EZEK. xvii. 24.

[ADVERTISEMENT BY THE AUTHOR]

[THE *Querist* was first printed in the year one thousand seven hundred and thirty-five; since which time the face of things is somewhat changed. In this edition some alterations have been made. The three Parts are published in one; some few Queries are added, and many omitted—particularly of those relating to the sketch or plan of a National Bank, which it may be time enough to take again in hand when the public shall seem disposed to make use of such an expedient. I had determined with myself never to prefix my name to the *Querist;* but in the last edition was overruled by a friend, who was remarkable for pursuing the public interest with as much diligence as others do their own. I apprehend the same censure on this that I incurred upon another occasion, for meddling out of my profession. Though to feed the hungry and clothe the naked, by promoting an honest industry, will, perhaps, be deemed no improper employment for a clergyman who still thinks himself a member of the commonwealth. As the sum of human happiness is supposed to consist in the goods of mind, body, and fortune, I would fain make my studies of some use to mankind with regard to each of these three particulars, and hope it will not be thought faulty or indecent in any man, of what profession soever, to offer his mite towards improving the manners, health, and prosperity of his fellow creatures.]

THE QUERIST

Query 1. WHETHER there ever was, is, or will be, an industrious nation poor, or an idle rich?

2. Whether a people can be called poor, where the common sort are well fed, clothed, and lodged?

3. Whether the drift and aim of every wise state should not be, to encourage industry in its members? And whether those who employ neither heads nor hands for the common benefit deserve not to be expelled like drones out of a well-governed state?

4. Whether the four elements, and man's labour therein, be not the true source of wealth?

5. Whether money be not only so far useful, as it stirreth up industry, enabling men mutually to participate the fruits of each other's labour?

6. Whether any other means, equally conducing to excite and circulate the industry of mankind, may not be as useful as money?

7. Whether the real end and aim of men be not power? And whether he who could have everything else at his wish or will would value money?

8. Whether the public aim in every well-governed state be not that each member, according to his just pretensions and industry, should have power?

9. Whether power be not referred to action; and whether action doth not follow appetite or will?

10. Whether fashion doth not create appetites; and whether the prevailing will of a nation is not the fashion?

11. Whether the current of industry and commerce be not determined by this prevailing will?

12. Whether it be not owing to custom that the fashions are agreeable?

13. Whether it may not concern the wisdom of the legislature to interpose in the making of fashions; and not leave an affair of so great influence to the management of women and fops, tailors and vintners?

14. Whether reasonable fashions are a greater restraint on freedom than those which are unreasonable?

15. Whether a general good taste in a people would not greatly conduce to their thriving? And whether an uneducated gentry be not the greatest of national evils?

16. Whether customs and fashions do not supply the place of reason in the vulgar of all ranks? Whether, therefore, it doth not very much import that they should be wisely framed?

17. Whether the imitating those neighbours in our fashions, to whom we bear no likeness in our circumstances, be not one cause of distress to this nation?

18. Whether frugal fashions in the upper rank, and comfortable living in the lower, be not the means to multiply inhabitants?

19. Whether the bulk of our Irish natives are not kept from thriving, by that cynical content in dirt and beggary which they possess to a degree beyond any other people in Christendom?

20. Whether the creating of wants be not the likeliest way to produce industry in a people? And whether, if our peasants were accustomed to eat beef and wear shoes, they would not be more industrious?

21. Whether other things being given, as climate, soil, &c., the wealth be not proportioned to the industry; and this to the circulation of credit, be the credit circulated or transferred by what marks or tokens soever?

22. Whether, therefore, less money, swiftly circulating, be not, in effect, equivalent to more money slowly circulating? Or, whether, if the circulation be reciprocally as the quantity of coin the nation can be a loser?

23. Whether money is to be considered as having an intrinsic value, or as being a commodity, a standard, a measure, or a pledge, as is variously suggested by writers? And whether the true idea of money, as such, be not altogether that of a ticket or counter?

* * * * * * *

52. Whether small gains be not the way to great profit? And if our tradesmen are beggars, whether they may not thank themselves for it?

53. Whether some way might not be found for making criminals useful in public works, instead of sending them either to America, or to the other world?

54. Whether we may not, as well as other nations, contrive employment for them? And whether servitude, chains, and hard labour, for a term of years, would not be a more discouraging, as well as a more adequate punishment for felons than even death itself?

55. Whether there are not such things in Holland as bettering houses for bringing young gentlemen to order? And whether such an institution would be useless among us?

56. Whether it be true that the poor in Holland have no resource but their own labour, and yet there are no beggars in their streets?

57. Whether he whose luxury consumeth foreign products, and whose industry produceth nothing domestic to exchange for them, is not so far forth injurious to his country?

* * * * * * *

85. If all the land were tilled that is fit for tillage, and all that sowed with hemp and flax that is fit for raising them, whether we should have much sheep-walk beyond what was sufficient to supply the necessities of the kingdom?

86. Whether other countries have not flourished without the woollen-trade?

87. Whether it be not a sure sign, or effect of a country's thriving, to see it well cultivated and full of inhabitants? And, if so, whether a great quantity of sheep-walk be not ruinous to a country; rendering it waste and thinly inhabited?

88. Whether the employing so much of our land under sheep be not in fact an Irish blunder?

89. Whether our hankering after our woollen-trade be not the true and only reason which hath created a jealousy in England towards Ireland? And whether anything can hurt us more than such jealousy?

90. Whether it be not the true interest of both nations to become one people? And whether either be sufficiently apprised of this?

91. Whether the upper part of this people are not truly English, by blood, language, religion, manners, inclination and interest?

92. Whether we are not as much Englishmen as the children of old Romans, born in Britain, were still Romans?

93. Whether it be not our true interest, not to interfere with them; and, in every other case, whether it be not their true interest to befriend us?

94. Whether a mint in Ireland might not be of great convenience to the kingdom; and whether it could be attended with any possible inconvenience to Great Britain? And whether there were not mints in Naples

and in Sicily, when those kingdoms were provinces to
Spain, or the house of Austria?

95. Whether anything can be more ridiculous than for
the north of Ireland to be jealous of a linen manufacture in the south?

*   *   *   *   *   *   *

142. Whether it be not certain that from the single
town of Cork were exported, in one year, no less than
one hundred and seven thousand one hundred and sixty-
one barrels of beef; seven thousand three hundred and
seventy-nine barrels of pork; thirteen thousand four
hundred and sixty-one casks, and eighty-five thousand
seven hundred and twenty-seven firkins of butter? And
what hands were employed in this manufacture?

143. Whether a foreigner could imagine that one-half
of the people were starving, in a country which sent out
such plenty of provisions?

144. Whether an Irish lady, set out with French silks
and Flanders lace, may not be said to consume more beef
and butter than a hundred of our labouring peasants?

145. Whether nine-tenths of our foreign trade be not
carried on singly to support the article of vanity?

146. Whether it can be hoped that private persons
will not indulge this folly, unless restrained by the
public?

*   *   *   *   *   *   *

271. Whether there be any country in Christendom
more capable of improvement than Ireland?

272. Whether we are not as far before other nations
with respect to natural advantages, as we are behind
them with respect to arts and industry?

273. Whether we do not live in a most fertile soil

and temperate climate, and yet whether our people in general do not feel great want and misery?

274. Whether my countrymen are not readier at finding excuses than remedies?

* * * * * * *

351. Whether all men have not faculties of mind or body which may be employed for the public benefit?

352. Whether the main point be not to multiply and employ our people?

353. Whether hearty food and warm clothing would not enable and encourage the lower sort to labour?

354. Whether, in such a soil as ours, if there was industry, there could be want?

355. Whether the way to make men industrious be not to let them taste the fruits of their industry? And whether the labouring ox should be muzzled?

* * * * * * *

370. Whether it would be a great hardship if every parish were obliged to find work for their poor?

371. Whether children especially should not be inured to labour betimes?

372. Whether there should be not erected, in each province, an hospital for orphans and foundlings, at the expense of old bachelors?

* * * * * * *

378. Whether it be an impossible attempt to set our people at work, or whether industry be a habit, which, like other habits, may by time and skill be introduced among any people?

379. Whether all manner of means should not be employed to possess the nation in general with an aversion and contempt for idleness and all idle folk?

380. Whether it would be a hardship on people destitute of all things, if the public furnished them with necessaries which they should be obliged to earn by their labour?

381. Whether other nations have not found great benefit from the use of slaves in repairing high roads, making rivers navigable, draining bogs, erecting public buildings, bridges, and manufactories?

382. Whether temporary servitude would not be the best cure for idleness and beggary?

383. Whether the public hath not a right to employ those who cannot, or who will not find employment for themselves?

384. Whether all sturdy beggars should not be seized and made slaves to the public for a certain term of years?

* * * * * * *

475. As wealth is really power, and coin a ticket conveying power, whether those tickets which are the fittest for that use ought not to be preferred?

476. Whether those tickets which singly transfer small shares of power, and, being multiplied, large shares, are not fitter for common use than those which singly transfer large shares?

477. Whether the public is not more benefited by a shilling that circulates than a pound that lies dead?

478. Whether sixpence twice paid be not as good as a shilling once paid?

479. Whether the same shilling circulating in a village may not supply one man with bread, another with stockings, a third with a knife, a fourth with paper, a fifth with nails, and so answer many wants which must otherwise have remained unsatisfied?

480. Whether facilitating and quickening the circulation of power to supply wants be not the promoting of

wealth and industry among the lower people? And whether upon this the wealth of the great doth not depend?

481. Whether, without the proper means of circulation, it be not vain to hope for thriving manufactures and a busy people?

482. Whether four pounds in small cash may not circulate and enliven an Irish market, which many four-pound pieces would permit to stagnate?

* * * * * * * *